Contents

Contents

Contents

Introductory

Introduction

Welcome to Volume Two of *The Film Finance Handbook*. The first volume was a "Practical Guide to Film Financing", a continuous narrative taking the reader through a step-by-step evolutionary process: from script to finished product to the big screen. The second volume is a "Reference Book", a manual purposely designed to complement the first, to assemble all the components written about therein and give them shape and purpose.

This book has a clearly-defined structure of four independent sections, bound together by the common purpose of providing you with the resources you need to understand the intricacies of film production, and the knowledge which should lend your enterprise credibility. The sections are as follows:

1. **Statistics.** An overview of the European market. Written in collaboration with Elisabetta Brunella of Media Salles and *Moving Pictures International*.
2. **Preparing the business plan.** A guide to harnessing creative talent with sound business sense, to supporting your business with coherent financial planning and long-term corporate management strategies. Templates for producing a document which will announce that you're a player with a vision and a strategy, which will attract investment and product alike. Written by Bernie Stampfer of EMDA, Linda Beath of Ideal Filmworks, and Luis Jiménez of Arthur Andersen.
3. **Legal and business affairs.** Unravelling the labyrinth of keeping your business legally watertight. Written by Peter Dally of Bird & Bird, an established legal expert.
4. **Directory.** Exhaustive listings of industry contacts and information on the pan-European and national funding mechanisms.

In keeping with the Volume One of *The Film Finance Handbook*, the Media Business School has mined a rich vein of collaboration with industry experts to produce what is hopefully a comprehensive manual for you, the independent film producer, to exploit and return to again and again. Peter Dally, a partner in the Media and Entertainment Group of Bird & Bird has provided us with an invaluable chapter on the legal and business affairs involved in film production. Elisabetta Brunella, Bernie Stampfer, Linda Beath, and Luis Jiménez have lent us their considerable expertise, and Damjana Finci from Moving Pictures International lightened the burden by providing the "Festivals and markets" section.

Europe is a vast amalgamation of cultures, traditions and aims. The film industry in Europe is the result of the evolution of successful industries developing in parallel. The aim of this book was to try to bring together the manifold experiences of the European industry as a whole, to assist the producers of the future meet the challenges facing them in this melting-pot of an industry, bound to feature so prominently in our lives in future years.

This book has been written with the support of the MEDIA Programme of the European Union, whose aim is to strengthen the circulation of audiovisual works throughout Europe, and to help professionals in Europe reach the maximum level of competitiveness. In this task, we have also counted on the collaboration of the Spanish Ministry of Culture and Education and the Culture Secretary of the Andalusian government, which had the foresight to realise that helping to build Europe is a positive step forward in the building of national industries.

But the complexity of Europe is also manifested in the difficulty of gathering data and processing it in a way that is comprehensible for everybody. In that sense, I have to thank again the incredible dedication of Ana Durández and Charles Balfour at the MBS, and Mike Downey in London, who together have managed to assemble this extremely coherent, demanding and complex guide. To all of them the appreciation of the MBS and, I guess, the professionals in Europe

Antonio Saura
Director, MBS
Madrid, November 1999

Foreword

If William Goldman's maxim that when it comes to the film business "nobody knows anything" were true, then there would be little point producing a book like this.

In the introduction to the first volume of *The Film Finance Handbook* I made the point that there are as many ways of producing films as there are films themselves. Things have changed little in the intervening few months.

On the one hand, we live in a world in which web sites exist that can digest a film's subject, genre, cast and director and then regurgitate its potential box office returns; also a it is a world in which a Tibetan lama film director, who is the reincarnation of a 19th century saint, can create an international box-office hit by making his artistic and practical decisions by using the Buddhist equivalent of drawing straws. So, it does make one wonder.

We have, in producing this, the second volume of *The Film Finance Handbook* for European Film Producers, tried to be a little more practical and follow da Vinci's maxim to "look to the facts" – though not, we hope, in the process completely losing our imagination.

In no other single publication will the European film producer find such a plethora of compressed information, data and documentation directly related to the hands-on, nuts-and-bolts production of internationally-minded motion pictures. And in keeping with the spirit of the Media Business School, and of the MEDIA Programme of the European Union, we have tried to present that information in as straightforward and as user-friendly a way as possible. This is designed to complement the narrative, step-by-step approach that appeared in the bestselling Volume One.

In a business that is notorious for the arbitrary giving and taking of credit, I'd like to make it very clear that this book exists largely because of the efforts of Charles Balfour, and for that I would like to give him thanks. The same goes for Jonathan Preece, and indeed the whole team at Moving Pictures whose forebearance has been much appreciated.

Finally, to Antonio Saura and Ana Durández at the Media Business School who continue to have the vision for projects such as this and also the drive and enthusiasm to find the means for their production.

Mike Downey
Editor
London, November 1999

Introductory

Media Business School

What is the Media Business School?

One of the foremost training and R&D centres in Europe, the Media Business School has the backing of the MEDIA Programme of the European Union, the Instituto de la Cinematografía y de las Artes Audiovisuales de España (ICAA), and the government of Andalucía.

As a training centre, the MBS has had a lasting impact on the careers of over 2,000 European audiovisual (AV) professionals. The courses organised by the MBS offer the highest available standard of training and are designed to boost the projects and careers of AV professionals and cater to both the needs of entry-level AV professionals as well as those of experienced producers and executives of the industry.

The MBS regularly co-operates with professionals and institutions from Europe and Latin America and has a longstanding tradition of recruiting some of the world's leading AV professionals as instructors.

Activities

The MBS offers a complete set of training activities that range from entry-level specialisation courses to intensive training for the experienced producer. The MBS runs three highly-regarded consulting and training programmes and the prestigious Master in European Management. In addition, the MBS organises many training activities for and with a number of institutions and organisations. These activities and the MBS publications are outlined below.

Project-based courses

The key component of the MBS intensive courses is consultation. These courses are project-based and place emphasis on formulating a finance plan for each participant's project. They are designed to serve the needs of working AV professionals who have acquired a certain experience in the industry: AV producers and executives who have already produced projects for the international market and who seek training in specific areas.

They offer AV professionals the opportunity to gain in-depth feedback and consultation for their projects from an international team of leading industry players, and to widen their knowledge of the latest trends in financing and management of AV projects. One of the defining characteristics of these courses is the extremely high standard of the team of instructors and tutors who come from all over Europe and the United States. The instructor to participant ratio on these courses is typically no less than 1:2.

The intensive training programmes are:

- Film Business School
- Television Business School
- Interactive Media Business School

Master course

The **Master in European Audiovisual Management (MEGA-MEDIA)** addresses the needs of professionals wishing to specialise in the audiovisual industry. The MEGA provides specific know-how in the fields of company management and independent film, TV and multimedia production, as well as the tools needed to up-date, recycle and expand their skills. Participants of the MEGA typically receive instruction from over 40 experts during the theoretical part of the course.

Other training programmes

The MBS also designs and organises various other intensive training programmes in collaboration with several AV organisations and institutions.

Publications

The MBS is the publisher of the *Media Business File*, as well as numerous reference guides and textbooks.

The *Media Business File* is a user-friendly and practical management guide targeted at professionals which is published three times a year. It deals with financial, legal and marketing aspects of the production process of audiovisual projects (film, TV and interactive media sectors). The *Media Business File* is published with the support of the MEDIA Programme of the European Union and is available by subscription for a nominal fee.

Forthcoming MBS publications include *Making Things Happen*, a collection of interviews with successful film producers, and *The European Television Producer's Handbook*, based on sessions of the TVBS.

Contact

Media Business School
Velázquez, 14
28001 Madrid
Tel: +34 91 575 95 83
Fax: +34 91 431 33 03
E-mail: fcm@mediaschool.org
Website: www.mediaschool.org

The MEDIA Programme of the European Union

Taking over from the MEDIA 95 Programme, the MEDIA II Programme, adopted for a period of five years (1996-2000), aims at promoting and developing the European audiovisual programme industry. It focuses on three priority areas, grouping about 20 action lines:

- the continuous training of European professionals
- the development of production projects aimed at the European and world market
- the transnational distribution of European works.

The sums earmarked for the implementation of these measures amount to € 265 million for the "development and distribution" part and € 45 million for the "training" part of the programme.

General description of the programme

Drawing on the lessons of the five years of the MEDIA I programme, MEDIA II focuses on three sectors which hold the key to the competitiveness of the European audiovisual programme industry:

- the training of professionals: films and television programmes
- the development of promising works
- and their transnational distribution on the European market.

By avoiding fragmentation and a preoccupation with the microeconomic aspects, the measures implemented will try to produce a constructive impact on the industry in the medium and long term.

Development

MEDIA II support in the field of project development is directed primarily at film and television drama, documentaries and animation. Producers and creators of works with commercial potential on the European market are eligible for financial and technical assistance for scriptwriting, for putting together the financial package and producing the business plan. One of the programme's prime objectives is to encourage the emergence of big-budget European productions capable of winning back market share for European films and so producing a knock-on effect for the kind of productions that – while possibly less ambitious – go to make up the characteristic diversity of European cinema.

Production companies are also being encouraged to improve their organisational structure, to develop medium-term production plans and to seek European partners to set up new networks. This approach is particularly relevant to companies in the new technology sectors (computer graphics, special effects, multimedia), animation and audiovisual archives, which are urged to co-ordinate their efforts under the umbrella of a common sectoral development plan.

Distribution

In the priority area of distribution (cinema, video, television), MEDIA II aims to encourage distributors to invest in the production of promising films to add to their catalogues and to enhance their chances of worldwide distribution by increasing the number of copies available and the amount spent on promotion. One of the best ways of doing this is to build strong and lasting links between distributors and to encourage multilingualism by means of dubbing and subtitling. Incentives are also being offered for the creation of networks of commercial cinemas with a policy of showing mainly European films.

MEDIA II is focusing its effort in the television sector on independent production companies. These are capable of producing high-quality works which can be shown outside their country of origin, provided they are backed from the outset by the various national television channels in Europe. Loans will be available for co-productions bringing together independent production companies and broadcasters who agree to show their programmes in their particular area.

A series of other services and measures are being introduced to promote independent productions and improve their access to the market, mainly through film and television markets, fairs and festivals.

Training

To help professionals adapt to the demands of a European market, the MEDIA II training programme will support initiatives to improve skills in the economic and commercial management of audiovisual projects and companies, including the legal aspects. The development of course modules on screenplay techniques and the use of new technologies is also being encouraged, to help creative artists produce programmes of high artistic and commercial quality. Finally, the programme will support co-operation and exchanges of know-how between training institutions, professionals and of course companies themselves.

Assistance under the MEDIA II programme is mostly given in the form of advances on earnings and repayable loans, but subsidies are awarded for multilingualism and training. Assistance may cover up to 50% of the project costs, rising to 75% for certain kinds of training projects. These measures will complement regional and national initiatives by the member states, so generating a genuine European component of added value in the audiovisual sector.

Who can participate in the programme ?

The MEDIA II Programme is addressed to all professionals of the programme industry in the 15 Member States of the European Union.

In accordance with the Council decisions, the Commission will ensure that the involvement of professionals in the programme is geographically balanced and reflects Europe's cultural diversity.

Special attention will therefore be paid to the specific needs of countries with only a small production capacity and/or a limited language audience and to the development of the SMEs

Introductory

(small and medium-sized enterprises) which represent the dynamic element in independent production and distribution.

MEDIA is also open to the participation of the associated countries of central and eastern Europe as well as to Cyprus, Malta and the EFTA countries members of the EEA Agreement (Iceland, Norway, Liechtenstein) in line with the agreements each of these has signed with the European Union.

The programme will also be open to co-operation with other non-member countries which have concluded agreements with the European Union containing audiovisual clauses.

The network of MEDIA Desks and Antennae, the bureaux set up throughout Europe to keep professionals informed, will ensure that information on the programme reaches the greatest possible number of professionals in Europe, regardless of where they are based.

Amounts available

The financial resources available for the programme amount to € 310 million over five years :

- € 45 million to support training initiatives;
- € 265 million to support development of projects and companies as well as distribution.

Financial support granted to companies takes the form of loans or subsidies up to a maximum of 50% of the costs of operations, although support given to training initiatives will in certain cases cover as much as 75% of costs and will in all circumstances take the form of non-repayable grants.

How does the programme work?

The programme is open to all operators in the market.

It operates through calls for proposals containing detailed guidelines and specifications which are issued periodically by the Commission to European professionals for the award of specific community aid to the different sectors concerned. These calls for proposals are published in the Official Journal of the European Communities and relayed to professionals in the field by the network of MEDIA Desks and Antennae.

Depending on the deadline laid down, each call for proposals involves a separate selection procedure and the appointment of a committee of independent experts specialised in the various areas covered by the programme. They are convened by the Commission to access the intrinsic value of the projects, their feasibility, financial viability, distribution potential, etc.

The Commission is responsible for the final decision on the allocation of Community funding; it makes the selection in the light of the expert committee's advice and in conjunction with the MEDIA committee, – which is made up of representatives of the member states of the EU and associated countries (Norway, Iceland and Hungary) – whenever the cost of a project exceeds a certain threshold: € 200,000 for training, € 300,000 for development and € 500,000 for distribution.

To assist it in its work, the Commission has decided to call on the expertise of recognised professionals: intermediary organisations, selected by invitation to tender, help it to carry out certain tasks necessary for the smooth running of the programme, such as:

• preparing measures to be implemented
• technical evaluation of applications for funding submitted by professionals
• administrative management of the projects selected by the Commission
• monitoring the market (sectoral studies, subsequent evaluation of projects granted support)
• providing information for professionals.

To make the programme as transparent as possible and enable all European professionals to participate fully and actively on an equal footing, the Commission enhanced the role of the MEDIA Desks and Antennae. This network of information offices set up across Europe under the MEDIA I programme has redoubled its efforts in the field of communication and information among professionals in the countries, communities and regions of the European Union (publicising the guidelines for measures under the programme, maintaining contacts with the press and the professional associations), in particular using new channels of communication such as the Internet.

The MEDIA Desks and Antennae also liase permanently with the different support agencies in the member states to ensure that MEDIA II measures complement national support schemes.

See the Directory for further details on MEDIA Development, and for contact details.

Statistics

1

1.1 Cinema exhibition in Europe in 1998

By Elisabetta Brunella, MEDIA Salles
Extract from the Media Business File

Introduction

Although still provisional, the 1998 data on cinema-going shows that audiences in western Europe are on the increase: 844 million, compared to 792 million in 1997 (+6.6%). This offers further confirmation of a trend towards the general increase in cinema attendance which, apart from the slight "hiccup" in 1995, has characterised the 1990s.

The modernisation of facilities and the availability of successful home-produced films continue to be elements of the greatest importance for attracting audiences. This was added to, in 1998, by the "*Titanic* effect".

France

This is particularly true for France which, in 1998, gained as many as 21 million spectators, recording an increase over 1997 of 14.2%. The origin of this success is certainly due to the spectacular results of *Titanic* (20 million tickets sold) but there are also the excellent results achieved by three domestic productions: *Le Dîner de Cons, Les Visiteurs 2, Taxi*, which sold respectively nine million, eight million and six million tickets. With 170 million spectators, France not only confirms itself as the most important market in Europe, but also increases its lead over the other four territories that each count more than 100 million tickets sold.

Germany

Of these four, the most important in terms of number of spectators (148.9 million in 1998,

compared to 143.1 million in 1997), is Germany. Attendance increased by 4% in one year, whilst the number of screens increased by 2.8%. The balance of closures and new openings shows an increase of 116 screens. Whilst there is still a tendency for traditional cinemas to close down, the multiplex phenomenon is experiencing a true boom: in the second half of the year 20 new complexes were opened, for a total of 186 screens.

Italy

1998 was a record year for Italy, too, where the provisional data shows a market with a 16.3% growth rate. Having passed the 100 million threshold the previous year, the number of spectators is now touching the 120 million mark. In the meantime, the transformation of the Italian exhibiting theatres continues: the splitting of single-screen cinemas, which has been going on for some years now, has been accompanied over the past two years by the building *ex-novo* of multi-screen complexes by both Italian and foreign exhibiting companies.

Spain

The increasing affirmation of the multiplexes was one of the main features of the situation in Spain in 1998. From July to December six new complexes were opened for a grand total of 95 screens. Of these, three may be considered true megaplexes, according to the definition proposed by MEDIA Salles. Beyond the 16-screen threshold are the complexes built in Tenerife (18 screens), Madrid (25 screens) and Barcelona (24 screens), by, respectively, Union Cine Ciudad, the most important Spanish exhibitor, by the Belgian group Kinepolis and by AMC, both newcomers to Spain and supporters of the megaplex model. Although to a lesser extent than screens (14.9%), the number of tickets sold also increased on the Spanish market: +3.2% compared to 1997. If Spain's 1998 growth rate in terms of spectators was lower than the European average, it is equally true that this is the tenth consecutive result that improves on the previous year's. This means a 55% increase in attendance over the last 10 years.

The United Kingdom

The United Kingdom provided a slightly negative exception within this broadly positive overall picture. With total admissions of 135.2 million in 1998, audiences there fell by almost four million (2.7%) as compared to the previous year. On the other hand it is true that 1997 was a unique year: cinema-going had increased by 12.5% compared to 1996 and the tickets sold had reached a record value of 138.9 million. It would be necessary to look as far back as 1974 to find such a high attendance rate. As from this date a process of disaffection for cinema-going began, causing per capita attendance to plunge to around 0.96 in 1984. In '97, instead, every citizen in the United Kingdom had come to purchase an average of 2.4 tickets, placing the country amongst the highest consumers in Europe (the average for western Europe was, in fact, 2).

In 1998, too, notwithstanding the drop in audiences, with a per capita rate of cinema-going of around 2.3, Great Britain still manages to stay above the European average (2.2). During a year of ups and downs, distinguished by the success of *Titanic* in the first half of the year and then by the negative effect of the World Cup football finals, screens increased by 8.9%, compared to 1997. By the end of 1998, there were 113 multiplexes, for a total of 1198 screens. While 38.9% of screens were situated in multiplexes in 1997, in 1998 this percentage rose further: 46.4%. The trend for the near future is towards a further increase: in 1999 around 20 new complexes are foreseen. The decrease in audiences – an isolated phenomenon regarding Great Britain alone in 1998 – might raise the question of whether the British market has begun to suffer from too high an offer of screens. It seems, however, that such a conclusion is at least premature.

Belgium

Belgium, the other European territory in which the multiplex phenomenon is just as strong (43% of the country's screens are concentrated in 16 multiplexes), has in fact recorded a considerable increase in audiences. In 1998 ticket sales increased by around 13%. Of the almost three million extra spectators, a very considerable number can be attributed to Antwerp, thanks to the opening of the 17 screens at the Gaumont in the city centre at the end of 1997.

Ireland

Cinema-going is on the increase in Ireland, too, which is another country with a high incidence of multiplexes (accounting for around 28.2% of screens), and reaches a total of 12.4 million tickets sold (+7.8% compared to 1997), confirming, with 3.4, its position as the European territory with the highest per capita rate of cinema-going (apart from Reykjavik).

Luxembourg

Cinema-going in Luxembourg is also increasing at a giddy rate, reaching a per capita attendance of 3.3. The number of tickets sold in two years in the Grand-Duchy has almost doubled.

Austria, Cyprus, the Netherlands, Greece

The increase in audiences is also above the European average in Austria (+10.9% compared to '97) and in Cyprus (+8.8%). The Netherlands is growing at a slower rate (+6.2%) and remains amongst those European territories where the per capita ticket sales are more limited (1.3 a year). Also growing at a slower rate are Portugal (+3.6%) and Switzerland (+2.2%). From estimations of cinema-going in Greek cinemas, the situation proves to be more or less stable.

Scandinavia

1998 is a positive year for Scandinavia, too. All Scandinavian countries, including Sweden and Norway, which saw a drop in audiences during 1997 of respectively 1.2% and 4.7%, increased their audiences. The increases vary from 1.5% in Denmark, to 4% in Sweden and 5.3% in Norway, which regains all the spectators lost in 1997 and obtains one of the best results of the nineties, to 6.3% in Finland, where ticket sales cross the six-million threshold for the first time since 1991. In Finland, 1998 was marked by the inauguration of the first multiplex, a Sandrew Metronome investment, together with local partners. Still further north, a slight dip in cinema-going is recorded in Reykjavik (-1%), where, however, the legendary annual per capita rate of cinema-going does not drop below eight tickets.

Central and eastern Europe

The situation of central and eastern European countries is a clear contrast to the positive picture in western Europe. Whilst in 1997 a distinct difference was recorded between countries where cinema-going was on the increase and which tended to assume the features of the western market, and countries still marked by a drop in cinema-going and considerable reductions in the number of exhibiting theatres, in 1998 there was a drop in audiences almost everywhere.

On the basis of the data available, only Slovakia seems to be holding its own (+1%) amidst the overall slump, varying in extent from country to country, on the eastern markets: -13% in Bulgaria and Hungary, -16% in Poland, -28% in Romania.

The balance between closures and openings of new screens tends to vary more: still positive in Hungary (+6.5%) and in Poland (+1.9%) but extremely negative in Bulgaria (-12.4%) and Romania (-16%). Nevertheless, the faith of investors in a revival of central and eastern European cinema-going continues to be firm.

In 1998 three new multiplexes were opened in Hungary, for a total of 29 screens. These markets are also in the sights of the Kinepolis-Cinemaxx alliance, which, with the fledgling Kinemaxx trade mark, has announced a programme that foresees the building of 20 complexes over the next three or four years in northern and eastern European countries. Poland is amongst Kinemaxx's first objectives – a market where further UCI complexes and those of important international companies such as Ster-Kinekor are soon to be added to the multiplex opened by UCI.

Number of screens and admissions: 1997–1998 (I)

	Screens			Admissions (x 1,000)		
	1997	1998	Var. %	1997	1998	Var. %
A	424	-	-	13,717	15,219	10.9%
B	475	498	4.8%	22,073	ca 25,000	13.3%
CH	503	518	3.0%	15,552	15,894	2.2%
D	4,128	4,244	2.8%	143,122	148,876	4.0%
DK	320	331	3.4%	10,843	11,011	1.5%
E	2,584	2,968	14.9%	105,045	108,440	3.2%
F	4,659	4,762	2.2%	148,935	170,110	14.2%
FIN	321	325	1.2%	5,943	6,317	6.3%
GR	340	360	5.9%	Ca 11,600	ca 11,500	-0.9%
I	2,401[1]	ca 2,500[2]	4.1%	102,805	119,569	16.3%
IRL	228	259	13.6%	11,491	12,386	7.8%
IS	26	-	-	1,330	1,317	-1.0%

Number of screens (continued)

	Screens			Admissions (x 1,000)		
	1997	1998	Var. %	1997	1998	Var. %
L	26	21	-19.2%	1,186	1,415	19.3%
N	395	393	-0.5%	10,948	11,526	5.3%
NL	444	461	3.8%	18,934	20,100	6.2%
P	ca 400	ca 390	-2.5%	ca 14,000	ca 14,500	3.6%
S	1,164	1,167	0.3%	15,210	15,819	4.0%
UK	2,369	2,581	8.9%	138,922	135,200	-2.7%
Total	-	-	-	791,656	844,199	6.6%
BG	121	106	-12.4%	2,685	2,333	-13.1%
CY	23	25	8.7%	931	1,013	8.8%
HU	523	557	6.5%	16,818	14,578	-13.3%
PL	825	841	1.9%	ca 23,700	19,900	-16.0%
RO	451	379	-16.0%	9,456	6,799	-28.1%
SK	296	296	-	4,041	4,082	1.0%

1) Screens with more than 60 days of activity per year.   2) Idem.
Source: MEDIA Salles. 1997 figures European Cinema Yearbook – 1998 edition (http://www.mediasalles.it).
1998 data is provisional.

Market shares by film origin: 1997–1998

	Domestic films		European films		US films		Other films	
	1997	1998	1997	1998	1997	1998	1997	1998
B[1]	3.6%	1.3%	13.4%	22.1%	82.1%	76.1%	0.9%	0.5%
CH	2.3%	2.5%	21.0%	21.7%	73.6%	72.3%	3.1%	3.5%
D	16.7%	9.1%	11.5%	5.7%	70.5%	83.9%	1.3%	1.4%
DK	18.8%	12.8%	13.1%	9.1%	66.5%	77.8%	1.7%	0.4%
E	13.0%	11.9%	17.6%	8.4%	67.9%	78.6%	1.5%	1.1%
F	34.2%	27.0%	10.0%	7.2%	52.5%	64.0%	3.3%	1.9%
I[2]	31.3%	23.6%	15.9%	10.8%	48.7%	65.2%	4.2%	0.4%
NL	3.4%	5.6%	10.5%	4.1%	84.5%	89.8%	1.6%	0.5%
S	17.8%	14.4%	14.9%	8.7%	66.7%	76.3%	0.7%	0.5%
BG	0.4%	0.4%	3.7%	7.8%	96.0%	91.5%	-	0.3%
PL	20.4%	9.1%	7.8%	4.4%	71.4%	85.9%	0.4%	0.6%
RO	2.7%	0.9%	1.5%	2.5%	92.2%	95.4%	3.6%	1.2%
SK	2.1%	1.1%	20.4%	3.5%	74.6%	95.3%	2.8%	0.1%

1) Brussels only.   2) Cinetel data.

Source: MEDIA Salles.
1997 figures European Cinema Yearbook – 1998 edition
(http://www.mediasalles.it).
1998 data is provisional.

Reference:
Elisabetta Brunella is the Secretary General of MEDIA Salles. MEDIA Salles is the project operating within the framework of the European Union's MEDIA II Programme and with the support of the Italian Government, which addresses cinema theatres and the promotion of European films. More information at: http:///www.mediasalles.it

1.2 Film figures 1997–98

Extracts from the study "Watch your figures" *conducted by the MBS and* Moving Pictures International, *issue December 1998. Published in the* Media Business File

This article collates cutting-edge figures on film production, distribution and exhibition sectors in four major markets in Europe, plus most of Benelux and Scandinavia. Where available, published figures are for 1998. The sheer number of sources used illustrates the difficulties in compiling a current analysis of European film. Crucial sources include Screen Finance, SPIO, France's CNC, the Spanish ICAA film institute, the Norwegian, Swedish and Danish film institutes, Blickpunkt Film, to name just a few. Box office or admission figures usually run to October 1998. Barring surprises, the figures comprise a substantial take on the state of European film and film markets over 1998.

But before we let you get into some hardcore number crunching for yourself, here's what we think the data on the following pages really means...

(1)

The upward trend in film admissions and box office in Europe looks set to continue, although 1998 will not mean a bumper rise for cinema-going in Europe, despite fervid multiplexing. Of Europe's five largest territories – Germany, France, the UK, Italy and Spain – which accounted for some 81% of admissions in western Europe in 1997, all looked on target to equal or better their 1997 takings. But performances vary.

In the UK, total tickets sold up to the end of August 1998 – 92.9 million – put the UK on target for a 138-140 million total for the year,

roughly level with 1997 (139.5 million). Rising ticket prices should see a 5% growth in total box office.

Spanish box office saw a spectacular 41% increase over January-April 1998 as compared to 1997. The total rise in box office will be down on this figure but should beat 1997's $391.3 million, thanks to a quartet of bows including Fernando Trueba's La Niña de tus Ojos (*The Girl of Your Dreams*).

Tickets sold in France were up 26% to 91 million by June 1998 as compared to the first half of 1997. Total admissions for 1998 should reach around 180 million, which would be the highest figure for the decade.

German admissions for the first half of 1998 – 74.1 million – put the country in sight of reaching or passing the total tickets sold for 1997: 143.1 million.

The biggest rise in 1998 could, however, be registered in Italy. Admissions have gone up 35% – some 15 million – over the first 10 weeks of the new box-office season, 1 August-4 October, putting Italy on target to reach some 120 million admissions for 1998, up from 102.8 million last year.

(2)

The rise in box office and admissions was driven in the early part of the year by *Titanic*. Yet initially some local industries – the UK and Germany – failed to maintain their large rise in domestic market shares over 1997.

Others, such as French and Spanish pictures, have sold an equal number or more admissions over the first part of 1998 but seen market shares decrease (from 43% to 34% over the first half of 1998 in France) or remain stable (as in Spain's 13% share) because of the *Titanic* phenomenon. Recent releases attest, however, to the continuing vitality of Europe's local

1

industries. September saw strong bows in Germany – from *Lola Rennt*, and *Das Merkwuerdige Verhalten* – and Spain, from *Los Amantes del Círculo Polar* (*The Lovers of the Arctic Circle*), *Barrio* (*Neighbourhood*) and *Los Años Barbaros* (*The Stolen Years*). *Lock, Stock and Two Smoking Barrels* ($25.8 million by October 15) suggests "Cool Britannia" has yet to become "Cruel Britannia" as far as the much-vaunted renaissance of European film-making is concerned.

(3)

France remains the bastion of popular local film-making with three films, two produced by Gaumont, taking over $35 million this year: *Les Visiteurs 2: Les Couloirs du Temps* ($48.1 million), *Le Dîner de Cons* ($48.0 million) and *Taxi* ($35.2 million).

Equally, the language of foreign films in the UK is French. Nine of the top 10 European films in the UK last year were French (co-) productions. Beyond the UK, however, top 10s of non-national European films are dominated by two British films – *Tomorrow Never Dies* and *The Full Monty* – in Spain and Scandinavia. Germany suggests, however, more widely varied tastes, with films from the UK (*Spice World*), France (*Les Visiteurs 2, Taxi*) and Spain (*Live Flesh*) in the lists of top films from other parts of Europe.

(4)

News of the demise of Europe's *auteur* tradition is exaggerated. Witness the performance of Pedro Almodovar's *Live Flesh* in the UK or Germany this year. Yet the attractiveness of European films is now more diverse, at home and abroad. The top three French films, for example, comprise a popcorn movie (*Les Visiteurs 2*), an upscale adaptation of a stage hit (*Le Dîner de Cons*) and an actioner with an *auteur* touch (*Taxi*). Local films in the British charts are dominated by

feature debuts (*Sliding Doors, Lock, Stock..., and Martha – Meet...*) all loosely cast in a commercial mould. German cinema suggests a similar generational renewal, with *Lola Rennt* flying the flag for a shift from local comedies to more ambitious drama.

The success of *Character* at home (84,770 admissions in The Netherlands by October 1998) and abroad ($420,000 so far) underscores the value of a US Academy Award on distribution in Europe as well as the US.

In Spain, strong marketing is positioning *auteur* pictures like *Lovers of the Arctic Circle* and *Neighbourhood* as mainstream must-sees. Long arraigned for its *auteurist* indulgences, European cinema is now firing on far more cylinders, both in terms of genre and style.

(5)

Even for the biggest multinational companies in Europe, the US studios, there is as yet no common market. The box-office returns of their national sub-branches vary wildly from one territory to the next. Results for 1998 in some territories (cf. Germany) suggest, though, that Fox may have a bumper year in 1998.

(6)

In broad terms, Europe's ratios of population per screen and TV-homes per screen are still vastly higher than in the US. Annual *per capita* cinema visits are, hence, way lower in Europe, between 1.22 in The Netherlands and 2.62 in Spain. Average yearly visits to the cinema in the US come in at 5.62. The brute force of these statistics suggests that Europe will remain a multiplexing target for both local and US companies.

All in all, 1998 looks set to be a record year for admissions in the 1990s. But it will probably be surpassed very shortly...

Statistics

Belgium

Top five domestic films (Brussels only) July 1997–June 1998	
Title	Admissions
1. Oesje!	39,560
2. Ma Vie en Rose	11,973
3. Le Rêve de Gabriel	10,651
4. Licht	10,026
5. Left Luggage	6,284

Top five European films (Brussels only) July 1997–June 1998	
Title	Admissions
1. Tomorrow Never Dies	140,733
2. The Full Monty	140,119
3. Les Visiteurs 2	113,544
4. Le Diner de Cons	95,405
5. Bean	93,819

Top five grossing films, Brussels July 1997–June 1998	
Title	Admissions
1. Titanic	474,262
2 Tomorrow Never Dies	140,733
3. The Full Monty	140,119
4. Men in Black	134,841
5. The Lost World	131,658

Top ten grossing films 1997 (by admissions), all Belgium		
Title	Gross (Bfr)	Admissions
1. The Lost World	168,970,000	845,000
2. Men in Black	141,513,360	744,807
3. 101 Dalmations	130,900,000	700,399
4. Oesje!	117,566,150	635,493
5. Ransom	112,900,000	633,149
6. The English Patient	113,876,139	615,546
7. My Best Friend's Wedding	114,139,305	600,733
8. The Fifth Element	117,400,000	571,548
9. Space Jam	92,854,765	515,860
10. Face/Off	91,300,000	490,000

Denmark

Top ten films 1997 (Denmark)		
Title	Distr.	Admissions
1. Frøken Smillas ornemmelsefor sne Smilla's Sense of Snow (Ger/Den/Swe)	All Right/Scanbox	411,000
2. The Lost World: Jurassic Park II (US)	UIP	371,000
3. Barbara (Den)	Nordisk Film	358,000
4. Sunes familie (Sune's family)	Grasten Film	349,000
5. Bean (US)	All Right/Scanbox	323,000
6. Men in Black (US)	Nordisk/Col-Tristar	320,000
7. The English Patient (US)	Nordisk Film	280,000
8. Ransom (US)	Buena Vista Intl	273,000
9. 101 Dalmatians (US)	Buena Vista Intl	266,000
10. Det store flip (Wild Flowers) (Den)	Nordisk Film	250,000

Top five national films 1997 (Denmark)

Title	Distr.	Admissions
1. Froken Smillas fornemmelse for sne (Smilla's Sense of Snow)	All Right Film	411,000
2. Barbara	Nordisk Film	358,000
3. Sunes familie (Sune's Family)	Grasten Film	349,000
4. Det store flip (Wild Flowers)	Nordisk Film	250,000
5. Jungledyret Hugo - Den store filmhelt (Amazon Jack – The Movie Star)	Nordisk Film	199,000

France

Top ten domestic films in France, 1998

Title	Distr.	Gross	Admissions*	Released
1. Les Couloirs du Temps	GBVI	$48,143,220	7.7m	2/98
2. Le Dîner de Cons	GBVI	$47,969,256	7.6m	4/98
3. Taxi	ARP	$35,194,578	5.6m	4/98
4. Une Chance sur deux	UFD	$6,334,878	1.0m	3/98
5. Paparazzi	AMLF	$5,566,872	0.9m	4/98
6. L'Homme est une Femme comme les	PolyGram	$3,003,126	0.5m	3/98
7. Autres Ceux qui m'aiment prendront le Train	Bac	$2,949,780	0.47m	5/98
8. Un grand Cri d'amour	AMLF	$2,719,284	0.44m	1/98
9. Restons Groupes	Bac	$2,517,096	0.4m	9/98
10. Dieu seul me voit	UFD	$2,074,818	0.33m	6/98

* Broad estimate based on box-office gross

Top ten grossing films in France up to 4 October 1998

Title	Distr.	Gross	Admissions*	Released
1. Titanic	UFD	$123,895,362	19.8m	1/98
2. Les Couloirs du Temps	GBVI	$48,143,220	7.7m	2/98
3. Le Dîner de Cons	GBVI	$47,969,256	7.6m	4/98
4. Taxi	ARP	$35,195,578	5.6m	4/98
5. Armageddon	GBVI	$24,857,268	4.0m	8/98
6. Lethal Weapon 4	Warner	$19,246,290	3.1m	7/98
7. Anastasia	UFD	$16,545,906	2.6m	2/98
8. Man in the Iron Mask	UIP	$13,575,048	2.2m	4/98
9. Scream 2	Bac	$12,466,518	2.0m	7/98
10. Jackie Brown	Bac	$7,853,124	1.3m	4/98

* Broad estimate based on box-office gross

Germany

Top ten German films in 1998			
Title	Distr.	Released	Admissions
1. Comedian Harmonists	Senator	25/12/97	2,236,302
2. Lola Rennt	Prokino	20/08/98	1,815,983
3. Das Merkwuerdige Verhalten	BVI	27/08/98	1,220,863
4. Pippi Lamgstrumpf	Col/Tri	22/01/98	1,056,082
5. Der Campus	Constantin	05/02/98	714,570
6. Bin Ich Schön?	Constantin	17/09/98	549,437
7. Zugvögel	Prokino	09/08/98	377,286
8. Frau Rettich die Czerni und Ich	Jugend Film	14/05/98	223,521
9. Sieben Monde	BVI	21/05/98	165,900
10. Freundinnen und andere Monster	Polygram	09/07/98	160,639

Source: SPIO, original research

Top ten films up to 30 September 1998			
Title	Distr.	Released	Admissions
1. Titanic	Fox	08/01/98	17,785,539
2. Armageddon	BVI	16/07/98	5,187,341
3. Tomorrow Never Dies	UIP	18/12/97	4,467,892
4. My Best Friend's Wedding	Col/Tri	04/12/97	3,582,468
5. Hercules	BVI	20/11/97	3,210,442
6. Deep Impact	UIP	14/05/98	3,080,506
7. As Good As It Gets	Col/Tri	12/02/98	3,002,826
8. Comedian Harmonists	Senator	25/12/97	2,766,325
9. Godzilla	Col/Tri	10/09/98	2,678,924
10. Ballermann 6	Constantin	16/10/97	2,445,475

Source:Blickpunkt:Film/EDI

Top ten European films in 1998

Title	Distr.	Released	Admis
1. Spice World	PolyGram	01/01/98	951,751
2. Les Visiteurs 2	Tobis	30/07/98	225,752
3. Taxi	Tobis	20/08/98	146,606
4. Live Flesh	Prokino	07/05/98	143,802
5. Rien na va plus	Concorde	08/01/98	136,105
6. Wings of the Dove	Scotia	23/07/98	134,689
7. On Connait la chanson	Pandora	09/04/98	128,699
8. Elles	TiMe	12/03/98	94,503
9. Jerusalem	MFA	02/07/98	93,220
10. Dobermann	Senator	07/05/98	72,828

Source: SPIO

The Netherlands

Top eight grossing films, October 1997–October 1998

Title	Admissions
1. Titanic	3,331,374
2. Tomorrow Never Dies	961,977
3. Seven Years in Tibet	854,101
4. Armageddon	687,29
5. The Lost World	606,528
6. Hercules	555,895
7. Flubber	528,312
8. Deep Impact	523,94

Top eight European films, October 1997–October 1998

Title	Admissions
1. Spice World	243,187
2. The Full Monty	202,461
3. A Life Less Ordinary	96,427
4. Pippi Longstocking	81,902
5. Bean	53,807
6. Wilde	50,850
7. L'Appartement	29,514
8. Brassed Off	27,393

Top eight domestic films, October 1997–October 1998

Title	Admissions
1. Left Luggage	208,644
2. Character	84,770
3. Little Tony	65,341
4. The Polish Bride	59,848
5. Tropic of Emerald	58,719
6. Siberia	43,844
7. Lagrimas Negras	29,922
8. The Tango Lesson	22,201

Norway

Top five national films 1997

Title	Distrib.	Admissions
1. Budbringeren (Junk Mail)	SF Norge	145,357
2. Salige er de som tørster (Blessed Are Those Who Thirst)	NFD	143,857
3. Insomnia	NFD	67,619
4. Maja Steinansikt (Maya Stoneface)	NFD	56,357
5. Brent av frost (Burnt by Frost)	SF Norge	33,119

Top ten films 1 January 1998–30 June 1998

Title	Distrib.	Admissions
1. Titanic (US)	KF/Fox	1,331,959
2. As Good As It Gets (US)	Egmont Col-TriStar	328,625
3. Tomorrow Never Dies (UK/US)	UIP	315,691
5. Scream 2 (US)	SF Norge	182,478
6. Home Alone 3 (US)	KF-Fox	178,896
7. I Know What You Did Last Summer (US)	Egmont Col-TriStar	178,126
8. Deep Impact (US)	UIP	159,310
9. Spice World, The Movie (UK)	KF	130,736
10. Anastasia (US)	KF	122,275

Spain

Top ten domestic films, 1 January 1998–11 October 1998

Title (distributor)	BO	Admissions (m)
1. Torrente, el brazo tonto de la Ley (CTSI)	$12.9m	3.2
2. Abre los Ojos (Warner Sogefilms)	$5.6m ($7.5m)*	1.4
3. Cha, Cha, Cha (Warner Sogefilms)	$3.3m#	0.9
4. Los Amantes del Círculo Polar (Alta)	$2.4m#	0.6
5. Los Años Bárbaros (Warner Sogefilms)	$1.7m#	0.4
6. Cosas que Dejé en la Habana (Alta)	$1.5m	0.4
7. Secretos del Corazón (Alta Films)	$1.4m ($4.6)*	0.4
8. Lucky Star (Alta Films)	$0.9m ($2.6m)*	0.3
9. Mensaka (Alta Films)	$0.7m	0.2
10. Barrio (Warner Sogefilms)	$0.7m#	0.2

* Released in 1997, cumulative in brackets; # still on major release

Statistics

Box-office gross of top ten European Films, 1998

Title, Country (distributor)	BO	Admissions (m)
1. Tomorrow Never Dies, UK (UIP)	$7.3m	1.7
2. The Full Monty, UK (Fox)	$3.8m ($15.6)	0.9
3. The Boxer, Ireland (UIP)	$1.7m	0.4
4. Les Visiteurs 2, France (BVI)	$1.5m	0.4
5. The Borrowers, UK (Warner Sogefilms)	$1.2m	0.3
6. Les Miserables, France (Tripictures)	$1.1m	0.3
7. Up'n'Under, UK (UIP)	$0.6m	0.2
8. Misadventures of Margaret, UK/Fr (UIP)	$0.5m	0.15
9. The Winter Guest, UK (Tripictures)	$480,000	0.1
10. Firelight, UK (BVI)	$448,626	0.1

NB. List is not inclusive

Top ten grossing films, 1 January 1998–11 October 1998

Title (distributor)	BO	Admissions (m)
1. Titanic (Fox)	$44.2m	11.1
2. As Good As It Gets, (Col-TriStar)	$14.6m	3.5
3. Torrente, The Dumb Arm of the Law (Col-TriStar)	$12.9m	3.1
4. Six Days, Seven Nights (BVI)	$12.6m#	3.0
5. Armageddon (BVI)	$10.5m	2.6
6. Godzilla (Col-TriStar)	$9.6m	2.4
7. The Man In the Iron Mask (UIP)	$9.4m	2.4
8. Misadventures of Margaret, UK/Fr (UIP)	$0.5m	0.15
9. Saving Private Ryan (UIP)	$7.7m#	2.0
10. Jackal (UIP)	$7.6m	1.8

 # Still on major release

Sweden

Top five national films 1997

Title	Distrib.	Admissions
1. Adam & Eva (Swe)	SF	648,242
2. Pippi Långstrump (Pippi Longstocking)	SF	290,314
3. Ogifta par... en film somskiljer sig (Unmarried couples... a comedy that will break you up)	SF	280,237
4. Svensson, Svensson	SF	221,142
5. Lilla Jönssonligan och Cornflakeskuppen (Young Jönsson Gang)	Sonet Film	183,299

Top ten films 1 January 1998–30 June 1998

Title (distributor)	BO	Admissions (m)
1. Titanic (US)	Fox	2,020,078
2. Tomorrow Never Dies (UK)	UIP	387,164
3. Hamilton (Sweden)	BVI	369,165
4. As Good As It Gets (US)	Col-TriStar	346,567
5 Svensson, Svennson (Sweden)	Svensk Filmindustri	300,392
6. The Full Monty (UK)	Fox	292,720
7. Anastasia (US)	Fox	207,041
8. Good Will Hunting (US)	Svensk Filmindustri	191,885
9. Devil's Advocate (US)	Warner	189,654
10. I Know What You Did Last Summer	Col-TriStar	189,654

Total ticket sales: 8.1 million (last year, 6.7 million). Up 21%

The United Kingdom

Top ten UK films released up to October 14 1998

Title	Released	Distrib.	BO
1. Sliding Doors*	1/5/98	UIP	£12,298,655
2. Lock, Stock...*	28/8/98	Polygram	£8,892,208
3. Up 'n' Under	23/1/98	Entertainment	£3,126,317
4. Martha – Meet...	8/5/98	Film Four	£2,641,174
5. The Wings of the Dove	2/1/98	Buena Vista	£2,072168
6. Girls' Night	26/6/98	Granada	£653,115
7. The Land Girls*	28/8/98	Film Four	£624,032
8. Love and Death...*	3/7/98	Pathé	£393,857
9. The Winter Guest	9/1/98	Film Four	£250,583
10. TwentyFourSeven	27/3/98	Pathé	£235,126

* Co-productions. Source: Screen Finance

Top ten US films at the UK box office, 1998

Title	Released	Distrib.	BO
1. Titanic	23/1/98	Fox	£68,513,593
2. Doctor Dolittle	31/7/98	Fox	£18,269,485
3. Godzilla	17/7/98	Columbia	£15,831,198
4. Armageddon	7/8/98	Buena Vista	£15,180,876
5. Flubber	6/2/98	Buena Vista	£10,538,779
6. Lost In Space	31/7/98	Entertainment	£10,402,001
7. Deep Impact	1/5/98	UIP	£10,200,806
8. As Good As It Gets	13/3/98	Columbia	£9,599,292
9. The Wedding Singer	5/6/98	Entertainment	£9,241,078
10. MouseHunt	3/4/98	UIP	£8,306,940

Up to 11-20 September. Source: Screen Finance

Top ten European films in the UK, 1997

Title	Origin	Distrib.	Admissions
1. (22) The Fifth Element	France	Pathé	7,097,243
2. (83) Ridicule	France	Alliance	722,900
3. (96) Kolya	UK/Czech/Fra	Buena Vista	498,870
4. (101) L'Appartment	France	Artificial Eye	421,172
5. (104) Ma Vie En Rose	UK/Fra	Bluelight	409,095
6. (115) Beyond The Clouds	Fra/It/Ger	Artificial Eye	268,372
7. (117) Microcosmos	France	Pathé	259,853
8. (118) A Self-Made Hero	France	Artificial Eye	246,477
9. (143) Unhook The Stars	France	Artificial Eye	117,422
10. (149) Smilla's Feeling For Snow	Ger/Den/Swe	Fox	99,684

Figures in brackets indicate where a film stands in overall year rank

Preparing the business plan

2

2.1 Outline of the business plan

By Bernie Stampfer, EMDA
Extract from the Media Business File

Successful business planning is becoming, now more than ever, an indispensable part of the development of any audiovisual project. Confronted with the prospect of writing a business plan, a European independent film producer will most probably ask himself, first, "why write a business plan at all", followed by, "how can business plans be written within such an unpredictable environment". As more and more producers are facing up to the challenge of writing full-scale business plans – normally covering a period of five years – they are finding out how helpful and important this exercise is. A well-constructed business plan:

- helps to analyse and focus on business ideas on a corporate and creative level.
- helps to clarify management structure and activity over a number of years.
- creates benchmarks against which to plan controlled growth and expansion.
- is the ideal document to underline the company's seriousness and to attract product and finance alike.
- forces the producer to think like an entrepreneur and to develop a mid- to long-term business strategy (as opposed to day-to-day or project-to-project operation).

As outlined below, a full-scale plan deals with a lot of issues and the next question normally is "who should write the plan?"

Depending on the country or even city a producer is working in, there are business consultants almost everywhere but only very few specialised in the film and television business; and then again, they might be very knowledgeable on the accounting and auditing side but not necessarily when it comes to innovative and competitive strategies. My advice would be to write the essentials of the plan yourself, together with your closest collaborators or your management team. The plan is written for *you* and it must be *your* plan as it will be about *your* work and even *your* life.

Yet, external advisors must be involved. Solicitors will look into legal pitfalls and opportunities, accountants will be needed for the financial projections and all tax-related decisions you'll have to consider (they can, of course, also advise on financial matters such as venture capital and equity investment).

Marketing experts are needed almost as *conditio sine qua non*, as this field (still) represents the biggest weakness and challenge in European film-making. Depending on the particularities of a plan, other experts – for mergers, acquisitions, MBOs and MBIs – might be called in.

There are no rules about the length of a business plan and I often compare it with the writing of a script: it can be short, it can be a one-hour drama, a ninety-minute feature or an epic: the plan should cover the business idea and strategy adequately, but it must be short enough to maintain the interest of the reader.

Who are the readers?

First of all, it is the producer himself, putting a (hopefully) crystal-clear mirror in front of his/her face and then basically everybody you want to attract to your particular business (and that can also mean luring people away from competitors...): creative people, financiers, distributors, broadcasters, banks, investors, etc. A good plan is fun to read and is certainly a document to be proud of: it contains, of course, highly confidential information, and confidentiality agreements might be of the same importance as copyright protection.

All these readers will open a business plan with the same questions and curiosity:

1. What makes this company different from all the others I know?
2. Will this company still be around in a few years?
3. Will it be a great company to be associated with?
4. Do these people have a vision and do they know how to go about it?

Four simple questions which may change your (business and private) life.

All areas included here should represent questions which management will need to consider and be able to answer at some stage. The outline gives general guidance only and should not be applied mechanically.

Section 1 – Executive summary

1. Purpose of the plan.
2. Brief description of the company and its marketplace. Highlights of financial projections for the next two to five years. Summary of funding requirements, when money will be needed and how it will be spent. Brief description of background and attributes of key managers or key talent (writers, directors) attached.

The summary should provide a concise overview of the important aspects of the plan. Keep it short – two pages maximum.

Section 2 – History

1. Brief summary of progress since incorporation. Films or programmes the company has developed and marketed and the success of each. Relevance of current funding application. Details of current capital: equity/loans/options.
2. Brief description of the founders, stressing their relevant experience and their roles in the company. Previous and current involvement of outside shareholders, partners or investors (if any). Any outstanding share options, warrants, royalty obligations, leases or other financial commitments, including those involved and principal terms of those commitments.

This section will help to look at your future potential by first looking at your past performance. It should be brief, but should point out any past success *and* failure of the company. If however there are good reasons to believe that past performance may not be a reliable indicator of future potential, these should be noted briefly here, and developed elsewhere in the plan.

Section 3 – Products

Description of principal: new films or products or services. Potential markets and exploitation opportunities. This section should define precisely what is to be developed and marketed. Its length will vary according to the number of products, etc.

1. **Significant distinctive competitiveness.** Although the competitive environment will be dealt with at a later stage, it is important to establish clearly the advantages of your products or services. Low production cost, superior technology, niche market potential or the ability to react quickly to customer needs (for example).
2. **Current market position.** This information should be analytical rather than descriptive – detailed specifications, diagrams or documents can be attached as appendices. Its purpose is to give the prospective investor an idea of the network within

which the company operates, its position in the marketplace and similar.

3. **Future developments.** Need for change of strategy or product, need of additional personnel, possibility of emergence of competitive technologies, research and development, new products, resources required.

Avoid the common mistake of comparing the product you hope to launch in 18 months' time with what was on the market some time ago or what is on the market now, instead of addressing the likely competition of that time.

Section 4 – Markets and marketing

Markets and marketing will be critical to all companies. The business plan should recognise this, and ensure that appropriate weight is given to all the factors mentioned in this section which are relevant to an understanding of the company's operations. If this would result in a statement of excessive length in the body of this plan, parts or even the whole of this section should be included as an appendix.

1. **Description and outlook.** Description of the media industry environment in which you operate (minimum or maximum finance available, minimum or maximum licence fees, box-office results, video rental and sell-through results, etc.). What is the historic (last five years) and forecast (next five years) rate of growth for each market segment? Major business applications. Who are your customers? Who would you want as new customers?

Keep this section brief, but be precise. In the case of generically new products market research may be required to give meaning to the size and nature of the expected initial and future market. This section should describe the results of such research. Use reliable forecasts from industry, trade associations or government sources.

2. **Segmentation.** What target market segments are to be penetrated? What are their current sizes and projected growth rates? Where are your present and future markets: regional, national, international?

3. **Characteristics of each target segment.** How will you sell to each market segment: agents, distributors, representatives, company sales force, direct response, multiple distribution?

Avoid: using statistics of the market size which in reality relate to a wider market than the target. Over-optimistic sales targets which will rapidly lead to financial difficulties. This is particularly applicable where such targets are used to justify the creation of a fixed overhead structure which is not sufficiently flexible to cope with the failure to achieve budgeted sales.

4. **The competition.** Identity and market share of current competitors. Strengths, weaknesses and potential of current competitors. Comparison of products/services with current competitors. Planned counter-response. Principal competitive factors in marketplace, e.g. reliability, offers of unique product, delivery, service, merchandising, price. Trends in marketplace, danger of future market entry by new competitors.

The nature, intensity and ability of the competition will prove critical to the prospects of any company. This will be especially important in the case of small companies entering markets dominated by mature organisations with far greater resources. Your business plan should indicate the share of the market which you expect to capture in the first three to five years and spell out your rationale for these projections. It is important to define the niche you expect to fill in the market and summarise the strategy you intend to employ to gain your share of an existing market. Common mistakes include: the failure to consider the response of potential entrants and existing competitors to your plans; over-estimation of your competitive strengths, and under-estimation of your weaknesses.

5. Marketing and sales

I *Market positioning:* how will products/services be positioned in relation to competitors (in terms of price, quality, audience, etc.)? Pricing policy, current and future.

Develop a comprehensive marketing plan, both on an annual and a long-term basis. Name the executives who will be responsible for marketing. Summarise your goals, quantitative, realistic and consistent with the market analysis described above.

II *Distribution channels:* agents, in-house sales force, distributors, broadcasters, etc. Size and geographical coverage of sales force. Commission structure, recoupment structure, break-even and profit share structure. Collection of revenues.

Formulate your sales strategy and the potential partners involved. Produce projections which should be built up in as much detail as possible and practicable, to act as a cross-check against the sales agents developed from the market analysis process outlined above.

6. Interest shown by prospective customers and/or partners. This section should be sketched out in summary only, with all details shown in appendix (letters of interest, intent, conditional commitments and similar).

Section 5 – Development, production and operations

1. Sources of supply: significant dependence on source materials (scripts, novels, skilled labour), alternative or additional sources of supply and projected costs.
2. In-house capability, today, projection.
3. Description of facilities, production capacity (current and future, compared to growth plans).

Efficient development and production will be a major factor in your company's success – or lack of it. This section should summarise the nature, quality and extent of operating facilities, emphasising those areas which will be critical to future success.

You must indicate the timing, cost, extent and importance of any planned expansion and show related financing issues and tax implications. Use tables and spread-sheets which can be presented as appendix.

Section 6 – Management

1. Owners and directors. Degree of control held by managers. Experience and role of non-executive directors (if any).
2. Summary of planned staff numbers (broken down by key functions).
3. Future recruitment plans.
4. Strategies to develop and retain staff (e.g. share option schemes, profit participation, etc.).

The importance of this area cannot be over-emphasised. Show experience and competence of each current and future key management executive. Detailed CVs attached as an appendix. CV of company attached as appendix. If you apply for a personnel loan, you must deal with the issue here, outlining your planned management structure in chart form and providing detailed job descriptions and minimum qualifications for each unfilled spot. You should also indicate the level of compensation for each open position and indicate when and how you expect to fill it.

Section 7 – Financial analysis

1. Summary of key data in forecasts (sales, profit before tax, profit and loss, fixed cost pattern, impact on profitability, cash-flow, peak cash requirements, impact of capital expenditure on cash generation, sensitivity/break-even analysis, funds required (timing and uses), anticipated gearing (if any), possible exit routes for matching fund investors (public offering, takeover, MBO, etc.).
2. Provide personal comments to figures.

In this section, you will bring together all of the company's sales, market and cost projections in a summary-type financial format. Where appropriate provide a parallel set (or sets) of financial projections and comment in Section 8. You may use a sensitivity analysis which calculates a minimum performance necessary to cover all fixed costs, assuming anticipated margins. The ratio of forecast versus break-even can be a valuable performance indicator to EMDA.

Remember that these figures will determine payments to be made by MEDIA and also the re-payments. Inaccurate projections will affect your own matching fund projections and might lead to an early collapse of the support scheme.

Section 8 – Risks and reward

1. **Risks** – and how management plans to minimise them. Rewards – possible worth of the company if forecast results are achieved.

Show that management is aware of all major potential pitfalls and can react appropriately to minimise their effects. Contrast this with the potential upside. Comment on the above section.

2. **SWOT analysis.** SWOT stands for:

- *strength*
- *weaknesses*
- *opportunities*
- *threats.*

This analysis method is widely used and offers a very simple tool to assess not only your business but also your own capabilities and those of your personnel. Objectives in such an exercise should be:

- *maximise strengths*
- *turn weaknesses into strengths*
- *be aware of current business opportunities and anticipate future ones*
- *analyse threats and find ways how to react efficiently.*

Section 9 – Milestones

Timetable and detailed key deadlines, for each major segment of the business plan (products, marketing, producing, facilities, management, etc.).

Appendices (as applicable)

- Glossary of terms
- Summary – technical data, new products, etc.
- Marketing plan
- Current shareholders
- Organisation chart
- CVs of senior management
- Company profile
- Financial projections
- Audited accounts of last business year, summary

Preparing the business plan

Points to watch

Having assessed more than a hundred business plans of European independent production companies I can draw up a list of the most common weaknesses and reasons for failure:

1. Under-capitalisation.
2. Lack of demand for products.
3. Poor development strategy.
4. Poor or non-existent development structure.
5. Lack of expertise in the field of international distribution/sales.
6. Lack of access to source material and rights.
7. Lack of access to talent (writers, directors, actors).
8. Under-use of specialist expertise.
9. Management over-stretched in day-to-day duties.
10. Poor management of debt.
11. Poor management accounting.
12. Skill shortages of staff.
13. Competitor behaviour.
14. Poor forecasting.
15. High overhead costs.
16. Lack of language skills.

I also want to list some early warning signs of failure which you may check against your present situation and your business plan:

1. You pay a supplier only when a writ is issued and your suppliers are refusing to sell you any more goods.
2. You are (permanently) near or above your overdraft limit at the bank.
3. Your liabilities are greater than your assets.
4. The boss takes no advice.
5. The skills of the business are unbalanced.
6. There is no strong financial person.
7. There is no budget, cash-flow plan or costing system for the company.
8. The business is failing to respond to change.

Reference:
Bernie Stampfer is project monitor at EMDA (European Media Development Agency), the intermediary organisation of the MEDIA II Development Programme that aims to support the development of audiovisual projects and companies.

2.2 Business plans for feature film, television programmes and multimedia projects

By Linda Beath, Ideal FilmWorks Inc.
Extract from the Media Business File

Why?

The production costs of the majority of European feature films, television programmes and even the smaller documentaries and CD-ROMs have climbed, particularly in the last decade. The acquisitions budgets for most European industry users – broadcasters, publishers, wholesalers and distributors – have remained stagnant or have decreased. The number of European companies, especially those producing less than one project per year, has risen. This combination of elements has caused consolidation throughout the EU: many countries have recently formed large production companies generating a high percentage of annual production.

In order to survive in this situation, single producers have to become more competitive than ever before. Long-term stability depends on a good strategy for rights ownership and company managers who can avoid crises and capitalise on opportunity. The main elements of success in this industry remain high-calibre content and creative talent. Now these elements need to be supported by good organisation, a sensible balance between cost and market, and reliable, professional production personnel and methods.

Producers are used to their work being associated with writing and revising the "blueprint" – a script for a film or a series, a treatment for a documentary or a CD-ROM. Now they are having to start preparing the equivalent "blueprint" – a business plan – for the organisation of the creative process and the financial area from high-risk development to high-cost production to revenue, break-even and, yes, profits. Deals are more complex and have to be negotiated, on both sides, by people who are well-informed and who have thought through the potential variables. Marketing strategies, advertising materials and target audiences or consumer groups have to be defined before production, not while a project is being completed.

Informal requests for some of the main elements of a standard business plan appear in applications to state funding bodies while major broadcasters throughout Europe are beginning to ask for all or part of a business plan.

External reasons for business plans are a good motivation to start using this tool, but producers soon find they are better at negotiating deals, understanding the timing of the various production stages and dealing with the pitfalls of development, production and sales.

To be a business plan, it has to have four key units: an objective, an action plan, a cash-flow and a list of key benchmarks (aka measuring success). It can contain many or few other units. A high-budget feature film that will use funding from a variety of industry and non-industry sources could include the following:

Sample units of a business plan for a feature film

Unit 1: **The objective of the business plan**
A short explanation of the goal of the business plan.

Unit 2: **The mission statement**
"Pitch" your film. Include the status of the production:
I. where it is in its development
II. who has been signed
III. who will sell it, etc.

Unit 3: **The executive summary**
A one- to two-page summary of the business plan.

Unit 4: **The industry - current and future trends**
Information on the country's current production activities and trends; a written survey of the production sector of the feature film industries:
I. internationally
II. in Europe
III. in the country or countries of production.
And additional material on:
IV. future trends in the film industry.
This unit is used for non-industry investors only.

Unit 5: **The project**
This unit may include:
I. a short synopsis of the contents
II. a long synopsis of the contents
III. cast, crew, special locations, etc.
IV. a description of the production values
V. the scope of the project, including budget
VI. delivery dates, languages, etc.

As your publicists, distributors and marketing people come on board, this material will be used as the basis for most of the promotional materials worldwide. The short synopsis will be quoted frequently, for years, and the long synopsis will become one of the units or chapters in your film's press kit.

Unit 6: **The market for the film**
• The term market does not mean the public audience or retail buyers, but rather the companies that will buy or pre-buy your film such as funding agencies, distributors, television sellers/networks, video wholesalers, etc.
• This is one of the units that will appear in some copies of the business plan, but not others. This particular unit is valuable and necessary for non-industry sources of financing, but may be modified or deleted for industry financiers.

Unit 7: **The creative elements**
In the early stages of development it would be your list of four to six top candidates for all the key creative roles in the production. Closer to production and contracting of cast and crew, this unit would become a collection of resumés, one for each of the main creative personnel working on the film.

Unit 8: **The business affairs elements**
• This is a list of the people, accompanied by addresses and phone, fax and e-mail numbers, who will do the business affairs functions for your project. Here you include your lawyer, accountant, insurance agent and bank.
• This unit can have a second section, a schedule of legal

contracts that need to be signed, in chronological order. By the time the financing stage is reached, this series of legal contracts forms the "chain of title" and may become a separate document.

Unit 9: Timeline and action plan

- The timeline is a list of dates, events, money and jobs that follows the sequential order you will use to research, develop, produce, market and sell your project. It is an elaborate "to-do list" that is not included in the business plan you circulate, but which is the basic of the action plan and cash-flow.
- The action plan is constructed from the timeline: the dates and events listed on the timeline are given further detail including deadlines and the person responsible for getting the work done.

Unit 10: Cash-flows

- A cash-flow is the main accounting schedule: the horizontal columns are divided into dates, ones that correspond to the events and dates you established on the timeline. The vertical rows are divided into two main categories, revenue and expenses, each of which is subdivided into more detailed categories.
- There are totals of each of revenue and expenses then a grand total of revenue minus expenses at the bottom of each date/event column. For more clarity there is a second total below each column's grand total which is the cumulative total (the total of column 1 plus or minus

column 2 appears at the bottom of column 2, that plus or minus column 3 is the cumulative total at the bottom of column 3, etc.).
- Additional cash-flows may be included in a business plan. For example: different cash-flows for different budget levels; optional cash-flows for shooting in one country rather than another; analysis of using high interest bank finance or not; if your film is picked up for distribution by a major studio or by a smaller boutique you may want to include two cash-flows with different revenue forecasts.

Unit 11: Measuring the success of the business plan (aka benchmarks, milestones)

Frequently measuring success is done simply by comparing how closely the expenses and revenues match the projected cash-flows in the business plan. Although it is obviously a more relevant tool for a company than a film production (where filming is often the ultimate success), this unit can be valuable in two ways:

I. If there are choices to make (alternatives for development, production or sales which the authors included to allow more flexibility), this unit would lay out the criteria for moving from one option to another.

II. For a project that is being developed or produced with shaky or private or incomplete financing, it may be that this unit is solely the definition of when the project has to be stopped so that personal bankruptcy is not only the result.

Unit 12: Distribution and marketing

This is a combination of written and financial summaries.

I. A short summary of the key market for the film.

II. The distributor – either a company profile or a description of self-distribution plans.

III. Key marketing elements which can be expanded to include sample artwork: title treatments, photographs, posters.

IV. Estimates of potential revenue and of probable expenses per market, media or territory.

V. Distribution expenses (for self-distribution) or the financial terms of the distribution deal.

Unit 13: Proposed financing structures

- The first page is a statement of development costs followed by a list of the amounts and sources of the money to be used to pay these costs.

- The next page, a schedule of production costs followed by a list of the amounts and sources of the money used to cover these costs. Since production money usually comes from several sources and each source usually negotiates one of a limited number of different deals for the return of its money, similar deals are grouped together.

- If distribution costs are to be a producer expense, include a plan for how they will be paid in a separate schedule.

- To avoid the collapse of a project and to give clear parameters for negotiating, it is a good idea to do two alternatives for each of the development, production and distribution schedules. Do a Plan A (your preference) and a Plan B (an acceptable but less attractive alternative) for covering the costs of each stage.

Unit 14: Revenue projections

This is the place to estimate the sales of your film, deduct the costs and fees paid to others and arrive at reasonable estimates of net income and...net profits.

Unit 15: Investment proposal

This unit applies to private equity investors; it outlines the request for money, the terms, timing and conditions of the investment, share ownership, profit participation, controls, and it usually analyses the potential RoI – Return on Investment.

Unit 16: Appendices

This is a collection of supporting documentation that would slow down the reader's understanding of the main points of the business plan, but are important to the arguments included in the plan.

2.3 Practical tips

By Linda Beath
Extract from the Media Business File

Practical tips on language

Use:

- a tone that is realistic but positive, confident and decisive
- concise and precise language – point form summaries, charts and graphs, illustrations in place of lengthy descriptions
- professional rather than personal language (Robert De Niro, not "Bob", even if he is your best friend)
- the present tense is compelling, so use it whenever possible
- statistics in place of descriptions and only credit the source for the statistics.

Avoid:

- pronouns (use "the company will be profitable in Year Three" rather than "we predict profits in Year Three")
- superlatives ("the company will make the best film of the year" is not credible)
- as many adjectives and adverbs as possible ("the film is an independent, low-budget feature aimed at the youth audience" is fine, but describing it as "a big box-office, highly entertaining, action-packed thriller" provokes suspicion from the industry and non-industry investors; forget the word "very")
- using specialised industry language and terms when possible and define those that are unavoidable in an easy-to-find glossary
- equivocation (always "the company is" rather than "the company might").

Practical tips on presentation

Style:

- the opulence of the business plan should match its aims (simple black and white text on ordinary paper for a low-budget project or operation; glossy colour on heavy paper for a new company aiming to capture a large market share)
- the business plan is a showpiece for abstract as well as concrete information, so find ways to demonstrate conservative management of money, time and resources; wise decision-making, quality organisation and good planning skills.

Expect your readers to use and abuse the business plan:

- it should be easy to understand who has prepared the business plan, why it has been prepared and how to contact the principals
- each page should have a label (the name of the company or project) and date as well as be numbered
- the table of contents should be easy to find and easy to use
- the executive summary is the only thing some senior executives will read and it becomes the base for verbal descriptions of the project or company by others; after writing it carefully, test it on valued advisers
- use colour and highlighting for sections you do not expect to be photocopied and avoid it in those areas that will be
- financial summaries are often circulated to specialists so make sure they are complete, that assumptions and non-standard forecasts or methods are outlined, and that the complete unit can be photocopied easily
- keep the essential parts of the business plan lean and easy to understand by using the appendices to provide supporting information (a sentence or two about the director, producer, writer, etc., can appear in the front while complete filmographies go in the "creators" appendix).

Practical tips on writing a project business plan

- Like company business plans, project business plans usually take five drafts, 100 hours and result in approximately 100 pages of well thought-out, well presented information. They can be drafted over a much longer time frame than corporate documents.

- Start a timeline before deciding on whether to develop the project, refine the timeline as development proceeds and use it as a constant organisational tool in the financing, pre-production and production stages.

- When the first script work starts, begin with the table of contents – a good way to test the evolution of a logical argument in favour of the project.

- As development progresses, use the timeline to draw up an action plan detailing the deadline, job description and person responsible.

- During development, set up folders for each of the chapters (units) of the business plan to collect information, articles, resumes, contract, etc.

- During development, list similar projects and find case studies or research the economic elements of these projects.

- In the middle to late stages of development, write the main units and lay out the formats for the market and sales financial summaries. These units usually require some research or consultation with industry experts.

- In the final stages of development and prior to beginning to raise funding, start work on the financial summaries and complete the written sections.

- When the script or treatment, budget and schedule are complete, finalise the last draft of the business plan.

Reference:
Linda Beath specialises in the financing and business organisation of international productions. She founded Ideal Filmworks Inc., which finances development and arranges the financing of projects of a small number of talented producers, directors and writers. She is currently an instructor at the Television Business School.

2.4 Company business plans

By Luis Jiménez, Arthur Andersen
Extract from the **Media Business File**

The business plan of an audiovisual company does not differ significantly from that of an audiovisual project. The only difference is that since an audiovisual company usually groups together several audiovisual projects, the preparation of its business plan, rather than being more complex simply involves more work, and aspects peculiar to the company itself (its financing, tax matters, legal expenses, etc.) must be taken into account.

We will focus on the two matters which usually give rise to most difficulties when preparing a business plan for any company and which, unfortunately, are usually those which are least well addressed. These are:

1. The gathering and analysis of all the information needed to prepare the business plan itself and how this information is set out in the plan.

2. The preparation, within the document in which the business plan is described, of the financial statements which must be included in any company's business plan, i.e. the cash-flow statement, the projected balance sheet and the projected income statement.

First things first: the ingredients

What is needed to prepare a company's business plan?
The list of ingredients would include:

• A clear and quantifiable idea of the business to be undertaken.

• A complete list of the resources required to undertake it.

• A quantified and sensible financial plan, in consonance with the business.

The first advantage of preparing a business plan is that it helps to obtain the three ingredients in a sensible and balanced fashion, somewhat like fitting together the pieces of a giant jigsaw puzzle. The preparation of a business plan is, in itself, one of the most powerful and useful management tools available to the person setting up any business.

Note that it is critical "to quantify" the ingredients. The preparation of a business plan is not only to prepare an attractive, well presented document describing objectives, giving an overview of the project, explaining its virtues and benefits. A company business plan is not just a presentation of a project, although it is that too; it is, above all, an exercise in economic planning which sketches from that standpoint the profile of the business over time and gives an estimate of its profitability.

The business

The audiovisual business, despite the special features it may have, is a business like any other. This phase of the preparation of ingredients consists of defining the key variables of the business, which, like any other business, are as follows:

• The product or products/services that are to be sold.

• The market at which they are aimed and their potential demand.

• The distribution system or procedure for these products/services, i.e. the most appropriate procedure for making them known or getting them to potential clients.

In practice, the following procedure is required to properly define these variables:

1. **Obtain a clear idea of the product or service to be sold.**

This requires a clear identification of the appropriateness of the business, i.e. whether it offers a service or product for which there is a demand that is not, or is insufficiently, covered by current supply. For example, television fiction series were practically non-existent in most European countries in the early 1990s. Producers identified this opportunity and their efforts resulted in the creation of a new business that has proved to be highly profitable in the European countries. The point is that it is necessary to ascertain whether the business to be undertaken is sufficiently distinctive to generate earnings. Such distinctive businesses are waiting to be found and the primary mission should be to do just that. And this should be the axis around which the whole business plan revolves.

On occasions it is the product itself, but normally in the audiovisual industry it is other aspects of the business: the trademark, the marketing, the distribution, the people (above all), etc. This task calls for independent consideration which is not a captive of intuition and which must be reviewed by third parties. Most mistakes in business come from not understanding its "uniqueness", which is the real source of income.

2. **Next, it is necessary to understand the market.**

Understanding a market means, on the one hand, identifying the potential client for the products and, on the other hand, its economic size. If the size of the market and the value that the market may place on the product are not known, it is almost impossible to quantify the business as such. Therefore, a business plan must contain at least information on the economic size of the market and the reasonable share of the market that it is aimed to achieve for the product.

In the case of a feature film producer, both these aspects are easily identifiable. In the first place, what type of film it wants to make and for whom. It is not the same to produce commercial cinema, with more possibilities in the different marketing channels (box office, video, television) as it is to produce *auteur* cinema which has lower potential demand. Similarly, the size of the market must be taken into account. If the intention is to distribute films in international markets, it may well be necessary to embark on bigger projects with international casting and scant "cultural" references to the country of origin, which might limit the film's appeal in other countries. It is always essential to gauge the market; this is not a matter of judging or evaluating it qualitatively. It is necessary to measure it, correctly determine its size and adjust the business of the company accordingly.

3. **Finally, a study should be made of the mechanisms in place in the market to get the product to the final consumer.**

A film producer wishing to start up a business must have a good understanding of how films are distributed. If the film producer wishes to make films with a good potential for international distribution, the business plan must state how this distribution will be approached, the costs to be met to achieve it properly and, of course, the potential profit it is expected to obtain. The distribution plan for a film must be consistent with the type of film to be produced and the size of the market aimed at. A business plan for a producer intending to produce films for the European market which did not take into account the economic efforts needed for their distribution in such an extensive market with such complex distribution channels, would not be reasonable. Such a plan would be still less coherent if the type of film in question did not fulfil the expectations common to such a diversified market.

To summarise, the three variables must be analysed in full and their internal consistency evaluated; the business plan must always describe a quantifiable market in terms of size and a product with qualities consistent with this market and in line with its expectations, which can attain a reasonably profitable share of this market in distribution conditions consistent with the product and the market.

Resources

The undertaking of any business necessarily requires material and human resources. To evaluate these resources, it is essential to have a good knowledge of the company's business and to have previously analysed as rigorously as possible the business described above.

The number of factors to be considered is enormous. A list which is not intended to be exhaustive, of the main factors to be taken into account, is as follows:

1. **The human resources required for the business.**

   These are the people who will participate in production and the making of the film. It is necessary to know whether or not these people will provide services to the company on a permanent basis. The permanent staff of any successful production company in Europe is fairly small, whereas the number of people involved in the projects undertaken by these companies is quite large, and the people required are usually hired on a temporary basis. The hiring of temporary staff under contracts limited to the life of a project, rather than permanent employees, considerably reduces business risks and establishes a structure of variable costs depending on actual business activity.

   Which human resources should be permanent and which should not? There is no golden rule. The permanent staff should be those who contribute to the "uniqueness" of the company's business. For example, a producer of television game shows should try to enter into a permanent employment contract with the key people in the location and programme design department. Of course, there are other factors to be considered: tax advantages for companies that create permanent jobs, employee loyalty to the company, etc.

   In evaluating the size of a company's staff, all areas of the business should be considered, i.e. production, distribution, sales, marketing, company management, etc. Certain tasks can be out-sourced to other companies, such as: temporary employment agencies, which are widely used in some countries as suppliers of personnel in the production of television programmes, particularly in the areas of scenery, lighting and technical aspects; and administrative services agencies which provide administrative, accounting and tax return preparation services. The latter agencies are especially useful because they convert a company's typically fixed administrative costs into variable costs.

   Lastly, after the evaluation of the size it is essential to face its cost. This requires consideration of the quality of the people to be hired (professionals with superior credentials and experience are more productive, but cost more), the characteristics of such compensation and the tax and legal obligations, cost of which must be included in cost calculations.

2. **The physical assets directly involved in the business.**

   In this connection the audiovisual industry is highly complex because it has innumerable sub-industries, analysis of which would lead to all manner of conclusions, some mutually contradictory. For example, a company engaged in post-production services has to invest more in the equipment required for its activities. Moreover, the characteristics of the industry in which such companies operate obliges them to make major investments because a key success factor (their "uniqueness") is ownership of the most advanced machinery for providing post-production services to their clients on competitive terms. In this industry, a delay in renewing equipment which must be updated fairly frequently (every four to eight years) can lead to loss of market share and, more seriously, to the company losing its best people to more technologically advanced companies that offer better quality jobs.

In contrast, a film producer does not need to acquire studios, cameras, editing rooms, etc. Usually these are rented for each project so that the company has variable costs which depend on the projects undertaken.

The answer to the problem is different in every case, because it is the individual business which is the determining factor.

3. **Other physical assets used by the business.**

These are the offices housing the company's headquarters, furniture, office technology, communications, etc. They are generally the overhead costs of the business, essential for its functioning, and are usually fixed and not directly dependent on business volume.

In connection with these types of assets, it must be determined whether these physical resources will be leased or owned. These assets are not essential in the audiovisual business of a feature film producer and they are not a major asset group, so the rental of these assets may provide greater flexibility

to the business and prevent their presence from restricting business management. The cost of rental and the cost of ownership should be compared on the same terms and action taken accordingly.

4. **The services that the company will have to obtain from third parties to support both the business and the company itself**

These services vary widely in a film production company: script writers and script editors, communications, catering, editing and post-production services, laboratories, travel and accommodation, particularly for locations, presence in national and international markets, legal and tax counselling services, etc.

In short, what should be thoroughly analysed in this stage of information gathering is the resources required to undertake the business previously analysed and described in the business plan and whether the required resources are consistent with the proposed business. For example, a feature film producer intending to produce films with potential for international distribution must consider in the business plan that people who are more experienced in distribution in different markets with the resulting impact on staff numbers and costs. Also, it is likely that the average expenditure on films will be higher if are hired artists with greater potential appeal in different countries, which involves greater cost.

Financing

The next, and final, big question is how the company is to be financed.

Financing in the film production industry is a key issue: the projects have a long period of maturity up to the marketing stage in which they require less funding and where there is a risk that the project may not be successfully completed. Normally this is the most complicated part of the film-making challenge and it is required to be familiar with the customary mechanisms for its financing: advances from distributors and television channels on film rights, credit facilities obtained by pledging non-refundable subsidies as security, refundable subsidies from EU public-sector agencies, etc.

But the issue that must be undertaken in the business plan is the financing of the company as a whole. Curiously, it is much easier to obtain financing for a company than for a specific project. The reason is obvious: financing a company, which aggregates several projects, poses less risk of bad debts than the financing of a single project.

Proper evaluation of a company's financing requirements calls for the following analysis to be done in the following stages:

I. **Determine the volume of assets to be financed, i.e. the size of the company's average investment in operating assets each year.**

By assets is meant: the audiovisual projects undertaken, the investment in assets at the company (proprietary offices, furniture, etc.), etc. In determining the volume of assets to be financed for a feature film producer, consideration must be given to the amount invested in each project and in the assets the company needs and the average recovery period of the investment in those assets. If the period is long, the average volume of assets and, naturally, the financing must be higher. If, on the contrary, the asset recovery period is short, the financing requirements are smaller. For example, feature film production requires more financing, because the investment recovery periods are fairly long (two to four years, depending on the success of the film). In contrast, the financing needs of a television series producer are much lower because the investment recovery period is usually very short.

2. **Once this first task has been completed, the next question is how to go about the financing.**

The key issue is to design the most efficient financial structure in terms of financial risk and of cost to the company. Following are a couple of ideas to help the decision-making:

I. **The equity or capital invested in a company does not have a repayment date.**

However, it costs more. An equity investor will be willing to put money into a company if he has a reasonable expectation that it will be returned to him at some time and, above all, that the return on his investment will be higher than that on a no-risk investment such as government bonds. If a potential investor in a risky venture is only offered a return similar to that on low-risk assets, logically he will choose the latter and sleep better.

II. **Borrowed funds, or bank financing, have a maturity date.**

This, of course, causes concern to any businessman. But fortunately it has advantages. First, the cost of this capital is lower than that demanded by shareholders. Second, this cost is tax deductible in the corporate income tax return, so the effective cost of funds is reduced depending on the tax rate applicable in each case.

Accordingly, these factors have to be combined in the most appropriate "mix" of equity/debt financing, depending on the financial risk that the company can assume, so as to minimise the overall cost of financing. After all, the final objective is to optimise the return on the company's equity. This is not the same as maximising income. A simple example will illustrate this. Imagine that the average total assets of a company to be financed amount to 1000 monetary units (m.u.) and that operating income before taxes is 100 monetary units.

Suppose that the tax rate is 35%. If this business were financed exclusively with equity, the return on the business would be 6.5%, i.e. annual after-tax income of 65 m.u. is obtained from equity of 1000.

Suppose that half of the average operating assets are financed through bank debt with a cost of 8%. Income after taxes is 39 m.u. Remember that interest on this debt, and income tax after reporting the related interest expense, must be paid. Curiously, the return on equity is 7.8%, which is higher than previously. If the business is able to commit itself to repaying the bank debt on the agreed terms, this second financing structure seems more appropriate.

Though it could look very simple, it is not. There are numerous factors to be considered and they are not easy to handle. However, they must be analysed by the businessman as regards risk aversion and the risk mitigating factors.

3. **Finally, where can the company obtain financing?**

Here is where a company's business plan is a basic tool. It is the company's calling card. It is what enables a potential investor or financier to assess whether the business is or is not a viable proposition. And for this purpose, the company needs not only the ingredients, but must also have prepared them properly and present them even better. The following pages are set out in key ideas regarding their preparation and presentation.

Preparation of the business plan

So, now the ingredients are ready: the basic information for drawing up the business plan. Now it is essential to ensure that it all makes sense on paper.

In principle, the business plan should contain all the information obtained previously:

- A description of the business and its key variables in terms of market, product and expected demand.
- A description of the marketing and distribution plan.
- A description of the resources required by the company to carry out the different projects and for their correct functioning.
- The structure of the most appropriate funding required by the company.

These matters should be treated carefully and each of the aforementioned factors should be quantified as far as possible.

As mentioned above, this article does not explain how to prepare an attractive business plan for a company. Everything that has been said in this regard about the business plan for a single audiovisual project is equally applicable to the case at hand. We are going to focus exclusively on what is usually the most difficult part to prepare: the financial information for a business plan.

Remember that potential readers of a business plan seek to obtain the maximum amount of information about it. In addition to all the business description that it is essential to include, which must be presented as attractively as possible, it is necessary for the reader to "do his sums" and analyse that everything said about the business has an economic vision that is consistent with the plan and, more importantly, is acceptable. It should not be overlooked that the main readers of a business plan are financial backers, completion bonders and investors in general, who need to see these numbers before they approve the plan.

So, any company business plan should include at the end an economic and financial summary of how the company's business is expected to perform over time. For this purpose the following documents must be prepared:

- A statement of changes in the company's cash position, financing requirements and expected surpluses.
- The company's projected income statement.
- The projected balance-sheet structure.

In order to make the financial statement preparation process more understandable, a simple case is explained below.

The company in our example will undertake the production and distribution of three films in the next five years. The production costs will be 300 m.u., 360 m.u. and 400 m.u. The films will be produced in years 1, 2 and 3. The company's initial capital will be 150 m.u. and it is intended to finance two thirds of the films with bank loans and through advances from the various distribution outlets; equity will be used for the remainder of the financing. The loans will be repaid over five years in equal instalments (repayments). The interest rate of the bank financing is 5%. The advances from the various distribution outlets are always equal to one quarter of the cost of the films and are received when they are required for production.

The revenues from the first films are as in the table below.

All collections and payments are assumed to be made 30 days from the invoice date. However, for the sake of simplicity, all the collections and payments relating to a given year are assumed to be made during the calendar year, so there are no balances receivable or payable at year-end.

Advances are always received from the first distribution outlet (box office and video).

The company's general expenses not allocated to film production amount to 15 m.u. per year.

The company's required asset investment is 25 m.u. The assets are acquired in the first year and depreciated over five years. The tax rate on the company's income is 25%.

Any knowledgeable reader will of course realise that this example is somewhat unrealistic, particularly in the case of an independent producer. Our objective here is not to describe a "business case", but to illustrate in a simple example how to prepare the financial statements that should be included in all business plans.

One last comment before we move into the details of financial statement preparation.

Revenues from the first films				
	Estimated date of receipt of revenues	First film	Second film	Third film
Box office and video (including aid)	1st year of distribution	200	220	250
Pay television	2nd year	35	40	45
Free television	3rd year	70	80	110
International	3rd year	25	30	50
Free television (2nd run)	5th year	40	55	65
Total		370	425	520

It is recommended to prepare these financial statements at the same time as the business analysis is being made. The business in our example seems to be sound at an overall level: the films earn positive net revenues which in certain cases are excellent, the overhead costs are not very high, the initial investment in capital seems reasonable with respect to the production cost of the first film, etc. However, we will see that the preparation of financial statements based on the case data, supposedly obtained in the initial stage of business analysis, show that this business will run into serious financial difficulties that will seriously endanger its viability and will force us to go back and re-evaluate the cost structure, the production plan and all the financial arrangements.

Example: model cash-flow statement

	Year 1	Year 2	Year 3	Year 4	Year 5
OPERATIONS AND INVESTMENTS					
Operations					
Collections					
• *1st film*	75	125	35	70	25
• *2nd film*		90	130	40	80
• *3rd film*			100	150	45
Current payments & taxes	(15)	(15)	(15)	(15)	(23)
• *Surplus (deficit)*	60	200	250	245	127
Investments					
Investments in production	(300)	(360)	(400)		
Investments in fixed assets	(25)				
Surplus (deficit)	(325)	(360)	(400)		
Business surplus (deficit)	(265)	(160)	(150)	245	127
Capital stock					
Shareholders' contributions	150				
Dividends					
• *Net*	150				
Borrowed funds					
Credits and loans	125	150	167		
Interest		(6)	(14)	(18)	(14)
Repayment of credits and loans		(25)	(55)	(88)	(88)
• *Net*	125	119	98	(106)	(102)
Cash balance	10	(31)	(83)	56	81

Projected cash-flow statement

The cash-flow statement identifies over time the cash inflows and outflows generated by the business and is designed to identify cash surpluses and, above all, the cash requirements needed to be covered with borrowed funds or additional stockholders / investors.

What is essential when preparing this document is to know precisely when the collections and payments relating to the business will be made and when, from a cash standpoint, investments should be made, and to establish a plan for obtaining funds from banks or other entities or the company's shareholders.

This document is of great interest for financial backers or potential investors in the company, since it shows that the business is viable not only in terms of results but also from the strictly financial standpoint, and discloses the quality of the financial information formerly included in the financial statements described earlier.

It is relatively easy to prepare and structure. The model cash-flow statement (opposite) is included by way of an example.

As can be seen, the statement is divided into three main sections:

1. A section summarising collections and payments directly relating to the business: collections from sales, disbursements for business investments, current payments, etc.
2. A section summarising operations with shareholders of the company: their initial contributions and the dividends we can pay.
3. A section which evaluates, based on the cash deficit the company may have at a given time, its requirements for bank or other financing.

As can be appreciated in the case at hand, the company runs into serious financial difficulties in years 2 and 3, which is common in a feature film producer during film production periods. The statement is an excellent aid because it has enabled us to notice that, although overall the business may yield a positive cash-flow, in two years' time the company will find itself in a situation of insolvency. The solutions are various: increase contributions from shareholders or find financing from third parties to cover the shortfall; obtain additional short-term bank financing secured by rights-assignment contracts already signed with television companies, since these contracts are usually signed before the film has even been finished, on the basis of the script; set up a co-production structure in some of the films so that their cost can be met at lower risk; postpone the production plan for the second and third films, so that the cash-flow generated by the first film can be reinvested in the production of the second film; and so on. As can be seen, all these solutions involve decisions and considerations that should have been made in the previous stage.

The process of preparing a business plan is an indivisible whole and, although analysis has to begin somewhere, it does not have self-contained parts and the information generated in each stage feeds back to the previous ones.

The following are some of the additional advantages of preparing this statement:

1. It reflects the capacity of the business to generate cash. Collections and payments strictly relating to the business must be positive, so that investments, capital and repayment of financing from third parties can be financed in time. In our example, once the investments needed to build up a catalogue of films have been made, the business generates sufficient positive cash-flow to meet project expenses.

2. It makes it possible to evaluate when bank financing is required and when the business will be able to repay it. As has been noted, additional financing has to be obtained in years 2 and 3.

3. It enables the dividend policy to be evaluated. We must not forget that a company's business plan serves, among many other things, to convince potential shareholders of the company of the strengths of the business. Also, investors like to know when they will start obtaining returns on their money, even if they are relative. However, all the financial statements are needed to complete the relevant analysis. But at least the cash-flow possibilities of the business can be evaluated.

4. Lastly, it makes it possible to evaluate how the company intends to finance its investments.

As can be seen, it is a very useful tool which, as mentioned above, even helps the businessman to go back to the previous stage of gathering and analysing information for preparing the business plan so that he can correct any weaknesses that may run the business into a cul-de-sac.

The projected income statement

The income statement shows the income obtained or the loss incurred by a business during a particular period. For its preparation the business community has adopted a common language for recording and reporting the transactions on time, which is called accounting. It will be necessary to become familiar with this language in order to prepare the income statement in the context of a business plan and understand it properly.

Accordingly, bearing in mind the above, a company's projected income statement is simply an estimate, based on the best information available, of the income obtained or the loss incurred by a business over a certain number of future periods.

Unfortunately it is essential to have accounting grounds for preparation of the statement. In accounting, the economic facts are recorded when they take place, regardless of the monetary flow generated by them.

This is known as the accrual method. The following examples illustrate this principle:

- The purchase cost of an item of editing equipment is not recorded in the income statement at the time of purchase, but at the time of the economic event of its use, which in accounting terms is known as depreciation. As the equipment is used over a number of years, the cost of acquisition of this equipment is depreciated over the estimated years of use.

- The expense incurred in hiring a service is recorded at the time the service is received, regardless of when it is paid for.

- The sale or provision of a service is recorded when the sale is made or the service is provided, again regardless of when it is collected.

The income statement should be prepared using these accounting principles. Consequently, it is very important to know when the economic events will take place, which is not easy in the audiovisual industry. Let us take some examples:

Films are commonly funded by advances from future distributors or exhibitors of the film. For example, it is common practice for television companies to make advances on account on the future broadcast rights of a film which is going to be produced. These advances cannot be deemed to be sales in any case, since the service for which this monetary flow is being received has not yet been provided – the television company does not yet have anything, because nothing exists as yet. This advance, which at the time of receiving it can be deemed to be a loan, does not become a sale until the economic event of providing the service takes place, i.e. when a copy of the film is delivered for broadcasting.

The production expenses of a film are incurred a considerable time before it is marketed. These expenses cannot be recorded in the income statement at the time they are incurred, but rather are capitalised for future amortisation once the marketing of the film commences.

The time period to which the projected income statement relates should coincide with the period needed for the business activity to reach its normal level. The usual period is five years, but there is no hard and fast rule. Feature film producers are advised to use a longer period because of the long maturation period of their business.

The income statement structure should be as follows:

- Revenues, including the sale of rights or the provision of services of the company.
- The cost of sales, or costs directly relating to the revenues described above. For example, the sale of rights of a film entails the allocation as a cost of the portion relating to amortisation of the costs incurred in producing the film which, as indicated earlier, have been capitalised in the production period.
- Overheads, which are the costs necessary for the operation of the business and the company and which cannot be directly allocated to the production or the services provided by the company.
- Financial expenses. For this purpose it is necessary to know the financial structure of the business and its borrowing requirements. To this end it is essential to prepare, together with the projected income statement, the balance-sheet projections and the statement of funds, which are the documents that will provide us with the exact quantified measure of the external financing the company will require.
- Corporate income tax. In this connection, it should be emphasised that taxes are an expense item. Should losses be incurred these losses can be recovered in the subsequent years in which income is obtained.

Amortisation of the cost of films is critical to the preparation of this financial statement. In the case being used to illustrate the preparation of these financial statements, the percentage of the cost of the films amortised each year would be equal to the ratio of the annual revenues to the total revenues expected to be obtained during the film amortisation period. Amortisation of

Example: amortisation					
	Film 1		Film 2		Film 3	
Year	% Income	amortisation	% Income	amortisation	% Income	amortisation
1	54	162	52	187	48	192
2	9	27	9	32	9	36
3	19	57	19	69	21	84
4	7	21	7	25	10	40
5	11	33	13	47	12	48
Total	100	300	100	360	100	400

Example: income statement

	Year 1	Year 2	Year 3	Year 4	Year 5
Revenues from sales					
• *1st film*		200	35	70	25
• *2nd film*			220	40	80
• *3rd film*				250	45
Cost of sales					
• *1st film*		(162)	(27)	(57)	(21)
• *2nd film*			(187)	(32)	(69)
• *3rd film*				(192)	(36)
Overheads	(15)	(15)	(15)	(15)	(15)
Period depreciation and amortisation of fixed assets	(5)	(5)	(5)	(5)	(5)
Operating income (loss)	(20)	18	21	59	4
Financial expenses	(3)	(10)	(16)	(16)	(12)
Income (loss) before taxes	(23)	8	5	43	(8)
Corporate income tax				(8)	
Income (loss) for the year	(23)	8	5	35	(8)

the cost of the film must start when the film is in the market and able to generate revenue. In the example given, the amortisation would be as in the table on the previous page.

The amortisation of a film can be estimated beforehand. For example, most of the US "majors" are able to estimate the future revenue from a film with a 5% margin of error within a week of the premiere, based on the box-office takings in that period. It is not a stab in the dark or a lottery. It can be accurately estimated. My experience of independent film producers who use this method is that the errors in their estimates are usually small and concentrated on those films whose production costs overrun the budget.

The format of this income statement could be as in the table above.

Although the pattern of earnings may seem strange, it is usual in a feature film production business. The unevenness is because we are in the first years of production and earnings do not usually stabilise until the producer reaches a reasonable level of operations, which takes more than five years in the case of feature film producers.

It can also be observed that taxes are not paid in years 2 and 3, because the loss incurred in the first year was deducted.

Finally, no revenue was recorded in the first year, despite the advances received from the various distribution outlets. These advances must not be included in this financial statement until the actual sale is made, regardless of collection of these advances.

Balance-sheet projections

The balance sheet reflects the company's financial and net worth position at a given date. Unlike the income statement, which describes the result of "a film" – a time period – the balance sheet provides a "photo" of the company at a given moment in time.
The accounting recommendations indicated above for the preparation of the income statement also apply to the preparation of the balance-sheet projections.

The recommendations to be followed in preparing the balance sheet are as follows:

- First, it is necessary to know when the fixed-asset investments will be made in order to place them correctly in time. The time is important, since from that date they should be depreciated or amortised over the period of use in accordance with the methods laid down in accounting rules. This depreciation or amortisation should be correctly reflected in the projected income statement and the balance sheet should show at any given time to what degree the asset has been depreciated or amortised.
- The treatment of audiovisual rights production costs requires some explanation. A film is always the property of the production company, unless it sells the negative. What it sells are the rights to show or broadcast in the different media, but in no case ownership rights. As it is an asset of the company, the costs of producing it should be recorded on the asset side of the balance sheet and, as was said before, should be amortised over the period considered to be reasonable in which the rights to the film will be exploited.
- With regard to borrowed funds, it is necessary to know when they will be obtained and when it is estimated that the company will have to repay them. Evidently it is necessary to take into account when financing requirements

will arise which will oblige the company to borrow funds. This will make it possible to establish the financial burden to be borne by the company and the resulting impact on the projected income statement.

- Finally, we must estimate when collections will be made from clients and when the company will have to pay its suppliers and pay for the other resources used in carrying on its business activities, and to duly record in the balance sheet the accounts receivable and payable based on reasonable forecasts. For example, if it is estimated that customer receivables will be collected 30 days from the invoice date, approximately one-twelfth of sales in the period are normally recorded under accounts receivable in the projected balance sheet. However, more careful analysis must be carried out in the case of a feature film producer because its revenues and expenses do not have a stable monthly periodicity and usually arise at very specific points in time.

Accordingly, the projected balance sheet structure will look as follows (see next page). This structure is simple and can be easily understood by any reader. Some final recommendations regarding the balance sheet:

- The balance-sheet figures should interrelate to those in the income statement. The bank debt figure should be consistent with the estimated financial expenses used in preparing the projected income statement. The fixed-asset depreciation and amortisation should be consistent with the annual depreciation and amortisation expense recorded in the income statement. The cash balance is consistent with the one obtained in the projected cash-flow statement and so on.
- Current assets and current liabilities should normally be balanced. A permanent situation in which current liabilities exceeded current assets would disclose a potential liquidity problem. However, it is not unusual to find audiovisual production companies with

permanent negative working capital situations, due to the high turnover of fixed assets in the audiovisual industry. We should not forget that it is perfectly possible for a film to be 80% amortised by the end of the second year of exploitation. In the example given, it is seen that the overall business is in danger of folding in years 2 and 3 if it does not obtain additional financing to restore its financial position.

Example: projected balance sheet

	Year 1	Year 2	Year 3	Year 4	Year 5
ASSETS					
Fixed and other non-current assets					
Tangible fixed assets					
• *Cost*	25	25	25	25	25
• *Accumulated depreciation*	(5)	(10)	(15)	(20)	(25)
Audiovisual production rights					
• *Cost*	300	660	1060	1060	1060
• *Accumulated amortisation*		(162)	(376)	(657)	(773)
Total fixed and other noncurrent assets	320	513	694	408	277
CURRENT ASSETS					
Accounts receivable					
Cash	10	(31)	(83)	56	81
• *Total current assets*	10	(31)	(83)	56	81
Total assets	330	482	611	464	358
SHAREHOLDERS' EQUITY AND LIABILITIES					
Capital and reserves					
Capital stock	150	150	150	150	150
Previous years' income (loss)		(23)	(15)	(10)	25
Income (loss) for the year	(23)	8	5	35	(8)
• *Total capital and reserves*	127	135	140	175	167
Long-term debt					
Bank financing	100	195	274	186	98
Other accounts payable					
• *Total long-term debt*	100	195	274	186	98
Current liabilities					
Bank financing	28	62	97	95	93
Other accounts payable (advances & taxes)	75	90	100	8	
• *Total current liabilities*	103	152	197	103	93
Total shareholders' equity and liabilities	330	482	611	464	358

Final considerations

A company's business plan is above all a management tool, and should be considered as such. It enables objectives to be set and their obtainment to be measured.

Evidently everything looks better on paper, and many businesses appear to function *a priori* when set out in a plan. For this reason, when preparing a business plan we should be extremely sceptical and not fall into the trap of yielding to the temptation to delude ourselves. When an entrepreneur embarks on a business venture, the first requisite is to have faith in it. But it is equally necessary to be sufficiently sceptical regarding the strengths of the business in order to do everything possible to ensure that these strengths lead to solid results and are not frustrated.

The preparation of a business plan for a company will enable to be embodied both these qualities to an adequate degree in the most appropriate form.

I trust that the above has helped the reader to understand the advantages of preparing a business plan and structuring it around a company, and to swell the ranks of those independent producers who make films to earn money, which in the long run are those who make good films.

Reference:
Luis Jiménez is a partner and head of the Audit and Consultancy División in the Audiovisual Media Department at Arthur Andersen & Cia. S. Com.
Arthur Andersen is part of the Andersen Worldwide Organisation, the world's largest professional services provider. Arthur Andersen provides creative solutions for its clients through audit, tax, business advisory and specialty consulting services.

Preparing the business plan

Legal and business affairs

3

3.1   Introduction

This chapter is concerned with the legal and business affairs aspects of film and television production. As such it deals mainly with contracts, and since the law of contract varies from country to country it will be helpful to explain the contractual principles on which the following sections are based.

The laws of the United States and the United Kingdom are closely related and are similar in many respects. The legal system of these two countries is known as the common law system, and one of the key features is that the law is not to be found in statutes but in the decisions of the judges. In other words the system is based on precedent and is not codified in the way that, say, the French legal system is. Codified systems are often referred to as civil law systems. (This is necessarily an oversimplification: there is, of course, statute law in the US and the UK.)

One of the results of this difference is that agreements drawn up under the common law system tend to be longer than those drawn up under a civil law system. This is because a civil law contract can incorporate many legal concepts by reference to the code (or, indeed, certain legal concepts are incorporated without express reference). However, in a common law contract it is usually necessary to set out in full everything that the parties intend to govern their relationship.

The approach taken to the contracts that are discussed in this chapter is a common law one, but the essential questions that the checklists pose are ones that ought to be addressed whatever legal system applies.

Before proceeding it may be useful for some readers to learn about some of the basic principles of contract law in the common law system. Those readers who are already familiar with these principles should go straight to the next section.

The fundamental questions that are often asked are:

- How do I make a binding agreement? Does it have to be in writing? Does it have to be signed?
- What is the difference between a contract, a comfort letter and a letter of intent? Are any of them binding?
- How can I be sure that I have not entered into a binding agreement before I am ready?

What constitutes a binding agreement?

Under the common law systems a binding agreement can be created orally and need not be in any particular form nor, indeed, need it be in writing. Only certain special agreements need to be in writing to be enforceable (contracts for the sale of land, for example). All the agreements dealt with in this chapter (and, indeed, all the agreements that a producer will normally enter into) are ones that can be created orally. The value of writing is in proving that a contract has been entered into and establishing what the terms of that contract really are.

The essential elements of a binding contract are:
1. An offer by one party.
2. Acceptance of that offer by the party to whom it was made.
3. Consideration.
4. Certainty as to the essential terms of the contract.
5. An intention by the parties to create a legal relationship.
6. The absence of any public policy considerations which make the contract illegal.

Offer and acceptance

A contract will only be created if the offer is accepted in precisely the form that it is made. If the recipient of the offer accepts part of the offer but tries to vary one term no contract will be formed. Note: an offer can be withdrawn at any time before it is accepted.

Example
A producer offers the north American rights in a film he is proposing to make to a distributor for an advance of $1,000,000.

The distributor replies that he is delighted to accept but needs Mexico as part of the deal.

Result? This is a counter-offer, not an acceptance, so no contract is formed.

Consideration

This is an unfortunate legal term for which there is no simple equivalent in plain language. What is meant is that in return for one party's promise the other party must promise some benefit to that party.

This benefit need not be money, although it often is. Moreover it need not be equivalent to the value of what the other party has promised. So in English and American agreements you will often see the expression "in consideration of the payment of the sum of £1 (or $1) A agrees with B...". This is known as nominal consideration and is effective in creating a binding contract.

The legal rationale is that the law will not enforce mere gratuitous promises.

Example
In the example given above the $1,000,000 is the consideration.

If the producer had said $1 instead this would have been good "consideration" and a binding contract could have been formed.

If the producer had said "I promise to give you the north American rights in my film" there would have been no consideration and no contract.

Certainty

All the essential terms of the arrangement must be agreed at the outset before there can be a binding contract. An agreement to agree is not binding.

Clearly not every single thing that might happen in a business relationship can be anticipated and dealt with in the contract, but all the obligations on the parties that are essential to make the arrangement work must be spelled out.

Example
The producer asks for an advance of $1,000,000 in return for certain rights in the film, the precise extent of which are to be agreed at a later date. There is no certainty as to an essential term and therefore no binding contract.

Intention to create legal relations

This is not a hard test to satisfy. There is no need for the parties to expressly state that they intend to create a legal relationship between themselves: if all the other ingredients of a contract were present the court would normally imply an intention to create a legal relationship. If the parties do not intend to create a legal relationship they should clearly state so in the correspondence, deal memo or other documentation relating to matters between them.

Public policy

Gambling contracts and contracts with minors are examples of contracts that the courts will not enforce on public policy grounds.

Comfort letters, letters of intent and how to avoid entering into a binding contract until you are ready

Since a contract can be formed on the basis of correspondence, care must be taken with all letters that are not intended to create enforceable obligations. If the intention of the writer is to give comfort to the recipient that, say, the policy of the parent company is that all subsidiary companies honour their obligations without actually guaranteeing those obligations the letter should expressly say so.

If the writer intends to enter into a contract at a later date, say when finance is available, it is best to include a paragraph in the letter which makes it clear that no contract is to be formed until a written document is drawn up and signed by both parties. An acceptable (and in most cases effective) shorthand for this is to head all correspondence "subject to contract".

Conclusion

It is not the role of a book like this to be an exhaustive textbook on the law of copyright. However, it is hoped that an understanding of these very basic principles may help in understanding the sections that follow. If in doubt – consult your lawyer!

3.2 Copyright

3.2.1 International overview

Copyright has developed in different ways in different countries in response to varying cultural and economic influences. Two main systems of copyright law have evolved:

1. The *droit d'auteur* (civil law) system puts the emphasis on personal rights and the principles of natural justice.

2. The common law system emphasises the practical and economic argument.

One of the main differences between the systems is the civil law concept of moral rights which was introduced into the UK common law system in the Copyright, Designs and Patents Act 1988. However, under UK law such rights can be waived and are therefore of little practical effect.

The *droit d'auteur* or civil law system

Copyrights are essentially personal rights. The right in the work is seen as arising from the act of personal creation: the work is part of the personality of the author and remains linked to the author throughout his/her life. This intellectual and moral link with the author gives him the right to publish his work as he wishes, when he wishes and in such form as he wishes and to defend it against any distortion or abuses (these are the so-called moral rights).

Several important results flow from this concept:

Legal and business affairs

- Copyright is a natural right and thus, in theory, absolute and should not be restricted. In practice, if restrictions have to be imposed they must be kept to a minimum.
- Moral rights cannot be waived in order to protect the author against commercial pressures which he may find irresistible, particularly at the early stages of his career.
- Contracts between the author and those he has to deal with are put in a special category imposing safeguards for the author as the financially weaker party.
- Restrictions on the rights of authors, such as compulsory licences, are acceptable only in exceptional circumstances.

The most far-reaching consequence is that, because the *droit d'auteur* is a natural and therefore individual right, it can only originate in an individual and not in a company or corporation. This means that "making" a film or record or broadcast, which in most cases is done by a company, cannot give rise to a *droit d'auteur* in the company because companies cannot be authors. As a result, under this system, film companies have to gather in the copyright of those individuals who are classed as authors, including the stars, director, cameraman and cutters. Historically the concept of the *droit d'auteur* is a child of the French Revolution and has been applied most rigorously in French law, but other Latin countries such as Italy, Spain and Portugal have adopted the *droit d'auteur* system in a more or less pure form. The Germanic jurisdictions (Germany, Austria and Switzerland) while based on the concept of *droit d'auteur* show significant variations. The Nordic jurisdictions also stem from the *droit d'auteur* concept but are closer to German than to French law and have developed special traits, particularly in recent decades, under the influence of their own social philosophy.

The Anglo-Saxon or common law system

The philosophical foundations of the common law system are more humble. Copyright is simply the right to prevent the copying of physical material, and its object is to protect the owner of the copyright against any reproduction or use of that material which is not authorised. Copyright in its essence is a negative concept. It is the right to prevent people dealing with something that is yours and has been improperly taken by somebody else.

The main objective of the common law copyright system was to protect the investment of booksellers or publishers in the printing of written material. The economic argument has always been in the foreground and the system adapted easily to twentieth century technology. When film, photographs, records and broadcasting joined writing as a means of communication, the copyright system had no difficulty in applying itself to film producers, record producers, and in some cases, broadcasting organisations.

The general philosophy of common law copyright is that whoever takes the initiative in creating material and makes the investment to produce and market should be allowed to reap the benefit. He can only benefit if he is protected by law, because if he is not protected someone else can reproduce the same product at a lower cost. Thus the copyist will be unjustly rewarded and competitive creativity will not be encouraged.

The US copyright system is more closely related to the common law than the civil law system although it was, until recently, much more restricted, introverted and bureaucratic than the Anglo-Saxon common law system.

3.2.2 Harmonisation of copyright

In 1988 the European Commission embarked on a programme to harmonise copyright legislation between member states. The policy was motivated by two main needs:

1. The need to safeguard the highest level of author's rights and copyright protection in response to the multiplication of new media and the attendant challenge of controlling uses by third parties and the public at large (anti-piracy).
2. The need to harmonise the duration of copyright. Previously the life of a copyright work varied within the EC's member states between 50 and 70 years after the death of the longest surviving author or after the first act of publication.

The European Commission has adopted a number of directives harmonising copyright laws. The following are relevant and should now have been implemented in the national legislation of EEA* member states:

1. Directive on the Term of Protection of Copyright and Certain Related Rights 93/98 (the "Duration Directive").

2. Directive on Satellite Broadcasting and Cable Re-transmission 93/83 (the "Satellite and Cable Directive").

3. Directive on Rental and Lending and Neighbouring Rights 92/100 (the "Rental Rights Directive").

All these directives have now been implemented in UK copyright law, but some states have been slow in passing the necessary national legislation.

The European Commission is planning directives dealing with the protection of encrypted broadcasts, private copying,

droit de suite, and is now examining the impact of the information society on copyright which will probably lead to the need for further directives in order to ensure the harmonisation of copyright laws relating to online demand services throughout the EEA.

The Duration Directive

The European Commission believed that wide variations between member states raised an unnecessary obstacle to the free circulation of intellectual property goods and therefore distorted competition.

The basic term recommended by the International Conventions – the life of the author plus 50 years – was intended to protect the author and the next two generations of his descendants. The Commission felt that, the average for life expectancy having increased significantly, this term was too short to cover two generations. The Commission acted on the principle that no harmonisation should result in a reduction of the protection period for any authors in member states. Accordingly, the copyright period has been harmonised with that of Germany, which was 70 years after the death of the longest surviving author.

The main effects are:

1. The copyright in the works of authors who are nationals of EEA states is extended by 20 years.
2. The term of copyright in film and television productions could be very substantially lengthened, because it expires at the end of 70 years from the end of the year in which the last of the following dies:
   I.   the principal director
   II. the author of the screenplay
   III. the author of the dialogue
   IV. the composer of music commissioned specifically for the film.

Legal and business affairs

NB: No definition exists for "principal director", and in the UK no distinction is made between (II) and (III).

3. Many works which were in the public domain have had their copyright revived.

The extension and revival of copyright raises the question of who owns such copyrights for the extended or revived periods.

Under the UK regulations the owner of the extended period of copyright is the person who was the owner of the copyright in the work on 30 November 1996. However, if the person owning the copyright on that date owned the copyright for less than the then remaining full term of copyright, the extended period will belong not to that person but to the person to whom the copyright reverts.

The provision with regard to licences of extended copyright is dealt with in a slightly different way: the licence will continue after the expiry of the old copyright period for the length of the extended copyright unless there was an agreement to the contrary.

With regard to revived copyright, the person who was the owner of the copyright in the work immediately before it expired is, from 1 December 1996, the owner of any revived copyright in the work. The rights of such owners are restricted, however. Anyone can do what they want in relation to such work provided that they pay to the owner of the copyright such reasonable royalty or other remuneration as may be agreed or determined in default of agreement by the Copyright Tribunal.

In order to take advantage of this provision, the person who intends to use the work must give reasonable notice of its intention to the copyright owner stating when he intends to begin to do the acts. Failure to give such notice will result in his acts not being treated as licensed and will therefore constitute an infringement. If notice has, however, been given, the acts are treated as licensed.

The Duration Directive also dealt with ownership of the copyright in film. The legal systems of the UK and the USA have long accepted that the author of a copyright work, in particular a film, can be a non-human entity such as a company. The basic principle in the UK was that the first owner of copyright in a film was the "maker" and that the "maker" was the person who made all the arrangements for the production of the film. Since, in English law, a "person" includes a company and since the arrangements for the making of a film are invariably made by a production company, the result is that in virtually all cases films and television programmes made in the UK are treated as having been "made" by the production company and the production company is, therefore, the first owner of copyright.

In France, and much the rest of continental Europe, the legal theory is that the author of a copyright work can only be a "natural person", and typically the ownership of the copyright in a film is vested in the group of individuals who made the film.

This conflict has finally been resolved by the UK's adoption of the Duration Directive. The authors of a film made after 30 July 1994 are now the producer and the principal director, and a film is treated as a work of joint authorship unless these two are the same person. "Producer" is defined as a person by whom the arrangements for the making of the film are undertaken – normally the production company. There is no definition of "principal director", but under UK law an employer is the first copyright owner of a work made by an employee in the course of his employment. This applies to films, therefore the contract between the production company and the director will determine whether the director retains the right to be recognised as an author of the film.

Satellite and Cable Directive

There are two principal features of this directive, the most important being the issue of deciding the applicable law governing satellite broadcasts. There are two views. The Bogsch Theory maintains that the applicable law should be both that of the country of origin of the broadcast and that of the country of reception of the broadcast – the "footprint" country (the view favoured by rights holders). The alternative view is that only the law of the country of origin should apply and, subject to limited exceptions, this is the view adopted by the Commission.

The second feature of the directive concerns cable re-transmission rights. The directive provides that member states are to ensure that rights holders who are able to grant or refuse authorisation to cable operators for a cable re-transmission may exercise such rights only through a collecting society. The aim is to assist the negotiation of rights to re-transmit by cable by facilitating access to protected works.

One of the main purposes of the directive is to create a level playing field for the satellite and cable transmission of programmes. By clarifying the law governing the transmission as well as the setting up of minimum rights protections for works throughout the communities (see the Rental Rights Directive below) the Commission hopes to discourage any tendency for broadcasters to move to countries of origin when protection levels are unfairly low.

The Rental Rights Directive

This directive gives rental and lending rights to authors and performers. The distinction between "rental" and "lending" is financial. Rental means making available for use for a limited period of time for direct or indirect economic or commercial advantage; lending does not involve any such advantage.

At the time of the adoption and implementation of the directive it was thought by many (particularly in the UK and the USA, where no equivalent concept existed) that the unwaivable right of authors and performers to be paid equitable remuneration (see below) in respect of their rental rights would cause serious problems, particularly with the financing of feature films. This has not turned out to be the case, and what has become a standard "buy-out" clause (for an example, see below) seems to be effective, although these clauses may yet be challenged.

The rental right is the right:

- In the case of an author, to authorise or prohibit the rental of copies of his or her work.
- In the case of a performer, to authorise or prohibit the rental of copies of a recording of his performance to the public.

In both cases, the term "copy" includes the original.

A "recording" of a performance includes a film made directly from the live performance itself or from a broadcast or cable transmission of the live performance or directly or indirectly from another recording of the performance.

The rental right may be transferred to a third party, but for any assignment to be effective it must be in writing, signed by or on behalf of the person transferring the right.

There is special provision for film production agreements: performers and certain authors are presumed to transfer rental right to the producer, unless the agreement provides otherwise. This provision does not apply to agreement between the producer and:

- the author of the screenplay
- the author of the dialogue
- the composer of any music composed for and used in the film
- the principal director.

The best practice is to take express assignments from all performers and authors.

Notwithstanding any express or implied assignment, authors and performers retain the right to receive equitable remuneration in respect of the exercise of the rental right. The right to receive equitable remuneration cannot be assigned or transferred except to a collecting society.

Where an author is employed to create the work in question, the first owner of rental right will be the employer. It seems that in such circumstances the author will not be entitled to equitable remuneration since he will never be in a position to transfer the rental right.

Those entitled to equitable remuneration will be: the authors of any underlying work, of the screenplay or of the dialogue; the composers of any music used in the film (whether specially composed for the film or not); the principal director of the film and performers.

The directive does say how equitable remuneration is to be calculated: it simply says that equitable remuneration must take into account the importance of the contribution of the authors and performers to the film. This uncertainty, together with the unwaivable nature of the entitlement, was what caused concern. However, in practice there have been few, if any, problems. The following "buy-out" language has generally been accepted by agents acting for authors and performers as sufficient and effective.

"The writer/artist/author acknowledges that the compensation payable pursuant to this agreement includes equitable remuneration in respect of rental and lending rights and any similar rights to which the writer/artist/author may now or shall hereafter become entitled under the laws of any country in connection with the exploitation of the film. However, nothing in this agreement shall prevent the writer/artist/author from receiving any additional monies to which the writer/artist/author becomes entitled as determined by the United Kingdom Copyright Tribunal (or any equivalent tribunal in any other jurisdiction within the European Economic Area) whether administered by any bona fide collection society or otherwise."

It should be borne in mind, however, that this type of clause may still be capable of being successfully challenged. The effect of such a challenge would be to make the production company liable for the payment to such authors of equitable remuneration for the exploitation of their rental and lending rights.

3.3 Chain of title

3.3.1 Deal terms

A surprising number of independent producers' projects fail because of some problem with the ownership of the film or television rights in the underlying works (typically a novel, a play, or an original script). The documents evidencing ownership are usually referred to as "chain of title" documents. If you assume that your company's chain of title will be examined carefully by lawyers acting for the broadcasters, financiers, co-producers, distributors and guarantors involved in your project, you will understand the importance of creating an unbreakable chain.

The following are the main forms of agreement which comprise a typical chain of title:

- option agreement
- acquisition or licence agreement (sometimes called "the assignment")
- writing agreement (whereby the writer is commissioned to adapt a novel/play into a screenplay or to write an original script).

The following checklists propose a menu for negotiating the main terms of such agreements.

Note: subject to contract
If you do not intend a contract to be formed until the written agreement is signed all correspondence and draft agreements should be expressed to be "subject to contract".

3.3.2 Option agreements and acquisition agreements

You cannot commission a writer to adapt an underlying work which is still in copyright without having acquired the right to do so. Typically this right is obtained by entering into an option agreement. Usually an option agreement will have attached to it the acquisition agreement, with all terms fully negotiated so that it can be signed upon exercise of the option.

To be enforceable, all the principal terms of the acquisition agreement must be agreed at the time of entering into the option agreement, since many legal systems will not enforce an agreement to agree. Do not accept a free option because it may be unenforceable for lack of consideration, though £1 will be legally sufficient. Ensure that the option agreement grants you exclusive rights.

Checklist

Vendor/owner
(could be author or successor in title to author – ensure correct legal name if vendor is a company)
Contact name:
Address:
Tel:
Fax:
Email:

Agents/lawyers
Contact name:
Address:
Tel:
Fax:
Email:

Legal and business affairs

Title of work

Author
Author's date of birth:

Author's nationality
During writing:
At first publication:
On death:

Published or unpublished work
If published, who is the publisher?

First publication
Date:
Country:

Is work in copyright?
If in doubt, seek local legal advice. The information gained from the answers to the previous four questions will help determine the answer.

US copyright registration
Is the work already registered at the Library of Congress in Washington? A search can be conducted through a US agency such as Thompson & Thompson (www.thomson-thomson.com) or Dennis Angel.

Vendor's chain of title
If the vendor is not the author you must require the right to see documents proving the vendor is the owner and has the right to sell. Whether you should check at option stage or acquisition stage depends on the circumstances: for example, complexity of the vendor's chain of title, cost of the option, your financial circumstances.

Rights to be acquired
You should obtain an exclusive option to acquire sufficient rights to produce and exploit your project. These would normally include most of the following:
- Right to adapt, i.e. write a screenplay based on the work.
- Feature film rights
- TV rights: terrestrial, cable, satellite broadcasting, re-transmission, pay-TV, video on demand
- Video
- DVD
- Radio
- Internet
- Rental and lending
- TV spin-offs
- Re-make/sequel/prequel (in relation to the film)
- Author written sequels/prequels (in relation to the underlying work)
- Radio plays
- Stage plays
- Synopses for publicity purposes (limit on number of words; accept no less than 7500 words)
- Soundtrack albums
- Book of film (unlikely if the underlying work is a published novel)
- Publication of screenplay
- Merchandising
- Moral rights waiver (where legally possible)
- Interactive rights
- Games
- Use of author's name, likeness, biography
- Right to assign

Rights reserved to author/owner
Single-voice reading
Stage plays
Print publications rights if underlying work is a novel

Holdbacks
Where rights are reserved to author/owner: it is usual to delay the possible exploitation of rights which are reserved to the author/owner so as to avoid the film having to compete with these other forms of exploitation.

Territory
The countries in which such rights are acquired.

Languages

The languages in which the film can be made and/or dubbed/sub-titled.

Media

The methods by which the film can be exploited.

Credit

- Screen: position in respect to other credits
- Separate card or shared
- Prominence requirements: size, colour, duration
- Paid advertising (subject to usual exceptions)
- Special requirements, i.e. link to other(s) involved in the film

Publisher's quitclaims

If the underlying work has been published you should obtain written quitclaims from all publishers confirming that the publisher does not have the film and television rights or any of the rights you are seeking to acquire. This is because it was the practice for publishers to acquire film rights as standard in their publishing agreements. This is no longer common practice, but obtaining a publisher's quitclaim is still a sensible precaution and financiers will insist on seeing one at least from the publishers in the main English language territories.

Initial option fee

Amount: typically 10% of purchase price.
Is this to be credited against purchase price? Normally, yes.

Option renewal fee

Amount: typically a further 10%.
Is this to be credited against purchase price? Normally, no.

Option renewal date and periods

Initial period: frequently 12 months.
Renewal period: frequently 12 months.
Any subsequent periods? Not usual, but becoming so, e.g., third year if producer can demonstrate substantial progress.

Force majeure

Is there to be an extension of option for the happening of a *force majeure* event or for breach by vendor? The producer should ensure such an extension is included.

Purchase price

It is often difficult to agree on the appropriate figure for the purchase price. It is common, therefore, to agree that the purchase price will be a percentage of the budget of the film. A rough rule of thumb is that the story rights package (i.e. the underlying rights and the script rights) should cost 5% of the budget. So a typical deal for further underlying rights might be between 2% and 3% of budget, but subject to a floor and ceiling.

Your interest is to ensure that the budget is as low a figure as possible, so the budget should be tightly defined as the:

"final budget as certified by the completion guarantor and/or financiers – less contingency, completion guarantee fee, financing costs, legal and accounting costs, any overhead fees and any sums paid to the vendor".

Alternatively, the budget is sometimes defined for this purpose as the "below-the-line budget". Sums paid for the option which have been agreed can be set against the purchase price and will be deducted from this figure.

Usually a significant part, if not all, of the purchase price is payable on exercise of the option (a further amount may be due on commencement of filming if later). For this reason, the exercise of the option often takes place on the first day of principal photography.

Ensure that it is expressly stated that the purchase price includes equitable remuneration for rental and lending rights.

3

Additional fees

(e.g. remake, sequels, prequels, spin-offs)
Agents often insist on negotiating the fees for these additional forms of exploitation up front, even if you have no interest in using them. (See "Deal points", 7, V in "Commissioning a screenplay", page 81.)

Deferred compensation

This is unusual for authors/owners.

Profit participation

Typically between 2% and 5% of 100% of net profits.

Definition of net profits

It is not usually desirable to have more than one definition of net profits on a film, so it is common to agree that net profits be defined as in the principal production finance and distribution agreement. This avoids protracted negotiation with the vendor's agent, which may result in a definition that has to be amended anyway when the film is financed.

Other compensation

Expenses (not usual for vendors).

Method of payment

Currency and the frequency with which the purchaser will have to account for profits to the vendor.

Standard warranties and indemnities to be given by the vendor

1. Authority to contract.
2. Sole author/original work.
3. Work is protected by copyright, i.e. work is "in" copyright.
4. Not defamatory/blasphemous/obscene.
5. No threatened proceedings.
6. No unauthorised disclosure.
7. Author's citizenship/residence.
8. Exclusivity.

Special terms

For example, turnaround – whereby the rights revert to author/owner if no film is produced within a given period (say five or seven years) of exercise of option upon payment by the owner/author. Exactly what must be paid is subject to negotiations, but would typically be all sums paid to the owner/author under the agreement plus all other development costs plus interest (payable on the first day of principal photography) plus a share of profit for any film subsequently made.

Certificate of authorship

Required by French distributors for registration at the CNC, so obtain it now to avoid later delay.

3.3.3 Commissioning a screenplay checklist

Project name

Name of writer

Agent's name

Contact address

Tel:
Fax:
Email:

Contracting party

If the writer's services are provided by his loan-out company, you will need an inducement letter from the individual writer. For the principal terms of such a letter, see "Artist's engagement checklist", "Contracting party", page 107.

Preliminary considerations

1. What is the status of the writer? Do you know what the writer is currently being paid for similar work, i.e. have you obtained writer's quotes?

2. Is the writer or are you, the producer, subject to any union or guild regulations?

3. Is the screenplay to be based on an original work, e.g. a novel or play, or on a treatment or outline? Do you own the right to adapt that original work?

Deal points

1. Writing services – typical stages:
   - treatment
   - first draft [and revisions]
   - second draft [and revisions]
   - polish [and final polish].

2. Right of cut-off? If so, at what point(s)? Is it clear you can engage another writer?

3. Additional services prior to and during principal photography as required by producer.

4. Services exclusive during writing periods/ first call* during reading period/subject to prior professional commitments for additional services.

5. Delivery schedule of work product: this must include long enough reading periods for producer and financiers to read each draft and decide whether to commission revisions or a further draft. Time to be "of the essence".

6. Postponement of writer's services: producer should be allowed to postpone writer's services and not lose the right to require writer to perform at a later date subject to the writer's prior professional commitments.

7. Typical payment schedule:
   I. First draft: 50% on commencement
      25% on delivery
      25% on delivery of revised first draft or [x] weeks after delivery of first draft if no revisions requested.

   Second draft: as for first draft.

   Final polish: 50% on commencement
      50% on acceptance
      (or delivery)
      (unless polish is free, as it sometimes is).

II. First day of principal photography.

If the deal is that the writer is to be paid a percentage of the final, agreed budget (less usual deductions, e.g. contingency, completion guarantee fee, financing costs, legal and accountancy costs and any overhead fees), then the balance (i.e., percentage less sums previously paid) will usually be payable on first day of principal photography. A typical deal would be 2% to 3% of the budget (less agreed deductions) subject to a floor and ceiling. This is sometimes called a "picture bonus" or "budget escalator".

Full amount should be payable only if writer receives sole writing credit. Otherwise payment shared *pro rata* with other writer(s). Sometimes the agent will insist that the writer cannot be reduced below 70%.

III. Deferments – unusual for writers.

IV. Profit participation.

The writer of an adaptation of an existing work may not be offered a profit participation: if he is it will be relatively small.

If the work is an original screenplay by the writer and the writer receives sole writing credit the writer will usually expect 2.5% of 100% of net profits (also *pro rata* if credit shared).

V. Remakes/sequels/TV spin-offs.

Not normally offered initially, but agent will often insist that payment terms are negotiated at the outset. Standard terms (sometimes called passive royalties):

   a. Remakes: one-third of writer's fee and profit share.

   b. Sequels/prequels: one-half of writer's fee and profit share.

   NB: Consider whether you care about remake payments – you are not likely to be the one producing a remake. If you are an independent producer you are probably doing a very keen deal with the writer. If there is ever a remake it will probably be produced by a studio or large company, so to tie the writer's fee to a low base is unfair on the writer and does not affect you.

c. TV spin-offs.

This can become a very sophisticated subject, and since many films have no real potential for further exploitation/development as TV series it may be best to leave the fees to be negotiated in good faith.

However, typical fee structures would be:

i. Flat fee per episode on US network TV – $1,000-$1,750 per half hour ($2,000-$2,500 per hour), for first transmission – less for repeats.

ii. If non-network US TV, half the above. *Or* fee equal to 10% of highest script writing fee paid in series.

iii. US mini-series/movie of the week: $5,000-$10,000 per hour.

V. **Expenses** – reasonable travel and accommodation costs.

Rights acquired

1. **Grant of full copyright in perpetuity.**
   Reservations, if any: normally the writer could only hope to reserve the print publication rights in the screenplay. If other rights are reserved by the writer you should agree on holdback periods to protect your exclusivity.
2. Rental and lending rights.
3. Moral rights waiver to legally possible extent.
4. Use of name and likeness.
5. Turnaround? When and on what terms? See "Option agreement checklist", "Special terms", page 80.

Credit

Writers' Guild of Great Britain rules? These are often referred to if the writer does not have the sole writing credit.

Credit on film – position/single card/above/below main titles/size/size of lettering and percentage in relation to the title.

In paid ads – subject to customary distributor's exclusions.

Warranties to be given by writer

1. Authority to contract.
2. Sole author/original work.
3. That copyright exists.
4. Not defamatory/blasphemous/obscene.
5. No threatened proceedings.
6. No unauthorised disclosure.
7. Writer's citizenship/residence.
8. Exclusivity.
9. Writer to assist with E&O application.
10. Writer will comply with all rules/regulations.
11. Not to use producer's name to buy goods.

Termination

Usually the only grounds for terminating a writer's agreement are failure or refusal to perform the contracted services. The rights granted to the producer by the writer would normally remain vested in the producer despite termination.

No injunctive relief

It is very important to include a clause whereby the writer agrees that his only remedy in the event that you breach the agreement is an action for damages. Your financiers will be keen to be reassured that if, for instance, there is a dispute about the writer's credit or profit share that he cannot interfere with the distribution of the film.

Other documentation

1. Short-form assignment for US.
2. Certificate of authorship for France.
3. Power of attorney to execute on writer's behalf if he fails/refuses to execute.

3.4 Development finance agreement

3.4.1 Deal terms

The following is a list of the principal items that will be the most negotiated in a typical development deal with the provider of development finance (e.g. large production company or a broadcaster).

Definition of the development work

This will be as agreed between you and the finance provider but, typically, will include:

1. The acquisition of either an option to acquire sufficient rights in the underlying work upon which your project is to be based, e.g. novel, magazine article, etc., to realise your project, or the acquisition of those rights.
2. Agreement on the identity of a writer to write the script(s) for the project and the entering into an agreement with that writer on terms approved by the finance provider.
3. Undertaking on the part of your production company to procure the individual producer (i.e. you) to spend sufficient time with the writer to ensure proper supervision of his services.
4. The provision by you of a list of personnel whose services would be required for the project and who the finance provider would wish to approve, e.g. the potential director, cast and heads of technical and management departments.
5. The necessary location research and travel that is provided for in the development budget to view potential locations.
6. The requirement that you prepare a detailed budget, schedule and financing plan for the production of the project and provide detailed accounts for the development period.

Chain of title

The finance provider will normally expect you to demonstrate your ownership of any underlying works at this stage.

Inducement letter

Where the production company is essentially a vehicle for an individual producer, and/or producer/director, the finance provider will require that individual to make certain direct personal undertakings to the finance provider, principally:

1. He is director of the production company.
2. He will be personally involved in carrying out the development work and will use all reasonable endeavours to ensure that the production company carries out the development work to the highest standards and honours its agreements.
3. If the production company is dissolved or ceases to exist or fails or refuses to perform the terms of the development agreement, he will be substituted as a direct party to the development agreement.
4. He will look solely to the production company for all compensation and not to the finance provider.
5. He assigns all copyright that the individual producer may possess personally to the production company.

The development budget

The items that are included in a typical development budget are also a matter of negotiation and will directly reflect the contents of the agreed "development work". It is unusual for the production company to receive any significant fee, either for the company itself or to cover the services of the individual producer. Only nominal sums are usually paid by way of a contribution to overheads. However, development finance providers will generally cover the full cost of the acquisition of options and/or rights in underlying material and of engaging writers and of paying retainers to key personnel whose services are required during the development period, e.g. a director, production accountant or production manager for the preparation of budget, schedule, etc. You should include an amount for legal costs in acquiring the rights and engaging key personnel, but be aware that the finance provider is unlikely to accept the cost to you of negotiating the development agreement. They will not fund you to negotiate against them.

Co-production

If it is contemplated or expected that there will be a co-producer or co-financier involved in the making of the project, then any specific or special requirements of such co-financier or co-producer should be dealt with in the development agreement.

Assignment

The finance provider will normally expect to own the development work which it pays for.

Further development / production

Ensure that the finance provider can commission only you to undertake further development or produce the project.

Turnaround

It is vitally important to negotiate as short a period as possible during which the finance provider has to indicate to you whether it wishes to proceed with either further development or with production. The document should then go on to specify your right to utilise the property to try to make alternative arrangements for its financing and broadcasting. The important points here are:

1. Length of period in which the finance provider has to make decisions.
2. The cost of exercising the turnaround right, e.g. cost plus interest.
3. When the cost is payable (ideally it should be postponed until first day of photography).

3.5 Rights clearances

3.5.1 Legal principles

Producers must acquire, or "clear", the rights to the products of the services of all contributors to film and television productions so as to permit the contributions to be exploited, as part of the film or programme, by all the means and in all the media contemplated. Permission must also be obtained for the inclusion of any pre-existing material such as film clips, pre-recorded music or photographs.

The importance of proper rights clearance surfaces in two very practical ways: in the warranties that the producer will have to give to financiers and distributors and in the application for Errors and Omissions (E&O) insurance.

A selection of warranties that a producer may be asked to give is attached to this section as Exhibit A. These particular warranties were extracted from the production financing and distribution agreement of a British broadcaster and relate to a low-budget, independently produced film intended for television release. They may be harsh, but they are by no means untypical.

The producer's ability to obtain E&O insurance will depend in large part on the thoroughness with which the producer has conducted the process of rights clearance. A standard E&O insurance application form is attached as Exhibit B. It is clear, from the questions asked and the clearance procedures set out at the end of the form, that insurers address very closely the issues which are discussed below.

Distinguish "clearing" from "paying"

It is not always necessary/advisable/possible to pay in advance for clearance for all media throughout the world. Producers should clear and pay for all uses reasonably foreseeable or contractually required by the commissioning broadcaster/international distributor/financier and clear all other uses (or as many as possible) with a right to pay a pre-agreed fee at a later date if the film or programme is to be exploited in additional media/territories.

3.5.2 Rights to be cleared

Copyright

Generally speaking the work of writers is protected as *literary copyright*, the work of designers as *artistic copyright* and the work of composers and lyricists as *musical works of copyright*.

Artistic works (paintings, sculptures), works of craftsmanship and photographs are also protected by copyright and will have to be cleared, as will extracts from pre-existing film/sound recordings.

Music

Musical works are protected by copyright, but the issues are complex and require separate consideration.

Moral rights

Now exist in all jurisdictions within the European Union. For a fuller analysis of the waivability of moral rights in Europe, see Exhibit C.

Rights in performances

The copyright law of the UK protects the rights of live performers by requiring the consent of the performer to the making of a film or sound recording of any performance given by him or her. The right to consent (or withhold consent) is also extended to any person who has an exclusive recording contract with a performer, in respect of that performer's live appearances. That person will usually be a record company.

Rental and lending rights

Rental right is the right:

- in the case of an author, to authorise or prohibit the rental of copies of his or her work
- in the case of a performer, to authorise or prohibit the rental of copies of a recording of his or her performance to the public.

In both cases, the term "copy" includes the original.

A "recording" of a performance includes a film made directly from the live performance itself or from a broadcast or cable transmission of the live performance or directly or indirectly from another recording of the performance.

Rental right may be transferred, but for any assignment to be effective it must be in writing, signed by or on behalf of the person transferring the right.

There is special provision for film production agreements whereby performers and certain authors are presumed to transfer their rental right to the producer unless the agreement provides otherwise. Note, though, that this provision does not apply to agreement between the producer and:

- the author of the screenplay
- the author of the dialogue
- the composer of any music composed for and used in the film
- the principal director.

The best practice is to take express assignments from all performers and authors.

The author or performer retains the right to receive equitable remuneration in respect of the exercise of any rental right transferred by him. The right to receive equitable remuneration cannot be assigned or transferred except to a collecting society (but refer to the "buy-out" language on profit in 3.2 "Copyright", page 76).

Where an author is employed to create the work in question, the first owner of rental right will be the employer. It seems that in such circumstances the author will not be entitled to equitable remuneration since he will never be in a position to transfer the rental right.

Other property rights

Where locations outside a studio are used for filming, the producer will need consents from the owner of the property to be present there. Otherwise, any activities on the owner's property will be trespass. In addition, there may be other consents to obtain, such as from the police or local authorities.

3.5.3 Clearing rights

Copyright

Assignment or licence?

An *assignment* is an outright transfer of property from one person to another.

A *licence* is an authority or permission to do something which would otherwise be unlawful.

Copyright can only be transferred by assignment in writing (the exceptions are by will and by operation of law) and an assignment of copyright can be limited in certain ways:

1. an assignment may be limited to one or more of the infringing acts, e.g. it is possible to assign the broadcast rights in a novel
2. an assignment may be limited to part of the period for which copyright subsists.

A simple licence need not be in writing, but it can be withdrawn or terminated by the person granting it. Also, since the person granting the licence retains the copyright that person can still assign it to a third party, and if that third party has no notice of that licence, the licence will be defeated and the licencee will lose his rights. He will have an action in damages against the licensor, but this may be worthless. If a licence is all that is on offer, ensure that it is exclusive, irrevocable, in writing, signed by the person granting the licence, and, if possible, for the full period of copyright.

When copyright clearances may not be required

Fair dealing exceptions

UK copyright law allows certain exceptions to the normal rule that copying or exhibiting a work of copyright requires a copyright owner's permission. The main exceptions are known as the "fair dealing exceptions" because they each allow the use of works of copyright or parts or extracts from them when it is for:

- criticism or review
- reporting on current events.

In either case, the use must be fair. If it is for criticism or review, an acknowledgement must also be given to the work and its author. If the use is in reporting current events and the work is shown as part of a film, broadcast or cable programme, no such acknowledgement is actually required by law.

The current events exception does not apply to photographs, so specific consent from the owner of the copyright in a photograph will be necessary for its use in news and current affairs programmes.

Public display of artistic works

UK copyright law permits the inclusion in films and television programmes of buildings, sculptures, models for buildings, works of artistic craftsmanship, in each case permanently situated in a public place or in premises open to the public.

Incidental inclusion

If a work of copyright (of any kind) is incidentally included in a film, broadcast, sound recording or artistic work, no permission is required of the copyright owners. However, the meaning of "incidental" is not expanded on. The view is generally taken that it applies only to the inclusion of works over which the maker of the film or sound recording had no control (i.e. accidental).

Music

Music in films can either be specially commissioned or pre-existing. In both cases the producer must clear the right to:

- record and synchronise the recording with the film (the synchronisation right)
- perform the music by exhibiting/distributing the film (the performing right).

If the producer wishes to use a pre-existing recording which is still protected by copyright, the producer must also clear the right to dub the sound recording (i.e. to copy it on to the soundtrack of the film as well as the performing right).

Note that when using compositions by a classical composer the work may well be out of copyright, because the composer has been dead for the requisite number of years. If so, this will remove the need for a music synchronisation licence, but not for a licence in respect of the recording, unless the producer makes a new recording, as the recording is quite likely to still be in copyright.

Moral rights

Waiving moral rights
English law enables authors to give general or specific waivers, to give them conditionally or unconditionally, irrevocably or revocably. Although English law is not clear on the point, it is recommended that any waiver be obtained in writing.

Performance rights

For actors, consent is given as part of a standard-form actor's engagement contract. For all other performers (including sportsmen) it is advised to obtain consent in writing.

Rental and lending rights

Include express reference to rental and lending rights in assignments, licences or consent clauses. For language "buying out" equitable remuneration, see page 76.

Other property rights

Filming in public places will usually require permission from the local government authority and probably the police.

Films on private property will require a licence from the property owner – usually called a location agreement – covering:
1. the fee
2. insurance
3. details of the proposed filming, including the duration
4. details of access and parking, if any
5. which parts of the property can be used and which remain private
6. what temporary alterations are proposed and a timetable for reinstatement
7. an express waiver of privacy rights by the owner
8. an express right to use the footage of the property in the finished film and in all publicity and promotion.

Film and television clips

All film and television clips intended for use in a film or television programme should be cleared, even if the use is only intended to be in the background.

Film clip licences are granted according to media, territory or licence period required.

Note that the owner of a physical copy of the material in question may not actually be the copyright owner of the film embodied on the material. Thus, even if a fee is agreed with the owner of the copy for providing it, this fee will not necessarily clear the right in the underlying copyright in the film. Such clearance must be undertaken separately.

Further consents may be needed, for example, the use of certain clips featuring performers (musicians and actors) or clips featuring music. Performers' rights and rights to use the music will also have to be separately cleared (i.e. the synchronisation right in the music itself and, if the music was not especially recorded for the original production from which the clip is taken, the dubbing right in respect of the pre-existing recording which was used). These separate permissions would not, of course, be necessary if the producer of the original material, from which the clip is taken, contracted with the performers of the music on terms which allowed its use by all means and in all media.

Television commercials and music video

The rights in commercials and music videos will also have to be cleared if extracts are to be used in a film or television programme. These may be controlled by the record companies or collecting societies.

General

Review the wording of any clip licence provided by the rights owner. Try to ensure that the rights owner gives full warranties that they own all the rights and are entitled to grant them for the use contemplated.

Photographs and other artistic works

If the artistic work is protected by copyright, then permission to feature it in a film or television production will be needed, unless the use is one which exempts the user from having to obtain permission, e.g. fair dealing or incidental inclusion.

3.5.4 Exhibit A – producer's warranties

The producer warrants, represents, agrees and undertakes that:

The producer is the sole owner of the entire worldwide copyright in the film and the ancillary rights and sole legal and beneficial owner without any limitation whatsoever of all rights granted and assigned hereunder in and to the film and the ancillary rights and shall have (prior to delivery) obtained all rights required for the production, synchronisation, exhibition, performance, distribution, marketing and exploitation of the film and the ancillary rights pursuant to this agreement throughout the territory and during the term (subject to the right of the Performing Right Society Limited and its overseas affiliates and in this respect the producer agrees that prior to delivery it shall enter into a theatrical performance licence with the Performing Right Society upon terms approved by the financier).

The film shall be produced in accordance with all applicable laws, statutes, ordinances, rules and regulations (including, without limitation, those contained in any relevant trade agreements), and requirements of all governmental agencies and regulatory bodies both domestic and foreign having jurisdiction with respect to the production of the film and all ancillary products relating thereto.

With respect to all persons rendering services in connection with the film, the producer has or will before delivery hereunder have the right to issue publicity concerning them and the right to use, reproduce, transmit, broadcast, exploit, publicise and exhibit their respective names, photographs, likenesses, biographies, voices, sound effects and the products of their services generally as well as recordings, transcriptions or other reproductions thereof in connection with the distribution, exhibition, advertising and exploitation of the film and any books, records, music or merchandise derived therefrom.

Neither the film nor any part thereof nor any materials contained therein or synchronised therewith nor the title thereof nor the exercise of any right, licence or privilege herein granted violates, infringes or invades or will violate, infringe or invade any trade mark, service mark, trade name, contract, agreement, copyright, patent, literary, artistic, dramatic, musical, personal, private, civil or property right or right of privacy or right of publicity or amoral rights or rights of confidentiality or any law or regulation or other right whatsoever of, and that the film is not and will not be blasphemous or obscene and does not and to the best of the producer's knowledge and belief having made due and diligent enquiries will not slander or libel, any person, firm, company or association whatsoever including their heirs, successors in title or personal representatives of any person, firm, company or association whatsoever.

At the time of delivery of the film all of the following to the extent that the same are or have become due and/or payable will be fully paid or discharged:

- All claims and rights of owners of copyright in literary, dramatic, musical and artistic rights and other property or rights in or to all stories, plays, scripts, scenarios, themes, incidents, plots, characters, locations, dialogue, music, words and other material of any nature whatsoever appearing, used or recorded in the film.
- All claims and rights of laboratories, owners and inventions and patent rights with respect of the recording of any and all dialogue, music and other sound effects

embodied in the film and with respect to the use of all equipment, apparatus, appliances and other materials used in the photography recording or otherwise in the manufacture of the film.
- All claims and rights with respect to the use, distribution, performance, exhibition and exploitation of the film and the ancillary rights throughout the territory.
- All costs of producing and completing the film.

Except as expressly provided for in this agreement, there are no restrictions relating to the film and the ancillary rights which would or might prevent the financier from distributing or otherwise exploiting the film and the ancillary rights in accordance herewith and there are not and will not be any payments (out of any part of any revenues from the distribution or exploitation of the film or otherwise) which must be made by the financier to any actors, musicians, directors, writers or to other persons who participated in the film or to any union, guild or labour organisation for any right to exhibit the film or as compensation in connection with such exhibition or for any other use of the film of the ancillary rights or any of the rights therein and thereto granted hereunder.

The producer will be solely responsible for all costs in connection with the production of the film including all music synchronisation and master use licences in all media whether now known or hereafter devised and for all costs in connection with the delivery of the film to the financier hereunder (except for any performing rights payments due to the Performing Right Society Limited and its foreign affiliated societies).

The copyright in the film will be valid and subsisting throughout the world for the full period of copyright and all renewals and extensions thereof and no part of the film is in the public domain except such public domain music as may be contained in the film and such other underlying material as has been expressly approved by the financier.

There is no present or prospective claim, proceeding or litigation in respect of the film or the title of the film or ownership of or the copyright in the film or any underlying material on which the film is based which might in any way impair, limit, diminish or infringe upon any of the rights hereby expressed to be granted.

The financier will quietly and peacefully enjoy and possess each and all of the rights, licences and privileges herein granted or proposed to be granted to it throughout the term and the territory without interference or hindrance on the part of the producer and/or third parties.

There is no reason known to the producer which would prevent or cause any liability to arise upon the use of the title of the film in connection with the film.

The producer hereby indemnifies and agrees to keep the financier and its officers, directors, shareholders and employees fully and effectually indemnified, from and against any and all losses, costs, actions, proceedings, claims, damages, expenses (including reasonable legal costs and expenses and VAT thereon) and liabilities suffered or incurred, directly or indirectly, by the financier in consequence of any breach, non-performance or non-observance by the producer of any of the agreements, conditions, obligations, representations, warranties and undertakings on the part of the producer contained in this agreement.

3

3.5.5   Exhibit B – E&O application form

Television and Film Errors and Omissions Insurance Proposal

YOUR BUSINESS

1.   Name of insured

_____

2.   Date of establishment

_____

3.   Address of insured

_____

Postcode

_____

4.   Name of partners or directors   Years in the industry

_____

_____

_____

THE PRODUCTION

5.   Title of production

_____

_____

6.   Names of writer or author

_____

Names of producer

_____

Names of executive producer

_____

7. Is this production based on another work?   Yes ☐   No ☐

   If yes, explain and list title, date and name of author of such work

   _____

   _____

8. The production is:

   ☐ Television "entertainment"
   ☐ Television factual (but not investigative)   ☐ Television factual (investigative)
   ☐ Television drama
   ☐ Children and religious
   ☐ Daytime
   ☐ Other. Please give details

   Film for:
   ☐ Cinema release   ☐ Television release

9. If any of the above are a "series", how many episodes?

   _____

10. Running time of production?

   _____

11. Initial release or air date?

   _____

12. Territory of broadcast or distribution?

   _____

13. Is the agreement for distribution subject to US law?   Yes ☐   No ☐

14. Is the production

   ☐ Entirely fictional?
   ☐ Entirely fictional, but inspired by specific events and/or occurrences?
   ☐ A portrayal of actual facts which includes significant fictionalisation?
   ☐ A true portrayal of actual facts or happenings?

   Other than above (explain)

   _____

   _____

   _____

15. Brief description of storyline

_____

_____

16. The time frame for the setting of the plot is (e.g., the present, ten years in the future, within the last twenty years, etc.)

_____

17. Estimated gross annual turnover derived from the programme £

_____

CLEARANCE PROCEDURES

18. Has a title report been obtained from any title clearance service?   Yes ☐   No ☐

If yes, please indicate the name of service and attach copy. If no, explain

_____

_____

19. Have copyright reports been obtained?   Yes ☐   No ☐

If yes, are there any ambiguities,
gaps or problems in the chain of title?   Yes ☐   No ☐

If no copyright report has been obtained, please explain the reason

_____

_____

20. Is the production based upon, or does it include, any literary
or musical works which were first published or registered for
copyright prior to 1 January 1978?   Yes ☐   No ☐

If you answered yes, please provide the title, writer's name, and year of first publication (or registration) for each such pre-1978 work, and then answer questions (a) and (b) below. If you answered no, disregard the rest of this question

Title   Writer's name   Year

_____

_____

_____

(a) Did you clear each of the words identified above to be   Yes ☐   No ☐
certain that your production will not infringe
(now or in the future) the renewal copyrights to those works in light
of the United States Supreme Court in Stewart vs Abend, 110 S.Ct.1750 (1990)
(commonly referred to as the "Rear Window" case)?

(b) If you answered "yes" to question (a), please describe the clearance procedures you used
to be certain that your production will not infringe (now or in the future) the renewal
copyrights to those pre-1978 works.

_____

If you answered no to question (a), please explain why not. (Attach additional sheets for
your response, if necessary.)

_____

21. Is the name or likeness of any living person used in the production?   Yes ☐   No ☐

If yes, have clearances been obtained?   Yes ☐   No ☐

If no, explain

_____

_____

22. Is there a plausible risk that a living person could claim   Yes ☐   No ☐
(without regard to the merits) to be identifiable
in the production (whether or not the person's name or likeness
is used or the production purports to be fictional)?

If yes, have clearances been obtained?   Yes ☐   No ☐

If no, explain

_____

_____

23. Is the name or likeness of any deceased person used in the production?   Yes ☐   No ☐

If yes, have clearances been obtained from personal
representatives, heirs or owners of such rights?   Yes ☐   No ☐

If no, explain

_____

_____

Legal and business affairs

24. It is hereby confirmed that we have carried out   Yes ☐   No ☐
a full negative check which has been confirmed
as satisfactory by our lawyers who are party to this application.

If no, please explain

_____

_____

If yes, have all necessary changes been made?   Yes ☐   No ☐

If no, please explain

_____

_____

25. Will any film clips be used in this production?   Yes ☐   No ☐

If yes, have licences and consents for the film clips been obtained as follows:

From copyright owners?   Yes ☐   No ☐

From writers and others?   Yes ☐   No ☐

From performers or persons appearing in clip?   Yes ☐   No ☐

From music owners?   Yes ☐   No ☐

If any of the answers above is no, please explain

_____

_____

26. Are any photographs used in the production?   Yes ☐   No ☐

If yes, have licences and consents been obtained as follows: Yes ☐   No ☐

From individuals or businesses depicted?   Yes ☐   No ☐

From copyright holders?   Yes ☐   No ☐

If any of the answers above is no, please explain

_____

_____

27. Have the following musical rights been cleared:

(a) Recording and synchronisation?   Yes ☐   No ☐

(b) Performing rights?   Yes ☐   No ☐

(c) Right to distribute for all forms of distribution
     contemplated (home video, etc.)?   Yes ☐   No ☐

     If the response to any of the above is no, please explain

_____

_____

_____

28. Has a music cue sheet been prepared?   Yes ☐   No ☐

     If no, explain

_____

_____

_____

29. If original music has been commissioned,
     has a "Hold Harmless*" been obtained from the composer?   Yes ☐   No ☐

     If no, explain

_____

_____

_____

30. Will a soundtrack album be produced?   Yes ☐   No ☐
     If yes, answer the following:

(a) Have you acquired all necessary rights and licences?   Yes ☐   No ☐

(b) Have you acquired separate insurance coverage for this recording?   Yes ☐   No ☐

     If the response to any of the above questions is no, please explain

_____

_____

Legal and business affairs

* In other words, a warranty and indemnity whereby the composer warrants that he has the rights, and that he can grant them to the producer, and agrees to compensate the producer if there is a claim for breach of this warranty. Both the warranty and the indemnity are standard terms in a composer's agreement.

31. Will any merchandise (i.e. toys, dolls, clothing, etc.)   Yes ☐   No ☐
be created from this production

(a) If yes, describe

_____

_____

(b) If merchandise is to be created and distributed   Yes ☐   No ☐
based upon the production, have all necessary consents
and licences been obtained from performers, authors,
artists, etc., to produce and distribute this merchandise?

If no, explain

_____

_____

(c) Has additional or separate insurance coverage for this   Yes ☐   No ☐
merchandise been obtained?

If no, explain

_____

_____

32. Will there be any computer version of this production   Yes ☐   No ☐
(i.e. computer game, video game, interactive CD)?

(a) If yes, describe

_____

_____

(b) If a computer version of this production is to be created   Yes ☐   No ☐
and distributed based upon the production, have all
necessary rights been obtained from the performers,
authors, programmers, etc., to produce and distribute
this version in all territories and software platforms contemplated?

If no, explain

_____

_____

(c) Has additional or separate insurance coverage
for the computer version been obtained? Yes ☐ No ☐

If yes, explain

_____

_____

33. Have you or any of your agents been unable to obtain Yes ☐ No ☐
or been refused an agreement or release after having
(a) negotiated for rights in literary, musical or other materials,
or (b) negotiated for release from any persons with the production?
If yes, explain

_____

_____

LAWYERS USED FOR CLEARANCES

34. Name, address and telephone number of your lawyers (if a firm, also name individual at firm)

_____

35. Have your lawyers read and agreed to use their best Yes ☐ No ☐
efforts to ensure that the "Clearance Procedures"
attached are followed?

If no, explain

_____

_____

CLAIMS DECLARATION

36. Has any claim been brought against you arising out of:
invasion of privacy, infringement of copyright Yes ☐ No ☐
(statutory or common law), defamation,
unauthorised use of titles, formats, characters, plots,
idea, other programme material embodied in any production,
or breach of implied contract arising out of the alleged
submission of any literary or musical material?

If yes, please give details

_____

_____

Are you aware of any existing or threatened claims   Yes ☐   No ☐
or legal proceedings of any kind, based on the
production to be insured or any material contained
in or upon which such production is based?

If yes, please give details

_____

_____

DECLARATION

1. I/we declare that (a) this proposal form has been completed after proper enquiry, (b) its
    contents are true and accurate, and (c) all facts and matters which may be relevant to the
    consideration of our proposal for insurance have been disclosed.
2. I/we undertake to inform you, before any contract of insurance is concluded, if there is
    any material change to the information already provided or any new fact or matter arises
    which may be relevant to the consideration or our proposal for insurance.
3. I/we agree that this proposal form and all other written information which is provided are
    incorporated into and from the basis of any contract of insurance.

_____

Signature of principal/partner/director   Date

AS LAWYERS FOR THE ABOVE INSURED, WE BELIEVE THE STATEMENTS CONTAINED IN
THE PROPOSAL FORM ARE CORRECT. WE ARE FAMILIAR WITH THE UNDERWRITERS'
STANDARD CLEARANCE PROCEDURES, WHICH ARE ATTACHED TO THE PROPOSAL FORM,
AND WE HAVE BEEN RETAINED BY THE INSURED TO, AND WILL, USE OUR BEST EFFORTS
TO SEE THAT THOSE CLEARANCE PROCEDURES ARE FOLLOWED.

_____

Signature of lawyer(s)   Date

CLEARANCE PROCEDURES

Your lawyers should assure themselves of the following before first exhibition of the insured production:

1. A copyright report must be obtained, covering domestic and foreign copyright, as well as all extensions and renewals thereof, for all literary material (other than original and unpublished) contained in the production. If the insured is acquiring the production as a completed work (such as a pick-up of a motion picture), a copyright report must also be obtained covering the completed work. In the case of an unpublished original work, the origin of the work must be traced in order to ascertain that the insured has all required rights in the work.

2. Written agreements must exist between the insured and the creators, authors, writers and owners of all material, including quotations from copyrighted works, used in the insured production, authorising the insured to use all the material in the insured production.

3. If the production is in any way based on actual facts, it must be ascertained is the source material is primary (e.g., direct interview court records) and not secondary (e.g., another copyrighted work). Use of the secondary sources may be permissible, but full details must be provided by the company in an attachment to the application.

4. Written releases must be obtained from all persons who are recognisable or who might reasonably claim to be identifiable in the insured production, or whose name, image or likeness is used, and if such person is a minor, the minor's consent must be legally binding. If the recognisable or identifiable person is deceased, releases must be obtained from the personal representative of such person. Releases of the type described in the preceding two sentences may not be required in certain instances, but full details must be provided by the company in an attachment to the application. Releases are not necessary if the recognisable person is part of a crowd or background shot and his image is not shown for more than a few seconds or given special emphasis.

5. Where the work is fictional in whole or in part, the names of all characters must be fictional. In certain limited instances, particular names need not be fictional, but full details must be provided by the company in an attachment to the application.

6. Where scenes are filmed depicting or referring to distinctive businesses, personal property or products identifiable with a person, film or corporation, or depicting or referring to distinctive real property of any person, firm or corporation, written releases must be obtained from such person, firm or corporation granting the insured the right to film and use such property in the insured production. In certain instances releases may not be required, but full details must be provided by the company in an attachment to the application. Releases are not necessary if property is non-distinctive background only.

7. All releases must give the insured the right to edit, modify, add to and/or delete any or all of the material supplied by the releasor. Releases from recognisable persons must grant the insured the right to fictionalise the insured's portrayal of the releasor.

8. All contracts and releases must give the insured the right to market the production for use in all media and markets (e.g., video discs, cassettes, supplemental markets), except to the extent the insured qualifies the application to exclude insurance coverage for particular media.

9. Synchronisation and performance licences must be obtained from the composer or copyright owner of all music used in the insured production. Licences are unnecessary if the music (and its arrangement) is in the public domain. Licences must also be obtained for the use of previously recorded music.

Legal and business affairs

10. If the production contains any film clips, the insured must obtain authorisation to use film clip from the owner of the clip who has the right to grant such authorisation, and must obtain authority from the appropriate persons for "secondary use" of all material contained in the film clip, e.g., underlying literary and musical rights, performances of actors and musicians.

11. A report (generally known as a "title report") covering the title of the production must be obtained from a recognised source setting forth prior uses of the same or similar titles, and the title of the production must be changed to avoid any conflict.

12. It must be determined whether the applicant, or any of its officers, directors, partners or agents, received any submission of any similar material or production, and if so, the company must be fully advised of all circumstances relating to each occurrence, in an attachment to the application.

13. It must be determined that the insured production does not contain any material which constitutes defamation, invasion of privacy or violation of the right of publicity or of any other right of any other person, firm or corporation.

14. Prior to any public exhibition of the production, it must be previewed to assure that the Clearance Procedures have been followed.

15. To the extent that any information required to be furnished pursuant to these Clearance Procedures is not known at the time of the application, such information must be furnished in writing to the company as soon as known.

The foregoing Clearance Procedures are not exhaustive nor do they cover all situations which may arise, given the great variety of productions. You and your lawyers must continually monitor the production at all stages, and in light of any special circumstances, make certain that the production contains no material which could give rise to a claim.

3.5.6 Exhibit C

Waiver of moral rights by country

Belgium

Moral rights are inalienable, except for integrity right.

France

Moral rights are inalienable though the author can waive temporarily the paternity right. The author is not forced to reveal himself as the author of a literary work.

Germany

Moral rights are waivable but the author is protected in case of gross distortion on the work.

Greece

Dissemination of the work, alterations and access to the work are waivable in certain cases and by written contract.

Italy

Moral rights are inalienable. The author can waive authorship of a commissioned work when another person finishes it.

The Netherlands

Author can waive right to be named, to restrain publication under his name and to restrain modifications of his work. The rights against distortion and mutilation prejudicial to reputation are not waivable.

Spain

Moral rights are inalienable.

Sweden

Moral rights are waivable for specified uses of the work.

Switzerland

Integrity right can be waived, though the author is protected from changes that prejudice personal interests.

The UK

Statutory moral rights can be waived by contract or in an informal way.

3

3.6 Engaging the director

3.6.1 Director's engagement checklist

Project name

Name of director

Agent's name

Contact address
Tel:
Fax:
Email:

Contracting party
Is the agreement with the director or his loan-out company? If the director's services are to be provided by his loan-out company, you will need an inducement letter from the director, the principal terms of which are the same as for an actor – see "Actor's engagement checklist", page 107.

Address

Preliminary issues
1. Have you asked for a quote of the director's fees?
2. Are you engaging the director for the development period or just the production?
3. Will the engagement be "pay *or* play" or "pay *and* play"? If the latter, for how long?
4. Nationality of director: if the director is a US citizen he will likely be a member of the Directors' Guild of America ("DGA"). If the director is French you will have to

accept that he has unwaivable moral rights, at least in France.
    Are any visas or work permits required?
5. Is the director, or are you, the producer, subject to any union or guild regulations? If the director is a DGA member the DGA will seek to have jurisdiction over the terms of his engagement even if the film is wholly European and the director's services are to be rendered in Europe. In which case you will not be able to contract out of the obligation to pay residuals or make contributions to his pension, health and welfare fund. Also the DGA Basic Agreement gives the director other rights, in particular the Basic Agreement gives the director certain cutting rights and rights to choose the first assistant director. It may be possible to avoid the jurisdiction of the DGA if it can be shown that not only are the services to be rendered outside the US but the deal was initiated and negotiated outside the US. To achieve this the director must have a non-US representative (i.e. agent or lawyer).
6. Is the engagement conditional? If so, upon what?

3.6.2 Deal points

Subject to contract
The correspondence/deal memo should be headed "subject to contract" so that no contract is entered into until the written agreement is signed.

Development

1. **Start date.**
2. **Services required:** e.g. supervision of the writer; attending script meetings; being involved in casting; attending auditions; visiting potential locations.
3. **Compensation:** the director's fee for development services is not generally a

large one and should be offset against their directing fee when the film goes into production. Sometimes it may be necessary to agree to an abandonment payment if the film is not made.

4. **Are the director's services exclusive or non-exclusive?** They will usually be non-exclusive during development.

5. **Expenses** (if any).

6. **Terms of "attachment" to project.**
What does attachment really mean?
You will want an option over the director's services so that you can ask him to direct the film when you have raised the finance. This is unlikely to be acceptable to an established director who will want the right to decline if he is not going to be available when you want him. Also the director will not want to be forced to direct unless he is happy with the script and possibly also the cast.

7. **Copyright.**
If the director has supervised the writer during development, or has otherwise made a contribution to the script he will probably own the copyright in his contribution unless the development agreement contains an assignment of his copyright. If there is no such assignment, either because the development agreement did not contain one or because there was no written development agreement, there may be a problem if the film is made with another director. The director may require payment in order to induce him to assign his copyright to you.

Production

1. **Start date**
Usually commencement of pre-production.

2. **Services exclusive/non-exclusive**
   - *Pre-production:* should be exclusive.
   - *Principal photography:* must be exclusive.
   - *Post-production:* should be exclusive at least until delivery of the answer print.

3. **Period of principal photography**

4. **Publicity services**
Try to agree that the director will support the release of the film by giving interviews and attending premieres and markets. Such services should be free except for payment of travelling and accommodation expenses, and be subject to the director's prior professional commitments.

5. **"Pay or play"/"pay and play"**
(For definition of pay and play, see Glossary in *Volume 1*, page 213).

6. **Compensation**
Fixed fee. Example: say 20% during pre-production; 60% in weekly instalments during production; 10% on delivery of the answer print; and 10% on complete delivery.

Overages (if any): the fixed fee should ideally be a fee for directing the film and not for a fixed number of weeks of services, and so no overage payment should be made in the event that making the film takes longer than anticipated.

Deferments: payable when and from which funds?

Profit share: it is usual to give the director a share of the profit, particularly if he has been involved in the production throughout the development period.

The possibilities are:

- *Out of gross:* only "A" list directors working below their normal rate can demand this. And you can only agree it if the financiers and distributors agree.

- *A percentage of 100% of net profits:* this is what the director's agent will want to protect against you giving too big a share to the financiers.

- *A percentage of the producer's share of net profits:* in other words the share that you are left with after the financiers have taken their share (but before you have shared profits with the other talent). This is best for the producer, but you will usually have to give a larger percentage.

7. **Approvals**

The director may ask for approval over the script, principal cast, director of photography, editor and other elements. Whatever you agree to must be subject to the financiers' final approval, although the reality is that a director will not normally direct a script that he does not consider ready, whatever the contract may say.

8. **Cutting rights**

Only major directors are in a position to insist on final cut. If you are being forced to accept that the director has final cut make sure that your financiers and principal distributors understand and approve. Even if you give the director final cut you must retain the right to cut for censorship, television timing and airline versions, although you could give the director the first opportunity to make these cuts if he is available.

A director will usually prepare the director's cut and have the opportunity to make further cuts in consultation with the producer, but the producer will have the right to make the final cut. If the director is reasonably well established as a feature director, and if the budget allows, he may be offered the opportunity to have a number of previews (which may be private or public) and to make cuts consequent on those previews.

9. **Director's obligations**

The director will normally agree to:
- consult with the producer on the script
- assist in preparing production schedule and budget
- assist in casting
- make the film in accordance with the script and budget
- ensure that the film is delivered on time, with the correct running time and able to qualify for the specified censorship rating
- supervise editing, titling, scoring, dubbing and completion

- assist in the making of promotional films, trailers and any "making of…" film.

10. **Rights**

The director must assign the copyright in all his contributions including full waiver of moral rights and grant of rental and lending rights.

The director should also give his consent to the use of his name and likeness in connection with ancillary exploitation and for purposes of publicity and promotion of the film.

11. **Credit**

On film:
- *possessory:* only for established major directors, e.g. "a Steven Spielberg film".
- *"directed by":* the standard position is on a single card, last in the main title before the film, size and prominence tied to the individual producer.

In paid ads – subject to customary distributors' exclusions.

In ancillary exploitation, e.g. on video box, on soundtrack album cover, on merchandising. These can be the subject of negotiation.

12. **Expenses**

Per diem?
What does it cover?

13. **Accommodation**

Who pays? Who organises?

14. **Travel**

Class?
This is often tied to individual producer and/or principal cast.

15. **Ground transportation**

Exclusive/non-exclusive? It is usual to give the director an exclusive car because it can be awkward for him to have to travel with the cast after a "difficult" day.

16. **Office**

The agent will often ask for the director to have an office and secretary during pre-production and principal photography. It is good to be able to agree this if the budget can cover it.

17. **Premieres/festivals**

The director will often ask for the right to be invited to premieres, festivals and markets, or at least be tied to the producer in this respect. You will almost certainly not have money in your budget to cover the expense of doing so. You should turn it around and oblige the director to attend, if required, and only ask him to attend if a distributor is willing to underwrite the cost. A director would not normally be paid for these services but would certainly expect travel and accommodation expenses (and probably *per diems*) to be paid on the same basis as for production services.

18. **Videotape**

You may be asked to provide the director with a videotape of the film; you should only agree to do so when one is commercially available.

19. **Right to direct sequels and/or remakes**

If there is the possibility of a remake or sequel it will probably be because the original film was successful. It is fair, therefore, to agree that the director should have the first opportunity to direct any such further film. The offer should be conditional upon the director not having been in breach of this agreement, having received the directing credit on the original film, and him still being an active director of feature films. The obligation to make the offer should only last for seven years after the release of the film and the director should only have a limited time (say 14 days) in which to decide to accept the offer.

3.7 Engaging the cast

3.7.1 Artist's engagement checklist

Project

Role

Name of artist

Agent

Contact address

Tel:
Fax:
Email:

Contracting party

If loan-out company, you will need an inducement letter from the individual artist, the principal terms of which are:

- the artist agrees that there is an agreement between the artist and the loan-out company and the loan-out company is entitled to provide the artist's services
- the artist has read the main agreement and agrees to perform in accordance with its terms
- the artist will look only to the loan-out company for payment
- if the loan-out company ceases to exist for any reason or breaches the main agreement the artist will be deemed to be a direct party to the main agreement
- the artist assigns any rights (including rental and lending rights) he may have to the production company and waives moral rights to the extent possible.

Address

Legal and business affairs

3.7.2 Deal points

Preliminaries

1. Have you asked the agent for the artist's quotes? For example, what fees did the artist get for recent roles? Check the quotes to the best of your ability. Did the producer really pay the amount quoted? What were the budgets of the films quoted? Were they British or US, independent or studio? Did they perform well at the box office?

2. Will the engagement be pay or play (see Glossary in *Volume 1*), or subject to contract or conditional on the occurrence of specific events?

3. Nationality of artist. Are any visas or work permits required?

4. Is the artist, or are you, the producer, subject to any union or guild regulations?

5. Are there any tax issues to be considered? For example, withholding tax, or perhaps the artist is American and seeking an indemnity from you against any tax liabilities that might arise in your country.

6. Is the artist a minor? If so, what are the consequences in terms of working conditions, location films, especially filming abroad? Local legal advice indicated.

The engagement

1. **Start date**
   Start of principal photography of the role. Usually seven days prior to or after a given date.

2. **Scheduled period of principal photography**
   How many weeks have you scheduled and budgeted for the shooting of the role?

3. **Period of rehearsals**
   Must rehearsal days/weeks be immediately prior to the start date?

4. **Post-production services**
   Exclusive/non-exclusive? Subject to artist's prior professional commitments? Once nominated by you then services should be on exclusive basis.

5. **Stop date**
   Is there a date beyond which the artist will not work? If so, the completion guarantor and the financiers must be asked to approve.

6. **Publicity services**
   Often distributors will require the producer to procure that artists give press conferences and attend premieres/festivals. Expenses will be paid on the same basis as for acting engagement.

7. **"Free" days/weeks**
   Agents may agree a (small) number of free post-production days. Sometimes agents will agree a free principal photography week in order to keep the artist's quote up for future engagements.

8. **Services exclusive/non-exclusive**
   Exclusive during principal photography, "free" weeks and additional period of photography, and for nominated post-production days.

Compensation

1. **Fixed fee**
   Payable in weekly instalments during the scheduled period of principal photography.

2. **Overage**
   Daily/weekly rate payable if principal photography extends over scheduled period.

3. **Deferments**
   Payable when and from which funds?

4. **Profit participation**
   Not all actors are awarded a share of profits, but sometimes the principals are given shares and sometimes, on very low, or so called "no budget" films all the cast will be given a profit share.
   The possibilities are:
   - *Out of gross*: only "A" list cast working below their normal rate can demand this and you can only agree it if the financiers and distributors agree.
   - *A percentage of 100% of net profits*: this is what the agent will want, to

protect the artist against you giving too big a share to the financiers.

- *A percentage of the producer's share of net profits*: in other words the share that you are left with after the financiers have taken their share (but before you have shared profits with the other talent). This is best for the producer, but you will usually have to give a larger percentage.

5. **Other**

    For example, a box-office bonus which would have to be paid to the artist by the distributor(s).

6. **Withholding tax?**

    The tax authorities in some countries require producers to withhold a percentage of payments being made to foreign persons and companies. If you are agreeing to make payments to foreigners, check whether withholding tax applies.

Pay or play

If the engagement is pay or play, then the producer will be bound to pay the fixed fee. Unless failure to produce the film is caused by the artist's death, incapacity or default or for *force majeure* reasons.

Rights

1. **In the performance**

    All rights in all media now known, or hereafter devised, throughout the world in perpetuity, including full waiver of moral rights.

2. **Name and likeness**

    In connection with ancillary exploitation and for purposes of publicity and promotion of the film. Does the artist have any approval rights?

3. **Dubbing and doubling**

    Any restrictions? For example, rights for the artist to dub in own language(s).

Credit

1. **On film**

    Position; single card; above/below main titles; size; size of lettering; and percentage in relation to the title.

2. **In paid ads**

    Subject to customary distributors' exclusions.

Expenses and working conditions

1. *Per diem*

    What does it cover?

2. **Accommodation**

    Who pays? Who organises?

3. **Travel**

    Class?

4. **Ground transportation**

    Exclusive/non-exclusive?

5. **Dressing room/trailer**

    Exclusive?

6. **Premieres/festivals**

    Check with distributor; don't accept obligations to invite; obtain obligations to attend.

7. **Wardrobe**

    Does artist have to supply?

    Can artist keep?

8. **Nudity**

    Is any nudity/simulated sex involved? If so, discuss with agent. There may be union/guild requirements to observe. The agent may impose conditions.

3.8 Sales agency and distribution agreements

Sales agency agreements should be distinguished from distribution agreements. A sales agency is where a producer appoints an agent to sell a film in more than one territory, whereas under a distribution agreement the distributor acquires rights only in its own territory.

Since sales agents increasingly want to acquire distribution rights for re-sale (as opposed to mere agent's authority to sell on the owner's behalf), discussions with a sales agent should clearly identify which type of deal is on the table. Sales agents are often referred to as international distributors, particularly if they have acquired distribution rights, rather than agency rights.

Very different scenarios are possible. The sales agent may simply agree to arrange the sale of a completed project or may become involved before production and be part of the financing by providing a minimum guarantee or advance. The role of the sales agent (or international distributor) and the terms of the agreement will differ – possibly substantially – in each case.

The role of the sales agent is central in a number of other situations. For instance, if the production finance or part of it is to be raised by means of a bank loan to cover a gap, the bank (or insurers if an insurance policy is part of the collateral) will want to see satisfactory sales estimates from a reliable sales agent. Also the appointment of a sales agent can be a condition to obtaining finance from some subsidy-giving bodies.

3.8.1 Sales agency checklist

Subject to contract

If you do not intend a contract to be formed until the written agreement is signed, all correspondence and draft agreements should be expressed to be "subject to contract".

Producer

Full name and legal status of party granting the rights:
Address:
Tel no:
Fax no:
Email:

Sales agent

Correct legal name and form (i.e. company/partnership/individual):
Place of incorporation if a company:
Contact name:
Address:
Tel no:
Fax no:
Email:

Programme/film

Territories granted to sales agent

Territories reserved to producer

Authorised languages

Nature of appointment

(Agency or grant of distribution rights.)

Scope of agency

Distribution contracts – can producer approve?
Marketing campaign – who devises?

Sales agent's responsibilities

Marketing.
Sales.
Delivery to distributors.
Collection from distributors.

Sales agent's obligations

To prepare marketing plan.
To spend agreed minimum on prints and advertising.
To maximise receipts.
To achieve pre-agreed minimum prices.
To provide sales information.
To allocate between different projects contained in same package on a fair/arm's length basis.
To attend certain markets.

Restrictions on sales agent

Not to sell below agreed minimum prices.
Not to spend more than agreed maximum on prints and advertising.
Not to cut or edit without consent.
No packaging.
No sub-agents.
Observe windows/holdbacks.

Sales agent's approval rights

If the sales agent is paying a minimum guarantee or advance and the programme has not been produced at the time of entering into the agreement, the sales agent will usually require approval over:
• screenplay (and changes)
• budget (and variations)
• principal cast (and substitutes)
• director (and substitute)
• production and post-production schedule
• heads of department
• completion guarantor (if any).

Rights granted

Television: standard; non-standard TV/digital.
Video: sell-through; rental.

Video on demand.
Theatrical: conventional cinema.
Non-theatrical: hotels/ships and aeroplanes.
DVD.
Internet.
Ancillary rights: merchandising; soundtrack; music publishing; print publishing; interactive; computer games.
Right to edit? For all purposes or just censorship, TV and airline versions?

Rights reserved

Particularly future media?

Term

Initial term.
Sales threshold for extension of term.
Extension period.

Producer's rights

Sales
Right to approve sales agent's form of contract.
Right to approve all sales/or just sales below agreed minimum.
Right to approve identity of distributor.
Right to approve all financial terms.
Do approvals apply to all territories or just key territories?
Is there a mechanism for deemed approval?

Marketing campaign
Approval/consultation of overall strategy?
Approval/consultation of whole campaign?

Delivery date

Date by which the film must be delivered to the sales agent.

Delivery materials

Access.
Print materials.
Documentary materials.
Who pays?

Ownership of physical materials

Who owns:

1. Delivery materials.
2. Materials generated by distributor.

Advance/minimum guarantee

Total amount.

Timing of payment.

Is the advance or minimum guarantee supported by a letter of credit, provided by the sales agent?

Sales commission

Commission rates will generally be lower if the sales agent is not taking the risk of putting up an advance.

Inclusive/exclusive of sub-agent's commissions?

Expenses

Capped?

Interest on expenses.

Gross receipts

It is important to agree the definition of gross receipts since it forms the basis on which the sales agent will account to the producer.

Gross receipts should obviously include the receipts arising from the exploitation of all the rights granted; so if, for example, merchandising rights are granted, then the merchandising income should fall into gross receipts.

The sales agent will want to ensure that it only has to account for monies actually received from distributors, and the producer will want to ensure that the sales agent does not calculate its commission on monies which are not received because of the effect of withholding tax.

Typical definition: *"all receipts, revenue and income of every kind payable to the sales agent from the exploitation of the rights granted and actually received into the collection account including without limitation all non-returnable minimum guarantees, advances, fees and overages net of withholding tax, VAT and import duties".*

Division of gross receipts

Order of application: typically commission, then expenses (including residuals if paid by sales agent), then recoupment of advance, then to producer (either 100% or in agreed back-end ratio).

Payment direction

To whom should distributors (i.e. territorial distributors to whom the sales agent sells rights) make payment? To:

- sales agent
- producer
- joint account (producer and sales agent)
- sales agent's bank
- producer's bank
- collection agent.

From the producer's point of view, payment to the sales agent or their bank should be avoided, because in the event of the sales agent's insolvency the producer's share may be lost. It is unlikely that the sales agent will agree to payment into the producer's bank or even to establish a joint account, and so a collection agent is often the best solution. The distributor should be required to acknowledge the payment direction and waive rights of set-off and counter-claim by distributor.

Accounting

Trust account (rare).

Accounting periods.

Currency of account.

Accounting after expiry of term.

Reporting

Frequency.

Detail.

Audit rights

Right to audit sales agent:
• frequency
• detail.

Sales agent to pay if audit shows significant discrepancy (say 5% or 10%)?
Right to require the sales agent to audit distributors/licencees.

Insurance

Production insurance.
E&O.
Materials.

Warranties and indemnities

Standard warranties.

Essential elements

Are there any essential elements?
Pre-approved substitutes: or mechanism for approving substitutes.

Insolvency

Material adverse change.
Right to terminate.
Effect of insolvency on: agency: commission.

Sub-licensing

If permitted, is commission inclusive of sub-licencee's commission?

Termination

Producer's right to terminate:
• sales agent's failure to make payments
• material breach by sales agent
• failure by sales agent to reach pre-agreed targets
• length of cure period for sales agent to remedy breach if capable of remedy
• insolvency of sales agent.

Sales agent's right to terminate:
• material breach
• cure period.

Effect of termination on agency: how will agreements made by sales agent on producer's behalf be serviced?

Governing law/jurisdiction

Governing law.
Jurisdiction.

Who is to draft the contract?

Deal memo.
Long-form agreement.
Time frame.

3.8.2 Distribution agreement checklist

Distributor

Full correct legal identity:
Address:
Tel:
Fax:
Email:

Territory

Countries.
Exclusive?
Languages?

Term

Length of agreement.
Can distributor sub-licence for period greater than the term?

Rights granted

Nature of grant: licence or assignment?
Is grant of rights conditional on payment of a minimum guarantee or advance?

Which rights?

Television: standard; non-standard TV/digital.
Video: sell-through; rental.
Theatrical.
Non-theatrical: hotels/ships/aeroplanes.
DVD.
Internet.
Media hereafter invented.

Ancillary rights

Merchandising.

Games rights: can these rights be exploited on a territorial basis?
Soundtrack.
Music publishing: is distributor the party best equipped to exploit these rights?
Print publishing.

Promotion rights

Right to publicise.
Right to dub/sub-title.
Right to use photographs, biographies and star likenesses for advertisements.
Right to advertise on the Internet.

Rights reserved

Particularly future media.
Soundtrack?

Restrictions on distributor

Release date: is distributor prevented from releasing before release in another territory? Controlling the sequential release of the film in different media should help to maximise the film's earnings. This is done through a system of holdbacks and windows, the principal ones being:
• theatrical window
• video sell-through window
• video-rented window
• pay-per-view window
• pay-TV window.

Distributor's commitments

P&A (prints and advertising).

Expenditure

Minimum.
Maximum.
Financial guarantee of expenditure, e.g. Letter of Credit.

Prints

Minimum and maximum number of prints on which the film will be released.

Key cities for release

Campaign strategy

Does producer have approval?

Cutting and editing

For what reasons can this be done?

Use of sub-distributors

Is this permitted? What element of control does the producer want over this?

Distributor's approval rights

If distribution agreement is a pre-sale, the distributor will want approval over at least the following elements:
• screenplay
• budget
• director
• leading costs
• delivery date
• substitutes for above.

Commission, expenses and application of receipts

Gross receipts definition

Does it include ancillary exploitation, e.g. merchandising?

Net receipts definition

Does it exclude fees to sub-licencees/sub-distributors?
Taxes/levies?

Commission

What is the distributor's rate of commission? Is it uniform or does it vary according to territory/medium?

Distribution expenses

Sub-titling/dubbing.
Transportation.
Print manufacture.
Less any discounts?
Overall maximum?

Order of application

Do the producer and distributor share receipts after deduction of distribution expenses? Or does the distributor charge commission on 100% of receipts then deduct its expenses and then account to the producer?

Which method is best for the producer? (It will depend on the level of receipts.)

Any minimum guarantee or advance will usually be recouped out of the producer's share.

Payment direction

Does the distributor pay the producer, bank or collection agent?

Distributor's acknowledgement of payment direction/distributor's waiver of rights of counter-claim: is usually a separate document but could be in the distribution agreement if the bank's requirements are known.

Minimum guarantee/advance

Total fixed amount.

Stage payments, i.e. 10% on signature, 80% on "mandatory" delivery, balance on full delivery.

Supported by Letter of Credit?

Non-refundable?

Delivery

Delivery date.

Delivery materials:

1. Essential delivery materials to trigger minimum guarantee or advance (i.e. "mandatory delivery")
2. further delivery materials
3. documentary delivery items:
   I. copies of chain of title documents
   II. cast contracts
   III. lab access letter
   IV. credit obligations
   V. copyright registration
   VI. music cue sheets
   VII. certificate of nationality.

Ownership of physical materials

Who owns:

1. Delivery materials?
2. Materials generated by distributor?

Accounting and audit rights

Trust account?

Accounting periods?

Currency of account?

Accounting after expiry of term?

Frequency of reporting?

Detail of reporting?

Frequency of audit rights?

Payment of shortfall – plus interest?

Insurance

E&O: naming distributor as additional insured.

Materials: who insures?

Termination

Producer's right to terminate

Distributor's failure to pay minimum guarantee or advance.

Material breach by distributor

Length of cure period (opportunity to remedy breach, if breach is capable of remedy).

Insolvency of distributor.

If the distributor has paid an advance or provided a minimum guarantee, they will not permit termination until recoupment of the advance or release from the minimum guarantee commitment.

Distributor should not be entitled to continue to receive their commission if the agreement is terminated by the producer as a result of the distributor's breach.

Distributor's right to terminate

Producer's material breach.

Length of cure period.

Effect of termination on grant of rights: how will third-party licence agreements be serviced?

3

3.8.3   Delivery items

Schedule 1 – the delivery materials

Suggested material for a feature film

Film elements (1)

Physical delivery of the following in respect of the film:

1. 35mm interpositive (taken from complete and fully graded original negative).
2. 35mm internegatives (from interpositive, capable of making one light prints).
3. 35mm stereo optical soundtrack negative (synchronised with the picture negative).
4. 35mm English colour print (show print) made from the original negative, final gradings with combined stereo sound track.
5. 35mm English colour combined stereo check print from items 2 and 3 above.
6. 35mm master of magnetic SVA two-track English stereo soundtrack of the film.
7. (a) 35mm master of magnetic stereo four-track and effects track (effects must be comprehensively filled)
    (b) 35mm copy of magnetic stereo four-track M&E.
8. 35mm non-stereo three- or four-track magnetic master with separate dialogue, separate music and separate effects.
9. 35mm internegative and interpositive of textless backgrounds for main titles, end titles and any captions or sub-titles contained in the film – to include all optical fades and dissolves, to length of titled sequences.
10. D2 (Digital) PAL master videotape – first generation from graded TV quality print, with the English stereo mix on audio channels one and two, and the international stereo M&E on audio channels three and

four, and with the textless title backgrounds on the end of the same tape.

11. (Three-quarters) inch PAL U-Matic cassette of the completed film (whenever possible taken from item 10 above, but in any case a straight run-through excluding leaders).
12. In respect of the trailer of the film:
    (a) 35mm interpositive
    (b) 35mm optical soundtrack negative
    (c) 35mm textless internegative
    (d) 35mm four-track magnetic master of the soundtrack containing separate narration/dialogue/music/effects
    (e) 35mm mono mixed magnetic master of the soundtrack
    (f) post-production script.
13. Such out-takes, trims and spares and TV cover shots as shall be reasonably required of negative, print and sound elements.

Film elements (2)

Laboratory access letter* to:

14. 35mm original negative of the full and final film.
15. 35mm six- to twelve-track magnetic of stereo masters of the English soundtrack.
16. All master music specifically recorded for the film on original multi-track, plus 1 x 1/4" mix-down of same.
17. 35mm low-contrast, combined-print suitable for TV mastering.

Trailer elements

Physical delivery of:

18. 35mm print.
19. 35mm action negative of trailer.
20. 35mm optical sound track negative of trailer.
21. 35mm master interpositive of trailer.
22. 35mm textless interpositive and internegative of trailer (if applicable).
23. 35mm four-track magnetic master of the soundtrack of the trailer containing separate narration/dialogue/music/ effects.
24. 35mm SVA mixed magnetic master of the trailer soundtrack.

25. 35mm four-track stereo M&E master (L/C/R/S).

26. Digital PAL and NTSC video masters of the trailer (configured as per the film in item 12 above).

27. Post-production script of the trailer.

Publicity material

Physical delivery of:

28. All artwork or logo material available. (The grantor shall ensure that fully cleared rights to reproduce have been secured.)

29. Contact sheets of all B&W stills photographs, plus 100 negatives (to be selected from the contact sheets by the distributor and having full use approval as applicable).

30. One 10" x 8" B&W still from each of the selected 100 negatives, each with a detailed identity caption.

31. 100 selected original colour transparencies (35mm) each with a detailed identity caption (having full use approval).

32. EPK and TV spots to be supplied on PAL, BETA SP tape or better.

33. If a poster exists, one sample plus access to key elements such as poster art transparency and PMT of poster ad block.

Written material (1)

Physical delivery of:

34. Fully timed post-production script including spotting information (master + 8 copies).

35. Final shooting script.

36. Music cue sheet (giving details of all music contained in the film with title, composer/arranger, publisher, performer, pre-recorded source reference, usage category and duration).

37. Copies of all the fully executed music licences (synchronisation, performance and mechanical) pertaining to all music in the film.

38. Copies of all fully executed licences, contracts, assignments or permission for all film clip, archive footage or photographic materials contained in the film.

39. A complete statement of all screen and paid advertising credit obligations, together with a layout of the proposed screen and advertising credits and a statement of all contractual restrictions as to the use of name and likeness or otherwise of any contributor together with excerpts from any agreement agreeing to give screen and/or paid advertising credit.

40. A complete list of all contributors (i.e. cast and crew) identifying, where appropriate, their union or guild.

41. A statement of all persons whose worldwide rights in all media have been "bought out" and a statement of any residual, re-use or future payment obligations.

42. Contact list for principal players, director, producer and writer.

43. Four (4) original notarised certificates of origin (if non-EEC film) or certificate of nationality (if EEC film).

44. Four (4) original notarised producer's attestation/chain of title.

45. Certificate of authorship – in English and in French.

46. Biographies of principal cast and crew.

47. Long-form synopsis (three pages) and short synopsis (two paragraphs).

48. Production information/production notes/ interviews, etc.

49. Statement of dubbing restrictions.

50. Final audited cost statement – this item to be delivered within three months after the date of delivery of the film.

51. Errors and Omissions insurance certificate.

52. Title and copyright search and reports.

53. Copyright registration certificate for the script.

54. Copy of grantor's application for copyright registration.

55. Copyright registration certificate for the film (this item to be delivered as soon as

the same is available to the grantor, the grantor having used reasonable endeavours to obtain the same as early as possible).

56. Copies of all documents evidencing the grantor's claim of title, including proof of payment and, if required by the grantee, an independent legal opinion from a reputable lawyer qualified in the relevant jurisdiction confirming that the chain of title is satisfactory and adequate.

57. Copy of the Dolby licence.

58. Copy of the MPA rating certificate.

Written material (2)

Copies of:

59. Editor's marked-up shooting script, and dubbing cue sheets.

60. Music score and band parts for any original music recorded for the film.

61. All original artwork and materials used in the manufacture of the titles.

Laboratory letter

62. A letter addressed to the laboratory in the form set out in Schedule 2 signed by the grantor and the laboratory.

Suggested material for TV programming

1. One PAL D3 broadcast quality videotape master of the film, complete with soundtracks as follows:
   (a) If mono soundtracks:
      Channel one – Full mix with English dialogue
      Channel two – Full music and effects (M&E) track
   (b) If stereo soundtracks:
      Channel one – Full mix with English dialogue (left)
      Channel two – Full mix with English dialogue (right)
      Channel three – Full mix M&E (left)
      Channel four – Full mix M&E (right)

2. One one-inch 625 PAL C videotape broadcast quality videotape master of the film complete with soundtracks as follows:
   Channel one – Full mix (English dialogue) (monoed from stereo)
   Channel two – Full mix M&E (monoed from stereo)

3. One PAL D3 broadcast quality videotape master of the film with neutral textless title background for the main and end titles.

4. A master music cue sheet.

5. A complete statement of all screen and paid advertising credit obligations together with a layout of the proposed screen and advertising credits and a statement of all contractual restrictions as to the use of name and likeness or otherwise of any contributor together with excerpts from any agreement agreeing to give screen and/or paid advertising credit.

6. A complete list of all contributors identifying, where appropriate, their union or guild.

7. A statement of all persons whose worldwide rights in all media have been "bought out".

8. One sample copy of all advertising and publicity information created by the grantor, including one pressbook, actor/actress biographies and synopsis of the film.

9. A minimum of 20 action 8" x 10" colour still photographs with transparencies.

10. A minimum of 20 action 8" x 10" black and white production still photographs.

11. Errors and Omissions insurance certificate.

12. One copy of the English-language script conforming to the film as delivered.

13. A list of timecodes to facilitate foreign-language titling.

14. A letter addressed to the laboratory in the form set out in Schedule 2, signed by the grantor and the laboratory.

Schedule 2

Laboratory letter

From: [*Laboratory*]

To: [*Distributor*]

Dear Sirs,

Re: [""] ("*the film*")

[ ] ("*the grantor*") has informed us that it has entered into an agreement ("*the agreement*") with you under which you have been granted certain distribution rights in the film.

1. For good and valuable consideration, receipt of which is hereby acknowledged, we hereby confirm and agree for your benefit that:
   (a) the materials listed in exhibit 1 annexed [   ] (hereafter referred to as "the Materials") are in our possession, and that they are now ready and suitable in all respects for the making of technically acceptable release prints, videograms and duplicating material, including all usual elements and soundtracks;
   (b) we will retain possession of the materials and will not part with possession of any of them except in accordance with your and the grantor's written instructions;
   (c) neither you nor the grantor shall in any event be responsible or have any liability or any indebtedness to us for any laboratory services or materials ordered by the other party with respect to the film;
   (d) we presently have no past due charges with respect to the film or the materials, nor insofar as you are concerned will we assert or impose any claim or lien against the film or any of the materials except in respect and to the extent of any unpaid charges for work done on your written instructions;
   (e) we will fulfil all orders received from you for prints, duplicates and other materials in connection with the film and the materials notwithstanding any lien we may have with respect to any other party, subject only to payment by you of our customary charges for services rendered to you.
2. This agreement is irrevocable and may not be altered or modified except with your and our prior written consent.

Please confirm your acceptance of the foregoing by signing and returning the enclosed copy of this letter.
Yours faithfully,

For and on behalf of
[*laboratory*]

Accepted and agreed   Consented to

Signed by: Signed by:
For and on behalf of [*distributor*]   For and on behalf of [*grantor*]

Schedule 3

Instrument of transfer
Note: to be used if rights were "granted"

For one pound (£1.00) and other good and valuable consideration, the receipt and adequacy of which is hereby acknowledged, [   ] ("owner") hereby grants, sells and assigns to [   ] ("distributor") by means of this instrument of transfer, the sole and exclusive rights [throughout the world] [in the territory of [   ] ("territory") as defined in the distribution agreement dated [   ] ("the distribution agreement") [for [   ] years] ("term") to exploit and distribute the film entitled ["   "] ("the film") [theatrically and] by means of [standard/non-standard] television, videograms and non-theatrically as more particularly set out in the distribution agreement.

The distributor and its successors and assigns are hereby empowered to bring, prosecute, defend and appear in proceedings of any nature concerning the infringement or interference with any of the rights granted to it under the distribution agreement. This instrument is executed in connection with and is subject to the distribution agreement.

Dated: [   ]

By:

Title:

Short-form licence

Note: to be used if rights were "licensed"

For one pound (£1.00) and other good and valuable consideration, the receipt and adequacy of which is hereby acknowledged, [   ] ("owner") hereby licences to [   ] ("distributor") by means of this instrument of licence, the sole and exclusive rights [throughout the world] in the territory of [   ] ("territory") as defined in the distribution agreement dated [   ] ("the distribution agreement") [for [   ] years] ("term") to exploit and distribute the film entitled ["   "] ("the film") [theatrically and] by means of [standard/non-standard] television, videograms and non-theatrically as more particularly set out in the distribution agreement.

The distributor and its successors and assigns, are hereby empowered to bring, prosecute, defend and appear in proceedings of any nature concerning the infringement or interference with any of the rights granted to it under the distribution agreement. This instrument is executed in connection with and is subject to the distribution agreement.

Dated: [   ]

By:

Title:

3.9 Bank finance

3.9.1 Discounting distribution agreements

Introduction

Distribution agreements are possibly the most important agreements that a producer enters into. They not only provide the revenues to pay off the production finance but they can also be used to provide the means of raising the production finance in the first place.

They do this because they can, if properly drawn up, be discounted – i.e. lent against – by a bank. Below is an explanation of what discounting is, how it works and why various sides of the industry might want to do it.

It is important to understand from the outset that bank finance is almost invariably loan finance, not investment finance. The role of banks in film financing is crucial, but banks are not "investors". They do not provide finance for film production because they are impressed by or have confidence in the script, cast or director. They lend against collateral and they want to be secured. The collateral that they are looking for almost invariably takes the form of distribution agreements; and the security they want is over the underlying rights, the film itself and the exploitation rights. The bank will want to be certain, if it is not itself providing 100% of the production finance, that the rest of the finance has already been advanced before it starts to lend, and it will want to be repaid before any investors recoup their investment. The bank will want to be sure that all of its loan, including potential interest charges, and

its costs, including its legal costs, are covered by reliable sources of repayment. And the bank will want to be insured against all risks including the risk that the producer will not complete and deliver the film to the distributors on time, or at all. Whilst all this may seem very restrictive, in practice most banks active in this area are extremely supportive of producers and once they take on a deal will work very hard with the producer to create a bankable package to enable the film to be financed and produced.

What is discounting?

To form part of a bankable package a distribution agreement (or a number of them) or sales agency agreement entered into before production must conform to the following:

1. The agreement must contain a promise to pay an advance.
2. The advance must be for a fixed or fixable amount payable on a specific day. This must be a day which is bound to happen or can be guaranteed to happen, e.g. £10m on delivery. *Not* on theatrical release or first broadcast – either of which may not happen.
3. The advance must be non-refundable – but can be recoupable.
4. In this context discounting means the process whereby the bank decides how much to lend against the distribution agreement(s).
5. The biggest single factor will be the interest that the bank thinks will accrue on the loan from the date of the first advance until repayment.
6. If delivery is the date on which the advance is payable, and if delivery can be delayed for *force majeure* reasons, the bank will look to the last possible date – i.e. the outside date in the completion guarantee (more of which later), when making its calculation.
7. The interest rate in most production loans is arrived at by taking base rate, or

LIBOR (see glossary in *Volume 1* for definition), and adding the agreed margin (typically 2%). For the purpose of discounting the bank will also add a cushion to protect it against variations in the underlying rate.

8. Other factors:
   I. bank costs
   II. bank fee if the bank is lending it – which it usually will
   III. bank's legal costs
   IV. withholding tax – which is applicable to payments between certain countries
   V. allowance for possible delay in payment being made.
9. The bank then adds up all these factors and deducts the sum from the face value of the agreement(s) – i.e. the advance(s).

A typical definition of discounted value would be: 100% of the amount payable as an advance or minimum guarantee under approved distribution agreements or sales agency agreements less the allowance made by the lender for:

1. interest up to the outside date for repayment of the loan at the loan rate plus any "cushion" required by the lender
2. the lender's fees, expenses, costs and legal fees
3. the possibility of late payment
4. withholding taxes, if applicable
5. any other matters affecting the value of the net revenues, minimum guarantees, or advances.

The lender's certificate as to the discounted value will be final.

Why discount distribution agreements?

Pre-selling forces producers to face up to whether there is a market for their film.

For producers

Discounting can be cheaper. Typically discount finance costs 10% to 12% of the budget, but the producer doesn't have to give away 70% of the back-end. Once the bank is repaid it has no further interest in the film – it does not have any ownership interest or share of profits.

For distributors

Distributors need product, but they don't like paying for it in advance, because:
- they don't know how it will turn out
- they want to bring payment as close as possible to the point where they begin to earn income.

Thus discounting offers the opportunity to avoid risk of over-the-budget costs, late delivery and non-delivery. Plus the obligation to pay need not be noted on the distributor's balance sheet.

For banks

Banks don't invest – they lend. If done correctly it is safe. But because of the perceived risky nature of film finance, banks are able to charge higher fees and margins than they can on a lot of their other business.

How to do it

Banks lend to producers on the basis of the producer's track record and the strength of the "paper" offered.

The operation only really works if there is a completion guarantor. The completion guarantor underwrites the producer's obligations and guarantees to complete the film on time, on budget and in accordance with the distributors' and sales agents' requirements. So the bank is only taking the credit risk on the distributor and sales agent.

The producer must provide the bank with the means of assessing the project. This means giving the bank details of:
1. the producer's track record
2. the budget

3. the finance plan
4. **the** synopsis
5. details of the agreements offered as a source of repayment
6. the completion guarantor.

The bank will also want a number of other conditions fulfilled, and a typical list is set out at the end of this section.

The distribution agreements offered as collateral should ideally cover the cost of production, including interest fees and costs. If this is not the case but there are other sources of finance, the bank will want full details of those sources at the outset. The bank will want to be reasonably sure that the film is financed before committing time and energy to try to structure the deal. The bank will, as mentioned, want to be absolutely sure that the film is financed before it begins advancing its loan.

In some circumstances some banks will lend even if the cost of production is not covered by the aggregate of the amount that it is prepared to lend against the distribution agreements and other sources of finance. In other words if there is a "gap". The banks which are prepared to entertain gap financing do so on a different basis. They will expect a higher fee on the gap amount and they will insist the gap is covered by minimum sales estimates from a reliable sales agent in respect of unsold territories in an amount greater than the gap. The ratio between the gap and the aggregate sales estimates varies between banks, but is somewhere between 150% and 200%.

Some banks will also require an insurance policy to cover the possibility that the sales estimates will not be achieved – so-called insured gap financing. The policy usually pays any shortfall in actual sales against the estimates two years from delivery of the film.

Negotiating the distribution agreement

The negotiation will be more satisfactory if both producer and distributor know at the outset that the agreement is going to be discounted. The basic principle is that an agreement will not be discountable if the distributor can avoid or reduce payment on grounds not covered by the completion guarantee. The criteria for payment must be objective, so,

- it can be: "starring Ewan McGregor or approved replacement"
- it cannot be: "artistic quality equal to *Trainspotting*"
- it should be: "on delivery" *not* "on acceptance" (except acceptance of technical quality).

1. Payment should not be dependent on achieving a certain level of censorship certification, because completion guarantors are unwilling to guarantee anything but the most restrictive rating in the US and the UK and none elsewhere.
2. Payment of the advance cannot be dependent on achieving a level of P&A spend or achieving theatrical release targets (unless these are guaranteed by reliable third parties).
3. The distribution rights should not pass until the full advance is paid (or at least ensure that they revert automatically if the advance is *not* paid).
4. Avoid granting the distributor a security interest (this is usually impossible with north American distributors). If the distributor is granted a security interest they will have to be a party to the interparty agreement (see below).
5. Try to obtain the highest signature payment. The more the distributor has

paid on signature, the less likely they are to try to avoid payment of the balance on delivery.

6. Insert a term in the distribution agreement whereby the distributor agrees to sign the bank's standard form of acceptance of notice of assignment.

7. Ensure that the benefit of the distribution agreement can be assigned by the producer (at least by way of security), but not the distributor.

8. Ensure that the governing law of the distribution agreement is acceptable to the bank.

The assignment

The whole operation depends on the ability of the producer to make an effective assignment of the advance and of the bank to obtain priority over third parties for payment of that advance.

English law provides that debts may be assigned and that priority is determined by the giving of notice – i.e. the first to give notice gains priority over other creditors. Either the producer or the bank may give notice, but the practice has grown up to require the producer to give notice to the distributor that the advance has been assigned and to require the distributor to provide written acknowledgement of receipt notice of the assignment.

However, problems could arise if the producer owed the distributor monies in respect of some previous failed transaction. So the bank will require the distributor to waive all rights of set-off and counter-claim at the same time as acknowledging the assignment. Obtaining a satisfactory acknowledgement can be the most difficult part of any discounting operation.

Other problems surround the assignment:

- If the distributor makes payment of the advance to the bank but later discovers a fundamental problem – e.g. a flaw in the chain of title which cannot be remedied and which would entitle it to repayment of the advance by the producer – can the distributor obtain repayment from the bank? The English courts have held no: the payment is unrecoverable in the hands of an assignee.

- Or, if the distributor does not like the film when delivered and seeks to avoid payment on the grounds that the acknowledgement that it signed was the bank's standard-form and is unenforceable as unfair. This has been raised as a defence by distributors, but the issue has not yet been resolved.

The biggest problem is enforceability. Most agreements offered for discounting are not English (the UK is very small part of the world market for films). So even if the acknowledgement is made expressly subject to English law, the problem of enforcement in foreign jurisdictions remains. Foreign legal opinions can be obtained, but the best protection for a bank is to obtain letters of credit in support of the distributor's payment obligations.

3.9.2 The interparty agreement

The foregoing is a doctrine of perfection and is not always achievable. In which case there may need to be an interparty agreement, and this is often where the distribution agreement is made bankable.

The underlying concept is that the distributor may be willing to agree things with the bank that it would not agree with the producer. For example, it may be willing to waive its right to withhold payment for certain breaches as against the bank while retaining the right to sue the producer.

This is sometimes called the intercreditor agreement; but should be distinguished from a mutual funding agreement, which is properly an agreement among financiers whereby the financiers agree with each other that they will fund in accordance with their agreements with the producer.

In the interparty agreement the barriers to discounting the agreement are dismantled:

- the distributor's rights of approval are exercised or waived
- the assignment is acknowledged and rights of set-off and counter-claim are waived
- the vesting of rights in the distributor is postponed until payment
- the bank is given the right to terminate and take back the distributor's territory in the event of breach
- security interests are regulated and prioritised
- the parties agree not to disturb each other's rights as long as the other is not in breach
- the definition of delivery may be narrowed – i.e. the delivery schedule may be reduced to a limited number of essential items, delivery of which trigger payment of the bulk of the advance (say 90%)
- the method of resolving disputes about delivery is agreed.

The completion guarantor will normally join in the interparty agreement so that the bank can acknowledge its takeover rights and so as to subordinate its security interest to that of the bank.

The interparty can therefore act as a "bandage" safely wrapping up the whole operation.

3.9.3 Typical document requirements in a distribution agreement discounting transaction

Document	Document summary	Bank's requirement
Offer letter	Drafted by bank	
Loan agreement and security agreement	Drafted by bank's lawyers; will include all deal points from offer letter, plus bank's standard terms concerning security	Original
Bank mandate	Form supplied by bank, but authorised and signed by director of the borrower	Original
Certificate of incorporation and memorandum and articles of association of the borrower Resolutions of the board of directors of borrower approving the terms of the loan authorising the borrowing and execution of the loan agreement	Ensure that borrower has the right to produce, borrow etc.	Certified copy
Full and unfettered contracts for the services of: (a) the principal cast (b) the director (c) the producer (d) the composer	Confirming availability in accordance with the specification for the film if pre-contracted	Originals or certified copies
Full chain of title documentation including title clearance and US copyright search	Establishing that the borrower owns all rights necessary to complete and deliver the film and to give security to the bank	Originals
Music synchronisation licences	Music synchronisation licences	Originals

Document	Document summary	Bank's requirement
A laboratory pledgeholder letter from all laboratories where film materials will be processed and held	Whereby the laboratory holding the physical materials pledges to hold those materials to the order of the bank	Originals
Distribution/sales agency agreement	With aggregate discounted value sufficient to cover the loan	Originals
Letters of Credit	Securing payment by distributors	Originals
Notices to all distributors	Notifying distributor of assignment of advance to bank	Copy
Acknowledgements from all distributions	Acknowledging assignment and waiving set-off rights	Original
Completion guarantee	Guaranteeing completion and delivery of the film to the distributor, in accordance with the distribution/sales agency agreement(s)	Original
Loss payee endorsement/cut-through/parent company guarantee	Insuring the obligations of the completion guarantor	Original
Certificate of endorsement as additional insured	Naming bank as additional insured party on all production insurances and the E&O policy	Original
Letter from bank holding production account	Agreeing not to set-off money in production account against any debts of borrower and acknowledging bank's security interest in the production account	Original
Interparty agreement	Regulating security interests between e.g. bank, completion guarantor, north American distributor	Original
Mutual funding agreement	Whereby any other financiers agree with bank to make their advances when due	Original

3.9.4 Checklist – loan agreements

This checklist is designed to be used to work out a deal for bank cash-flow against the collateral of amounts due under the terms of contracts already entered into (principally distribution pre-sales), i.e. a bank discounting package. Some of the figures will need to be proposed by the bank in the light of its calculation of fees and interest. It is important to bear in mind that the amount of the *bank's advance* will (because of fees, interest, etc.) be less than the amount of the *bank loan facility* and this may in turn (because of risk discounting) be less than the *collateral face value*. It is net amount of the *bank's advance* which needs to correspond to the producer's *cash-flow requirement*. If the proposed advance falls short of the cash-flow requirement, then the cash-flow requirement needs to be trimmed (e.g. budget cuts or deferments) or extra collateral found (e.g. extra pre-sales). Alternatively, it might be possible to close the gap with financing based on sales estimates or parallel cash-flow or studio facilities for deferred payments, but in each case the discounting bank will require appropriate assurances.

Subject to contract

The bank will normally insist that no contract is formed until the loan agreement is signed. All correspondence and drafts will, therefore, be "subject to contract".

Name of lender

Contact name:
Contact address:
Tel:
Fax:

Details of film

Title:
Producer:
Director:
Stars:
Writer:

Commercial terms

1. The advance

   I. Principal amount: to be advanced to the producer by the bank.

   II. Drawdown method: procedure by which money is forwarded to the production account.

2. Bank fees

   I. Arrangement or facility fee charged by the bank.

   II. Bank expenses:

- legal fees – it may be possible to cap these fees
- other expenses – for instance sometimes the bank will employ an insurance expert to renew the producer's insurance arrangements. In this case the bank would be entitled to recover the cast as a third-party expense.

3. Interest rate

   I. The margin plus base rate or (if in foreign currency) the margin plus LIBOR (see glossary in *Volume 1*).

   II. Interest period in months, e.g. 1/3/6.

   III. Interest reserve.

   IV. Bank's margin.

4. Currency

   I. Currency of loan/currency of expenditure/currency of collateral.

   II. Exchange rate fluctuation risk – how great? This can be covered by forward exchange contracts.

5. Term

   Final repayment date.

Security

1. Completion bond

   I. Completion guarantor – approved by financiers.

   II. Rebate fee – held by the bank?

III. Strike price.

IV. Re-insurance endorsement (ie. cut-through to completion guarantor's insurers or loss payee endorsement on completion guarantor's insurance policy – only required if bond is not given by insurance company).

V. Completion guarantor's recoupment/security.

For more detail on the completion guarantee, see part 3.10.

2. Collateral/source of repayment

Sales agency agreement
I. Territory.
II. Sales agent.
III. Minimum guarantee/advance.
IV. Deferral of all or part of sales agent's fees and expenses until bank is repaid or gap closed.

Distribution agreement
I. Territory.
II. Distributor.
III. Minimum guarantee/advance.
IV. Letters of credit/corporate guarantee.
V. Withholding tax? This will affect the bank's advance.

3. Legal security taken by the bank
I. Security assignment over film copyright and physical materials.
II. Assignment of distribution/sales, agreements and notices and acceptances of assignment.
III. Is endorsement of the bank's interest on the production and E&O insurance required?
IV. Is essential element insurance required?
V. Laboratory pledgeholder agreement – to inform the laboratory who has control over physical materials held by the laboratory.

VI. Charge over bank's production collection account.

VII. Production bank set-off letter.

VIII. Other (for instance, a parent company guarantee or – rarely – a personal guarantee).

Interparty / security priority agreement

1. **Parties:** typically the bank providing the production cash-flow, the north American distributor, the producer, the completion guarantor, any other holder of a security interest, possibly the bank putting up the distributor's letter of credit.

2. **Terms:**
   I. the distributor acknowledges assignment of the distribution agreement by the producer to the bank
   II. the distributor waives rights of set off, counterclaim and cross-collateralisation as against the bank
   III. the distributor confirms that it has exercised all its approval rights under the distribution agreement (or waives them as against the bank)
   IV. the distributor confirms that the producer is not in default under the terms of the distribution agreement
   V. the distributor and the bank agree that they will not interfere with completion and delivery
   VI. the distributor agrees that it will not acquire any rights in the film until it has paid its advance
   VII. the bank is given the right to terminate the distribution agreement if the distributor does not pay the advance
   VIII. the bank agrees not to exercise its rights in such a way as to distribute the rights of the distribution or completion guarantor so long as they are not in default of their respective agreements
   IX. the parties agree on how any insurance recoveries are dealt with

X. the bank's security interest is put into first position

XI. the procedure for arbitrating disputes about delivery may be agreed.

Typical Conditions precedent to bank making loan

1. Signed loan agreement.
2. Incorporation documents/legal opinions/ board minutes of production company.
3. Approval of chain of title.
4. Service agreements for director, producer, heads of department and main cast.
5. Sales agency agreement and/or distribution agreement(s).
6. Completion bond.
7. Legal security.
8. Interparty agreement.
9. Insurances – policies and endorsements.
10. Is all other finance already advanced into production account? If not – mutual funding agreement.

3.10 Completion guarantees

Completion guarantees are most often required by financiers, i.e. typically by:

• lending banks
• commissioning broadcasters
• investors
• some national funding bodies.

A completion guarantee is sometimes required by distributors, especially if the distributor has paid part of the minimum guarantee (e.g. a signature payment) or if it has expended, or plans to expend, a significant amount on advertising before delivery.

In a co-production the minority co-producers are often well advised to require a completion guarantee in order to protect themselves against non-performance by the lead producer.

The completion guarantor's obligation is twofold:

1. It guarantees – subject to exclusions (e.g. chain of title, music clearances, post-delivery cutting, currency fluctuations, over-budget legal costs) – that the film/programme will be delivered in accordance with an agreed set of criteria: usually in accordance with a specified distribution agreement (or a number of such agreements), including delivery by a specified delivery date, and that it will provide any sums over and above the budget required to achieve this. Usually, the delivery date may be extended for a fixed period (between 60 and 90 days) if there is an event of *force majeure*, but the beneficiary of the guarantee will always insist on there being a final outside delivery date.

2. It guarantees that if the producer fails to deliver it will either complete and deliver the film/programme itself or will pay the beneficiary a sum equal to its advances to the production.

A completion guarantee is *not* a guarantee that all the finance required to fund the agreed budget will be available. It is simply a guarantee of delivery and the provision of over-budget finance, if required. *Nor* is a completion guarantee a credit guarantee: it does not guarantee that a distributor will pay if the film/programme is delivered. This credit risk is taken by the financier.

In order to be able to give such a guarantee the completion guarantor very carefully examines all aspects of the production, including the script, budget, cash-flow, shooting schedule, locations and production insurances and may require that the budget be increased if it feels that the amounts provided are inadequate. The guarantor will also insist that a contingency allowance is included in the budget.

There are certain uninsurable risks that a completion guarantor will not guarantee, such as the risk of war and the risk of nuclear catastrophe.

Before giving its guarantee the guarantor will also enter into an agreement with the producer whereby the producer gives the guarantor (*inter alia*):

• the right to have information about the production
• the right to countersign cheques on the production account
• the right to have personnel on set/location
• the right to make changes to the cast, crew, script, budget, etc.
• the right to take over the production and complete it in the name of the producer

- security rights (in second position to the financier) in the film/programme.

Unless the guarantor is itself an insurance company it will usually insure its liabilities with Lloyd's or another major insurance market. The beneficiary of the guarantee will usually require access to these insurance arrangements. This is achieved either by endorsement on the guarantor's insurance policy or a letter of undertaking from the guarantor's insurers. This arrangement is sometimes referred to as a "cut-through" or a "loss payee endorsement". Its effect is to enable the beneficiary to claim directly from insurers in the event that the guarantor does not meet its financial obligations.

The level of fee charged by the guarantor – usually between 5% and 6% – is affected by the risk involved and the track record of the producer as well as market conditions prevailing in the completion guarantee business. Typically the guarantor will rebate 50% of the fee if there is no claim. Often the guarantor will not require the full fee to be paid at the outset but the producer must ensure that the budget includes the full completion guarantee fee so that the deferred portion can be paid in the event of a claim.

The requirement for a completion guarantee is very common in English and American film and television production, even when the producer is experienced and successful.

Definitions

Completion guarantee

A guarantee, usually backed by financial strength and insurance underwriting, that a particular production will be completed and delivered in accordance with certain delivery instructions (e.g. compliance with a specified distribution agreement, or an agreed delivery schedule and by an agreed date). The guarantee will usually be subject to certain standard exclusions, e.g. copyright title risk. This guarantee provides a financier with the assurance that it will be entitled to be re-paid from any contract receivable which is conditional upon delivery.

Also referred to as a "completion bond" or "bond".

Completion guarantor

The company which provides the completion guarantee and which in return receives a fee (usually between 5% and 6% of the budget of the film – of which 5% will be refundable if there is no claim). The completion guarantor will require approval of various items including the screenplay, the budget and the production and shooting schedules and will usually demand a contingency allowance of not less than 10% of the budget.

Also referred to as a "completion bonder" or "bondsman".

Legal and business affairs

3.11 Co-production agreements

3.11.1 Introduction

The reasons for entering into co-production arrangements are numerous and varied. Commonly the reason is to access national subsidies which are available only to official "treaty" co-productions. Sometimes it is because more can be obtained from a particular territory on a co-production basis than as a straight pre-sale. Occasionally it is because the subject matter suggests a co-production.

It follows, therefore, that the arrangements for the co-production vary greatly, from genuine co-productions where each co-producer is participating in the production process to what are essentially only co-financing arrangements.

In television, co-productions often take place between national or other major broadcasters in different countries. This kind of co-production is obviously different to a co-production between independent producers, but many of the points in the following checklist are nevertheless relevant.

With any proposed co-production it is important to choose the right partner. Producers should take time to find out about a potential co-production partner: by enquiring about track record, using available databases and talking to people who have worked previously with the potential co-producer. Potential co-producers should try to meet face to face as often as possible and, where relevant, should have joint meetings with third parties, particularly financing parties. This

is, of course, subject to reasonable budgeting considerations.

Throughout the negotiation, it is critical that the co-producers communicate clearly to each other, in writing, whether or not they are yet ready to enter a binding contract. A common problem in European co-production is that many meetings and telephone calls take place in different countries: letters and faxes are sent, letters of intent and deal memos are signed. Sometimes these communications contradict but do not expressly overrule previous exchanges. At a later stage it is very difficult to analyse what the true intention of the parties was or whether or not a binding written or unwritten contract was concluded. While different legal systems have different rules on how a binding contract is concluded, it is recommended that points discussed at meetings should be confirmed simply and clearly in writing and previous arrangements referred to and dealt with. Under some legal systems it is usual to add the words "subject to contract" to signal that a party does not yet intend to conclude a contract. When a document is signed which is intended to have contractual force, the parties should state this intention clearly.

It is generally possible for co-producers to sign a document declaring their joint intention that the co-production contract shall not enter into force until certain conditions precedent (e.g. conditional approval of co-production status from competent national film authorities) have been fulfilled. This device of a conditional contract may be useful to co-producers who urgently need a document to include in an application for co-production status.

It should be remembered that even if no contract is signed, there is still a risk, under the various legal systems, that an oral agreement has been concluded. Even if no contract was concluded, there may be a risk under some legal systems (e.g. Dutch law, German law) that legal consequences may flow from the breakdown of mere negotiations.

The issues of ownership should be addressed at an early stage. All the co-producers should satisfy themselves that the rights which are acquired at any early stage from a novelist and/or scriptwriter by one of the co-producers have been properly obtained (or are obtainable) and are adequate for the purpose of the co-production. It is often difficult (and expensive) to go back and remedy flaws or obtain additional rights at a later stage. It may be stating the obvious, but it should be borne in mind that the underlying rights, the negative or master tape of the film, the copyright in the film and the income from the film are all separate and usually can be owned in different ways and in different ratios irrespective of the co-producers' respective contributions.

The checklist which follows should be helpful in identifying the issues which need to be addressed and negotiated.

3.11.2 European co-production checklist

1. Parties

List the co-producers: their address, country of incorporation and the correct legal form (company/partnership/individual).

2. Underlying works

I. Who are the actual or proposed authors of the screenplay? What stage has the scriptwriting reached?

II. Is the screenplay based on any other literary work, e.g. novel or stage play? If so, who are the authors of that other literary work and has it been published? If published, where, when and by whom? Is it in copyright?

III. What underlying rights have already been acquired, by which co-producer and under which agreements? What is the extent of the underlying rights already acquired, e.g. option? Do the underlying rights include, or should they include, additional rights such as merchandising, novelisation, interactive, remake and sequel, television adaptation and spin-off rights?

IV. If an option has been acquired, what are the terms for exercising and extending the option: deadlines and payments? Which co-producer will be responsible for extending or extending any option? How will the cost of extending or exercising the option be dealt with?

V. What further underlying rights still need to be acquired – from whom, and by which co-producer?

VI. How is ownership of underlying rights to be shared between the co-producers?

VII. Have US copyright and title search reports been obtained? If not, consider whether it is necessary to do so.

VIII. Which co-producer will be responsible for arranging US copyright registration of interests in the underlying works if not already negotiated?

3. Treaty co-production

Is the co-production to be based on one or more co-production treaties? If so, which ones? What are the qualifying criteria?

4. Budget

I. What is the approved budget?

II. What does it include? (For example, does it include a realistic provision for financing and legal costs?)

5. Control

I. Which co-producer is to have financial and creative control over production? Will there be consultation with other co-producers? Does this comply with the relevant treaty criteria?

II. Are some matters to be decided jointly? If so, which co-producer will have the right to break deadlock?

III. Is the position different during principal photography?

IV. Is there a mechanism whereby a co-producer can exit from the co-production? If so, on what terms?

6. Overcost

If production threatens to go over budget, how will the responsibility for obtaining the necessary additional finance be allocated between the co-producers? Will there be a completion guarantor?

7. Completion guarantee

I. If there is to be a completion guarantee, which co-producer will be responsible for making the arrangements with the completion guarantor?

II. Is the form of guarantee to be approved by all co-producers? Who will be the beneficiaries of the guarantee?

III. Can a co-producer be a beneficiary of a completion guarantee? A financial co-producer will usually be able to be the beneficiary of a completion guarantee. However if the co-producer is actively producing the film, the guarantor will be reluctant to make him a beneficiary because it would amount to the guarantor guaranteeing to the producer that the producer will perform the contract.

IV. Will all co-producers be required to join in the agreement with the completion guarantor and give a security interest in their rights in the film to the completion guarantor?

V. How is any rebate of the completion guarantee fee to be dealt with?

8. Underspend

How will any underspend by allocated between the co-producers? Is there to be a facility for re-allocation of underspend between budget items?

9. Financing plan

I. What will be the breakdown of co-producer contributions to the financing plan?

II. Are the co-producers providing their contributions:
  • in cash from their own resources
  • in cash from a third-party financier
  • in kind, i.e. facilities.

III. How do the co-producers protect themselves against the failure of one or more of them failing to provide their contracted contribution? Letter of Credit? Cash deposit? Security interest?

IV. Where a co-producer's contribution is in fact coming from a third-party source, e.g. subsidy fund or bank, how does that co-producer protect its financier's interests?

10. National authorities/ public funds

I. Which co-producer will be responsible for applying to which authority or funding body?

II. How are the costs of such applications to be treated?

III. Are co-producers obliged to co-operate with one another to enable each other to obtain consents or funds?

IV. How do the co-producers want to proceed if faced with an initial refusal or a conditional approval followed by refusal of final approval?

11. Cash-flow

I. What are the currencies of funding?

II. What are the currencies of expenditure?

III. How will the risk of currency exchange rate fluctuation be covered?

IV. Which co-producer will set up which co-production account and where?

V. How will the money in production accounts be owned as between co-producers?

12. Screenplay

What will be the mechanism for approving the final screenplay?

13. Specifications

I. What creative elements and technical specifications need to be agreed by all the co-producers?

II. Which co-producer will be responsible for ensuring which creative elements or technical specifications?

III. What details have been pre-approved and what is the method for approving substitutes if necessary?

14. Third-party contracts

What parameters or approval requirements will be imposed on one co-producer by the other co-producers for talent agreements, e.g. moral rights waivers, attempted buy-out of rental rights? Will talent be on union terms; if so, which?

15. Insurances

I. Will usual production insurances be required?

II. Will E&O insurance be required? If so, which co-producer will be responsible for making the application? Is the cost budgeted? Are the co-producers to be named as principal insured parties or additional loss payees?

III. How will sums paid by insurers be applied?

16. Production schedule

I. What is the proposed start date of principal photography? How will the co-producers address the question of possible postponement of the start date? What will be the consequences of failure to commence principal photography by the start date?

II. How will the shooting schedule be agreed?

III. What will the original language version be? Will there be double original language versions?

IV. Will all co-producers have access to the set?

V. Who will control publicity about development and production?

VI. What happens if an event of *force majeure* happens?

VII. What will the delivery schedule be, and are all items budgeted?

VIII. Which co-producer will be responsible for delivery and to which parties? What is the delivery date? Will there be a margin for postponement of the delivery date?

IX. In which laboratory will the materials be available for access?

17. Ownership of rights in the film

I. How will the producers own the copyright in the film?

II. Will there be an agreed copyright by-line?

18. Distribution

I. What will be the co-production territory of each co-producer? How will satellite rights be exploited where they cross over the co-production territories?

II. How will the film be distributed to the rest of the world outside the co-production territories?

19. Theatrical release

I. Is it a requirement of any financier that the film be released theatrically in any territory in any country. If so, is there a release date?

II. Is there a P&A budget? How is it to be financed?

20. Physical materials

How will the negatives and other physical materials be owned as between the co-producers? Is there a treaty obligation which dictates how ownership should be dealt with?

21. Credit

I. What will be the form of credit for the co-producers? Will the order of names of the co-producers vary in the different co-production territories?

II. Will official co-production countries require credits?

III. Which third-party financiers require credits?

IV. Who will be entitled to the individual producer credit? Will it be shared? If so, how will it appear?

22. Recoupment and profit participation

I. What will be the recoupment position of each co-producer?

II. Out of which receipts will each co-producer recoup?

III. How will receipts be defined for purposes of recoupment?

IV. How will net profits be defined?

V. How will co-producers share in net profits?

VI. From which receipts or share of net profits will talent participation be paid?

23. Collection

I. How will receipts be collected? Will there be a collection agent?

II. How will interest accruing on collection accounts be allocated?

24. Records

I. Who will maintain the main records of production?

II. Will co-producers be entitled to audit each other? If so, on what basis?

25. Certification of costs

I. Will a certified cost statement be required? Will each co-producer be entitled to receive copies?

II. Which co-producer is to set up the arrangements?

26. Warranties

Will each co-producer give standard warranties to the others?

27. Insolvency

What should happen if a co-producer becomes or threatens to become insolvent? Particularly, if the other co-producers are not secured on the insolvent producer's rights.

28. Breach

What should happen if a co-producer is in breach of its obligations?

29. Assignment

Can the co-producers assign to a third party or mortgage their rights in the project to raise money without the written consent of the others?

30. Choice of law

Which national legal system is to govern the co-production contract?

31. Jurisdiction

How do the co-producers want to deal with any disputes under the governing law of the co-production contract?

32. Signatures

Who are the authorised signatories for each of the co-producers?

33. Draft co-production contract

Is there to be:

I. a short-form deal memo, or

II. a long-form co-production contract, or

III. a short-form followed by a long-form?

Which co-producer is to be responsible for proposing the first draft?

3.12 Collection agreements

A collection or escrow agreement is an agreement between financiers (including the completion guarantor), the producer and profit participants that all the receipts from a film or TV programme be administered through a bank or trust corporation, who will also join in as a party to the collection agreement.

A number of banks offer this service, as does the National Film Trustee Corporation, a sister company of British Screen Finance. Sometimes the parties are content for the broadcaster to act as collection agent. So long as the collection agent is of undoubted financial strength and probity the arrangement offers a number of advantages to all concerned:

1. Financiers can be sure that all receipts will be applied to recoupment. Where there is more than one financier the question of who collects and accounts to the others is avoided.

2. Profit participants can be reassured that the income will be collected by an independent organisation which will account to them openly and promptly.

3. Financiers and profit participants can be sure that their income will not be affected by the insolvency or actions of the producer because the income will be held, until distribution, on trust for the beneficiaries.

4. Producers are relieved of the administrative burden of setting up a system for collecting and distributing gross receipts and are free to wind up the production company if it is no longer required.

5. All parties benefit because the collection agent will keep track of payments due from distributors and some will chase payment if not received on time. The

collection agent will provide all beneficiaries with regular statements giving details of collections and disbursements and some are able to offer immediate online access to information about the collection account through an electronic banking facility. Also some collection agents operate withholding tax minimisation schemes.

The arrangement works because the producer undertakes to give irrevocable instruction to all distributors, and other parties from whom income may be received to make payment of all monies to the collection agent and the collection agent makes a declaration of trust of all monies received.

Collection agents typically charge 1% of gross receipts in first position, their expenses, plus (sometimes) a one-off setting up fee.

Definitions

Escrow

An arrangement whereby money or documents or other things are held by an agent until certain conditions are performed or satisfied and are then delivered to the party entitled.

Trust

A relationship between two or more persons (or companies) whereby property or money is vested in one person (the trustee) for the benefit of the other or others (the beneficiaries). Under English law the beneficiary has an enforceable interest in the property in the hands of the trustee and the trustee can only deal with the property in accordance with the terms of the trust. The insolvency of the trustee will not deprive the beneficiaries of their entitlement to the property and the insolvency of any one beneficiary will only affect that beneficiary's share.

Directory

4

4.1 MEDIA II

4.1.1 MEDIA Development

MEDIA Development is a part of the MEDIA II Programme which ends in 2000; the last deadline for calls for proposals is 14 April 2000.

Funding

The amount of the financial contribution awarded to each company by the Commission is determined with respect to the cost and nature of each proposed project. Under no circumstances may the amount of the financial contribution awarded by the Commission exceed 50% of the overall cost of the operation. The recipient company must provide guarantees for the remaining finance. Support will take the form of loans.

Project selection

The beneficiaries of Community support will be selected by the Commission.

The Commission has appointed the European Media Development Agency (EMDA) acting under the designation "Media Programme Development" to assist it with the processing of applications.

Definitions

For the purposes of this call for proposals, the following definitions shall apply:

Development

"Development" means all operations prior to the production proper or principal photography of an audiovisual work. This includes the writing of the script, the search for partners, preparation of the financing plan, and the formulation of the marketing and distribution plan.

For certain types of production, the following are also considered to be part of the "development" phase: graphics research and the making of a pilot (for animated works), archive research (for productions designed to enhance audiovisual heritage) and the development of specific software packages (for multimedia productions).

Independent production company

An audiovisual production company which does not have a majority participation link with a television broadcaster, either in capital or commercial terms. There is considered to be majority participation when more than 25% of the share capital of a production company is held by a single broadcaster (50% where several broadcasters are involved) or when, over a three-year period, more than 90% of a production company's turnover is generated in cooperation with any one broadcaster. In applying these criteria, account shall be taken of specific characteristics of member states' and EEA states' audiovisual systems.

European production company

A company whose main activity is audiovisual production and which is owned, whether directly or by majority participation, by nationals of the Member States of the European Union, the EEA or other European countries participating in the MEDIA Programme, and registered in one of these countries.

Types of support

Independent European audiovisual production companies can apply for two kinds of development support from the MEDIA Programme Development. These are:

1. support for development of production projects and
2. support for development of production companies.

Priority will be given to projects particularly concerned with developing the potential of countries or regions with low production capacity and/or a restricted geographical and linguistic area, as well as the development of an independent European production and distribution sector, in particular small and medium-sized enterprises (SMEs).

Support for the development of audiovisual works submitted by European independent production companies

Purpose and amount of the support

Applications are invited from independent European production companies submitting film or television projects in the form of a script or a treatment. The support is intended to encourage the development of one or more audiovisual work(s) aimed at the European or world market.

The selection criteria applied to every project are:

- quality and originality of concept (as demonstrated by the submitted treatment, script, storyboard, etc)
- track record of the applicant company and the members of its team (as demonstrated by the submitted CVs of the company and associated individuals),
- production potential (as demonstrated by the submitted one page presentation)
- transnational potential (as demonstrated by the submitted one page presentation).

Particular attention will be paid to productions of one of the above genres which are designed for children and young people in general.

For television series, applicants may only apply for one development loan for each series.

The proposed projects (individual works or series) must take the form of productions lasting at least twenty-five minutes and in the case of fiction films, in principle, at least fifty minutes.

Projects promoting violence, racism or pornography will not be considered.

The transnational potential of projects submitted will be assessed in the light of the interest shown or undertakings given by European distributors/broadcasters in respect of the proposed works.

In respect of all the schemes for the support of the development of projects the award granted cannot exceed 50% of the eventual development expenditure on the project.

All awards are loans repayable under the terms and conditions of the respective contracts, normally on first day of principal photography.

Single project funding (animation, documentary and fiction)

Applicants for single project funding in any of these three categories may request any of the following amounts: € 10,000, € 15,000, € 20,000, € 30,000, € 40,000, € 60,000 or € 80,000.

Applications will be considered only for the amount of loan requested in the application form.

Indications as to what level of support applicants should normally apply for in each category are given below. Applicants who wish to apply for an amount different from those indicated as normally applying should give a clear explanation as to why they wish to do so.

For the development of fiction projects applicants should normally apply for € 30,000. In exceptional circumstances applicants may apply for € 80,000 for the development of a fiction project. Applicants for this level of support will have to provide significant evidence that the project is at an advanced stage of development and that significant production financing for the project is in place.

Production companies may submit more than one project, up to a maximum of five, within the framework of the present call for proposals so long as they can prove they have the capacity to develop these simultaneously, and that they have completed at least two productions over the last 12 months.

The total loans granted to any one company will not exceed € 225,000 per deadline.

Since changes tend to occur in the course of a production's development, support will be granted in the form of two identical instalments:

- start-up support of 50% at the signature of the contract
- consolidation support (granted on the basis of a progress report on the project, and in particular the financing plan and the prospects for transnational distribution).

Reimbursement

Loans will be reimbursed normally as follows:

- 100% of the loan is due on the first day of principal photography;
- twenty-four months after the signature of the contract, if the project has not gone into production, all recipients must repay 25% of the loan
- in the event that the supported project goes into production after 24 months, the outstanding 75% of the loan is due on the first day of principal photography.

However, if it is established that the recipient has not demonstrated the level of professional diligence required in normal circumstances to complete the project, the total amount of the loan must be reimbursed.

The loans are interest-free, provided that the conditions for repayment are respected.

Presentation of proposals

The Commission reserves the right not to process proposals which lack the required documentation. Any applications rejected on these grounds may be resubmitted for the future deadlines.

Proposals have to be presented in triplicate by using the attached application forms and providing the required annexes.

Each proposal must consist of the following elements:

1. **Form 1:** applicant information
2. **Form 2:** project information (one form for every project)
3. **Form 3:** development budget (one form for every project)
4. One page presentation of the application relating to the creative team, production potential, sales potential (national/international) and market (intended audience), (to be given to the panel of experts organised by the Commission)
5. Checklist

The Commission reserves the right to request additional information from applicants before making a final decision on granting support.

In particular, short-listed applicants will be asked to supplement their application by the following information:

- company incorporation documents
- additional information about key personnel of the company as well as a detailed budget and guarantees concerning the company's capacity to provide matching funds
- rights documents (where appropriate).

Amount and payment of funding

The amount of funding awarded to each company by the Commission for each planned project may not exceed 50% of the overall cost of the operation. The recipient company must provide guarantees for the remaining finance.

The selection of an applicant does not oblige the Commission to grant the amount requested. In no circumstances will the amount granted exceed the amount requested.

Applicants will be informed whether or not they have been awarded financial support as quickly as possible. The Commission's decision will be final.

The Commission will issue a contract specifying, in particular, the amount allocated, the payment arrangements and the obligations of the recipient.

Submission of proposals

If production companies are submitting several projects in one application, the projects should not be bound together.

Please use application forms provided by the MEDIA Desks (listed below). Applications submitted without application forms will not be considered.

Proposals should be submitted in *triplicate* to the European Commission. The final deadline for applications is 14 April 2000.

Slate funding – simultaneous development of production projects

The selected companies will be proposed a contract giving them access to a budget of a maximum amount of € 125,000, which will be allocated to them on a dedicated interest-bearing account from which they will be entitled to draw down the sums necessary to co-finance the development of their projects. Those will have to be preliminary approved by the Commission (on the basis of an estimated budget) and conform with the development strategy described in the activity plan. The maximum amount of the Community contribution per project shall in no event exceed € 50,000 and 50% of the total cost of development.

Whenever such a developed project goes into production, the company is required to repay the Community loan on a dedicated bank account. These amounts will of course remain the company's property if duly reinvested in further productions. The repaid amounts will be added to the initial contribution of the Commission and could be used to finance the development of further projects. If the project in development does not succeed, the company will be required to justify the reasons for its abandonment and the amount of aid will be regarded as lost.

The financial contribution of the Commission will be paid in two instalments:

1. During the first stage a contribution of € 125,000 will be paid credited to dedicated account.
2. An additional contribution of € 125,000 (Stage 2 funding) may be granted to the company for the implementation of activities planned for the second year, on the condition that it fulfils the requirements of the contract (activity reports) and subject to the agreement of the Commission.

It should be noted that, during all the implementation of the contract, no application will be selected by aforementioned company under the "single project funding", if they are developed within the slate.

Selection criteria

- Stability and financial potential of the company.
- Track record of the company and/or its team in the production sector, in particular on the international market.
- Quality and feasibility of the action plan.
- Potential of the projects in development of the European and international markets at the time of submission.

Information to be provided by the companies

- A detailed business plan covering a five-year period and comprising a work programme envisaged regarding the development of production projects and production activities. It will include a provisional budget for the first year of implementation of the activity plan.
- Detailed description of the company's activities during the last two years.
- The accounts of the company for the last two years.

Support for the development of European independent production companies

Purpose and amount of the support

This type of support is made available for European independent production companies developing and producing projects aimed at the European or world market. Such audiovisual production activities can be in the field of fiction, documentary, archive-based programmes, new technology or animation.

The objective of the support is to assist in creating "an environment favourable to the taking of initiatives by companies, in particular small and medium-sized businesses and their development," by assisting companies with strong plans for the development and growth of their audiovisual production activities.

The amount loaned cannot exceed the amount invested for the same purpose by the company itself from its own funds, or by other parties.

The loan may be used *inter alia* for the purposes of investment in agreed plans for company expansion such as:

- expansion of the company into new areas of production
- expansion of the company into new markets - geographical or sectorial
- significant increases in the company's use of external expertise
- acquisition of assets such as other companies or shares in other companies, rights and options
- joint ventures with other companies.

It would normally be assumed that such plans would involve investment in new activities and an injection of funds into the company so that, after repayment of the loan the company would be significantly strengthened.

There are two types of support available:

1. Companies with viable ideas for the development of their companies may apply for support regarding the *Preparation of a Business Plan*. The support granted will be for a maximum of € 10,000 or 50% of the invoiced cost of the preparation of the business plan, whichever is the lower. The Commission's contribution is up to a maximum of 50% of the costs of the preparation of the

business plan external to the company and does not include any costs incurred directly by the company itself in the preparation of the business plan.

2. Companies may apply for *Company Development Support*. This type of support is granted on the basis of a business plan. The preparation of these business plans may have been supported through the scheme for support for the preparation of a business plan or may have been paid for by the company exclusively. The loan is for a minimum of € 30,000 and a maximum of € 150,000, but in any event not more than 50% of the total cost of the implementation of the plan.

1. Support for the Preparation of a Business Plan will be granted on the basis of the following selection criteria:

I. the financial stability/potential of the company
II. the production track record of the company and/or the individuals who make up the company
III. the quality and feasibility of the company's business ideas.

Payment conditions

Support for the writing of a business plan will be normally paid in two instalments, the first of 50% on signature of the contract, the second on acceptance of the business plan prepared in line with the guidelines and after approval of a final report accompanied by invoices certified as paid from the accountants or business consultants who have prepared the plan.

Acceptance and payment by the Commission of business plan support does not automatically entitle the company to receive a company development loan to implement that business plan.

2. Company Development Support will be granted on the basis of a detailed business plan and the following selection criteria:

I. the quality of the company's proposal as reflected in the submitted business plan
II. the growth and profit potential of the company
III. the anticipated impact on the long-term stability of the company as a result of the expansion plan
IV. the business and production track record of the applicant company and/or the people involved
V. the quality of the production projects in development
VI. the European and international perspectives of the plan.

Payment conditions:

The loan will be paid on the basis of an agreement negotiated between the Commission and the company which in turn is based on the submitted business and development plan.

Payment will normally be made in two equal instalments of 50%. The first payable on signature of the contract, the second nine months later on production by the company and acceptance by the Commission of a progress report in a form decided by the Commission.

Reimbursement

Support for the Preparation of a Business Plan is granted as a subsidy to companies located in a country or region with low audio-visual production capacity and/or a restricted geographical and linguistic area.

For companies not falling within the category above, the *Support for the Preparation of a Business Plan* is repayable in the event that the company subsequently applies for a company loan under the MEDIA Programme and is selected. In this case the amount of the business plan support will be incorporated into the company development loan and will be repaid as part of that scheme.

Loans for Company Development Support will be reimbursed normally as follows:

- 100% of the loan is due in accordance with the terms of a negotiated agreement between the Commission and the company.

These will include at least the following minimum terms:

- Repayment will be made either in two payments six months apart or (for larger loans) in three payments six months apart, in any event so that the last payment is due four years after the signature of the contract.

- The loans are interest free, provided that the repayment conditions are respected.

Presentation of proposals

The Commission reserves the right not to process proposals which lack the required documentation. Any applications rejected on these grounds may be resubmitted for the future deadlines.

Proposals have to be presented in triplicate by using the attached application forms and providing the required annexes.

Each proposal must consist of the following elements:

I. Form 1 : applicant information
II. Form 2 : finance plan
III. Checklist

The required annexes to the forms should be submitted in French or English, where possible.

The application form is also available from the MEDIA Desks (listed below).

The Commission reserves the right to request additional information from applicants before making a final decision on granting support.

Amount and payment of funding

The amount of the financial contribution awarded to each company by the Commission for each planned project may not exceed 50% of the overall cost of the operation. The recipient company must provide guarantees for the remaining finance.

The selection of an applicant does not oblige the Commission to grant the amount requested. In no circumstances will the amount granted exceed the amount requested.

Applicants will be informed whether or not they have been awarded financial support as quickly as possible. The Commission's decision will be final.

The Commission will issue a contract specifying, in particular, the amount allocated, the payment arrangements and the obligations of the recipient.

Submission of proposals

Proposals should be submitted in *triplicate* to the European Commission. The final deadline for applications is 14 April 2000.

4.1.2 MEDIA Programme contact list

Head of unit
Jacques Delmoly / +32 2 295 84 06

Deputy head of unit
Costas Daskalakis / +32 2 296 35 96

Development
Jean Jauniaux / +32 2 299 91 48
Assistant: Hughes Becquart / +32 2 295 20 81

Training
Neal MacCall / +32 2 299 11 97

Distribution
Anne Boillot / +32 2 295 28 62

Cinema networks/festivals
Clotilde Nicolle / +32 2 299 91 23

Promotion
Elena Braun / +32 2 296 03 96

Management
Phat Minh Tang / +32 2 295 78 64
Assistant: Ulrike Haermeyer / +32 2 296 59 54

Information and MEDIA Desks
Alvaro Mason / +32 2 299 91 51

Legal affairs
Roberto Olla / +32 2 296 46 62

---

200 rue de la Loi (T120-1/2)
1049 Brussels
Tel: +32 2 299 91 47
Fax: +32 2 299 92 14
Website: http://europa.eu.int/comm/dg10/avpolicy/media/index_en.html

---

Intermediary organisations

The intermediary organisations assist the Commission in administering and processing applications as well as in monitoring the market in the following sectors:

MEDIA Training
Fernando Labrada
Claudio Coello 42 – 2ºD
28001 Madrid
Tel: +34 91 577 94 04
Fax: +34 91 575 71 99
Email: mrc@mad.servicom.es
Website: www.mrc.es

MEDIA Development
Michael Presscott
39c Highbury Place
London N5 1QP
Tel: +44 171 226 99 03
Fax: +44 171 354 27 06
Email: emda@compuserve.com
Website: www.futurenet.co.uk/emda

MEDIA Distribution
John Dick (head of office)
Rue Père de Deken, 33
1040 Brussels
Tel: +32 2 743 22 30
Fax: +32 2 743 22 45
Website: www.d-and-s.com
CINEMA: Antoinette Desclaubes
Tel: +32 2 743 22 34
PROMOTION: Frèdèrique Westhoff
Tel: +32 2 743 22 41
TELEVISION: Robert Strasser
Widenmayerstrasse 32
80538 Munich

Tel: +49 89 21 21 48 48
Fax: +49 89 21 21 48 49
VIDEO: Ashlyn Ward
Studio Building
Meeting House Square
Temple Bar
Tel: +353 1 679 96 52
Fax: +353 1 679 96 57

MEDIA Assistance

Bruno Nguyen
45-51 rue de Trèves
1040 Brussels
Tel: +32 2 282 08 30
Fax: +32 2 282 08 38
Email: mediaassistance@compuserve.com

Animation platform

Cartoon

Corinne Jenart/Marc Vandeweyer
418, Bd Lambermont
1040 Brussels
Tel: +32 2 245 12 00
Fax: +32 2 245 46 89
Email: cartoon@skynet.be
Website: www.cartoon-media.be

Cinema networks

Europa cinemas

Claude-Eric Poiroux
54 rue Beaubourg
75003 Paris
Tel: +33 1 42 71 53 70
Fax: +33 1 42 71 47 55
Email: europacinema@magic.fr
Website: www.europa-cinemas.org

Euro kids network

Elisabetta Brunella
Via Soperga 2
20127 Milan
Tel: +39 02 66 98 44 05
Fax: +39 02 669 15 74
Email: infocinema@mediasalles.it
Website: www.mediasalles.it

4.1.3 MEDIA Desks and Antennes

Media Desks and Antennes compose an information network on aids granted by the MEDIA Programme as well as on European initiatives supporting the European audiovisual industry.

Austria

MEDIA Desk Austria

Gerlinde Seitner
Österreichisches Filminstitut
6, Spittelberggasse 1070 Vienna
Tel: +43 1 5269730-406
Fax: +43 1 5224777
Email: media@filmminstitut.or.at

Belgium

MEDIA Desk Belgique (Communauté française de Belgique)

Gilbert Dutrieux
44, Boulevard Léopold II - 1080 Brussels
Tel: +32 2 413 22 45
Fax: +32 2 413 20 68
Email: mediadesk.belgique@cfwb.be
Website: www.cfwb.be/mediadesk

MEDIA Desk Belgie (Vlaamse Gemeenschap)

Christine Berckmans
18, Quai du Commerce - B2 - 1080 Brussels
Tel: +32 2 219 31 25
Fax: +32 2 219 31 53
Email: flanders.mediadesk@pophost.eunet.be
Website: www.flanders-image.com

Denmark

MEDIA Desk Danemark

Soren Stevns
Vognmagergade,10
1120 Copenhagen

Tel: +45 33 743442
Fax: +45 33 743465
Email: media@centrum.dk
Website: www.dfi.dk

Finland

MEDIA Desk Suomi

Kerstin Degerman
Finnish Film Foundation
K 13 Kanavakatu, 12
00160 Helsinki
Tel: +35 89 62203013
Fax: +35 89 62203070
Email: kerstin.degerman@ses.fi
Website: www.ses.fi

France

MEDIA Desk France

Françoise Maupin
Rue Hamelin, 24
75116 Paris
Tel: +33 1 47271277
Fax: +33 1 47270415
Email: mediafr@club-internet.fr
Website: www.cst.fr/mediafr

MEDIA Antenne Strasbourg

Catherine Buresi
1, Place De L'Etoile
67070 Strasbourg
Tel: +33 388609297
Fax: +33 388609590
Email: media@cus.sdv.fr
Website: www.cst.fr/mediafr

MEDIA Antenne Rennes

Jacqueline Irlande
10 bis, Avenue Henri Fréville
35200 Rennes
Tel: +33 299531105
Fax: +33 299531256
Email: media-bretagne@dial.oleane.com
Website: www.cst.fr/mediafr

Germany

MEDIA Desk Deutschland

Nikola Mirza
Friedensalle, 14-16 - 22765 Hamburg
Tel: +49 40 3906585
Fax: +49 40 3908632
Email: mediadesk@compuserve.com
Website: www.mediadesk.de

MEDIA Antenne München

Carola Zimmerer
Schwanthaler StraBe,69
80336 Munich
Tel: +49 89 54460330
Fax: +49 89 54460340
Email: media_antenne_muenchen@compuserve.com
Website: www.mediadesk.de

MEDIA Antenne Düsseldorf

Anne Marburger
Kaistrasse, 14 - 40221 Düsseldorf
Tel: +49 211 9305014
Fax: +49 211 930505
Email: media@filmstiftung.de
Website: www.mediadesk.de

MEDIA Antenne Berlin-Brandenburg

Gabriele Brunnenmeyer
c/o Filmboard Berlin-Brandenburg
26-53 August Bebel Strasse
14482 Potsdam-Babelsberg
Tel: +49 331 7212858
Fax: +49 331 7212883
Email: mediaantenne@filmboard.de
Website: www.mediadesk.de

Greece

MEDIA Desk Hellas

Ioanna Haritatou
44 Vas. Konstantinou Street - 11635 Athens
Tel: +30 1 7254056
Fax: +30 1 7254058
Email: media-he@otenet.gr

Iceland

MEDIA Desk Iceland

Sigridur Vigfusdottir
Tungata,14
101 Reykjavik
Tel: +354 5626366
Fax: +354 5627171
Email: mediadesk@centrum.is
Website: www.centrum.is/mediadesk

Ireland

MEDIA Desk Ireland

Siobhan O'Donoghue
Eustace Street, 6
Dublin 2
Tel: +353 1 6795744
Fax: +353 1 6709608
Email: info@mediadesk.ie
Website: www.iftn.ie/mediadesk

MEDIA Antenne Galway

Eibhlín Ní Mhunghaile
C/O Galway Film Centre
Cluain Mhuire Monivea Road
Galway
Tel: +353 91 770728
Fax: +353 91 770746
Email: mediaant@iol.ie
Website: www.iftn.ie/mediadesk

Italy

MEDIA Desk Italia

Giuseppe Massaro
286, Viale Regina Margherita
00198 Roma
Tel: +39 06 4404633
Fax: +39 06 4402865
Email: produzione@mediadesk.it
Website: www.mediadesk.it

MEDIA Antenne Torino

Alessandro Signetto
Piazza Carignano, 8
10123 Turin

Tel: +39 011 539853
Fax: +39 011 531490
Email: media@antennamedia.to.it
Website: www.antennamedia.to.it

Luxembourg

MEDIA Desk Luxembourg

Françoise Poos, Maison du Cassal
5 Rue Large
1917 Luxemburg
Tel: +35 2 478 21 70
Fax: +35 2 22 09 63
Email: francoise.poos@sma.etat.lu

The Netherlands

MEDIA Desk Nederland

Veroniek Schaafsma
Post Box 256
1200 Hilversum
Tel: +31 35 6238641
Fax: +31 35 6218541
Email: avpmedia@euronet.nl
Website: www.avp-mediadesk.nl

Norway

MEDIA Desk Norge

Sidsel Kraakenes, Filmens Hus
Dronningens Gate, 16
Box 482, Sentrum
0105 Oslo
Tel: +47 22 474570
Fax: +47 22 474597
Email: sidselk@nfi.no
Website: www.nfi.no/mediadesk

Portugal

MEDIA Desk Portugal

Amelia Tavares
Rua Sao Pedro Alcántara, 45
1200 Lisboa
Tel: +351 1 347 86 44
Fax: +351 1 347 86 43
Email: mediadesk@ip.pt

4

Spain

MEDIA Desk España

Jesus Hernández
P° de la Castellana,163 6ª Planta
28020 Madrid
Tel: +34 91 5711712
Fax: +34 91 5711751
Email: mediasp@mail.ddnet.es
Website: www.cinespain.com

MEDIA Antenne Barcelona

Aurora Moreno
Dcció. Gral. Promoción Cultura,
Portal Sta. Madrona, 6-8
08001 Barcelona
Tel: +34 93 3162780
Fax: +34 93 3162781
Email: kcpc0002@correu.gencat.es

MEDIA Antenne Sevilla

Carmen Illana
Levíes, 17
41071 Sevilla
Tel: +34 95 441 33 28
Fax: +34 95 442 01 56
Email: mediasev@arrakis.es

MEDIA Antenne Euskalherria

Verónica Sánchez-Nevejans
Ramón María Lili,7 - 1B
20002 San Sebastian
Tel: +34 943 326837
Fax: +34 943 275415
Email: mediaeusk@coverlink.com

Sweden

MEDIA Desk Sverige

Antonia Carnerud
Svenska Filminstitutet
5, Borgvagen
10252 Stockholm
Tel: +46 8 6651205
Fax: +46 8 6663748
Email: antonia.carnerud@mediadesk.sfi.se
Website: www.sfi.se

UK

MEDIA Desk UK

New Desk to be set up soon

MEDIA Antenne Cardiff

Jason Tynan
c/o SGRÎN
The Bank, 10 Mount Stuart Square
Cardiff CF1 6EE
Tel: +44 1222 33 33 04
Fax: +44 1222 33 33 20
Email: antenna@sgrinwales.demon.co.uk
Website: www.screenwales.demon.co.uk

MEDIA Antenne Glasgow

Louise Scott
249, West George Street
Glasgow G2 4QE
Tel: +44 141 302 1776
Fax: +44 141 357 2345
Email: louise.scott@dial.pipex.com

MEDIA Antenne Glasgow

Service: England
Chris Miller
249, West George Street
Glasgow G2 4QE
Tel: +44 870 0100791
Fax: +44 141 3572345

MEDIA Antenne Glasgow

Service: Northern Ireland
Heike Meyer Döring
21, Ormeau Avenue
Belfast BT2 8HD
Tel: +44 1232 232444
Fax: +44 1232 239918
Email: media@nifc.co.uk

4.2 Eurimages

4.2.1 Regulations for the support of co-production: full length feature films, animation and documentaries

Eligibility criteria for both schemes

1. Projects for feature films and animation, together with documentaries of a minimum length of 60 minutes which are intended for cinema release, are eligible.

2. The projects must originate from one of the fund's member states and be co-produced by at least two independent co-producers, established in different member states of the fund.

3. The participation of the majority co-producer must not exceed 80% of the total co-production budget, and the participation of the minority co-producer must not be lower than 10% for multilateral co-productions and 20% for bilateral co-productions.

4. However for budgets exceeding €5.4m (FF35m), bilateral co-productions applying for the first scheme may present a majority/minority co-production proportion of 90%/10%.

5. If additional co-producers from non-member states of the fund are involved in the project, their combined co-production percentage cannot exceed 30% for multilateral co-productions (i.e. involving at least three Eurimages member states) and 20% for bilateral co-productions (i.e. involving at least two Eurimages member states).

6. Projects must display artistic and/or technical co-operation between at least two co-producers from different member states of the fund. *(This co-operation will be checked before the payment of the first instalment of the support and will be assessed on the basis of the different posts mentioned in Appendix II of the European Convention of Cinematographic Co-production, i.e. authors, principal and secondary roles, main crew as well as the provision of technical services.)*
However bilateral financial co-productions are also eligible on condition that they have access to national accreditation in the co-producing countries (the award of national accreditation will be checked before the payment of the first instalment of the support).

7. The director of the film must be a European *(i.e. to be in possession of a valid passport or to have European resident status).*

8. The project must be European in terms of cultural origin, of investments and rights.

9. The European character of the project will be assessed on the basis of the points system mentioned in the European Convention on Cinematographic Co-production, taking into account the provision of technical services.

10. European co-production companies must have a European majority shareholder.

11. The majority (i.e. at least 51%) of the total financing of a project must come

from sources within the Eurimages' member states. The remainder of the financing (i.e. at most 49%) may come from sources outside Eurimages' member states on condition that no more than 30% of this financing does not come from sources outside Europe or from one single European non-Eurimages member state. The Executive Secretary will ensure that control of the project remains in the hands of the Eurimages member state majority producer.

12. The projects submitted must show that decisions concerning the final cut are coherent with the valid law of author's rights in the European co-producing countries.

13. The negative must belong undividedly to all co-producers.

14. If appropriate, Eurimages can demand a completion guarantee.

15. In order to be eligible for financial assistance, co-producers who have previously received financial support from Eurimages must have met all their contractual obligations to the fund, in particular, the submission of income statements for any film(s) previously supported by Eurimages and the reimbursement of any outstanding amounts.

16. Financial assistance may only be awarded to natural or legal persons governed by the legislation of one of the fund's member states, whose principal activity consists in producing cinematographic works, whose origins are independent of public or private broadcasting organisations.

17. Applications are eligible only if principal photography has not commenced at the time of the Board of Management's examination of the application, and is

scheduled to commence no later than six months after this date.

18. The projects submitted must conform to the cultural objectives of the fund.

19. Projects of a blatantly pornographic nature or those that advocate violence or openly incite to a violation of human rights, cannot be awarded any assistance from Eurimages.

Additional eligibility criteria for the first scheme: assesses the projects submitted primarily on the basis of their international circulation potential

In addition to the eligibility criteria common to the two schemes, the projects submitted for the first scheme must respect the following:

1. At least 75% of the financing must be confirmed in the majority co-producing country and 50% in at least each of the other co-producing countries. This should be confirmed by formal undertakings or agreements in principle (contracts, deal memos, letters of intent, confirmation of national support). However, a bank guarantee cannot be the sole means of reaching the financing threshold. *(Except in the case of a financial co-production: in this case the Executive Secretary will check the capacity of the producer to find financing in his/her own market.)*

2. The project must be accompanied by a sales projection by a credible sales agent. *(A sales agent's credibility will be assessed on the films he has previously sold and distributed.)* The producer must provide this projection when submitting his/her application.

3. The distribution in at least three countries (in the form of a minimum guarantee, pre-sale to television or worldwide pre-sale) must be justified by

means of a contract, deal-memo or a letter of intent. The definitive contracts must be provided for the payment of the second instalment of the support.

Additional eligibility criteria for the second scheme: assesses the projects submitted specifically in light of the cultural and economic diversity of European cinema

In addition to the eligibility criteria common to the two schemes, the projects submitted for the second scheme must respect the following:

1. At least 50% of the financing must be confirmed in each of the co-producing countries. This should be confirmed by formal undertakings or agreements in principle (contracts, deal memos, letters of intent, confirmation of national support). However, a bank guarantee cannot be the sole means of reaching the financing threshold. *(Except in the case of a financial co-production: in this case the Executive Secretary will check the capacity of the producer to find financing in his/her own market.)*

2. The projects should have the benefit, in each of the co-producing countries, of either national support or a pre-sale to television or a financing arrangement verifiable by, and acceptable to, the Executive Secretary.

Selection criteria

The Executive Secretary will provide the Board of Management with a systematic and detailed analysis of each project.

The Board of Management will select the projects according to the cultural objectives of the fund. In doing so, it will carry out a comparative analysis of the applications submitted within the one scheme, upon the basis of the different criteria relating to each scheme.

1. Selection criteria for the first scheme
   I. For the first scheme, the Board of Management will particularly assess the commercial potential of the projects, their pre-sales and sales estimates, the number and quality of distribution commitments, the percentage of market financing confirmed and the experience of the producers and the director.
   II. The Board of Management will also take into account the artistic and cultural value of the project and the experience of artistic and technical teams.

2. Selection criteria for the second scheme
   I. For the second scheme, the Board of Management will particularly assess the artistic and cultural value of the projects, the experience of the director and also the artistic and technical teams.
   II. The Board of Management will also take into account the impact of the project in relation to the development of new co-production habits and practices between co-producing countries, and the language of the film: preference will be given to films shot in one of the co-producing countries' native languages. Furthermore, for both schemes, the Board of Management will pay attention to the degree of financing confirmed, the degree of artistic and/or technical co-operation and the manner in which producers have fulfilled their previous obligations towards Eurimages.

Submission of projects

1. Applications for financial assistance shall be submitted to the Executive Secretary of Eurimages by one of the co-producers, with the consent of all the co-producers attested in writing.

2. Applications should be submitted in French or English in typescript on the application form contained herein. *(Please follow the instructions given on the application form precisely and enclose all*

the documents required, otherwise the application will be considered void.) Any incomplete application will not be placed on agenda of the next Board of Management's meeting.

3. Application deadlines, fixed annually by the Board of Management, will be published in the major trade journals. Applications must be received by the Executive Secretary by the application deadline date at the latest (the date of receipt is valid).

4. The same project cannot be placed and withdrawn more than twice from the agenda of the Board of Management. A project can only be re-submitted a third time if it has been substantially modified in its structure.

5. In the same way, a project previously rejected by the Board of Management can only be re-submitted if it has been notably modified, compared to the initial application.

6. It must be noted that a project withdrawn from the agenda will not automatically be placed on the agenda of the next Board of Management's meeting. Any request for re-submission must be made in writing by the delegate producer within the timescales mentioned in (3) above.

7. The co-producers must contact their national representatives on the Board of Management of Eurimages at the earliest opportunity. If one of the representatives concerned has not been contacted, the project will not be placed on the agenda.

Conditions of support

1. Financial assistance is provided in the form of an advance on receipts and allocated to each co-producer according to the proportion of his/her financial participation in the co-production.

2. To assist producers established in member states with low cinematographic production levels, Eurimages' financial support can be allocated disproportionately between the co-producers, with the exception of purely financial co-producers. In such a case Eurimages' contribution shall not exceed 50% of the total financing of any of the co-producers. However, such disproportionate allocation of financial support to one of the co-producers shall not be lower than 10% nor exceed 50% of the total amount allocated by Eurimages to the co-production concerned. The repayment of the amount awarded will, however, be in proportion to each co-producer's co-production percentage.

3. Payment of the co-producers' share of the sum awarded shall be made by Eurimages, either to the respective bank accounts opened specifically by each co-producer for the co-production in question, or to the bank account opened specifically by the delegate co-producer, on condition that written consent is received from each of the co-producers concerned.

Amounts and payment of the support instalments for the first scheme

1. The maximum support shall not exceed €610,000 (FF4m) for budgets lower than €5.4m (FF35m) and €763,000 (FF5m) for budgets higher than €5.4m (FF35m). *(The budget, the financing plan and the amount of support requested will be assessed and verified by the Executive Secretary.)*

2. Unless otherwise agreed by the Executive Secretary, payment will be made in three instalments.
   The first instalment of 50% of the total amount awarded is payable on:
   • the first day of principal photography and approval of the definitive financing plan

- the signature of the support agreement
- the confirmation of the artistic and/or technical co-operation and provision of the employment contracts of the principal actors and technicians or, in case of financial co-production, the confirmation of the award of national accreditation.

The second instalment of 25% of the total amount awarded is payable:

- on receipt of exploitation guarantees (i.e. distribution contracts announced)
- after approval of the credit list by the Executive Secretary
- on receipt of the confirmed answer print from the laboratory.

The third instalment of 25% of the total amount awarded is payable:

- after confirmation of the cinema release in the co-producing countries, or television broadcast, if appropriate, for documentaries
- after receipt and approval by Eurimages of an audit of the total costs of the production and the expenditure of each co-producer, certified by a qualified chartered accountant independent from the production companies involved, and showing any variations to the cost compared with the budget approved by the Board of Management
- after receipt and approval by Eurimages of the video cassette and publicity material.

3. Should the final costs of the production of the film be less than the budget approved by the Board of Management, Eurimages reserves the right to reduce its contribution accordingly.

Amounts and payment of the support instalments for the second scheme

1. The maximum support shall not exceed €380,000 (FF2.5m) for budgets lower than €3m (FF20m) and €460,000 (FF3m) for budgets higher than €3m (FF20m). *(The budget, the financing plan and the amount of support requested will be assessed and verified by the Executive Secretary.)*

2. Unless otherwise agreed by the Executive Secretary, payments will be made in at least two instalments:

The first instalment of 75% of the total amount awarded is payable on:

- the first day of principal photography
- the signature of the support agreement
- the confirmation of the artistic and/or technical co-operation and provision of the employment contracts of the principal actors and technicians or, in case of financial co-production, the confirmation of the award of national accreditation.

The second instalment of 25% of the total amount awarded is payable:

- after approval of the credit list by the Executive Secretary
- after confirmation of the cinema release in the co-producing countries, or television broadcast, if appropriate, for documentaries
- after receipt and approval by Eurimages of an audit of the total costs of the production and the expenditure of each co-producer, certified by a qualified chartered accountant independent from the production companies involved, and showing any variations to the cost compared to the budget approved by the Board of Management
- after receipt and approval by Eurimages of the video cassette and publicity material.

3. Should the final costs of the production of the film be less than the budget approved by the Board of Management, Eurimages reserves the right to reduce its contribution accordingly.

Repayment of advance

1. The amount awarded is repayable, from the first penny, from the net receipts of each of the co-producers at a rate equal to the percentage of Eurimages' share in the financing of the film, and after deduction of the amount of the distribution guarantees and/or pre-sales. However these distribution guarantees and/or pre-sales must form part of the financing plan approved by the Eurimages' Board of Management or can be to compensate for the difference in the Eurimages' support requested and that actually awarded. They must genuinely and demonstrably be applied to the production of the work. The Executive Secretary must have received valid documentation before the beginning of shooting.

   The following are considered as co-producers' net receipts.

   I. All receipts resulting from the exploitation of all or part of the film in the territories exclusively allocated to the co-producers, in any form whatsoever, after deduction of *(all deductions must be approved by the Executive Secretary)*:
      - the distribution commission
      - the costs involved in the manufacture of release prints of the film and the costs of promotional expenses for the launch of the film, upon receipt of all items of evidence of these costs
      - non-deductible taxes, censor's fees, customs duties and fees to professional organisations, insofar as they are directly related to the film concerned.

   II. All receipts resulting from the exploitation of all or part of the film in the territories other than those exclusively allocated to the co-producers, in any form whatsoever, after deduction of *(all deductions must be approved by the Executive Secretary)*:
      - sales agents' commissions, up to 25% per set of rights sold in one territory
      - the distribution commission
      - the costs involved in the manufacture of release prints of the film and the costs of promotional expenses for the launch of the film, upon receipt of all items of evidence of these costs
      - the costs of the manufacture of a foreign language version of the work.

   The participation of the director, the producers, the scriptwriter(s) and the actors, up to a reasonable level in accordance with standard practice, shall be accepted as deductions.

   All such costs should be duly specified in the financial statements provided by the distributors and/or sales agents and shall be subject to verification.

   Each co-producer is obliged to provide Eurimages with a copy of all contracts for the exploitation of the film or any part thereof.

2. Each co-producer shall be proportionally responsible for the repayment of the part of the financial assistance allocated to him/her. Repayment is due up to 100% of the amount awarded. In the case of disproportionate allocation of Eurimages' financial support (see above, "Conditions of support (2)), the repayment of the amount awarded will be in proportion to the co-production percentages.

3. Should a collection agent be appointed, Eurimages must be a signatory to the subsequent agreement.

Award agreement

1. An agreement between the co-producers involved and the Executive Secretary, acting on behalf of Eurimages, shall stipulate the terms on which the financial support is awarded.

   The award agreement shall be prepared by the Executive Secretary of Eurimages upon receipt of the necessary documents and should be finalised at the latest two months after the end of shooting. The co-producers must submit to Eurimages, for prior approval, all documents which may affect the artistic, technical, legal or financial arrangements of the project as approved by the Board of Management (revised financing plan, addenda to the co-production contract(s), contracts relating to the exploitation of the film, revised cast and crew lists, etc.).

Any substantial modification to the artistic or financial structure of the project (change of director, principal actors, co-producing countries, budget decrease, etc.) must be approved by the Board of Management, and supporting documentation provided.

2. The validity of any decision taken to support the co-production of a cinematographic work, will expire if no agreement between Eurimages and the co-producers has been entered into, within a period of nine months from the date of the Board of Management's meeting at which the decision was taken. This period may be extended by the Executive Secretary by a maximum of three months if there are valid grounds for so doing.

Accounting currency

1. The accounts of Eurimages are kept in euros, and the amount of financial assistance is expressed in euros. Moneys shall be payable either in euros or, should the beneficiaries so desire, in any other convertible currency to the equivalent value of the amount expressed in euros.

2. In determining the equivalent in euros of the total production costs, of the contribution of each co-production partner and of the amount of financial assistance applied for, the only applicable exchange rate for foreign currencies into euros, is that regularly fixed by the Finance Division of the Council of Europe.

Reference to Eurimages' support

1. Eurimages' support must be mentioned clearly and visibly in the main credits at the beginning of the film, as high as possible after the producers and according to its financial contribution, as well as in the major publicity material for the film.

2. The draft credits must be submitted to Eurimages for prior approval. Otherwise, Eurimages reserves the right to refuse payment of the outstanding balance of support awarded.

3. On completion of the work, the publicity material and a video copy (VHS) of the film, subtitled in English or French, must be submitted to the Executive Secretary.

Termination or cancellation

1. The financial assistance given by Eurimages shall be cancelled if the film is not completed and shown publicly in the co-producing countries within the time limit set in the award agreement. It shall similarly be cancelled or immediately repayable if a producer fails to meet the terms of these regulations or the obligations upon him/her under the terms of the award agreement.

2. If, however, the Board of Management considers that the beneficiaries have valid reasons for failing to complete the film, or for exceeding the time limit set, it may decide not to withdraw its financial assistance.

Disputes

1. There can be no appeal against a decision of the Board of Management not to support a request for financial assistance.

2. Any dispute relating to the execution of any agreement concluded pursuant to these regulations shall be submitted, failing a friendly settlement between the parties, for decision to an arbitration board composed of two arbitrators, each selected by one of the parties, and a presiding arbitrator, appointed by the other two arbitrators.

If a presiding arbitrator is not appointed under the above conditions within a period of four months, the president of the European Court of Human Rights shall make the appointment.

3. However, the parties may submit the dispute for a decision to a single arbitrator chosen by them by common agreement or, failing such agreement, by the president of the European Court of Human Rights.

4. The board referred to in (2) above or, if appropriate, the arbitrator referred to in (3), shall determine the procedure to be followed.

5. Failing agreement between the parties on the law applicable, the board, or if appropriate, the arbitrator, shall decide *ex aequo et bono* in the light of general legal principles, as well as observing customs used in the cinematographic and audiovisual field.

6. The arbitration decision shall be final and shall be binding on the parties.

Interpretation and amendment

It is up to the Board of Management to interpret and amend these regulations.

4.2.2 Eurimages Secretariat

Mme Mireille Paulus, executive secretary
mireille.paulus@coe.int

M. Jean-Claude Lazaro, deputy to the executive secretary - jean-claude.lazaro@coe.int

Conseil de l'Europe – Eurimages

Avenue de l'Europe
67075 Strasbourg Cedex
Tel: +33 3 88 41 26 40
Fax: +33 3 88 41 27 60
Email: Eurimages@coe.int
Website: culture.coe.fr/eurimages/

4.2.3 Eurimages national representatives

President

Avv. Gianni Massaro
63 Via Aureliana
00187 Rome
Tel:+39 06 4880988
Fax:+39 06 483596

Austria

Mme Iris Heller
Österreichisches Filminstitut
Spittelberggasse 3
1070 Vienna
Tel: +43 1 526 97 30 407
Fax: +43 1 526 97 30 440
Email: oefi@filminstitut.or.at

Directory

Mme Anissa Baraka
Abteilung II/3
Freyung 1
1010 Vienna
Tel: +43 15 31 20 75 32
Fax: +43 15 31 20 75 38
Email: anissa.baraka@bmwf.gv.at

Belgium

Mme Paule Caraël, Chargée de mission
Ministère de la Communauté française
Service général de l'Audiovisuel et des
Multimédias
Espace 27 Septembre
44 Boulevard Leopold II
1080 Brussels
Tel: +32 2 413 22 47
Fax: +32 2 413 20 68
Email: sgav@cfwb.be

M.Walther Lerouge, Directeur
d'Administration Media et Film
Ministère de la Communauté flamande
Kunstlaan, 52
1000 Brussels
Tel: +32 2 553 45 88
Fax: +32 2 553 46 72
Email: walter.lerouge@wim.vlaanderen.be

Substitute(s)
M. Emmanuel Roland, Chargé de mission
Ministère de la Communauté française –
Service général de l'Audiovisuel et des
Multimédias - Espace 27 Septembre
44 Boulevard Leopold II
1080 Brussels
Tel: +32 2 413 22 31
Fax: +32 2 413 20 68
Email: sgav@cfwb.be

Denmark

Mr Thomas Stenderup,
Director of Development and Production
Danish Film Institute
Vognmagergade 10 - 1120 Copenhagen

Tel: +45 3374 3434 / 3374 3430
Fax: +45 3374 3697
Email: thomass@dfi.dk

Substitute(s)
Mr. Henning Camre, Managing Director
Danish Film Institute
Vognmagergade 10
1120 Copenhagen
Tel: +45 3374 3434 / 3374 3430
Fax: +45 3374 3435

Finland

Mr Erkki Astala, Head of Production
Finnish Film Foundation
Kanavakatu 12 K 13
00160 Helsinki
Tel: +358 9 62 20 30 25 / 962 20 30 0
Fax: +358 9 62 20 30 50
Email: erkki.astala@ses.fi

Substitute(s)
Mr Jouni Mykkänen, Managing Director
Finnish Film Foundation
Kanavakatu 12 K 13
00160 Helsinki
Tel: +358 9 62 20 30 0
Fax: +358 9 62 20 30 50

France

Mme Paule Iappini,
Directeur des Affaires européennes
et internationales
Centre National de la Cinématographie
12 rue de Lübeck - 75784 Paris Cedex 16
Tel: +33 1 44 34 38 96 / 1 44 34 34 40
Fax: +33 1 44 34 36 59

Substitute(s)
Mme Cécile Telerman, Attachée
Centre National de la Cinématographie
12 rue de Lübeck
75784 Paris Cedex 16
Tel: +33 1 44 34 36 88 / 44 34 34 40
Fax: +33 1 44 34 36 59

Germany

Dr Max Dehmel
Ministerialrat,
Bundesministerium für Wirtschaft
Scharnhorststrasse 36
10115 Berlin
Tel: +49 30 20 14 72 40 / 30 20 14 9
Fax: +49 30 20 14 70 10

Mr Rolf Bähr, Managing Director
Filmförderungsanstalt
Budapester Strasse 41 - 10787 Berlin
Tel: +49 30 25 40 90 0
Fax: +49 30 25 40 90 58
Website: www.ffa.de

Substitute(s)

Mr Winfried Görisch
Bundesministerium für Wirtschaft
Scharnhorststraße 36
10115 Berlin
Tel: +49 30 20 14 72 43 / 30 20 14 9
Fax: +49 30 20 14 70 47
Email: Goerisch@berlin1.bmwi.bund.400.de

Ms Petra Wersch
Filmförderungsanstalt
Budapester Strasse 41
10787 Berlin
Tel: +49 30 25 40 90 20
Fax: +49 30 25 40 90 57 / 30 25 40 90 58

Mme Isabelle Birambaux
Filmförderungsanstalt
Budapester Strasse 41 - 10787 Berlin
Tel: +49 30 25 40 90 20
Fax: +49 30 25 40 90 57

Greece

M Kostas Vrettakos
Greek Film Centre
10 Panepistimiou Avenue
10671 Athens
Tel: +30 1 361 01 09 / 363 17 33
Fax: +30 1 361 43 36

M.Yannis Bacoyannopolous, Special
Counsellor on Cinematography
Hellenic Republic, Ministry of Culture
5 Metsovou Street
10682 Athens
Tel: +30 1 82 53 611
Fax: +30 1 82 53 604

Substitute(s)

M. Iannis Illiopoulos
Greek Film Centre
10 Panepistimiou Avenue
10671 Athens
Tel: +30 1 363 50 86 / 363 17 33
Fax: +30 1 361 43 36

Ireland

Mr Christopher O'Grady,
Principal Officer Arts
and Culture Section
Department of Arts,
Culture and the Gaeltacht
"Dún Aimhírgin" Mespil Road
4 Dublin
Tel: +353 1 667 07 88 / 667 08 19
Fax: +353 1 667 08 27

Mr Rod Stoneman, Chief Executive
The Irish Film Board
Rockfort House,
St Augustine Street. Galway
Tel: +353 91 561398
Fax: +353 91 561405
Website: www.iol.ie/filmboard
Email: film@iol.ie

Italy

Dr Mario Liggeri, Vice Direttore Generale
Direttore Ufficio i relazioni internazionali
Ministero dei Beni e delle Attività Culturali
Dipartimento dello Spettacolo
51 Via della Ferratella in Laterano
184 Rome
Tel: +39 06 704 75 45 0 / 773 24 92
Fax: +39 06 773 24 92 / 704 92 602

Luxembourg

M. Joy Hoffmann, Responsable Cinéma
Centre National de l'Audiovisuel
5 rue de Zoufftgen, BP 105
3402 Dudelange
Tel: +352 522 424-25 / 522 424-1
Fax: +352 520 655

Netherlands

Mr Ryclef Rienstra, Managing Director
Dutch Film Fund
J. Luykenstraat 2
1071 Amsterdam CM
Tel: +31 20 570 76 76
Fax: +31 20 570 76 89
Email: Filmfund@xs4all.nl

Substitute(s)

Ms Barbara Stroink
Dutch Film Fund
J. Luykenstraat 2
1071 Amsterdam CM
Tel: +31 20 570 76 76
Fax: +31 20 570 76 89

Portugal

M. Pedro Berhan Da Costa
Instituto do Cinema, Audiovisual &
Multimedia ICAM
Rua S. Pedro da Alcântara 45, 1.
1269 Lisboa 138
Tel: +351 1 323 08 00 / 323 08 02
Fax: +351 1 343 1952 / 342 8717
Email: Re@mail.Terravista.pt

Spain

M. Carmelo Romero de Andres,
Subdirector General del Promoción y
 Relaciones Internacionales
Instituto de la Cinematografica y de las Artes
Plaza del Rey 1 - 28004 Madrid
Tel: +34 91 701 72 58
Fax: +34 91 532 39 40

Mrs Rosario Alburquerque, Consejera Tecnica
Unidad de Apoyo Direccion General
Ministerio de Educación y Cultura
Instituto de la Cinematografica y de las Artes
Plaza del Rey 1
28004 Madrid
Tel: +34 91 701 72 59
Fax: +34 91 523 19 13

Sweden

Mr Peter Hald
Svenska Filminstitutet Filmhuset
Borgvägen 1-5 Box 27126
102 52 Stockholm
Tel: +46 8 665 12 01
Fax: +46 8 660 38 04
Email: peter.hald@sfi.se

Substitute(s)

Mr Gunnar Carlsson,
Head of Drama Department
SVT - Göteborg
405 13 Göteborg
Tel: +46 31 837 190
Fax: +46 31 837 230

4.3 Sources of film finance

4.3.1 Austria

Österreichisches Filminstitut/Austrian Film Institute

Gerhard Schedl

Spittelberggasse 3 - 1070 Wien

Austria

Tel: +431 526 97 30

Fax: +431 526 97 30 440

Email: oefi@filminstitut.or.at

Website: www.filminstitut.or.at

Who can apply

Austria citizens with permanent residence; if legal entity or partnership, must be registered in Austria, managed by Austrian citizens, and equity participation of at least 51%. Residents of countries participating in the EEA enjoy equal treatment to Austrian citizens.

Requirements

1. If the project can not be realised without proper award of funding or if realisation would be inadequate.
2. In the case of production funding, the applicant must contribute to the production cost approved by the film institute in advance.
3. The project to be supported must relate to an Austrian film, an Austrian co-production or an Austrian participation in a non-Austrian film.

Development funding

1. For script/treatment for the author a maximum of ATS 100,000 (€ 7,300) income tax-free grant.

2. For script development in team a maximum of ATS 170,000 (€ 12,400) or half the development cost.
3. For project development a maximum of ATS 500,000 (€ 36,300).

Production funding

No maximum amount. The average funding given by the Austrian Film Institute is around ATS 6 million (€ 436,000).

Automatic subsidies

The automatic scheme entitles those production companies to financial support which have already produced an economically or artistically successful film. A film is considered economically successful if it has achieved at least 35,000 admissions in Austria (next levels: 60,000, 120,000 or more than 200,000 admissions). Artistically successful films are those invited to or awarded prizes at specific international film festivals. A list of festivals and awards is an integrative part of the AFI's guidelines and is evaluated once a year. Depending on the "level of success", automatic support varies from ATS 5 to 9.5 million (€ 363,000 to € 390,000).

Structural funding

Maximum ATS 3 million (€ 218,000) loan.

Distribution

Maximum of ATS 500,000 (€ 36,300) or 50% of the distribution cost.

Training

Case by case decision of the selection committee.

Wiener Filmfinanzierungsfond (Vienna Film Financing Fund)

Wolfgang Ainberger

Stiftgasse 6/2/3 - 1070 Wien

Austria

Tel: +431 526 50 88/11
Fax: +431 526 50 88/20
Email: wff@wff.at
Website: www.wff.at/wff

The funding guidelines are currently being redesigned and should be published in Autumn '99. Should prospective applicants require further information, please contact WFF directly. From 2000 on, the WFF's yearly budget will be ATS 110 million (€8m).

4.3.2 Belgium

Films in Flanders Fund/Fonds Film in Vlaanderen

Daniël De Craecker
Ministerie van de Vlaamse Gemeenschap
Administratie Economie, Markiesstraat 1
1000 Brussels
Tel: +32 2 553 37 65
Fax: +32 2 553 37 88
Website: www.flanders-image.com

This fund has an annual budget of BFr427.8 million (€10.6m) to support the audiovisual policy of the Flemish Government, including support measures in the form of script grants, production grants, grants on the basis of gross receipt and advance on receipt (*avance sur recette*) of obligatory 75%.

Productions eligible for financial support

In order to be eligible for support from the *Fonds Film in Vlaanderen*, the audiovisual (co-) productions must be recognised as belonging either to the Flemish Community, or to a country or region of the Council of Europe, or to a country or region where co-productions belonging to the Flemish Community are eligible for subsidies.

Criteria for Flemish production or co-production

The criteria for recognising an audiovisual production or co-production as belonging to the Flemish Community are the Dutch-language original version, ownership of the copyrights, subject, director, script-writer, delegated producer, cast, crew, locations, post-production and suppliers. A recognisable Flemish identity must be established on the basis of a number of the criteria listed above. The subsidy is awarded on this basis and its amount is in proportion to the Flemish identity.

Following an advice by the Flemish Audiovisual Selection Committee, the following grants can be awarded:

- A script grant to the author, for writing a script with a view to the realisation of an audiovisual (co-) production (a feature film or a long creative documentary).
- A production grant awarded to a Flemish independent producer, for pre-production, shooting and post-production (a separate grant for one or more stages of the production process or a grant after production are also possible). For feature films, the production grant also includes a subsidy for the costs of promotion and distribution.
- A grant on the basis of gross receipt can be awarded to the (co-) producer of a feature film. This grant amounts to 25% of the cinemas' gross receipt, but may in no case be higher than the own contribution of the independent producer or co-producer who belongs to the Flemish Community.
- An interest-free loan for:
  I. financing the costs of distribution and promotion for a short or medium-length film
  II. financing of exceptional promotion campaigns for a feature film.

The Flemish Audiovisual Selection Committee/Afdeling Media en Film– Vlaamse Gemeenschap

Adriaan Heirman
Parochiaanstraat 15-23 - 1000 Brussels
Tel: +32 2 553 68 15
Fax: +32 2 553 68 59

Functions

In order to be eligible for support from the Film in Flanders Fund, a file must be submitted to the Flemish Audiovisual Committee. The Selection Committee gives advice on two aspects: (1) it decides whether a production is eligible for subsidies, and (2) it gives advice on the form and amount of the subsidy.

Ministry of Culture of the French-speaking Community/ Ministère de la Communauté Française Centre du Cinéma et de l'Audiovisuel

Paule Carael,
Chargee de Mission Direction de l'Audiovisuel
Espace 27 Septembre
Boulevard Leopold II, 44 - 1080 Brussels
Tel: +32 2 413 22 19
Fax: +32 2 413 20 68

Production funding

Amount variable, but generally as follows:
1. Co-productions in which Belgian producer holds minority interest: Bfr12,000,000 to Bfr16,000,000 (€297,500 to €396,600).
2. Belgian productions: Bfr16,000,000 to Bfr25,000,000 (€396,600 to €619,700).

4.3.3   France

CNC (Centre Nationale de la Cinematographie)

Jean-Pierre Hoss
CNC Centre National de la Cinématographie
12 rue de Lubeck Cedex 16
75784 Paris
Tel: +33 1 44 34 34 40
Fax: +33 1 47 55 04 91
Website: www.cnc.fr

Legal form

A legally and financially independent public-sector agency

Financing

Manages the funds of the *Compte de Soutien Financier de l'Industrie Cinématographique et de l'Industrie des Programmes Audiovisuels* (COSIP).

Functions

1. Regulatory: the CNC establishes general regulations for the audiovisual industry and controls certain administative procedures.
2. Promotional: subsidies for various national and international events to promote the film industry and aid to finance educational programmes.
3. Economic: management and administration of public funds allocated to the film industry bu the Ministry of Culture and other bodies; encouragement of other indirect incentives to the film industry.

1998 budget – *compte de soutien* (support account)

Ffr2,425,200,000 (€370m)

Aid to the film industry

Ffr1,289,000,000 (€197m)

Requirements

L'agrément des investissements and l'agrément de production

There are two stages in the recognition of a film's status: the *agrément des investissements* (obligatory or optional depending on the sources of finance), and the *agrément de production* (issued after the film has been shot, obligatory for all films). Both are issued by the director general of the CNC.

Eligibility

The production company must be established in France and be authorised with directors being EU citizens or coming from a country which has signed a relevant treaty. The company may not be controlled from outside Europe.

Non-French people may set up a production in France and benefit from public support if they meet the criteria as outlined below.

The film

A film may qualify for support, the amount of which varies according to various points systems. 80 points out of a possible 120 are required for 100% support. The film:

- must be produced using French (or treaty co-producer) studio and laboratory facilities
- must obtain 14 points (for fictional works) on a scale of 18 points to qualify as a French or European work under the French broadcasting quota rules
- must obtain 25 points out of 100 which apply if the film is
  1. produced by a production company fulfilling the criteria above
  2. made using a certain number of writers whose contracts are under French law, and
  3. made using qualifying talent and technical personnel whose contracts are under French law.

Project development subsidies

Costs covered

Script

Remuneration of personnel involved in the development process

Location scouting

Amount

- up to Ffr1.5 million (€230,000)
- 10% of the project's estimated budget.

Requirements

1. The committee responsible for evaluating the project must consider it to be of sufficient cultural interest.
2. The producer must give a firm undertaking to complete the project
3. The film must be shot in French
4. The producer must hold at least an option on the script rights

Dead-line

Subsidy must be returned to CNC if shooting does not commence within 24 months of the date of notification of grant.

Automatic box-office revenue subsidies for qualifying feature-length films

Amount

130% of the tax (T.S.A) on cinema tickets. The features of this tax are:

- Amount: 11% of gross box-office revenues of French cinemas Ffr517,000,000 (€79m) in 1998.
- Aim: to transfer funds generated by foreign films to the national film industry.

Duration of subsidy

Five years from release.

Payment:

Each producer has an account with CNC.

The account is considered to be part of the producer's normal cash-flow and must be used to finance future films (reinvestment works).

Method of calculation
Film revenue x 11% (T.S.A) x130%.

Use of funds
Subsidy must be used for the following purposes:
1. Repayment of debts maturing within 18 months of commencement of shooting.
2. Investment in new projects.

Avance sur recettes

Interest-free loans for film projects ready to go into pre-production.

Amount
Loans of up to Ffr5 million (€760,000). The average loan in 1997 was Ffr2.5 million (€380,000).

Number of Loans
- 15-20 each year for first-time directors
- 30-35 loans each year for experienced directors

Payment
Dependent on type of project and production arrangements.
No aid is released until all the required documentation has been submitted and is generally paid in several instalments during shooting. In practice, the first payment is not usually made until 4 to 6 months after the loan is approved.

Requirements
1. The film must be shot in French
2. The producer must hold an option on the rights to the production and have the consent of the director of the film

Dead-line
The producer must commence shooting within 24 months from the approval of the loan.

Advances

Amount
Maximum of two instalments of up to Ffr 500,000 (€76,000)

Requirements
The producer may receive advances on the *avance sur recettes* production loan if it meets the following conditions:
1. The producer must submit an agreement evidencing assignment of copyright, a project budget and a financial plan.
2. The applicant must have produced a film in the past which received public-sector aid, either on its own or in conjunction with a co-producer.

Dead-line
If the loan is still pending approval 6 months after payment of the advances, the producer is required to refund the amounts received.

Interest-free loans on completion of shooting

Amount
Up to Ffr500,000 (€76,000), although in special circumstance this could be raised to Ffr1 million (€152,000) for first films.

Number of loans
In 1996, 12 loans were granted, out of 30 applications.

Payment
Dependent on the conditions pacted by the producer and CNC

Requirements
1. The film must have been completed
2. The producer must have entered into a firm distribution agreement
3. Compliance with nationality criteria

Aid for script rewriting

If the applicant does not feel that his script is sufficiently complete to qualify for a production loan, he may submit his script for supplementary improvement aid.

Amount
Average Ffr90,000 (€13,700) up to a maximum Ffr120,000 (€18,300).
In 1996, 40 awards were given.

The Ministry of Foreign Affairs, the Ministry of Cooperation (now Secrétariat d'État) and the Ministry of Culture (Centre National de la Cinématographie)

Fonds Sud Cinéma

Type of Support
Advances for film productions in developing countries

Amount
Average Ffr500,000 (€76,000), maximum Ffr1 million (€152,000)

Regions benefitting from aid
Africa
Latin America
Asia
Maghreb countries
Eastern Europe

Requirements
1. The aid is only designed to cover production costs incurred in France, including remuneration of French technicians
2. The director of the film must be a national of a country located in one of the beneficiary regions
3. A French producer must be appointed to administer the funds advanced

Dead-line
Shooting must commence within 18 months from notification of grant

Fonds Eco – Fonds d'aide aux co-productions avec les pays d'Europe Centrale et Orientale

As Fonds Sud, for central and eastern European countries.

Association Beaumarchais

Paul Tabet, director
11 bis rue Ballu
75009 Paris
Tel: +33 1 40 23 45 46
Fax: +33 1 40 23 46 64
Website: www.beamarchais.asso.fr

Type of Support
Script

Amount
30,000 Ffr (€4,500)

Requirements
The scriptwriter must be French or Francophone

PROCIREP – Société Civile pour la Perception et la Répartition des Droits de Représentation Publique de Film Cinématographique

Catherine Fadier,
chargée d'aide à la création cinéma
11 bis, rue Jean Goujon
75008 Paris
Tel: +33 1 53 83 91 91
Fax: +33 1 53 83 91 92

Type of support

Aid for script development in pre-production stage.

Amount

Between Ffr50,000 (€7,600) and Ffr300,000 (€45,700).

Average amount for 1996: Ffr155,000 (€23,600).

Number of projects approved

70 in 1996, about 70% of all projects submitted.

Limit

50% of script development costs, which are defined as:

1. Cost of acquiring film rights.
2. Remuneration of writers and script adapters.

Payment

Usually in two equal instalments on presentation of invoices paid to date

Special bank account

Aid funds are paid into a special bank account identified with the project being supported and cannot be used by third parties.

Repayment

Aid must be repaid in either of the following events:

1. The copyright to the work is assigned to a third party.
2. The project as developed fails to meet the "French film" requirements.

Requirements

1. The producer must be registered with the CNC.
2. The producer must be experienced – must have made 10 short films, or one feature-length film.
3. A dossier (one copy) must be submitted to Procirep with the following information:

- a completed official application form
- contracts with the scriptwriters and directors, registered with the CNC
- the contract giving the producer screen adaptation rights
- details of the agreement under which the screen adaptation rights will revert back to their owner
- copies of vouchers supporting payments made
- provisional statement of development costs
- film budget.

4. 18 copies of a dossier containing the following information must be submitted to the selection committee:
- data on the production company and its directors
- description of past films and films being currently developed
- contracts which the writer and the directors of the project for which aid is sought
- technical, artistic and financial details of the project and a description of the purpose for which the requested aid will be used
- project synopsis
- resumes of the main project participants
- summary of investments and incurred costs.

Restrictions

One project per production company per year

SOFICAs – Sociétés de Financement des Industries Cinématographiques et de l'Audiovisuel

Audiovisual investment companies licensed by the French finance ministry which attract capital by offering investors substantial tax write-offs.

The French tax authorities have agreed that audiovisual productions can be considered as depreciable assets. Therefore:

- Contributions to co-productions are exempt from VAT
- Film exploitation is subject to VAT at the reduced rate of 5.5%.

In 1998, SOFICAs were used in the financing of 59 films for total of Ffr182m (€27.75m). The average investment per film is Ffr3.1m (€472,600) , representing approximately 10% of each film's budget. SOFICAs are not equity investors as they are prohibited by law from owning a share of copyright.

There are three main SOFICAs, which provided 84% of total funding in 1998: Studio Images (Ffr74.6m (€11.37m)), Sofinergie (Ffr55m (€8.38m)), and Cofimage (Ffr23.6m (€3.6m)).

Cofimage

Tour Maine Montparnasse
33, avenue du Maine BP 176
75755 Paris Cedex 15
Tel: +33 1 40 64 22 00
Fax: +33 1 40 64 23 36

Sofinergie

48, avenue Raymond Poincarré
75116 Paris
Tel: +33 1 53 65 73 30
Fax: +33 1 53 70 87 07

Studio Images

17, rue Dumont d'Urville
75116 Paris
Tel: +33 1 53 78 60 10
Fax: +33 1 53 78 60 22

Tax-deductible amount

1. Individuals: their full investment, up to 25% of their total net income.
2. Companies: the depreciation charged on their investment. Up to 50% of the investment can be depreciated in the first year.

Forms of financing

1. Acquiring shares in production companies.
2. Entering into co-financing agreements with production companies.

Requirements

1. The initial deduction will only be permanent if the investment is held for at least for five years.
2. Any capital invested in a SOFICA must be managed by duly authorised financial institutions.
3. SOFICAS must be corporations (*sociétés anonymes*)
4. The share capital of a SOFICA must be approved by the French Economics Ministry and its activity must be subject to Government control.
5. No single corporate or individual shareholder can own more than 25% of a SOFICA's share capital.
6. A SOFICA can only invest in audiovisual projects which:
   - are shot in French
   - have EU nationality
   - have been approved by the French Ministry of Culture.
7. The contributions made by SOFICAs under co-financing agreements are payable before commencement of shooting.
8. All co-financing agreements entered into by a SOFICA must be registered in the Mercantile Register.
9. 50% of the project production costs must be incurred in France.

Exclusions

Promotional, propaganda and pornographic productions are excluded from the SOFICA system.

IFCIC – Institut pour le Financement du Cinéma et des Industries Cinématographiques

46, avenue Victor Hugo
75116 Paris
Tel: +33 1 53 64 55 55
Fax: +33 1 53 64 55 66

Financed by funds allocated to it by the CNC and the French Ministry of Culture

Main activities
1. To guarantee loans to the industry.
2. To act as an advisory body.

Other activities
- *SOFICAs*
  IFCIC has set up a number of specialised companies, including SOFICAS Investimage, to participate in film production.
- *Venture capital companies*
  Capital Images venture capital company - mainly TV productions and hi-tech audiovisual companies.
- *Club des Investisseurs*
  An investment fund created to foster the production of high budget films.
- *Completion bonds*
  Through its alliance with AGF, SCOR, Film Finance (London), SOCODEFILM and other specialist companies, the IFCIC offers producers various types of bond to guarantee the completion of their projects.

Specialised finance companies
Scope
Currently participate in the financing of approx. 70% of film productions.

Terms of loans
Short-term. Maximum term of loans is normally 24 months.

Interest rates
Loans are usually granted to the film producer at the interbank market rate plus 1.2%.
An average commission of 1.5% per annum is also charged.

Advantages
1. The terms of the loans granted by specialised finance companies match film production dates and periods more closely than that of bank loans.
2. Personal guarantees are not generally required.
3. In addition to interest and commissions, banks make other charges (e.g. for overdrafts, number of operations, etc.)

Main Specialised companies
COFICINE
Consortium Général de Financement et de Contrôle Cinématographique
COFILOISIRS
Compagnie pour le Financement des Loisirs
SODETE-UFCA
Société pour le Développement de la Télévision-Union pour le Financement du Cinéma et de l'Audiovisuel

The Investors' Club
Set up in 1989 to provide a new source of financing for film productions by pooling individual private investor funds.

The members of the Investors' Club are financial institutions.

Content
Invests in high budget films (over Ffr45,000,000 (€6.86m).
Backed by a guarantee fund which covers potential losses of between 50% and 70% of the investment fund.
The Club invests between Ffr7,000,000 (€1.07m) and Ffr12,000,000 (€1.83m) in each film.

Requirements

1. The project must have prospects of commercial success.
2. Investments in projects are approved by two committees chaired by the IFCIC:
   - A consultant committee consisting of 9 experienced and prestigious film producers.
   - A committee of bankers representing the individual private investors.

Local aid

What follows is a list of the regional, urban and departmental sources of aid for film production.

Regions

Conseil Régional d'Alsace

Direction de la Culture et des Sports
35, avenue de la Paix BP 1006
67070 Strasbourg Cedex
Tel: +33 3 88 15 69 40
Fax: +33 3 88 15 69 49

- Budget for 1999: Ffr2.3m (€ 350,000).
- Production support: maximum Ffr300,000 (€ 46,000) (15% of budget). Producer must provide 15% of budget.
- Scriptwriting & development: between Ffr10,000 (€ 1,500) and Ffr50,000 (€ 7,600). Applicant must be Alsace-based company or individual resident in Alsace.

The region of Alsace has two other support bodies: la Communauté Urbaine de Strasbourg and l'Agence Culturelle d'Alsace.

La Communauté Urbaine de Strasbourg

Monsieur Roland Ries, President
1, Place de l'Etoile - BP 1049/1050 F
67070 Strasbourg Cedex.

Budget of Ffr2 million (€ 305,000) (1999), which goes towards selective support for feature film production.

Contact

Catherine Buresi/Laurent Dené
Service de la Communication Externe/ Audiovisuel et Cinéma
Tel: +33 3 88 60 92 97
Fax: +33 3 88 60 98 57
E-mail: media@cus.sdv.fr

L'Agence Culturelle d'Alsace – Département audiovisuel

1, espace Gilbert Esteve
67601 Selestat Cedex
Tel: +33 3 88 58 87 58
Fax: +33 3 88 58 87 50
E-mail: films.alsace@culture-alsace.com
E-mail: comfilm@strasbourg-film.com

Support fund with yearly budget of Ffr500,000 (€ 76,000), reserved for first works and innovative projects.

Conseil Régional d'Aquitaine

14, rue François de Sourdis
33077 Bordeaux Cedex

Aid for:

- production, making a pilot (maximum Ffr100,000 (€ 15,000), or 1/3 of the budget)
- scriptwriting (maximum Ffr30,000 (€ 4,500).

Conseil Régional de Bretagne

283, avenue du Général Patton BP 3166
35031 Rennes Cedex
Tel: +33 2 99 27 10 10
Fax: +33 2 99 27 11 11

Direction de la Culture:
Direct tel: +33 2 99 27 11 68
Direct fax: +33 2 99 27 15 16

- Selective aid awarded to shorts, animation, or documentaries.
- Feature films are only supported in exceptional circumstances.
- The project must be linked to the region.

Conseil Régional du Centre

Service Culturel
9 rue Saint Pierre Lentin
45041 Orléans Cedex 01

See Loire Valley Film Commission (below) for information on A.P.C.V.L., the region's support body.

Conseil Régional de Franche-Comté

Michel David
(Direction de la Culture), Director
Chantal Fischer, Chargée de mission
(**direct tel:** +33 3 81 61 61 14)
Fonds d'Aide à la Production
Cinématographique et Audiovisuelle
4, square Castan 25031 Besançon Cedex
Tel: +33 3 81 61 61 61
Fax: +33 3 81 83 12 92

- 1997 budget: Ffr2m (€305,000).
- Aid awarded to feature films, shorts, TV-movies, and documentaries.
- Stipulates a majority of the shoot to take place in the region, using local technicians.

Conseil Régional d'lle-de-France / THÉCIF

Gilles Alvarez, Responsable cinéma
Françoise Linster, Adjointe cinéma

4, rue de la Michodière 75002 Paris
Tel: +33 1 42 65 11 55
Fax: +33 1 42 65 00 21
E-mail: thecif@imaginet.fr

- 1997 budget: Ffr2.4m (€366,000).
- Post-production support for feature films: maximum Ffr120,000 (€18,300).

Conseil Régional du Languedoc-Roussillon

Alain Seureau, Directeur de la Culture
(**Direct tel:** +33 4 67 22 80 84)
Annie Milhau (**Direct tel:** +33 4 67 22 94 12)
201, avenue de la Pompignane
34000 Montpellier
Tel: +33 4 67 22 80 00
Fax: +33 4 67 22 81 92

Aid for shorts and documentaries.

Conseil Régional du Limousin

Catherine Roche
Direction du Développement Culturel
27, boulevard de la Corderie
87031 Limoges Cedex
Tel: +33 5 55 45 18 59
Fax: +33 5 55 45 18 25

Aid for shorts and documentaries.

Conseil Régional de Lorraine

Dominique Laudien, Adjoint au Chef de Mission Culture, Tourisme et Sport
Place Gabriel Hocquard BP 81004
57036 Metz Cedex 1
Tel: +33 3 87 33 60 00
Fax: +33 3 87 32 89 33
Website: www.cr-lorraine.fr

Aid for "young film-makers".

Directory

Conseil Régional de Midi-Pyrénées

Alain Roth
Direction de la Culture et de l'Audiovisuel
(**Tel direct:** +33 5 61 33 52 04)
22, avenue du Maréchal Juin
31077 Toulouse Cedex
Fax: +33 5 61 33 52 66

FRACA – Fonds régional d'aide à la création audiovisuelle

- Scriptwriting aid: average amount Ffr30,000 (€4,600).
- Production aid: Ffr100,000 (€15,000) to Ffr500,000 (€76,000).
- Priority given to applicants from the region.

CRRAV Nord-Pas-de-Calais (Centre Régional de Ressources Audiovisuelles)

Catherine Droubaix,
responsable de la production
25, boulevard Bigo Danel - BP 89
59003 Lille Cedex
Tel: +33 3 20 17 04 50
Fax: +33 3 20 17 04 51
E-mail: doc-crrav@pictime.fr

- Eligible for aid are French-based production companies, who must contribute 15% of the budget.
- Scriptwriting and development aid: generally between Ffr20,000 (€3,000) and Ffr100,000 (€15,000) per project.
- Feature film production: average award Ffr700,000 (€107,000).

Conseil Régional de Basse-Normandie

Jean-François Bridel
(**Direct tel:** +33 2 31 06 98 58/98 44;
Direct fax: +33 2 31 06 97 61)
Place Reine Mathilde BP 523
14035 Caen Cedex

Aid for short-, medium- and feature-length films.

ARCA Haute Normandie

Annick Brunet Lefèvre
43, rue des Capucins
76000 Rouen
Tel: +33 2 35 89 49 62
Fax: +33 2 35 70 35 71
E-mail: arca@mcom.mcom.fr
Website: www.mcom.fr/arca

Contact for information on the ARCA Haute Normandie (*Association Régionale du Cinéma et de l'Audiovisuel*). ARCA manages a fund for first time features, available to film-makers from the region, or who want to shoot there. Production funding available: Ffr300,000 (€45,700) to Ffr500,000 (€76,000).

Conseil Régional des Pays-de-la-Loire

Clara Moussy
(**Direct Tel:** +33 2 40 41 40 34)
Thierry Moutier
(**Direct Tel:** +33 2 40 99 63 79;
Direct Fax: +33 2 40 99 63 80)
1, rue de la Loire
44266 Nantes Cedex 02
Tel: +33 2 40 41 41 41

Conseil Régional de Picardie

Zohra Guelfat
11, Mail Albert 1er BP 2616
80026 Amiens Cedex
Tel: +33 3 22 97 37 51
Fax: +33 3 22 97 39 03

- Scriptwriting: Ffr10,000 (€1,500) to Ffr20,000 (€3,000).
- Development: up to Ffr40,000 (€6,000).
- Exclusively for local film-makers.

Conseil Régional Provence-Alpes-Côte d'Azur

Nicole Reynaud, Service Culture
27, place Jules Guesde 13481
Marseille Cedex 1
Tel: +33 4 91 57 54 22
Fax: +33 4 91 57 54 15

Rhône Alpes Cinéma

Nathalie Huchard
Villa Gillet
Parc de la Cerisaie
25, rue Chazière
69004 Lyon
Tel: +33 4 72 98 08 98
Fax: +33 4 72 98 08 99

- Yearly budget of Ffr20m (€3m).
- Production: eight to ten projects supported annually, with an average investment of Ffr2m (€305,000).
- Scriptwriting and development: on average supports two projects per year, with an average investment of Ffr100,000 (€15,000).

Départements

Conseil Général des Bouches du Rhône

Emmanuelle Breaufrere,
chargée de mission audiovisuel
(Direct Tel: +33 4 91 21 17 57)
52, avenue de Saint-Just
13004 Marseille
Tel: +33 4 91 21 13 13
Fax: +33 4 91 21 23 99

Aid for shorts.

Conseil Général des Côtes-d'Amor

Madame George Mordelet
Service Enseignement, Culture, Loisirs, Espaces Naturels. Service des Affaires Culturelles et des Monuments Historiques.
Place du Général de Gaulle BP 2371
22022 Saint-Brieuc Cedex 1
Tel: +33 2 96 62 27 82
Fax: +33 2 96 62 27 79)

Aid for shorts and documentaries.

Conseil Général des Landes

Philippe Mary, Attaché Culturel
23, rue Victor Hugo
40025 Mont-de-Marsan Cedex
Tel: +33 5 58 05 40 40
Fax: +33 5 58 05 41 41

Aid for short-, medium- and feature-length films which have a link to the region.

Conseil Général de Loire-Atlantique

Mireille Lesaulnier,
Chargée de mission cinéma
(Direct Tel: +33 2 40 99 10 76)
3, quai Ceineray
44041 Nantes Cedex
Tel: +33 2 40 99 10 00
Fax: +33 2 40 99 11 70
E-mail: amdavid@cg44.fr

Aid for shorts, animation or documentaries.

Conseil Général du Puy-de-Dôme

Valérie Héraud, Chef du Service Culturel
Catherine Langiert
Mission départementale de
développement culturel
24, rue Saint-Esprit
63033 Clermont-Ferrand Cedex 01
Tel: +33 4 73 42 20 20
Fax: +33 4 73 42 23 08

Aid for shorts, animation or documentaries.

Conseil Général du Val-de-Marne

Marie Aubayle (Direct Tel: 01 43 99 73 69)
Service Culturel
Avenue du Général de Gaulle
94011 Créteil Cedex
Tel: +33 1 43 99 70
Fax: +33 1 43 99 73 92

Aid for shorts and documentaries.

Film commission network

Commission Nationale du Film France

Benoît Caron
30, avenue de Messine
75008 Paris
Tel: +33 1 53 83 98 98
Fax: +33 1 53 83 98 99
E-mail: comnat@filmfrance.com
Website: www.filmfrance.com

Bureau du Cinéma Centre Val de Loire

Jocelyn Termeau
Atelier de Production Centre Val de Loire
24, rue Renan - B.P. 31
37110 Château-Renault
Tel: +33 2 47 56 08 08
Fax: +33 2 47 56 07 77
E-mail: apcvl@creaweb.fr
Website: www.apcvl.com

Contact for information on the support body
A.P.C.V.L. (*Atelier de Production Centre Val de
Loire*), which provides development funding
(Ffr30,000 (€4,600) to Ffr50,000 (€7,600))
and production funding for first or second
feature films (Ffr350,000 (€53,400) to
Ffr500,000 (€76,200)).

Commission du Film de Normandie

Annick Brunet Lefèvre
ARCA Haute Normandie
43, rue des Capucins
76000 Rouen

Tel: +33 2 35 89 49 62
Fax: +33 2 35 70 35 71
E-mail: arca@mcom.mcom.fr
Website: www.mcom.fr/arca

Commission du Film de l'Eure

Agnès Sauvaget
Boulevard Georges Chauvin
27021 Evreux
Tel: +33 2 32 31 50 23
Fax: +33 2 32 33 68 00

Commission du Film Nord/Pas-de-Calais

Valérie Wroblewski
CRRAV
25, boulevard Bigo Danel - BP 89
59003 Lille Cedex
Tel: +33 3 20 17 04 50
Fax: +33 3 20 17 04 51
E-mail: vwroblewski@crrav.com
Website: filmcomnord.crrav.com

Agence Films Alsace

Gaëlle Jones
Agence Culturelle d'Alsace
1, espace Gilbert Estève
BP 25 - 67601 Sélestat Cedex
Tel: +33 3 88 58 87 57
Fax: +33 3 88 58 87 59
E-mail: films.alsace@culture-alsace.org

Commission du Film de Strasbourg

Franck Vialle
1, place de l'Étoile
BP 1049/1050 F
67070 Strasbourg Cedex
Tel: +33 3 88 43 61 82
Fax: +33 3 88 60 98 57
E-mail: comfilm@strasbourg-film.com
Website: www.strasbourg-film.com

Commission du Film de Bourgogne

Gaëlle Laurent
BP 91 – 89203 Avallon Cedex
Tel: +33 3 86 34 47 60
Fax: +33 3 86 34 46 16
E-mail: laurent.gaelle@wanadoo.fr

Commission Régionale du Film Franche-Comté

Chantal Fischer
Hôtel de la Région
4, square Castan
25031 Besançon Cedex
Tel: +33 3 81 61 61 14
Fax: +33 3 81 83 12 92
E-mail: commission.du.film@cr-franche-comte.fr

Bureau d'Accueil de Tournage du Limousin

Pascal Perennes,
Hôtel de la région
27, boulevard de la Corderie
87031 Limoges Cedex
Tel: +33 5 55 45 17 53
Fax: +33 5 55 45 17 50
E-mail: peutetre@club-internet.fr

Commission du Film Auvergne

Didier Jérémie
26, rue des Jacobins
63000 Clermont-Ferrand
Tel: +33 4 73 92 14 99
Fax: +33 4 73 92 11 93

Commission du Film Rhône-Alpes

Serge Tachon
Rhône-Alpes Film Commission
Villa Gillet-Parc de Cerisaie

25, rue Chazière
69004 Lyon
Tel: +33 4 72 98 07 98
Fax: +33 4 72 98 07 99

Commission Régionale du Film Provence–Alpes–Côte d'Azur

Gerard Medion
Carrefour de la Malle - CD 60 D
13320 Bouc Bel Air
Tel: +33 4 42 94 92 06
Fax: +33 4 42 94 92 01
E-mail: comfilmpaca@aix.pacwan.fr

Commission du Film du Var

Dana Théveneau
Montée de Villeneuve
83570 Entrecasteaux
Tel: +33 4 94 04 40 70
Fax: +33 4 94 04 49 98

Saint-Tropez Office

Michel Brussol
Tel: +33 4 94 54 81 88
Fax: +33 4 94 97 76 06
E-mail: filmcomvar@aol.com

Bureau du Cinéma d'Aix-en-Provence

Jean-Michel Paoli
Office du Tourisme
Place du Général de Gaulle
BP 160
13605 Aix-en-Provence Cedex 1
Tel: +33 4 42 16 11 61
Fax: +33 4 42 16 11 62
E-mail: aixtour@aix.pacwan.net

Bureau du Cinéma de Marseille

Christiane Laugier
Office de la Culture de Marseille
42, la Canebière - 13001 Marseille
Tel: +33 4 91 33 33 79
Fax: +33 4 91 54 28 84

Bureau du Cinéma d'Avignon

Gérard Lefeuvre
Avignon Film Office - Hôtel de Ville
Service Communication
84045 Avignon Cedex
Tel: +33 4 90 80 80 00
Fax: +33 4 90 80 81 50

Ciné 32 – Les Régies de Gascogne

Dominique Laffitte
17, rue Lafayette
32007 Auch Cedex
Tel: +33 5 62 60 61 11
Fax: +33 5 62 60 61 18

Aquitaine Tournages

Nicole de Pretto
Cité Mondiale
23, parvis des Chartrons
33074 Bordeaux Cedex
Tel: +33 5 56 01 78 70
Fax: +33 5 56 01 78 30
E-mail: anc@anc.cr-aquitaine.fr

Commission du Film des Pays de la Loire

Thierry Moutier
Hôtel de la Région
1, rue de la Loire - 44266 Nantes Cedex 2
Tel: +33 2 40 99 63 79
Fax: +33 2 40 99 63 78

4.3.4 Germany

Federal

Filmförderungsanstalt (FFA)

Rolf Bähr (Managing Director),
Kirsten Niehuus (Head of Funding)
Budapester Strasse, 41
10787 Berlin
Tel: +49 30 254 09 0-0
Fax: +49 30 254 09 0-57
Email: Niehuus@ffa.de
Website: www.ffa.de

Who can apply

Screenplay – Author backed by German or EU producer
Production – German or EU producer with subsidy in Germany

Budget

The FFA disposes of approximately DM 80 million (€ 40m) per year.

Film promotion areas

- Full-length German films (feature films, documentaries, children and youth films) which are supported with subsidies (*Referenzfilm*: previously successfully film) and conditionally repayable loan (*Projektfilm*: new project).
- Short films.
- Screenplay development.
- National and international distribution.
- Cinemas/video retail outlet.
- Vocational training.
- Research, rationalisation, innovation.
- Promotion of German cinema at home and abroad.

Screenplay

Funding

Grant up to maximum DM 50,000 (€ 25,500) (exceptional DM 100,000 (€ 51,000)) – 1/2 payable on allocation, 1/2 on delivery of script. For further development of the screenplay an additional DM 30,000 (€ 15,000) can be granted.

Application requirements

1. application (x6)
2. theatrical release
3. treatment and one shot-sequence with dialogue.

Production

Funding

Reference film principle

The producer/production company is entitled to financial support (subsidy) if it has previously produced a German film (or, in certain circumstances, a German co-production with another country) which, in the territory covered by the law, has achieved 100,000 admissions within one year from first release. Films awarded a certificate by the FBW (Film Assessment Board) or a prize at a film festival need only to register 50,000 admissions, documentaries, children and youth films, only 25,000 admissions within four years.

Project principle

Film project support is granted if the proposed film contributes to the improvement of the quality and profitability of German films. A grant commission consisting of eleven members is responsible for the selection. The support ranges from DM 50,000 to DM 2 million (€ 25,500 to € 1m) (exceptional cases). It is necessary for the production company to participate with its own investment amounting to a minimum of 15% of the budget. Financial support is granted in the form of a conditionally repayable loan. Recoupment is on a sliding scale, commencing at 10% of the revenues accruing to the production company after its initial recoupment of 20% of production costs.

Application requirements
General

1. one final copy of production in German
2. 70% of studio shooting in Germany

3. German director (or cast and crew – other than scriptwriter and 2 leading actors – are all German or EU

4. premiere in Germany

5. minimum equity for production company DM 200,000 (€ 100,000).

Referenzfilmförderung:
100,000 (exceptional 50,000) admissions within a year after premiere (up to 1.2million)

Projektfilmförderung (Project Principle):
1. Script, cast, budget, finance plan
2. Distribution agreement or LOI from distributor
3. Private funds at least 15%.

Beauftragter der Bundesregierung für Angelegenheiten der Kultur und der Medien (Bundesministerium des Innern)

MR Friedrich-Wilhelm Moog
Filmreferat K 35
Graurheindorfer Str. 198
53117 Bonn
Tel: +49 228 681-55 23
Fax: +49 228 681-55 04
Email: FriedrichWilhelmMoog@bmi.bund400.de

Who can apply

Script: scriptwriter
Production: producer

Screenplay

Funding
Non-repayable grant of up to DM 20,000 (€ 10,000) (exceptional DM 50,000 (€ 25,500))

Application requirements
1. The beneficiary must undertake to exhibit the film together with a German short film.
2. The film can not show on commercial and pay TV channels until at least two years after its cinema release.
3. A print of the film must be deposited at the Bundesarchiv (the Federal Archive) within a year from the receipt of the final instalment of aid.
4. The dossier (11 copies) must contain the following information:
   • previous scripts or projects
   • treatment of the script with a completed scene
   • indication of the original work, if appropriate.

Production

Funding
Non-repayable grant of up to DM 500,000 (€ 255,000)

Application requirements
The producer or production company must invest up 15% of the budget.

Kuratorium Junger Deutscher Film

Monika Reichel
Schloss Biebrich
Rheingaustrasse 140
65203 Wiesbaden
Tel: +49 611 60 23 12
Fax: +49 611 69 24 09
Email: kuratorium@t-online.de

Funding focuses on the promotion of children in film, but only German productions.
Provides loans totalling approx. DM 2m (€ 1m) per year.

Federal

Bayern

FilmFernsehfonds Bayern GmbH

Dr Herbert Huber, President
Dr Klaus Schaefer, Managing Director
Schwanthaler Str. 69
80336 München
Tel: +49 89 544 602 0
Fax: +49 89 544 602 21
Email: filmfoerderung@fff-bayern.de
Website: www.fff-bayern.de

Who can apply

Screenplay: author
Project Development: producer
Production: German producer for cinema,
Bavarian producer for TV

Screenplay

Funding
Loan up to maximum DM 30,000 (€ 15,000)
(exceptional DM 40,000 (€ 20,500)) – 1/2
payable on allocation, 1/2 on delivery of
script. (repayment on assignment of rights to
third party.)

Application requirements
1. application (x18)
2. treatment and one-shot sequence with
   dialogue
3. LOI of Bavarian producer to realise the
   project.

Development

Funding
Loan up to DM 200,000 (€ 102,000) (or 70%
development costs) – 3/4 payable on allocation,
1/4 on final report.
Repayment on first day of principal photography
or assignment of rights to third party.

Application requirements
1. application (x18)
2. script/treatment for cinema/TV
3. calculation for project development
4. realisation mainly in Bavaria.

Production

Funding
Loan up to DM 3m (€ 1.5m) 30% production
costs) for cinema.

Repayment: 50% of realised profits up to 5
years after film's premiere; applicant may
request a "success loan" (from amount of
loan repaid) up to 3 years following
repayment of first instalment of loan.

Application requirements
1. cinema or TV release
2. script, calculation, finance plan
3. private funds at least 5%
4. "regional effect" at least 1.5 times
   amount of loan.

LfA Förderbank Bayern (Referat Film)

Königinstrasse 17 - 80539 München
Tel: +49 89 21 24 24 29
Fax: +49 89 21 24 25 09

Berlin/Brandenburg

Filmboard Berlin – Brandenburg GmbH

Prof. Klaus Keil, Managing Director
August-Bebel-Strasse 26-53
14482 Potsdam Babelsberg
Tel: +49 331 743 87-10
Fax: +49 331 743 87-99
Email: filmboard@filmboard.de
Website: www.filmboard.de

Who can apply

German-based producer

Screenplay

Funding

Loan up to 70% of screenplay costs.
Repayment due on first day of principal
photography, or assignment of rights to third
party.

Application requirements

1. application (x2)
2. theatrical release
3. treatment and one shot-sequence (or first
   draft of the screenplay).

Development

Funding

Loan up to 70% development costs.
Repayment due on first day of principal
photography or assignment of rights.

Application requirements

1. application (x2)
2. script/treatment for cinema/TV
3. calculation for project development.

Production

Funding

Loan up to 50% production costs (60% for
budget under DM 3m (€ 1.5m) 70% for budget
under DM 0.5m (€ 250,000)). Repayment: 50%
of realised profits after applicant has recouped
his own private funds; applicant may apply for
a new loan to the amount of the repaid loan
within 5 years.

Application requirements

1. cinema or TV release
2. script, calculation, finance plan and
   distribution agreement in place
3. "regional effect" at least same amount as
   loan or generation of employment within
   the region.

Hamburg

FilmFörderung Hamburg GmbH

Eva Hubert
Friedensallee 14-16 - 22765Hamburg
Tel: +49 40 398 37-0
Fax: +49 40 398 37-10
Email: Filmfoerderung-hamburg@ffhh.de
Website: www.hamburg.de/economy/filmfoerderung

Who can apply

Script: producer and author
Project development: producer

Production
budget up to DM 1.3m (€ 665,000): producer
and director
budget over DM 1.3 m (€ 665,000): producer

Screenplay

Funding

Conditionally repayable loan up to DM
100,000 (€ 50,000).
Repayment due on first day of principal
photography, or assignment of rights to third
party. Applicant must apply to the film fund
for production support for the project
supported within 24 months of payment of
last instalment of loan.
If the script is not produced within 36 months
of the last instalment of the loan, all rights
revert back to the film fund.

Application requirements

Application must include treatment together
with one-shot sequence with dialogue or
outline of project.

Development

Funding

Conditionally repayable loan up to 80% of
costs (maximum DM 200,000 (€ 100,000).
Repayment due on first day of principal

photography, or assignment of rights to third party. Applicant must apply to the film fund for production support for the project supported within 24 months of payment of last instalment of loan.

Application requirements
Application must include screenplay and calculation of proposed budget.

Production
Funding
Project under DM 1.3m (€ 665,000): up to 70% of budget.
Project over DM 1.3m (€ 665,000): up to 50% of budget.
Repayable after producer's share has been recouped. Repayment term expires 8 years after theatrical release

Application requirements
1. theatrical release (German premiere in Hamburg)
2. finance in place
3. private funds at least 5%
4. "regional effect" at least 1.5 times amount of loan
5. Credit the FilmFörderung Hamburg GmbH in film credits & P&A.

Bremen

Filmförderung Bremen

Michael Flügger
Waller Heerstrasse 46
28217 Bremen
Tel: +49 421 387 67 40
Fax: +49 421 387 67 42
Email: filmbuero@is-bremen.de
Website: tunix.is-bremen.de/~film46/

Who can apply
Applicant must have "Bremen connection"

Screenplay funding
Up to DM 12,000 (€ 6,000)

Development funding
Up to DM 12,000 (€ 6,000)

Production funding
Up to DM 60,000 (€ 30,000)

Nordrhein Westfalen

Filmstiftung NRW GmbH

Herr Dieter Kosslick, Executive Director
Kaistrasse 14
40221 Düsseldorf
Tel: +49 211 930 500
Fax: +49 211 930 505
Email: info@filmstiftung.de
Website: www.filmstiftung.de

Who can apply
Screenplay: NRW-author or NRW-producer
Project development: NRW-producer
Production: producer

Screenplay
Funding
Loan up to DM 40,000 (€ 20,500) (DM 80,000 (€ 40,000) for two authors); 1/3 payable on execution of loan agreement, 1/3 on rough draft, 1/3 on delivery of script. Repayment due 6 months after principal photography, or assignment of rights to third party.

Application requirements
1. application (x10)
2. theatrical release
3. treatment and one shot-sequence with dialogue
4. NRW-author has to offer script to NRW-producer.

Development

Funding

Loan up to DM 200,000 (€ 100,000) (or 80% development costs). Repayment 6 months after first day of principal photography or assignment of rights. If film project is not realised 36 months after last instalment, rights will be assigned to NRW

Application requirements
1. application (x10)
2. script/treatment for cinema/TV
3. calculation for project development
4. realisation mainly in NRW.

Production

Funding

Loan up to 50% production costs. Repayment: 50% of realised profits after applicant has recouped his own private funds; applicant may apply for a new loan to the amount of the repaid loan.

Application requirements
1. cinema or TV release
2. script, calculation, finance plan
3. private funds at least 5%
4. "regional effect" at least 1.5 times amount of loan.

Filmbüro NW e.V.

Michael Wiedemann
Leineweberstrasse 1 - 45468 Mülheim
Tel: +49 208 44 98 41-44
Fax: +49 208 47 41 13
Email: filmbuero_nw@t-online.de
Website: www.filmbuero-nw.de

Ministerium für Arbeit und Soziales, Stadtentwicklung, Kultur und Sport

Frau Theda Kluth
Breite Strasse 31

40213 Düsseldorf
Tel: +49 211 86 18 50

Staatskanzlei Düsseldorf

Abteilung Medien und Telekommunikation
Stadttor 1
40219 Düsseldorf
Tel: +49 211 83701

Hessen

Hessisches Ministerium für Wissenschaft und Kunst

Frau Mehrfeld
Postfach 3260
65022 Wiesbaden
Tel: +49 611 32 34 58
Fax: +49 611 32 25 50

Filmbüro Hessen

Eva Heldmann
Schützenstrasse 12
60311 Frankfurt
Tel: +49 69 13 37 96 18
Fax: +49 69 13 37 99 98

Hessische Filmförderung

Am Steinernen Stock 1
60320 Frankfurt
Tel: +49 69 155 45 16
Fax: +49 69 155 45 14

Development

Hessische Kulturelle Filmförderung (HFF): grant up to maximum DM 30,000 (€ 15,000)
Hessische Rundfunk Filmförderung (HR-FF): up to maximum 50%

Production

Hessische Kulturelle Filmförderung (HFF): grant up to 90% of budget (maximum DM 150,000 (€ 77,000)).

Hessische Rundfunk Filmförderung (HR-FF): grants generally up to maximum DM 100-200,000 (€ 50-100,000), up to maximum 50%.

Niedersachsen

Ministerium für Wissenschaft und Kultur

Jochen Coldewey
Leibnizufer 9
30169 Hannover
Tel: +49 511 120 2555
Fax: +49 511 120 2801

Filmförderung des NDR in Niedersachsen

Frau Ursula Lotz
Hamburger Allee 4
30161 Hannover
Tel: +49 511-361 57 78
Fax: +49 511 361-92 97
Email: info@lts-nds.de
Website: www.lts-nds.de

Who can apply

Authors, producers, production companies with Niedersachsen residency

Screenplay

Funding:
Non-repayable grant of up to DM 30,000 (€ 15,000).

If script is sold within 5 years – must repay 50% of grant.

Application requirements
The application should include a synopsis, treatment, and explanation of funding

Development

Funding
Non-repayable grant of up to DM 30,000 (€ 15,000)

Application requirements
The application should include a synopsis, treatment, and explanation of funding

Production

Funding
Non-repayable grant of up to DM 250,000 (€ 128,000) (or 90% of budget).
More than DM 250,000 (€ 128,000) up to maximum DM 500,000 (€ 255,000): conditionally repayable loan (or 90% of budget)

Application requirements
Treatment, script or description of project. Producer's private funds at least 10%.

Film & Medienbüro Niedersachsen – Projektförderung/ Büro Hannover

Henning Kunze
Gerberstrasse 16,
30169 Hannover
Tel: +49 511 134 70
Fax: +49 511 701 15 54
Email: fmb.hann@t-online.de
Website: www.osnabrueck-net.de/fmb/
Website: www.filmbuero-nds.de

Schleswig-Holstein

Ministerium für Bildung, Wissenschaft, Forschung und Kultur des Landes Schleswig-Holstein – Referat Musik und Filmförderung

Gabriele Nogalski
Brunswiker Strasse 16-22
24105 Kiel
Tel: +49 431 988-58 43
Fax: +49 431 988-58 57

Kulturelle Filmförderung Schleswig-H. e.V.

Herr Jan Hammerich
Schildstrasse 12
23552 Lübeck
Tel: +49 451 716 49
Fax: +49 451 753 74
Email: filmbuerosh@t-online.de
Website: www.jessenlenz.com/filmfoerderung

Who can apply

Schleswig-Holstein film-maker/author
"Schleswig-Holstein connection".

Application requirements

All applications must include:
1. adequate description of project
2. calculation
3. financing plan
4. proof of "Schleswig-Holstein connection".

Development

Grant up to maximum DM 15,000 (€ 7,700)

Production

Grant up to maximum DM 100,000 (€ 50,000)

Saarland

Minister für Wirtschaft

Am Stadtgraben 6-8
66111 Saarbrücken
Tel: +49 681 50 100

Saarländische Investitionskreditbank AG

Gerhard Koch
Johannisstrasse 2
66111 Saarbrücken
Tel: +49 681 303 30
Fax: +49 681 30 33 100

Saarländisches Filmbüro e.V.

Nauwieser Strasse 19
66111 Saarbrücken
Tel: +49 681 36 04 7
Fax: +49 681 37 46 68

Gesellschaft zur Medienförderung Saarland (MFG), Saarland Medien GmbH

Werner Sosalla (Geschäftsführer)
Karcherstrasse 4 - 66111 Saarbrücken
Tel: +49 681 389 880
Fax: +49 681 389 8820
Email: sos@lmsaar.de

Currently no project/production funding. Only provides institutional funding

4

Rheinland–Pfalz

Kultusministerium

Bernd Braukfiebe
Mittlere Bleiche 61 - 55116 Mainz
Tel: +49 6131 16 28 27
Fax: +49 6131 16 41 51

Filmbüro Rheinland Pfalz

Günter Minas
Taunusstrasse 5 - 55118 Mainz
Tel: +49 6131 61 15 38
Fax: +49 6131 63 81 26
Website: www.mainz.de/filmbuero

Baden-Württemberg

Medien–und Filmgesellschaft Baden–Württemberg GmbH

Frau Gabriele Röthemeyer
Huberstrasse 4
70174 Stuttgart
Tel: +49 711 122 28 33
Fax: +49 711 122 28 34
Email: mfg@mfg.de
Website: www.mfg.de

Who can apply

Screenplay: producer or scriptwriter.
Development: producer resident in Baden-Württemberg or producer planning to film in Baden-Württemberg.
Production: producers.

General application requirements

The requirements to apply for production funding – other than the quality of the project – can either be a producer/co-producer based in Baden-Württemberg or a local reference of the project itself or reinvestment of at least 100% of the allocated aid by hiring local staff or facilities for production purposes. Also a co-production with SWR or ZDF/arte or with the French-German channel ARTE in addition to funding by another German film fund can be a further qualification.

Proof of the complete financing of the project. Financing must be proven within 18 months of award; the applicant must provide at least 5% of the production costs.

Screenplay
Funding
Success-related repayable loan up to DM 50,000 (€ 25,500). Repayment of the loan is due at the start of shooting or on transferral of rights; if the script is not produced within 36 months of the last instalment of the loan, all rights revert back to the film fund.

Development
Funding
Conditionally repayable loan up to 80% of the estimated project development costs (maximum DM 150,000 (€ 75,000)). Repayment of the loan is due at the start of shooting or should the rights be transferred; if project receives production loan, possibility of agreement: development loan incorporated in the production loan.

Production
Funding
Budget over DM 1m (€ 510,000): conditionally repayable loan up to 30% of costs (maximum DM 2m (€ 1m)). Repayable (in a MFG account) after producer's share has been recouped. Repayment term expires 8 years after theatrical release. Repaid funds are available to the producer to reinvest in new project, within 3 years following the repayment.

Budgets up to DM 1m (€ 510,000): conditionally repayable loan up to 70% of costs. Additional loan up to DM 250,000 (€ 128,000) can be offered for special projects with total production costs of up to DM 500,000 (€ 255,000).

Mecklenburg-Vorpommern

Mecklenburg-Vorpommern-Film e.V. im Landesfilmzentrum

Frau Gabriele Kotte
Frau Antje Nass
Röntgenstrasse 22
19055 Schwerin
Tel: +49 385 55 50 77
Fax: +49 385 557 41 47
Email: filmfoerderung@film-mv.de
Website: www.film-mv.de

Application requirements
Applicants must have "Mecklenburg-Vorpommern connection"

Screenplay funding
Up to DM 30,000 (€ 15,000)

Development funding
Up to DM 30,000 (€ 15,000)

Production funding
Up to DM 500,000 (€ 255,000).
Short film and documentary up to DM 200,000 (€ 100,000)grant.
Budget over DM 100,000 (€ 50,000): success-related repayable loan. Repaid funds available to producer for investment in subsequent project.

Thüringen/ Sachsen/ Sachsen-Anhalt

MDM Mitteldeutsche Medienförderung GmbH

Hainstrasse 19
04109 Leipzig
Tel: +49 341 269 87   0
Fax: +49 341 269 87 – 65
Email: ebecker@mdmfoerderung.de
Website: www.mdm-foerderung.de

Screenplay funding
Maximum DM 30,000 (€ 15,000)

Development funding
Maximum DM 200,000 (€ 100,000) (or 70% costs). Or to develop a slate of projects – maximum DM 300,000 (€ 150,000) (or 70%)

Production funding
Maximum 70% cost.

Kulturelle Filmförderung Thüringen, Thüringer Ministerium für Wissenschaft, Forschung und Kultur – Kulturabteilung

Frau Christel Schröder
Referat K3
Postfach 672
99013 Erfurt/Thüringen
Tel: +49 361 379 16 32
Fax: +49 361 379 16 99
Email: tmwfk.thueringen@www.de

Kulturelle Filmförderung Sachsen, Sächsisches Staatsministerium für Wissenschaft und Kunst

Frau Hedda Gehm
Wigardstrasse 17
01097 Dresden
Tel: +49 351 564 64 82
Fax: +49 351 56 46 40 65 00

Kultusministerium des Landes Sachsen-Anhalt

Dr Timm
Turmschanzenstrasse 32
39114 Magdeburg
Tel: +49 391 567 36 24
Fax: +49 391 567 38 55

4.3.5 Greece
Greek Film Centre

Manos Efstratiades
10 Panepistimiou St
Athens 10671
Tel: +30 1 363 1733
Fax: +30 1 361 4336
E-mail: info@gfc.gr
Website: www.gfc.gr

The Greek Film Centre (GFC) produces an average 15 films a year, with a total budget of DR2.2bn (€6.08m).

Funding regime

There has recently been a change in the funding regime of the GFC. The financing streams that are now in existence are:

Horizons II: six to seven high-budget films per year. The cost limit for a production that is made only with Greek producers is DR 250m (€760,000), and the GFC can award up to DR90m (€275,000).

Incentive II: six to seven feature-length films a year. The Greek Film Centre can award up to DR40m (€120,000) per film.

Micrography: nine short films, award of about DR10m (€30,000).

Motion: fund for animation. Per year: one short film, and one high-budget production (which can be a feature film, or TV-film/series). For the short film the GFC can award DR15m (€45,000), and for the high-budget production, DR90m (€275,000).

4.3.6 Ireland
The Irish Film Board– Bord Scannán na hÉireann

Mr Rod Stoneman
Rockfort House
St Augustine Street - Galway
Tel: +353 91 561398
Fax: +353 91 561405
E-mail: film@iol.ie
Website: http://www.iol.ie/filmboard

Budget

Approximately Ir£4m (€5m) in 1999. The board assists a number of films in development and provides production loans for eight to ten films a year.

Development

Up to a maximum of Ir£25,000 (€32,000). Repayable on first day of principal photography.

Teams (producer/director/scriptwriter) or individual scriptwriters may apply.

Production

Production finance is offered on the basis of repayable loan/equity participation of a proportion of the total budget. Producers/directors/companies may apply

Amount
- Up to 50% for budgets under Ir£1m (€ 1.3m).
- Up to 25% for budgets over Ir£1m (1.3m).
- Normally: 10-15% of budgets.

Department of Arts, Heritage, Gaeltacht and the Islands

Dermot Burke
43-49 Mespil Road - Dublin 4
Tel: +353 1 667 0788
Fax: +353 1 667 0827

The Department has an active role in the Section 481 investment incentive scheme, through the certification process.
Each film project is examined in the light of the contribution in three key areas:
1. creation of employment
2. value-added in the economy
3. and culture.

Section 481 of the Taxes Consolidation Act 1997

Formerly known as Section 35, this tax incentive presently has the following parameters (a distinction is made between peak and off-peak production periods, with a more favourable package available in off-peak periods):

1. Peak production periods (February to September inclusive)
   - 60% allowable for budgets of less than Ir£4m (€ 5m)
   - 50% allowable for budgets between Ir£5m (€ 6.3m) and Ir£15m (€ 19m) (subject to a maximum of Ir£15m (€ 19m), provided half of investment comes from corporations)
   - marginal relief applied to budgets between Ir£4m (€ 5m) and Ir£5m (€ 6.3m) .

2. Off-peak production periods (October to January inclusive)

- 66% allowable for budgets of less than Ir£4m (€ 5m)
- 55% allowable for budgets between Ir£5m (€ 6.3m) and Ir£15m (€ 19m) (subject to a maximum of Ir£16.5m (€ 20m), provided half of investment comes from corporations)
- marginal relief applied to budgets between Ir£4m (€ 5m) and Ir£5m (€ 6.3m).

3. 80% of investment tax relief for both individuals and corporates.

4. Re-investment by both individuals and corporates is allowed each year.

5. Corporates permitted to invest up to Ir£8m (€ 10m) (provided that Ir£5m (€ 6.3m) of this is invested in films with budgets of less than Ir£4m (€ 5m)).

6. Tax relief to commence from the start date of principal photography.

7. A production company must be established for the purpose of the production of one and only one film production.

8. A year-round uplift of 10% on the amount of tax relief may be applied for producers who carry out post-production work in Ireland.

4.3.7 Italy

Dipartimento del Turismo e dello Spettacolo

Dr Francesco Ventura
Via della Ferratella 51
00184 Rome
Tel: +39 06 7732 1
Fax: +39 06 7732 468
Contact: Mr Onori (Tel: +39 06 7732 489)

4

National subsidies or loans (maximum sum or % of budget)

- In order to qualify for state funds, the producer must have minimum capital of Lit40m (€20,700).
- Guarantee fund to films of "national cultural interest". Loan up to 90% film's budget (maximum Lit8bn (€4.1m)); the guarantee covers up to 70% of this sum.
- Guarantee fund to "Article 8/28" films (first or second film, with "artistic and cultural" bias). Loan up to 90% film's budget (maximum Lit2.5bn (€1.3m)); the guarantee covers up to 90% of this sum.
- Intervention Fund: loan at reduced rate; up to 70% of the budget, for films of "national production".
- Ordinary Fund: loan at regular bank rate, but the interest rate is reduced by Administration subsidy.
- Best screenplay prize – enhancing Italian cultural heritage Lit 40m (€20,700).
- Subsidy – 13% of gross box office for first 2 years of theatrical release (must be used to amortise film loans: the remainder must be invested in production of new films).
- Quality prize – bonus award to national films – Lit400m (€207,000) (71% to production company, 29% to other "authors" of the film).

4.3.8 Luxembourg

FONSPA (Fonds National de Soutien à la Production Audiovisuelle)

Guy Daleiden
5, rue Large
1917 Luxembourg
Tel: +352 478 2165
Fax: +352 220963
Email: guy.daleiden@sma.etat.lu
Web site: www.fonspa.lu

Tax incentive (CIAV – *Certificats d'Investissement Audiovisuel*)

- Company financing a production can recoup a proportion of qualifying production costs (incurred during production in Luxembourg) through tax certificates to the value of qualifying production costs
- if the holder of the certificate has no taxable income in Luxembourg, the company may sell the certificates to a resident corporation in order to obtain the financial benefit
- as Luxembourg's corporate income tax rate is around 30%, then the tax reduction available to a certificate-holding company will be 30% of its face value. The granting of the certificate is selective, subject to government criteria.

National Audiovisual Production Support (*Aide Financiére Sélective*)

- Selective loans in the form of advance on receipts.
- Available to Luxembourgish producer.
- Development/scriptwriting: maximum amount 2,000,000 Lfr (€45,000).
- Production: maximum amount 20,000,000 Lfr (€450,000) (10,000,000 Lfr (€225,000) in the case of a co-production); producer's equity participation should be no less than 10% of cost of production.

4.3.9 The Netherlands

Nederlands Fonds voor de Film/ Dutch Film Fund

Ryclef Rienstra
Jan Luykenstraat 2
1071 CM Amsterdam
Tel: +31 20 570 76 76
Fax: +31 20 570 76 89
Email: nff@filmfund.nl
Website: www.filmfund.nl

Facts

In 1998 the Dutch Film Fund supported the production of 15 feature length fiction films, along with 3 low budget film productions, 13 documentary films, 16 short films and 4 animation films. The 1999 budget of the Dutch Film Fund is approximately NLG 23,200,000 (€ 10.5m). The total amount available for feature film support is NLG 15,200,000 (€ 6.9m).

Who can apply?

The producer plays a crucial role in acquiring funds, while also being expected to invest substantially in his or her film. As a rule, these loans are made available through a Dutch-based producer, with a serious track-record in film production.

Requirements

Script and project development: development support is only available for an essentially Dutch project.

Co-production: assessment of artistic quality and financial viability of the project, the involvement of Dutch talent and facilities, possible contribution to Dutch film culture.

Script and project development

Development can be supported in various phases: from treatment to script, new versions, script doctoring, translations, production planning, research etc. Maximum of NLG 85,000 (€ 38,570) per project. However, development support is only available for an essentially Dutch project.

Production funding

Up to NLG 1,000,000 (€ 453,780) for feature length fiction films.

FINE B.V. (Film Investors Netherlands B.V.)

Gamila Ylstra
Sarphatikade 12
1017 WV Amsterdam
Tel: +31 (20) 530 4700
Fax: +31 (20) 530 4701
E-mail: info@fine.nl
Website: www.fine.nl

Fine B.V. (Film Investors Netherlands B.V.) was launched in January 1999 as an initiative of the Foundation for Film Investment Facilities established by the Dutch Ministry of Economic Affairs, in an attempt to stimulate the Dutch film industry.

Operating since spring 1999, Fine acts as an intermediary between film producers and potential investors, seeking venture capital for film projects through a network of financial institutions such as banks. Fine also acts as a consultant to banks and producers, helping to structure investment schemes which will benefit from the new Dutch tax incentives.

Fine additionally encourages film projects that fit the spirit and letter of the new tax laws. Fine's staff are available to provide advice on this issue to banks and investment companies.

On a modest scale, the company itself also invests venture capital in fully developed film projects, selecting projects which are expected both to be profitable and to have a beneficial impact on the Dutch film industry. For this purpose, the Ministry of Economic Affairs has provided a one-off interest-free subordinated loan of NLG 12.5 million (€ 5.7m).

Rotterdam Film Fund (Rotterdams Fonds voor de Film en Audiovisuele media)

Jacques van Heijningen
Rochussenstraat 3-C
3015 EA Rotterdam
Tel: +31 10 436 0747
Fax: +31 10 436 0553
E-mail: info@rff.rotterdam.nl
Website: www.rff.rotterdam.nl

The Rotterdam Film Fund (RFF) aims at stimulating and strengthening the audiovisual industry in the Rotterdam region. It has an annual budget of NLG 4 million (€ 1.8m).

Production funding

Interest-free loan, to be paid back from the revenue achieved through commercial exploitation of the film. As a rule, the maximum amount of the loan will be NLG 300,000 (€ 136,363).

Requirements

Applications are assessed in terms of the applicants' experience and quality, and the project's financial and technical viability.

At least 150% of the loan must be spent in the Rotterdam region, of which 3/4 must be spent in the audiovisual sector.

CoBo Fund

Jeanine Hage
P.O. Box 26444
1202 JJ Hilversum
Tel: +31 35 677 53 48
Fax: +31 35 677 23 10
Email: Jeanine.Hage@gsd.nos.nl

Fund encourages co-productions between national broadcasters and independent film producers.

Ministry of Economic Affairs

Bezuidenhoutseweg 30
Postbus 20101
2500 EC The Hague
Tel: +31 70 379 8820
Fax: +31 70 379 7287
E-mail: v.a.gilsen@minez.nl
Website: info.minez.nl/

The Ministry of Economic Affairs plays an important part in stimulating economical developments that contribute to Dutch industry's competitive position on the international scene. One of the key elements of its activities in this area is its market policy which aims to create favourable conditions for the Dutch industry sector.

Senter

Dokter van Deenweg 108
P.O. Box 10073
8000 GB Zwolle
Tel: +3138 455 3222
Fax: +31 38 454 0225
E-mail: J.G.vanderSluijs@minez.nl
Website: www.senter.nl

Senter is an agency of the Ministry of Economic Affairs. Senter takes care of the execution of the random depreciation facility of the production costs of movies. Information about the facility is available at Senter.

Ministry of Education Culture, and Science

Arts Directorate, Film Department
Europaweg 4
Postbus 25000
2700 LZ Zoetermeer
Tel: +31 79 323 4368
Fax: +31 79 323 4959
E-mail: r.j.h.docter@minocw.nl
Website: www.minocw.nl

The Ministry of Education, Culture and Science supports the Dutch film sector in a number of ways. It provides grants for the production, promotion, distribution, and screening of films of artistic quality, but also for the conservation of historic films and publications. The department provides financial support to organisations such as the Dutch Film Fund and Holland Film Promotion as well as to several film festivals.

Ministry of Finance

Korte Voorhout 7
Postbus 20201
2500 EE The Hague
Tel: +31 70 342 7540
Fax: +31 70 342 7924
Website: www.minfin.nl

The Ministry of Finance handles the random depreciation regulation. In connection with this, the State Secretary has issued a directive, intended both for the federal tax department and for taxpayers and their advisors. The department gives information about the random depreciation regulation and the directive.

4.3.10 Portugal

Instituto do Cinema, Audiovisual e Multimedia (ICAM)

Dr. Pedro Berhan da Costa (President)
Rua S. Pedro de Alcântara, 45 - 1º
1269 - 138 Lisboa
Tel: +351 1 323 08 00
Fax: +351 1 343 1952
Website: www.icam.pt

Production funding
- ICAM supports 10-12 features a year.
- Subsidy provided ranges from ESC90m

to ESC130 (approximately €450,000 to €650,000), per project (up to 80% of the film's budget).
- Subsidy money is issued on the first day of principal photography.
- Bank credits are available during the development stage.

4.3.11 Scandinavia

The Nordic Film and TV Fund

Svend Abrahamsen (from 1 January 2000)
Skovveien 2
0257 Oslo - Norway
Tel: +47 22 56 01 23
Fax: + 47 22 56 12 23

Established in 1990 by the TV networks and film institutes of all five Nordic countries. Annual budget DKK50 million (€6.7m).

NFTVF grants support to "Nordic productions" of high quality, suitable for theatrical, video and television release and which are likely to attract a broad public. There are no requirements with regard to the subject matter of the film having to be "Nordic" nor are there any requirements with regard to the make-up of the film's artistic and/or technical team.

However, for a feature film to be eligible for a grant, it is necessary that at least two theatrical agreements and two television distribution agreements have been entered into within at least two different Nordic countries.

The Fund contributes repayable capital. The producer is obliged to repay to the fund a share of the revenues corresponding to the fund's share in the funding of the film. However, the duty to repay arises only after the total private equity has been repaid to the producer including a 35% overhead to cover the producer's general costs.

---

* Technically, Scandinavia refers to Finland, Norway and Sweden. For the sake of convenience, we have used the term to refer to the Nordic countries (Denmark, Finland, Iceland, Norway and Sweden).

In 1996 10 feature films received support from NFTVT: 4 Swedish films, 3 Danish and 1 from each of Norway, Finland and Iceland. The total support granted to these features was DKK22 million (€2.96m), each individual contribution ranging between DKK500,000 (€67,260) and DKK4 million (€540,000).

Denmark

The Danish Film Institute

Thomas Stenderup
Vognmagergade 10
1120 Copenhagen K
Tel: +45 3374 3400
Fax: +45 3374 3401
Email: dfi@dfi.dk
Website: www.dfi.dk

Budget

For 2000: the total amount allocated to the DFI is DKK299 million (€40m), of which DKK185 million (€25m) is expressly for film.

Development

Development funding is granted to the producer on the same basis as with the two kinds of film production funds.

Consultant Model

Amount

In principle no limit to the amount awarded to each project, but generally awards loan of DKK6-10 million (€0.8m - €1.35m) per project. Development funding exceeding DKK500,000 (€67,250) is considered a production loan.

Requirement

Danish producer equity participation must be at least DKK1 or 2 million (€135,000 or €270,000) (deferred fee a possibility).

Basis of support

Artistic evaluation undertaken by a film consultant, who oversees the development of the film project from initial synopsis to finished picture.

60/40 Model

Amount

Can amount to maximum 60% of estimated production costs – calculated on basis of Danish investment – and cannot exceed DKK5 million (€670,000). Development funding cannot exceed DKK300,000 (€40,350), but can be supplied by loans to be paid back on first day of principal photography.

Criteria

Loan awarded without prior consultant approval – based on evaluation of whether film is likely to promote cinematographic art and culture in Denmark, and be able to attract a wide audience.

Finland

Finnish Film Foundation

Jouni Mykkänen
K13, Kanavakatu 2
SF-00530 Helsinki
Tel: +358 9622 0300
Fax: +358 9622 03050
Email: jouni.mykannen@ses.fi
Website: www.ses.fi

Who can apply

Support is available to a producer or production company holding the Finnish rights to the production in question - and can only be granted to productions which are "clearly domestic in terms of production and artistic contribution".

Directory

Production

- Non-repayable grant.
- Up to 70% of film's production costs – not exceeding FIM4 million (€673.000), including development support already granted to the project.
- Paid out in instalments.

Iceland

Icelandic Film Fund

Thorfinnur Ómarsson
Túngata 14
101 Reykjavik
Tel: +354 562 3580
Fax: +354 562 7171
Email: thorfinn@iff.is
Website: www.iff.is

Funds available to Icelandic producers. Fund's budget in 1997 was €2.13m.

Non-repayable subsidies for script development, pre-production and production funding are granted by the Awards Committee elected by the Board of Directors of the IFF.

As a main rule, grants are awarded to films with Icelandic dialogue, and produced by Icelandic parties, with co-production a possibility.

Norway

Norwegian Film Institute

Erling Dale
Filmens Hus, Box 482
0105 Oslo
Tel: +47 2247 4500
Fax: +47 2247 4599
Email: nfi@nfi.no
Website: www.nfi.no

Production

Distributes €4.85m of production support to feature-length theatrical fiction films. Documentaries for theatrical exhibition may also be eligible for support. Producers applying for grants must submit a shooting script and a production budget. The Feature Film Commissioning Executive of the NFI is charged with evaluating applications with regard to artistic merit, proposed and secured funding, and feasibility of the projects. Support may theoretically amount to 90% of approved production costs, but has averaged 65% over recent years. Grants are formally made by the Board of Directors of the Norwegian Film Institute on the recommendation of the Feature Films Commissioning Executive of the NFI.

Audiovisual Production Fund (Audiovisuelt Produksjonsfond)

Elin Erichsen
Filmens Hus
0152 Oslo
Tel: +47 22 47 46 50
Fax: +47 22 47 46 91
Email: av-fondet@av-fondet.filmenshus.no
Website: www.filmenshus.no/av-fondet

Production

Distributes €6.8m in production support to feature-length theatrical fiction films. In special cases, documentaries meant for theatrical exhibition as well as shorter fiction may also be eligible. All films supported by the fund will also be screened by the NRK or TV2 television channels. The Director of the AVPF is responsible for evaluating proposed projects with regard to artistic merit, proposed and secured funding, and the feasibility of the project. Support may theoretically amount to 90% of approved production costs, but is expected to remain at a lower level. Grants are formally made by the Board of Directors of the AVPF on the recommendation of the Director of the Fund.

Norsk Film a/s (gjelder langfilm)

Tom Remlov
Postbox 4
1342 Jar
Tel: +47 67 52 53 00

Production

Receives an allocation of € 3.9m for in-house production of feature films. Producers, individual filmmakers or writers may approach Norsk Film AS at any stage in the pre-production process. Following a formal decision by the board of directors of NF, on the recommendation of the managing director, the project will be launched either as a co-production between NF and an independent producer or as an NF in-house production

Sweden

Swedish Film Institute (Svenska Filminstitutet)

Hans Ottosson
Box 27 126
10252 Stockholm
Tel: +44 8665 1100
Fax: +44 8661 1820
Email: info@sfi.se
Website: www.sfi.se

Requirements

(Article 4 of SFI statutes):
1. "A film shall be regarded as Swedish provided that it has a Swedish producer

and that the contribution of Swedish artists is of obvious importance".
2. The term "Swedish producer" is defined as a person residing in Sweden, a branch of a foreign company, or other legal person registered in Sweden.
3. A film that has no Swedish producer is still regarded as Swedish provided that the Swedish investment in the film amounts to 20% of its production cost and that the contribution of Swedish artists is of obvious importance.

Production support

- Up to 70% of the production cost, max SEK 9 million (€ 1.05m).
- 1998 total support – SEK 119 million (€ 13.85m).
- Conditionally repayable only on theatrical income starting after 110,000 tickets sold.
- Repayment obligations lapse one year after the opening date of the film.

Box office bonuses

- Paid out within one year after the opening of the film on condition that the film has attracted at least 30,000 cinemagoers.
- Maximum support of SEK9 million (€ 1.05m) is payable after 110,000 visitors (1998 total support SEK 57 million (€ 6.63m)).

Terms of payment

Production support payable as follows:
1. 20% upon signing of of production agreement
2. 40% on first day of principal photography
3. 10% upon last day of photography
4. 20% upon commencement of mixing
5. 5% upon commencement of promotion
6. 5% upon delivery of copy of film and final accounts.

4.3.12 Spain

There are three main sources of public funding in Spain: ICAA, regional funding and funding from the Programme Ibermedia.

ICAA
Instituto de Cinematografía y Artes Audiovisuales

Ministerio de Cultura
Plaza del Rey, 1
28071 Madrid
Tel: +34 91 701 70 00
Fax: +34 91 522 93 77
Website: www.mcu.es/cine/index.html

ICAA has the following objectives:
- To encourage, promote and regulate the film and audiovisual activities in all issues related to production, distribution and exhibition.
- To promote Spanish films and Spanish audiovisual products.
- To recover, restore, preserve and circulate the film heritage.
- To enable the co-operation among professionals of different film specialities.
- To collaborate with similar institutions in other countries.
- To co-operate with the Autonomous Communities in all issues related to the film and audiovisual industry.

The selection process of script or project funding is done through committees of industry professionals and experts.

Script development

There are two different types of subsidies to develop screenplays available from the ICAA:

1. Authors and production companies presenting a project together. This subsidy is part of the agreement of the ICAA with various broadcasters.

2. Funding for individual authors.

Who can apply
1. Registered Spanish production companies and authors, temporarily associated to develop the script of the project.
2. Authors of scripts of films to be developed in any of the official languages of the Spanish territory.

Funding
1. Total funding available is Ptas. 90 million (€ 540,900). A total of 22 projects have been awarded Ptas. 4 million (€ 24,000) each in October 1999.
2. Total funding available is Ptas. 20 million (€ 120,200), for a total of 10 projects with Ptas. 2 million each (€ 12,000).

Application requirements
1. The author and company have to present a resume of their previous experience, synopsis, memory of the project, contract between author and company. The Jury will examine the background of the scriptwriter, the originality of the idea, the quality and viability of the project. Those companies receiving funding who have not started shooting within three years will have to reimburse 50% of the amount.
2. The author has to present a treatment, CV, synopsis and memory of the project. The Jury will evaluate the background of the scriptwriter, the originality of the story, the quality and commercial viability of each of the projects.

Production
Funding for upcoming directors and experimental projects
This selective subsidy is reserved for films of new directors, films with a small budget or films of an experimental character. New directors are those who have not directed more than two films already exhibited.

The amounts granted are fixed and the total amount can not be more than 50% of the declared budget or of the sum invested by the production company in the film up to a maximum of Ptas. 50 million (€300,500). It can be cumulative with regional aids.

Who can apply

Spanish production companies registered at the Official Registration Office. New directors are those who have directed less than three movies qualified for screening. Experimental projects are those which, due to their especial characteristics, are difficult to finance.

Funding

Funding will be for projects with a budget of less than Ptas. 125 million (€750,000). Total funding available is Ptas. 400 million (€2.4m).

Application requirements

1. Chain of title, script, budget, production schedule, certificate of Spanish nationality, and financial plan.
2. Company details: other subsidies awarded, other productions, investment plan and projections for the next two years.
3. Project details: project description, synopsis, and summary of the financial and commercial plan.

Automatic funding

Automatic subsidy calculated on the basis of box-office receipts. All films with Spanish nationality are entitled to receive an automatic aid equivalent to 15% of gross box office receipts during the first two years of screening in Spanish cinemas.

Additionally, films that have not received selective aid can be awarded one of the following:

1. An additional 25% of box office receipts during the first two years of commercial exploitation.
2. An amount equivalent to 33% of the producer's investment.

If the film has not received selective project funding, the total subsidy awarded can not exceed Ptas. 150 million (€902,000), nor 75% of the amount of investment made by the producer in this film nor 50% of the global cost of the film. Otherwise, the maximum amount is Ptas. 100 million (€601,000).

This subsidy is related to the credit system further explained in "Banking: guarantees and loans", below.

Who can apply

Production companies officially registered.

Funding

15% of box office revenues. Additionally 25% of box office revenues or 33% of the producer's investment.

Application requirements

To receive automatic funding the film must obtain the following box office revenues:

- Ptas. 50 million (€300,500) during the two years of commercial exploitation.
- Ptas. 30 million (€180,300) if the film has been directed by a new director or the budget is under Ptas. 200 million (€1.2m).
- Ptas. 20 million (€120,200) if it is screened in two Spanish languages and 5 million (€30,000) have been obtained in one of the official languages of Spain other than Castilian.

Regional Institutions

With the Statute of the Autonomous Communities created in 1982, the development of cultural policies was transferred to each of the autonomies. Some are more involved in the development of the local film industries. Catalonia, Galicia, the Basque Country, Valencia, Andalucía and Castilla y León are those most actively involved in financing feature films. Other Autonomous Communities like Navarra, Madrid, the Canary Islands and Asturias have small incentives for cultural projects, production or exhibition of features but not a formal audiovisual plan and have not been included in the analysis.

Generalitat de Catalunya

Direcció General de Promoció Cultural
Carrer del Portal de Santa Madrona, 6-8
08001 Barcelona
Tel: +34 93 316 27 80
Fax: +34 93 316 27 81
Website: cultura.gencat.es

The *Department of Culture* of the Generalitat of Catalunya was created in 1982 This department is responsible for supporting culture and makes financial backing available for the film and audiovisual sector in particular. It has also the responsibility of authorising and controlling measures related to co-productions, certification of nationality and box-office receipts.

Funding is awarded through the *Directorate General of Cultural Promotion*, the *Institució de les Lletres Catalanes* and through the *Directorate General of Linguistic Policy*. The Generalitat de Catalunya has been actively developing its film industry and acquiring more and more independence from the Central State.

From June 1999, the new Audiovisual Plan establishes the creation of the Catalan Institute of Cultural Industries – ICIC. The ICIC will join representatives from the Council of Culture, Industry, Commerce and Tourism, the Commission for the Information Society, the Catalan Institute of Finance and the Consortium of Commercial Promotion and the Catalan Radio Corporation.

The aim of the ICIC is to encourage the role of the broadcaster, ensure the quality of the productions, promote outside of Catalonia all Catalan productions, take advantage of all funding available in the EU and help new talent.

Script development

Through the *Institució de les Lletres Catalanes*, dependent from the Department of Culture, subsidies are granted to scriptwriters of audiovisual productions.

Who can apply
Scriptwriters with a script in Catalan.

Funding
Funding will depend on the interest and valuation of the project.

Application requirements
Application form, production plan, synopsis, script sample. The selection process is based on the following criteria:
1. The quality of the idea to be developed.
2. Use of stylistic resources.
3. Thematic interest and potential of the subject matter for other cultures.
4. Commercial viability.
5. Level of the language and general tone of the narration.

Development
Through the *Directorate General of Cultural Promotion*, dependent from the Department of Culture, subsidies are awarded to producers with the objective of designing the production of films (development and pre-production).

Who can apply
Any production company registered as such, based in Catalonia. The scriptwriter and director must be resident of Catalonia.

Funding
The maximum amount awarded will be of Ptas. 3 million (€ 18,000), if this does not exceed 50% of the cost of acquiring the rights, cost of design and research and scouting.

Application requirements
Application form. Budget, script, letters of interest of the director, proof of acquisition of rights.

Production
New talent
Subsidies for the production of feature films in Catalan directed by new talent.

Who can apply
The production company must be registered in Catalonia, using personnel and companies from Catalonia. The director must not have directed more than two films classified for screening in cinemas. The film must be screened for at least seven days in one of the normal screening cinemas in Barcelona in all sessions.

Funding
The amount of funding is Ptas. 15 million (€ 90,000) per film. This subsidy is incompatible with the aid to the production and to the credits granted by the Generalitat de Catalunya for film production.

Application requirements
Application form. The evaluation of the project is effected according to a system which awards points depending on the elements of Catalan interest involved in the production, e.g. shooting in Catalonia is worth 30 points, Catalan director, 10.

Feature films in Catalan
Subsidies for the production of feature films in Catalan.

Who can apply
Any production company registered as an official production company in Catalonia. Films must be screened in Catalan. Incompatible with the new talent subsidy. At least 40 points in the awards system.

Funding
Two types of funding:
1. Aid for premiering in Catalonia. Maximum subsidy of Ptas. 5 million (€ 30,000) for cost of prints and advertising.

2. Percentage of box office receipts of the Catalan version of the film. The percentage will be the same as the percentage of investment of the producer in the film (up to a maximum of 17% or Ptas. 30 million (€ 180,300)).

Application requirements
Application form with costs and official budget approved by the ICAA. The evaluation of the project is effected according to a system which awards point depending on the elements of Catalan interest involved in the production, e.g. shooting in Catalonia is worth 30 points, Catalan director, 10.

Xunta de Galicia

Consellería de Cultura, Comunicación Social e Turismo
Edificios Administrativos San Caetano
San Caetano s/n
15704 Santiago de Compostela
Tel: +34 981 545400
Fax: +34 981 544802
Website: www.xunta.es/conselle/cultura/consell/organig.htm

The Xunta de Galicia, through the Council of Culture, Communications and Tourism, establishes the measures to encourage the audiovisual industry. Total budget for the year 2000 is expected to be Ptas. 941 million (€ 5.7m).

The new Law Decree of the Audiovisual created the role of the *Consortium of the Audiovisual*: An independent institution set up to organise events to develop the audiovisual sector and set up a film commission.

The Law Decree also set up the *Assessment Council of Telecommunications and Audiovisual of Galicia*, which will unite some of the most active representatives to advise, assess, and serve as arbitration body and control in the contents of the audiovisual sector in Galicia. The Council has the mission of establishing different Commissions, the most immediate one the Commission of Galician Film to assess with the measures of support and action plans in the development, production, distribution, dubbing and exhibition of audiovisual products.

Subsidies for the development of feature films in Galician (an official language of the Spanish territory).

Who can apply

Authors resident in Galicia and production companies registered and domiciled in Galicia who have an agreement with a scriptwriter to develop a project.

Funding

It can never be more than 50% of the total cost.

Application requirements

Resume of company or author, project description, synopsis, memory of activities. The selection process will be based on the following criteria:
1. Artistic quality and interest.
2. Viability.
3. Match between financing and viability of the project.
4. Entrepreneurial capability of the applicant.

Aid for the production of feature films in the Galician language.

Who can apply

Production companies based and registered in Galicia.

Funding

40% of the cost of the feature film.

Application requirements
1. Memory of the project, synopsis, company profile, production schedule and financial plan.

2. The selection process will be based on the following criteria:
3. Artistic quality and interest of the project.
   • Viability of the idea.
   • Financial viability.
   • Company profile.

Basque Country

Departamento de Cultura del País Vasco
Avda. Duque de Wellington, 2 – Lakua
01010 Vitoria-Gasteiz
Tel: +34 945 01 81 14
Fax: +34 945 01 95 37
E-mail: Kultura@ej-gv.es
Website: www1.euskadi.net/helbideak/estru_gv/indice_c.htm

The *Department of Culture* of the Basque Country is in charge of all artistic and cultural activities. Through its *Direction of Creation and Dissemination of Culture*, the department establishes the means to promote activities, which encourage the production of fiction, animation and documentaries through a system of aids and subsidies.

In 1998, the *Department of Culture* announced the call to offer aids and subsidies for 1999. There are four different type of aids:

1. Scriptwriting.
2. Development of features, TV movies, animation and documentaries.
3. Production of features, TV movies, animation and documentaries.
4. Short movies.

Funding available for 1999 is Ptas. 100 million (€601,000) (6% development, 14% short movies, 10% development, 70% production).

Two different Commissions evaluate the projects presented. A *Consulting Technical Commission for Short Films, Development Projects and Production Projects* consisting of a representative from Basque television ETB, two representatives from the Producers' Association (IBAIA), a representative from the Association of scriptwriters, a representative from the Actors' Union, a representative from the international association of animation films and up to five professionals related to film promotion.

The *Technical Commission on Script Projects* will consist of two scriptwriters, two producers, a TV executive and a professional related to the film promotion.

Script development

Repayable loan for fiction, animation, TV movies or feature film scripts in any language.

Who can apply

Writers born in the Autonomous Community of Euskadi or who have been residents for at least a year.

Funding

Repayable loan of up to a maximum of Ptas. 2 million (€ 12,000). The subsidy is a repayable advance which will have to be returned two years after the completion of the script. Payment should be reimbursed for the amount plus interest related to the Consumer Price Index. Should the writer fail to repay the subsidy, the Basque Government will automatically retain 49% of the rights on the script.

Application requirements

Application form. The selection process is based on the following criteria:

1. The quality of the script to be developed (50%).
2. Interest of the project (30%) taking into account the commercial viability, its thematic interest, location and the use of Euskera in the original draft.
3. The background of the scriptwriter (20%).

Development

Repayable loan for the development of feature films, TV movies, fiction, animation and documentaries in any language. Development is understood as the preparation and design of an audiovisual production and is focused on the activities taking place before the production (script rewrites, looking for financiers, collaborations between the scriptwriters, team members and producer, preparation of the business plan, elaboration of the marketing and distribution plan, research).

Who can apply

Any production company with fiscal address in the Basque Country registered as an official production company.

Funding

The amount can not be more of 25% of the total fund for a single film and can not exceed 50% of the total costs estimated on development budget. The development budget can not amount to more than 20% of the whole production budget. 20% of the amount granted must be spent on the actual script.

The repayable loan must be returned with the following schedule:

1. 25% of the amount plus the Consumer Price Index accumulated fifteen days after the first day of principal photography.
2. 75% of the amount plus the CPI accumulated fifteen days after its first broadcast (theatrical or television).
3. If no shooting takes place, the Basque Government will retain 30% of the rights of the screenplay.
4. If it is not broadcast, the Basque Government will retain 49% of the rights on the economic exploitation of the film.

Application requirements

Application form. The selection process is based on the following criteria:

1. Evaluation of the production project (35%), taking into account the budget, the financial plan, co-production plan, distribution plan, the business resources,

the curricula of the producer, director, technicians and other professionals.

2. The quality of the script (25%).
3. Interest of the project (20%) taking into account its thematic and geographic interest.
4. The shooting in Euskera (20%).
5. The background of the scriptwriter (20%).

Production

Repayable subsidies for the production of feature films, TV movies, fiction, animation or documentaries in any language.

Who can apply

Any production company with fiscal address in the Basque Country registered as an official production company.

Funding

The amount of funding will be determined by the interest and evaluation of each project presented. It will not exceed 30% of the cost and real budget of the film. The cost of the movie has to be audited. The production company must repay the subsidy plus the CPI accumulated, three years after the last payment from the Government if it has obtained more than 80% of the cost of the film though the licensing of the rights. Otherwise, the Basque Government will retain a percentage of the rights of the film, equivalent to the percentage of the subsidy on the total cost of the film.

Application requirements

Application form. The selection process is based on the following criteria:

1. Interest of the project (40%) taking into account the new creative initiatives, its thematic interest, location and the use of Euskera in the original version.
2. Evaluation of the business plan (35%), taking into account the budget, financial plan, co-production and distribution plans, and human and business resources. The background of the production

company shall be taken into account, especially the box office, critics and feedback from the public of the films previously produced.

3. Quality of the script (25%)

Generalitat de Valencia

Conselleria de Cultura, Educación y Ciencia
Avda. Campanar, 32
46015 Valencia
Tel: +34 96 386 65 00
Fax: +34 96 386 65 75
Website: www.gva.es/consell/cult-c.htm

The Government of the Autonomous Community of Valencia has had a film division since 1984. Measures of support are implemented through the *Council of Culture, Education and Sciences.*

Current subsidies for 1998/99 total Ptas. 185 million (€1.1m). These cover subsidies for the production of feature films, short films and TV series. The Council of Education and Culture of Valencia is currently preparing the new guidelines for an updated film legislation.

Subsidies for the production of feature films, TV series and short movies.

Who can apply

Any production company registered as an official production company in the Community of Valencia.

Funding

With a total budget of Ptas. 185 million (€1.1m) for 1998/99, the only limitation is that the subsidised amount can not exceed the cost of the film.

Application requirements

The selection process is based on the following criteria:

1. Feasibility of the project.
2. Interest and quality of the script.
3. The use of human resources from the Community of Valencia.
4. Use of services based in the Community of Valencia.
5. Shooting in Valencia.
6. Shooting in *Valenciano* (Valenciano and Castellano are the two official languages of Valencia).

Junta de Andalucía

Consejería de Cultura
C/ Levíes, 17
41004 Sevilla.
Tel: +34 954 555 525
Fax: +34 954 555 527
Website: www.junta-andalucia.es/cultura/contenido.htm

The *Council of Culture* of the Junta de Andalucía is in charge of developing support plans and actions for the development of the audiovisual sector in the region. With the preparation of the Audiovisual Plan in 1997-98, the Junta decided to create the *Department of Audiovisual of the Public Company of Management of Cultural Programmes*, as the tool which then elaborates and executes the action lines in the audiovisual field. These action lines are currently production, distribution and exhibition, training, information and institutional collaboration.

Subsidies are currently available for short films, documentaries and training. Some one-off aid has been awarded for the distribution of Andalusian films in the rest of Spain. Benito Zambrano's *Solas* was awarded funding for the cost of the premiere in Madrid and for the recording of the soundtrack by the Orchestra of Málaga. Pilar Távora's *Yerma* was granted all the costs of contracting actress Irene Papas.

The funding system of the Junta de Andalusia is currently being reviewed and is expected to include around Ptas. 200 million (€ 1.2m) for funding of feature films.

Castilla y León

Consejería de Educación y Cultura
Autovía Puente Colgante, s/n.
Monasterio Ntra. Sra. de Prado.
47014 Valladolid
Tel: +34 983 41 1501
Fax: +34 983 41 1500.
Website: www.jcyl.es

Although there is currently very little help available for production companies in Castilla y León, the *Council of Education and Culture* of the Junta of Castilla y León has a small amount of funding available for audiovisual productions which are thematically related to this Autonomous Community. Total funding in 1999 was about Ptas. five million (€ 30,000). The new Film Commission has organised a workshop, which will study possible additional subsidies and investments in the audiovisual industry of this Autonomous Community.

Ibermedia

The co-production programme Ibermedia was developed by the Iberoamerican Federation of Film and Audiovisual Producers (FIPCA) and approved by the Conference of Iberoamerican Film Authorities, to set up a fund of around US$3.6 million (€ 3.5m). The Fund has the mission to encourage the development of co-production projects among Iberoamerican countries. Aids are distributed in the following areas of action:
1. Aid to co-productions.
2. Aid to distribution.
3. Aid for development of co-production projects.
4. Aid for training of professionals.

There are currently 10 countries participating in the fund with the following provisional monetary quantities:

Spain	$1,960,000	(€ 1.8m)
Argentina	$200,000	€ 193,000
México	$500,000	€ 480,000
Brasil	$233,000	€ 225,000
Venezuela	$202,000	€ 194,000
Cuba	$100,000	€ 96,000
Colombia	$100,000	€ 96,000
Uruguay	$100,000	€ 96,000
Portugal	$200,000	€ 193,000
Chile	$100,000	€ 96,000
TOTAL	$3,695,000	€ 3.5m

In 1998, a total of 118 production were subsidised. Fifteen projects received funding for co-productions, 40 for development, 25 for distribution and 30 for training.

Repayable loans for the development of Iberoamerican productions.

Who can apply
Production companies registered in any of the member countries of CACI which finance the Ibermedia Programme.

Funding
A maximum of US$15,000 (€ 14,500) per project.

Application requirements
Application form, budget, financial plan, resume of company, scriptwriter and director. The selection process will be based on the following criteria:
1. Quality and originality of the idea.
2. Experience of the production company and the professionals involved.

3. Viability of the project.
4. Possibility of transnational exploitation.

Repayable loans for the encouragement of Iberoamerican co-productions

Who can apply
Production companies registered in any of the member countries of CACI which finance the Ibermedia Programme. Feature film projects with at least three co-producers of the member countries. An exception can be made with co-productions between two member countries and distribution secured on a third one.

Funding
A maximum of US$200,000 (€ 193,000) per project up to a maximum of 50% of the total budget.

Application requirements
Application form, synopsis, director's comments, artistic and technical personnel, budget, financial plan, co-production structure, promotion strategy, contracts between the co-producers, script, accounts from other features produced which have been funded by Ibermedia. The selection process will be based on the following criteria:
1. Quality of the project
2. Finance already in place
3. Distribution arrangements already secured
4. In bilateral co-productions, expertise of the cast and crew
5. The director, scriptwriter and composer must be Iberoamerican unless otherwise justified.

Banking: guarantees and loans

BEX

Spanish banks are on the whole reluctant to invest in the film business. The main funding available is through the agreement of the Banco Exterior de España (BEX) and the ICAA. The ICAA will secure up to Ptas. 1,500 million (€ 9m) for credits granted by the BEX to the film industry. The aim is to provide bridge financing to projects rather than long-term financing to producers.

There are two different types of loans: discount loans and production loans.

1. Discount loans

Granted for a maximum amount of 90% of the standard project funding made available by the ICAA.

Who can apply

Production companies which have been granted project funding by the ICAA

Funding

90% of the funding made available by the ICAA.

The repayment term of the loan is nine months or the day the ICAA certifies the transfer of the funds. If the ICAA has not made available the funds within the nine months, the bank and the producer are free to renegotiate.

Interest rate: Euromibor+0.5%.

Application requirements

The bank will send a copy of the application to the ICAA, together with a viability study and an analysis of the financial situation of the company. The bank will be in charge of the decision and of the whole process of granting the loan.

2. Production loan

The aim of the production loan is to finance feature film projects likely to obtain automatic subsidies from the ICAA.

Who can apply

Production companies registered at the ICAA.

Funding

The principal can not exceed Ptas. 100 million (€ 600,000) per film or 40% of the film budget. Interest rate at Euromibor+0,5%.

Application requirements

Project description, budget, financial plan and cash-flows, production schedule, chain of title, certificate of Spanish nationality, company background. The bank will send a copy of the application to the ICAA, together with a viability study and an analysis of the financial situation of the company. The bank will be in charge of the decision and of the whole process of granting the loan.

Catalonia

Credits awarded through the *Instituto Catalán de Finanzas*, guaranteed by the Directorate General of Cultural Promotion, dependent of the *Department of Culture*, to production companies registered in Catalonia and with Catalan elements involved in the project.

Who can apply

Any production company with registered as an official production company in Catalonia.

Funding

Two different types:

1. A maximum of Ptas. 60 million (€ 360,000) or a 45% of the budget. Interest rate at Euromibor+0,35.
2. An amount equivalent to the interest during the first 12 months from delivery

by the bank of the first instalment (50% of the capital).

Application requirements

The selection process is based on the following criteria:

1. Companies which have produced at least a feature in the last three years and claim 50% of the points in the award system. The beneficiaries of the guarantee must mortgage all future earnings used as guarantee in favour of the Generalitat.
2. Background and solvency of the company.
3. Detailed budget.
4. Production and financial plan.
5. Script and chain of title.
6. Contracts and Points Awards Sheet.

4.3.13 The UK

The Film Council

Due to be launched in April 2000, the Film Council will incorporate the staff and activities of the British Film Commission (BFC), BFI Production and the Arts Council of England (ACE) Lottery Film Department. In addition, funding currently routed through DCMS (Department of Culture, Media and Sport) to other film organisations including British Screen Finance and the BFI – will in future be routed through the Film Council.

The film council will be chaired by Alan Parker; Stewart Till will be deputy chairman; and John Woodward, chief executive.

British Screen Finance

Simon Perry
14-17 Wells Mews
London W1P 3FL
Tel: +44 171 323 9080
Fax: +44 171 323 0092

Email: info@britishscreen.co.uk
Website: www.britishscreen.co.uk

Who can apply
Writer and/or producer must be EU resident.

Development finance
Screenplay loans; development loans; preparation loans.

Production finance
- Typically provides about 20% of a film's production budget (generally not in excess of £500,000 (€ 780,800).
- Applicant producer should supply the following: script, details of producer and director, casting ideas for principal roles, proposed schedule including start date for principal photography, proposed budget, details of finance in place.
- Loans together with interest (if requested) are repayable from the revenue of the film *pro rata pari passu* with other equity investors.
- British Screen is associated with a collection agency (The National Film Trustee Company) and a sales agency (The Sales Co).

European Co-Production Fund (ECF)

As above (administered by the British Screen Fund)

Who can apply
UK producer

Requirements
Eligible film must be structured as a co-production between at least two production companies (not linked by common ownership), one registered in the UK and one registered in another EU member state.

Production funding
- Loan up to 30% (maximum £500,000 (€780,800)).
- Application must include copy of the screenplay, one page outline, copy budget and production schedule, notes on proposed casting and detailed financing plan.

British Film Institute (BFI) Production

Roger Shannon
29 Rathbone Street
London W1P 1AG
Tel: +44 171 636 5587
Fax: +44 171 580 9456
Email: production@bfi.org.uk
Website: www.bfi.org.uk

Production funding
- Awaiting establishment of new Film Council to assess future funding schemes.
- Presently: script development schemes and support to regional production.

InSight - a low - budget feature film slate

InSight – Development Slate
c/o Lindsay Foster
bfi Production - 21 Stephen Street
London W1P 2LN

- Recently launched by BFI Production and BBC Films
- Script development initiative, for films intended for cinema release, and for broadcast on the BBC.
- Applicants should be debut feature film-makers from the UK.

The National Lottery

Arts Council of England

Sarah Macnee/Mark Dunford
14 Great Peter Street - London SW1P 3NQ
Tel: +44 171 333 0100

Fax: +44 171 973 6590
Email: lottery@artscouncil.org.uk
Website: www.artscouncil.org.uk

Arts Council of Northern Ireland

Contact: Lottery Unit
185 Stranmillis Road,
Belfast BT9 5DU
Tel: +44 1232 667 000
Fax: +44 1232 664 766

Arts Council of Wales

Contact: Lottery Unit
Holst House, Museum Place,
Cardiff CF1 3NX
Tel: +44 1222 388 288
Fax: +44 1222 395 284
E-mail: information@ccc-acw.org.uk
Website: www.ccc-acw.org.uk/

Scottish Arts Council

Contact: Lottery Unit
12 Manor Place,
Edinburgh EH3 7DD
Tel: +44 131 226 6051
Fax: +44 131 220 2724
E-mail: help.desk.sac@artsfb.org.uk
Website: www.sac.org.uk/

Production funding
- Lottery funding contribution in the region of 10-50% of the total cost (maximum £2m (€3.12m) although unlikely to exceed £1m (€1.56m)).
- Applications presently made to the Arts Council, but the Film Council, to be established in April 2000, will take over all responsibility for the Lottery film production funds.

National Lottery Film Franchises

- Film has to be approved both by the franchise and the Arts Council.
- Funds allocated mainly to production (up

to max. £2 million (€ 3.12m)), although development funding also available.

The three franchises are:

DNA Films Limited
Grace Hodge
30 Oval Road
London NW1 7DE
Tel: +44 171 485 4411
Fax: +44 171 485 4422

Pathe Pictures Limited
Andrea Calderwood
Kent House
Market Place
London W1N 8AR
Tel: +44 171 323 5151
Fax: +44 171 636 7594

The Film Consortium
Chris Auty
6 Flitcroft Street
London WC2 8DJ
Tel: +44 171 691 4440
Fax: +44 171 691 4445

Department for Culture, Media and Sport
Aidan McDowell or Peter Wright
Media Division (Films Branch),
4th Floor, 2-4 Cockspur Street,
London SW1Y 5DH
Tel: +44 171 211 6000
Fax: +44 171 211 6460

The Government department responsible for the audiovisual industries, the DCMS provides guidance and certificates of nationality (British and EC) for feature films.

Scottish Screen

John Archer
249 West George Street

Glasgow G2 4QE
Tel: +44 141 302 1700
Fax: +44 141 302 1711

Development funding
Script development up to max. £20,000 (€ 31,200). To be repaid on first day of principal photography plus 25%.

Production funding
Production finance for shorts and Gaelic films. Majority of feature film funding is provided through the Glasgow Film Fund.

The Glasgow Film Fund

Kevin Kane
Address as above

Production funding
Production investment up to £250,000 (€ 390,400).
Film must either be produced by Glasgow-based producer or filmed in the Glasgow area.

Isle of Man Film Commission

Hilary Dougdale
Illiam Dhone House
2 Circular House
Douglas, Isle of Man IM1 1PS
Tel: +44 1624 685 864
Fax: +44 1624 685 454

Production funding
Contact for details on the Isle of Man tax credit scheme ("Production Credit Scheme"), and possibility of investment by the Isle of Man Film and Television Fund. The tax credit scheme entails producer forming a company on the island and agreeing to spend one-fifth of the below-the-line costs there. Loans will be provided against sales estimates and the Isle of Man will take a first recoupment position. A completion bond is required.

Northern Ireland film development fund

Northern Ireland Film Commission
21 Ormeau Avenue
Belfast BT2 8HD
Northern Ireland
Tel: +44 1232 232444
Fax: +44 1232 239918
E-mail: info@nifc.co.uk

Feature films and television drama

- Established by the Northern Ireland Film Commission (NIFC) to offer loans to production companies for the development of feature films, television drama series or serials that are intended to be primarily produced in Northern Ireland.
- The subject matter does not have to be related to Northern Ireland, but the maximum exposure on screen of Northern Ireland locations in any eventual production will be an important consideration.
- The producer should be able to demonstrate a significant track record in feature film or television drama production.
- The writer should be appropriate for the project.
- The producer must have obtained – or be able to obtain – a minimum two-year option on the underlying rights to the project to be developed.
- In the case of a successful application the NIFC will offer a loan of up to 50% of the estimated cost of developing the project.
- Loans are unlikely to exceed £40,000 (€ 62,500) in total for television drama series or serial, or £15,000 (€ 23,400) in total for a single feature film. In many cases the loan offered may be less than these sums. The loan will be advanced in phases.
- The loan will be interest-free; it will normally be repayable to the NIFC, with a 50% premium, only if the developed project goes into production.

Sgrin

Sgrin - Media Agency for Wales,
The Bank, 10 Mount Stuart Square,
Cardiff Bay,
Cardiff CF1 6EE.
Tel: +44 1222 333300
Fax: +44 1222 333320
E-mail: sgrin@sgrinwales.demon.co.uk
Website: www.sgrinwales.demon.co.uk

In addition to offering advice to producers relating to development and production lottery funding, Sgrin is be responsible for assessing lottery applications and making funding recommendations to the Arts Council of Wales.

Regional aid

Eastern Arts Board

Martin Ayres
Cherry Hinton Hall
Cherry Hinton Road
Cambridge CB1 8DW
Tel: +44 1223 215355
Fax: +44 1223 248075
E-mail: cinema@eab.eastern-arts.co.uk
Website: www.arts.org.uk

First take films

Caroline Norbury
Anglia Television
Anglia House
Norwich
Norfolk NR1 3JG
Tel: +44 1603 615151
Fax: +44 1603 767191
E-mail: firsttake@angliatv.co.uk

Eastern Arts Board (EAB)'s specialist film and video production, scriptwriting, co-commissioning funding and development services are delivered through first take films.

East Midlands Arts Board

Annette Sotheran
Mountfields House
Epinal Way
Loughborough
Leicestershire LE11 0QE
Tel: +44 1509 218292
Fax: +44 1509 262214
E-mail: carol.clarke@cm arts.co.uk
Website: www.arts.org.uk

- Script Development Awards of up to £500 (€ 780) to assist with the development of scripts to a stage where projects may attract further development funds or production funding.
- Materials Awards of up to £1.500 (€ 2.340) for materials in support of new and innovative projects, including equipment hire, film/video stock and laboratory costs.
- Completion Awards of up to £1.500 (€ 2.340) to cover costs of film prints, video on-lines, duplication and clearance fees where theatrical or broadcast distribution is intended.
- Screen Test, a script appraisal service for short scripts.
- Co-Production Challenge Awards of up to £15.000 (€ 23.400) for short films for cinema release.
- First Cut broadcast initiative with Central Television for short projects, offering funding of up to £10.000 (€ 15.600).

East Midlands Media Initiative (EMMI)

Peter Carlton
c/o Intermedia Film and Video
19 Heathcote Street
Nottingham NG1 3AF
Tel: +44 115 955 6909
Fax: +44 115 955 9956

Development: Applications for awards of between £1.000 (€ 1.560) and £10.000 (€ 15.600) may be made. Films for cinema of any length or type, television, artists' film and video or multimedia works are all eligible. Applications may be from individual film makers, artists, writers or production companies. Applicants should normally be living or working in the East Midlands or will need to show a considerable potential production spend in the region.

Co-Production: Applications can be made for co-financing one-off productions of factual, drama and experimental work for television or theatrical release. EMMI will consider making investments of up to 25% of the total budget to a maximum of £100.000 (€ 156.000).

London Film and Video Development Agency (LFVDA)

Gill Henderson
114 Whitfield Street
London W1P 5RW
Tel: +44 171 383 7755
Fax: +44 171 383 7745
E-mail: lfvda@lfvda.demon.co.uk

London Production Fund

Only film and video makers living or working in London may apply. Full-time students are not eligible. Applications for production funding are invited in the spring of each year, and for development and completion funding in the summer. No retrospective awards will be made. £180.000 (€ 281.000) is available annually in the following categories:

- Development Awards: Support of up to £3.000 (€ 4.700) to assist development of scripts, story-boards, project packages.
- Production Awards: Support of up to £15.000 (€ 23.400) for production or part-production costs. Feature films are not eligible.

- Completion Awards: Support of up to £15,000 (€ 23,400). Completion awards are designed to finish projects already underway, not complete funding packages for projects in development.

MIDA (Moving Image Development Agency)

Poonam Sharma
109 Mount Pleasant
Liverpool L3 5TF
Tel: +44 151 708 9858
Fax: +44 151 708 9859
E-mail: enquire@mida.demon.co.uk

Primarily a funding organisation, which enables production through the management and distribution of production funds. MIDA manages public funds, working in partnership with organisations such as North West Arts Board, British Screen, Granada, BBC and Channel Four.

Merseyside Film Production Fund

Offers top-up finance to producers intending to produce feature films in the Merseyside area. Producers based in the area and outside producers wishing to film in the area are eligible to apply for fully-developed film projects of at least 60 minutes' duration with production budgets of at least £500,000 (€ 781,000). Terms of investment will be negotiated individually.

Northern Arts Board

Janice Campbell
9-10 Osborne Terrace
Jesmond, Newcastle upon Tyne NE2 1NZ
Tel: +44 191 281 6334
Fax: +44 191 281 3276
E-mail: nab@norab.demon.co.uk

Northern Production Fund

NPF occasionally offers funding to film makers originally from the region but now based elsewhere, seeking to make films within the region.

Feature film production

Support of up to £50,000 (€ 78,000) is available for the production of feature film projects by limited companies formally registered in the North East Objective 2 area. Applicants must demonstrate measurable economic benefits in terms of production spend, job creation, use of facilities and services. Out-of-region applicants must register a company in the Objective 2 area prior to application and demonstrate that they will spend a minimum of six times the grant awarded in the designated area.

Production

Support of up to £30,000 (€ 47,000) for production or part-production costs or completion costs.

Development

Support of up to £5,000 (€ 7,800) to assist development of scripts, story-boards, full treatments, pilot production and so on. This includes research and development for feature film, short drama, animation, documentary projects and innovative television drama.

Feature film development

A maximum of £10,000 (€ 15,600) for feature film development will be available each year. These awards will normally be made to Northern region production companies, working with an established writer, which are able to demonstrate their ability to match the Northern Arts contribution. Partnership funding may include the cost of feature film development expertise and/or the contribution of another funding partner.

Company support

Support for bona fide companies based in the Northern region is available to assist in the development of a programme of work.

North West Arts Board

Manchester House
22 Bridge Street
Manchester M3 3AB
Tel: +44 161 834 6644
Fax: +44 161 834 6969
E-mail: nwarts-info@mcr1.poptel.org.uk
Website: www.arts.org.uk/

Graphic House
Howard Rifkin
Duke Street - Liverpool L1 4JR
Tel: +44 151 709 0671
Fax: +44 151 708 9034

Supports shorts, documentaries and animation. Managed by MIDA (Moving Image Development Agency, see above).

Southern Arts Board

Jane Gerson
13 St Clement Street
Winchester Hampshire SO23 9DQ
Tel: +44 1962 855099
Fax: +44 1962 861186
E-mail: jane.gerson.southarts@artsfb.org.uk
Website: www.arts.org.uk

Fund for shorts.

South East Arts Board

Tim Cornish
Third Floor Union House
Eridge Road
Tunbridge Wells - Kent TN4 8HF
Tel: +44 1892 515210
Fax: +44 1892 549383
E-mail: tim.cornish.sea@artsfb.org.uk
Website: http://www.poptel.org.uk/arts/
Production Development Manager

Caroline Freeman
Lighthouse Media Centre
9-12 Middle Street
Brighton BN1 1AL
Tel: +44 1273 384222
E-mail: cfreeman@lighthouse.org.uk

Production fund offering around €5,000 (€7,800) grant.

South West Media Development Agency (SWMDA)

Sarah-Jane Meredith
59 Prince Street - Bristol BS1 4HQ
Tel: +44 117 9273226
Fax: +44 117 9226216
E-mail: swmda@eurobell.co.uk
Website: www.swmediadevagency.co.uk

Low – budget – awards

Awards are made annually for production, script development and completion, with no restrictions on genre or subject matter. The award for production and completion is £3,000 (€4,700) and up to £1,000 (€1,500) for script development.

Also awards for shorts, television drama, animation.

West Midlands Arts Board

Abigail Clements
82 Granville Street - Birmingham B1 2LH
Tel: +44 121 631 3121
Fax: +44 121 643 7239
E-mail: info@west-midlands-arts.co.uk

Yorkshire Arts

Terry Morden
21 Bond Street
Dewsbury West Yorkshire WF13 1AX
Tel: +44 1924 455555
Fax: +44 1924 466522

Website: www.arts.org.uk
E-mail: terry.morden.yha@artsfb.org.uk
Development awards
Awards of £500 (€ 780) are available to enable projects to be developed to a stage where applications can be made for production funding. An award can be used in any way which advances the project; for example script writing, research fees. Applications will be accepted from writers, producers or directors. The 1999 deadline is in October.

Yorkshire Media Production Agency (YMPA)

Colin Pons or Andy Curtis (Sheffield Office)
Ann Tobin (Sheffield and Bradford Offices)
Workstation
Paternoster Row - Sheffield S1 2BX
Tel: +44 114 272 0304
Fax: +44 114 249 2293
E-mail: ympa@workstation.org.uk

c/o Bradford Film Office
Mercury House
4 Manchester Road
Bradford BD5 0QL
Tel: +44 1274 754030
Fax: +44 1274 393426

YMPA offers support to a wide range of projects through the strands listed below. In most cases the maximum financial contribution made by YMPA to any project will be £80,000 (€ 125,000) or 25% of the total production budget, whichever is lower. However, in some cases YMPA will broker arrangements with other funders and the level will rise to 100%. Funds are usually loans repayable out of net profits or on the first day of principal photography.

Project development
Supports independent production companies to prepare and develop projects. It offers both development funding and development services and training.

Feature films
Encourages and supports the production of feature films in Yorkshire. It offers funding, complements the inward investment work of the Yorkshire Screen Commission, and encourages commercial investment in regional production companies.

Cultural Production
Encourages work with a strong cultural and artistic form and content, including fiction and documentary. Funding includes production for television as well as theatrical release.

Artists' film, video and multimedia
Supports a range of challenging and non-conventional film, video and multimedia work. It offers funding to support work by artists from all disciplines and encourages work that integrates audio-visual media with other arts. Work can be made for exhibition in a wide range of settings.

Film commission network

British Film Commission

Steve Norris, Commissioner
70 Baker Street, London W1M 1DJ
Tel: +44 171 224 5000
Fax: +44 171 224 1013
E-mail: info@britfilmcom.co.uk
Website: www.britfilmcom.co.uk

Bath Film Office

Richard Angell
Abbey Chambers,
Abbey Church Yard, Bath BA1 1LY
Tel: +44 1225 477 711
Fax: +44 1225 477 221
E-mail: Richard_Angell@bathnes.gov.uk

Central England Screen Commission

Cathie Peloe
Unit 5, Holliday Wharf,
Holliday Street,
Birmingham B1 1TJ
Tel: +44 121 643 9309
Fax: +44 121 643 9064
E-mail: info@central-screen.co.uk
Website: www.central-screen.co.uk

Eastern Screen

Julian Campbell, Maggie James,
Sarah Wheller
Royal Hotel,
Anglia Television,
Prince of Wales Road,
Norwich NR1 3JG
Tel: +44 1603 767 077
Fax: +44 1603 767 191
E-mail: productions@eastern-screen.demon.co.uk

East Midlands Screen Commission

Phil Nodding, Sarah Eccleston
Broadway, 14-18 Broad Street,
Nottingham NG1 3AL
Tel: +44 115 910 5564/65
Fax: +44 115 910 5563
E-mail: emsc@dccl.net
Website: www.dccl.net/emsc

Edinburgh Film Focus

George Carlaw, Ros Davis, Vikki McCraw
Castlecliff, 25 Johnston Terrace,
Edinburgh EH1 2NH
Tel: +44 131 622 7337
Fax: +44 131 622 7338
E-mail: edinfilm@ednet.co.uk

Film and Television Commission of North West England

Andrew Patrick, Helen Bingham, Julie Brown
Pioneer Buildings, 65-67 Dale Street,
Liverpool L2 2NS
Tel: +44 151 330 6666
Fax: +44 151 330 6611
E-mail: ftc@northwestengland.co.uk

Glasgow Film Office

Lenny Crooks, Helen Boyes
City Chambers,
Glasgow G2 1DU
Tel: +44 141 287 0424
Fax: +44 141 287 0311
E-mail: film.office@ced.glasgow.gov.uk
Website: www.glasgowfilm.org.uk

Herts Film Link

Roger Harrop, Chris Holt
The Business Centre,
Colne Way, Watford,
Hertfordshire WD2 4ND
Tel: +44 1923 495 051
Fax: +44 1923 333 007
E-mail: hfl@herts-filmlink.co.uk

Isle of Man Film Commission

Hilary Dugdale
Department of Trade & Industry,
Illiam Dhone House,
2 Circular Road, Douglas,
Isle of Man IM1 1PJ
Tel: +44 1624 685 864
Fax: +44 1624 685 683

Lancashire Film & Television Office

David Nelson, Lynda Banister
Enterprise plc, 17 Ribblesdale Place,
Preston PR1 3NA
Tel: +44 1772 203 020
Fax: +44 1772 252 640
E-mail: filmtv@lancsent.u-net.com

Liverpool Film Office

Lynn Saunders, Brigid Marray
Pioneer Buildings,
65-67 Dale Street,
Liverpool L2 2NS
Tel: +44 151 291 9191
Fax: +44 151 291 9199
E-mail: lfo@dial.pipex.com

London Film Commission

Christabel Albery, Jenny Cooper,
20 Euston Centre, Regent's Place,
London NW1 3JH
Tel: +44 171 387 8787
Fax: +44 171 387 8788
E-mail: lfc@london-film.co.uk

Manchester Film Office

Dawn Evans
Marketing Manchester,
Churchgate House,
56 Oxford Street,
Manchester M1 6EU
Tel: +44 161 238 4537
Fax: +44 161 228 2964
E-mail: mfo@marketing-manchester.co.uk

Mid Wales Film Commission

Mike Wallwork, Matthew Parry
Unit 6G, - Science Park,

Cefn Llan, Aberystwyth,
Ceredigion SY23 3AH
Tel: +44 1970 617 995
Fax: +44 1970 617 942
E-mail: mwfc@pcw-aber.co.uk

Northern Ireland Film Commission

Richard Taylor, Andrew Reid
21 Ormeau Avenue,
Belfast BT2 8HD
Tel: +44 1232 232 444
Fax: +44 1232 239 918
E-mail: info@nifc.co.uk

Northern Screen Commission

Dr Paul Mingard, Gayle Mason
Great North House,
Sandyford Road,
Newcastle NE1 8ND
Tel: +44 191 204 2311
Fax: +44 191 204 2209
E-mail: nfc@filmhelp.demon.co.uk

North Wales Film Commission

Hugh Edwin Jones, Peter J Lowther, Rhian Wyn Jones
Council Offices,
Shire Hall Street,
Caernarfon,
Gwynedd LL55 1SH
Tel: +44 1286 679 575
Fax: +44 1286 673 324
Email: film@gwynedd.gov.uk
Website: http://www.gwynedd.gov.uk/
adrannau/economaidd/Uned_Ffilm/english/
default.html

Scottish Screen

Kevin Cowle, Celia Stevenson
74 Victoria Crescent Road,

Glasgow G12 9JN
Tel: +44 141 302 1700/24/23
Fax: +44 141 302 1711
E-mail: info@scottishscreen.demon.co.uk
Website: www.scottishscreen.demon.co.uk

Scottish Highlands and Islands Film Commission

Tricia Shorthouse, Gordon Ireland
Cultural & Leisure Service,
The Highland Council,
Inverness Castle, Castle Hill,
Inverness IV2 3EG
Tel: +44 1463 710 221
Fax: +44 1463 710 848

Southern Screen Commission

Gerard Rosenberg, Sarah Bayliss
Brighton Media Centre,
9-12 Middle Street,
Brighton BN1 1AL
Tel: +44 1273 384 211
Fax: +44 1273 384 212
E-mail: southernscreen@medialan.co.uk
Website: www.adh.bton.ac.uk/SouthernScreen

South Wales Film Commission

Yvonne Cheal, Liam Hunt, David Lepla-Lewis
The Media Centre,
Culverhouse Cross,
Cardiff CF5 6XJ
Tel: +44 1222 590 240
Fax: +44 1222 590 511
E-mail: 106276.223@compuserve.com

South West Film Commission

Sue Dalziel, Sue Craig
18 Belle Vue Road, Saltash,
Cornwall PL12 6ES
Tel: +44 1752 841 199
Fax: +44 1752 841 254
E-mail: swfilm@eurobell.co.uk

South West Scotland Screen Commission

Kenny Eggo
Gracefield Arts Centre,
28 Edinburgh Road, Dumfries DG1 1NW
Tel: +44 1387 263 666
Fax: +44 1387 263 666

Yorkshire Screen Commission

Shuna Frood
The Workstation,
15 Paternoster Row,
Sheffield S1 2BX
Tel: +44 114 279 9115
Fax: +44 114 279 8593
E-mail: ysc@workstation.org.uk
Website: www.ysc.co.uk

4.4 Sales agents

Belgium

Brussels Ave

Jochen D Girsch, ceo
Rue des Visitandines 1/48
1000 Brussels
Tel: +32 2 511 9156
Fax: +32 2 511 8139

Denmark

Nordisk Film

Sanne Arlø, sales executive
Halmtorvet 29
1700 Copenhagen
Tel: +45 33 266 880
Fax: +45 33 266 889
E-mail: nfis@tvd.egmont.com

Trust Film Sales

Filbyen
Avedore Tvaervej 10
2650 Hvidovre
Tel: +45 36 86 87 88
Fax: +45 36 78 00 77
E-mail: post@trust-film.de
Website: www.zentropa-film.com

France

Artedis

Pierre-Richard Muller/Chantal Lam, directors
12 rue Raynouard
75016 Paris
Tel: +33 1 53 92 29 29
Fax: +33 1 53 92 29 20
E-mail: artedis@aol.com

Celluloid Dreams

Janine Gold
24 rue Lamarine - 75009 Paris
Tel: +33 1 4970 0370
Fax: +33 1 4970 0371
E-mail: info@celluloid-dreams.com
Website: www.celluloid-dreams.com

Eurocine

Daniel Lesoeur, chairman
Ilona Kunesova, head of acquisitions & development
33 Avenue des Champs-Élysées
75008 Paris
Tel: +33 1 42 25 64 92
Fax: +33 1 42 25 73 38
E-mail: eurocine@club-internet.fr

Les Films 26

Jean-Paul de Vidas
3 rue Campagne Premiere
75014 Paris
Tel: +33 1 5680 2626
Fax: +33 1 5680 2627

Films Distribution

Nicolas Brigaud-Robert/François Yon, vp
7 rue Daunou
75002 Paris
Tel: +33 1 42 92 0012
Fax: +33 1 42 92 0021
E-mail: infor@filmsdistribution.com
Website: www.filmsdistribution.com

Gaumont

Pierre-Ange le Pogam, president
Avenue Charles de Gaulle
92200 Neuilly sur Seine
Tel: +33 1 46 43 20 00
Fax: +33 1 46 43 20 33
Website: www.gaumont.com

Gemini Films

Paolo Branco, general manager
34 Boulevard Sebastopol
75001 Paris
Tel: +33 1 44 54 17 17
Fax: +33 1 44 54 17 25
E-mail: gemini@easynet.fr

Globe Trotter Network SA

10 Place Vendôme
75001 Paris
Tel: +33 1 53 45 54 48
Fax: +33 1 53 45 54 49
E-mail: stephan.dykman@wanadoo.fr

Flach Pyramide

Eric Lagesse, head of sales
5 rue Richepanse
75008 Paris
Tel: +33 1 42 96 0220
Fax: +33 1 40 20 0551
E-mail: elagesse@f p-i.net

FSO

Z.I. De l'Argile, Lot 23
460 av. De la Quiéra
05370 Mouans Sartoux
Tel: +33 4 9292 3939
Fax: +33 4 9292 3930

IDPL

Pascal Diot, president
7 rue René Bazin
75016 Paris
Tel: +33 1 45 25 99 50
Fax: +33 1 45 25 99 70
E-mail: IDPL@wanadoo.fr

M6 Droits Audiovisuels

Bernard Majani, director
89 Avenue Charles de Gaulle
92575 Neuilly sur Seine
Tel: +33 1 41 92 68 66
Fax: +33 1 41 92 68 69
E-mail: lmarty@m6.fr

Mercure Distribution

Jacques le Glou, manager
27 rue de la Botte aux Cailles
75013 Paris
Tel: +33 1 44 16 88 44
Fax: +33 1 45 65 07 47
E-mail: infos@mercure-distribution.fr
Website: www.mercure-distribution.fr

MK2 Diffusion

Sophie Bourdon, director of sales
55 rue Traversière
75012 Paris
Tel: +33 1 44 67 30 00/18
Fax: +33 1 43 41 32 30
E-mail: sales@mk2.com

Pandora Cinema

Ernst Goldschmidt, president
7 rue Keppler
75116 Paris
Tel: +33 1 40 70 90 90
Fax: +33 1 40 70 90 91

President Films

Jacques-Eric Strauss
2 rue Lord Byron
75008 Paris
Tel: +33 1 45 62 82 22
Fax: +33 1 45 63 40 56
Website: www.presidentfilms.com

Roissy Films

Raphäel Berdugo, chairman & ceo
58 rue Pierre Charron
75008 Paris
Tel: +33 1 5353 5050
Fax: +33 1 4289 2693
E-mail: roissy_f@club.internet.fr

Le Studio Canal+

Daniel Marquet
17 rue Dumont d'Urville
75116 Paris
Tel: +33 1 44 43 98 00
Fax: +33 1 47 20 29 67

TF1

Jean-Louis Capra, chairman
125 rue Jean-Jacques Rousseau
92138 Issy-les-Moulineaux
Tel: +33 1 41 41 25 72
Fax: +33 1 41 41 31 44
E-mail: gshapiro@tf1.fr

TVOR

Eric Giovannini
42 Avenue Kleber
75116 Paris
Tel: +33 1 44 05 14 00
Fax: +33 1 44 05 14 55
E-mail: tvor@wanadoo.fr

UGC

Patrick Binet, chairman & ceo
2 rue de Quatre-fils
75003 Paris
Tel: +33 1 40 29 89 00
Fax: +33 1 40 29 89 10
E-mail: hernst@ugc.fr

Unifrance

Daniel Toscan du Plantier
4 Villa Bosquet
75007 Paris
Tel: +33 1 47 53 95 80
Fax: +33 1 47 05 96 55
E-mail: info@unifrance.org

Germany

Atlas International Film

Dieter Menz, president & ceo
Rumfordstrasse 29-31
80469 Munich
Tel: +49 89 227 525/210 9750
Fax: +49 89 224 332
E-mail: mail@atlasfilm.com

Bavaria Film International

Michael Weber, head of sales
Bavariafilmplatz 8
82031 Geiselgasteig
Tel: +49 89 6499 2686
Fax: +49 89 6499 3720
E-mail: Michael.Weber@bavaria-film.de

Cine-International World Distribution

Lylli Tyc-Holm, president
Leopoldstrasse 18
80802 Munich
Tel: +49 89 39 10 25
Fax: +49 89 33 10 89

Cinepool

Dr Thomas Weymar, md
Sonnenstrasse 21
80331 Munich
Tel: +49 89 55 87 60
Fax: +49 89 55 87 61 88
E-mail: telepool@telepool.de

DBM Videovertrieb GmbH

Am Schornacker 66
46485 Wesel
Tel: +49 281 952 9214
Fax: +49 281 952 9266

Futura Film

Antonio Exacoustos Jr
Rambergstr. 5
80799 Munich
Tel: +49 89 38 17 00 30
Fax: +49 89 38 17 00 20
E-mail: futura_filmverlag@t-online.de

Media Luna

Ida Martins
Alter Markt 36-42
50667 Cologne
Tel: +49 221 139 22 22
Fax: +49 221 139 22 24

Metro International Distribution

Am Ochsenmarkt 41
24937 Flensburg
Tel: +49 401 461 2200
Fax: +49 401 461 2442

Progress Film-Verleih GmbH

Bettina Kunde, head of international sales
Burg Str. 27 - 10178 Berlin
Tel: +49 30 24 003 210
Fax: +49 30 24 003 222
E-mail: progress-film@snafu.de

ZDF Enterprises

Margrit Stärk, director, acquisitions & sales
Lise-Meitner-Str. 9
55129 Mainz
Tel: +49 61 31 991 221
Fax: +49 61 31 991 283
E-mail: sales.zdfe@zdf.de

Italy

Achab Film

Jeff Nuyts
Viale Gorizia 24c
00198 Rome
Tel: +39 06 85 47 230
Fax: +39 06 85 355 692

Adriana Chiesa

Adriana Chiesa di Palma, president
Via Barnaba Oriani 24a
00197 Rome
Tel: +39 06 807 0400/808 60521
Fax: +39 06 806 87 855

Anica

Viale Regina Margherita, 286
00198 Rome
Tel: +39 06 442 5961
Fax: +39 06 440 4128

Butterfly Motion Pictures Corp.

Via delle Milizie 138
00192 Rome
Tel: +39 06 372 2020
Fax: +39 06 372 2037

CDI–Compagnia Distribuzione Internazionale

Via Salaria, 292
Rome
Tel: +39 06 854 8821
Fax: +39 06 854 1691

Cecchi Gori Group

Faruk Alatan, head of acquisitions
Via Valadier 42
00193 Rome

Tel: +39 06 32 47 21
Fax: +39 06 32 47 23 00
E-mail: randi@cecchigori.com

Deluxe Italia

Via Palestro 24
00187 Rome
Tel: +39 06 4470 3788
Fax: +39 06 4470 3793

Dinamic Group

Via Aristofane 25/c
Rome
Tel: +39 06 5236 2161
Fax: +39 06 5235 3546

Eagle Pictures Srl

Via Buonarroti 5
20149 Milan
Tel: +39 02 481 4169
Fax: +39 02 481 3389

Europe Corporation Film Srl

V. le Parioli 55
00197 Rome
Tel: +39 06 3972 8480
Fax: +39 06 3973 0020

FilmExport Group International

Roberto di Girolamo, president
Via Polonia 9
00198 Rome
Tel: +39 06 855 4266/841 4724
Fax: +39 06 855 0248
E-mail: film.info@filmexport.it
Website: www.filmexport.it

Gold Pictures

Via Flaminia, 43
Rome
Tel: +39 06 361 2801
Fax: +39 06 361 0610

Gruppo Minerva International

Gianluca Curti, managing director
Via Domenico Amarosa 18
00198 Rome

Tel: +39 06 854 3841/3284/3382
Fax: +39 06 855 8105
E-mail: minervai@tin.it

HDH Communications
Via San Calimero 11
Milan
Tel: +39 02 5830 5949
Fax: +39 02 5830 9965

Incomat Company/FM Video
Via Nomentana 1018
00137 Rome
Tel: +39 06 410 3398
Fax: +39 06 411 0050

Intra Films
Paola Corvino, president
Via E Manfredi 15
00197 Rome
Tel: +39 06 807 7252/807 6428
Fax: +39 06 807 6156
E-mail: Intraf@tin.it

Istituto Luce
Via Tuscolana, 1055
00173 Rome
Tel: +39 06 7299 2283
Fax: +39 06 722 1127

Jolly Cinematografica
Via Amantea, 18
95129 Catania Ct
Tel: +39 095 321 186
Fax: +39 095 715 8879

Kodak
V. Le Matteotti 62
20092 Cinisello Balsamo Mi
Tel: +39 02 660 281
Fax: +34 02 6602 8406

Media Trade
Viale Europa 48 - Cologno Monzese
20093 Milan
Tel: +39 02 25141
Fax: +39 02 2514 9091

Medusa Film
Via Aurelia Antica, 422/424
00165 Rome
Tel: +39 06 663 901
Fax: +39 06 6639 0450

Movietime Srl
Via Nicola Ricciotti 11
Rome
Tel: +39 06 322 6709
Fax: +39 06 3600 0950

Onceas/Fuji Film Italia
Via de Sanctis 41
20141 Milan
Tel: +33 02 895 821
Fax: +33 02 846 4121

Rai Radiotelevisione Italia
V. le Mazzini 14
00195 Rome
Tel: +39 06 3686 4517
Fax: +39 06 321 9595

Rai Trade
Roberto di Russo, president
Via Novaro 18
00195 Rome
Tel: +39 06 374 981
Fax: +39 06 370 1343

Surf Film Srl
Massimo Vigliar, president
Via Padre G.A Filippini 130, 144
Rome
Tel: +39 06 526 2101
Fax: +39 06 529 3816

Uniexport Film International
Via Rubicone 27
00198 Rome
Tel: +39 06 841 6561
Fax: +39 06 841 9653

Luxembourg

CLT-UFA International

Heinz Thym, head of international
acquisitions and sales
45 Boulevard Pierre Frieden
1543 Luxembourg
Tel: +352 42 142 3935
Fax: +352 42 142 3771

The Netherlands

Fortissimo Film Sales

Wouter Barendrecht
Herenmarkt 10-2
1013 ED Amsterdam
Tel:+31 20 627 3215
Fax: +31 20 626 1155
E-mail: ffsales@globalxs.nl

Magus Entertainment

Rick Van Den Heuvel, president
Ampèrestraat 10 - 1221 GJ Hilversum
Tel: +31 35 6420 677
Fax: +31 35 6420 668
E-mail: magus@worldonline.nl

Norway

BV International Pictures

Bjørg Veland, managing director
Box 17
Kvalvågsveien 156
4262 Avaldsnes
Tel:+47 5284 2210
Fax: +47 5284 0119
E-mail: annette.stuen@bv-film.no

Spain

Aurum Productions

Francisco Ramos, ceo
Avenida de Burgos, 12 floor 10º
28036 Madrid
Tel: +34 91 768 4800
Fax: +34 91 768 4833
E-mail: mochaaguilar@aurum.es

Filmax-Sogedasa

Miguel Hernandez, 81-87
Poligono Pedrosa
08908 Barcelona
Tel: +34 93 336 8555
Fax: +34 93 263 4778
E-mail: s.elguer@filmax.com
Website: www.filmax.com

Kevin Williams Associates

Kevin Williams
Estrecho de Mesina 12, 2º
28043 Madrid
Tel: +34 91 388 5355
Fax: +34 91 300 2202
E-mail: kmade@mx2.redestb.es
Website: www.kevinwa.com

Radiotelevision Española

Edificio Prado, 3ª planta
Prado del Rey
28223 Madrid
Tel: +34 91 581 7759
Fax: +34 91 581 7757

Sogepaq

Margaret Nicoll, general manager
Gran Vía 32, 1ª planta
28013 Madrid
Tel: +34 91 524 7220
Fax: +34 91 521 0875
E-mail: ediederix@sogepaq.es

Sweden

Filmbox International

PO Box 9138
40093 Goteborg
Tel: +46 31 685 140
Fax: +46 31 685 144

Svensk Filmindustri

Rasmus Randstad, president & ceo
Dialoggatan 6
12783 Stockholm
Tel: +46 8 680 3500
Fax: +46 8 710 4460

Switzerland

World Sales Christa Saredi

Christa Saredi, president
Staffelstrasse 8
8050 Zürich
Tel: +41 1 201 1151
Fax: +41 1 201 1152
E-mail: saredifilm@compuserve.com

The UK

2 Match World Sales

Marie Hoy, sales & finance
18 Bruton Place
Berkeley Square, Mayfair
London W1X 7AA
Tel: +44 171 493 3345
Fax: +44 171 493 3997

Alibi Film International

Gareth Jones, md
12 Maiden Lane
London WC2E 7NA
Tel: +44 20 7845 0410
Fax: +44 20 7836 6919

Capitol Films

Sharon Harel, managing director
Jane Barclay, managing director
23 Queensdale Place
London W11 4SQ
Tel: +44 171 471 6000
Fax: +44 171 471 6012

ENTCO

Thierry Wase-Bailey
c/o RPC
24 Hanway Street
London W1P 9DD
Tel: +44 171 636 2251
Fax: +44 171 636 2261
E-mail: entco@ibm.net

The Film Company Ltd

Carey Fitzgerald, managing director
25 Elizabeth Mews
London NW3 4UH
Tel: +44 171 586 3686
Fax: +44 171 586 3117
E-mail: sales@highpoint-the-filmcompany.co.uk

Film Four International

Paul Webster, chief executive
Michael Jackson, chief executive
76-78 Charlotte Street
London W1P 1LX
Tel: +44 171 868 7700
Fax: +44 171 868 7766

Goldcrest Films International

John Quested, chairman
65-66 Dean Street
London W1V 6PL
Tel: +44 171 437 8696
Fax: +44 171 437 4448
E-mail: mailbox@goldcrest-films.com

Hanway Films

Thierry Wase-Bailey
24 Hanway Street
London W1P 9DD
Tel: +44 171 636 2252
Fax: +44 171 636 2261
E-mail: tmb@ibm.net

Hollywood Classics

Joe Dreier, director
John Flyn, director
8 Cleveland Gardens
London W2 6HA
Tel: +44 171 262 4646
Fax: +44 171 262 3242
E-mail: hollywoodclassics@compuserve.com

IAC Films

Guy Collins, managing director
23 Ransome's Dock
35/37 Parkgate Road
London SW11 4NP
Tel: +44 171 801 9080
Fax: +44 171 801 9081
E-mail: general@iacholdings.co.uk

Intermedia Pictures

Tim Haslam, president of distribution
9-13 Grosvenor Street
London W1X 9FB
Tel: +44 171 495 3322
Fax: +44 171 495 3993
E-mail: info@intermediafilm.co.uk

International Pictures

Heather Playford Denman
20 Earlham Street
London WC2H 9LN
Tel: +44 171 240 2511
Fax: +44 171 240 2599

Jane Balfour Films

Jane Balfour
Burghley House
35 Fortess Road
London NW5 1AQ
Tel: +44 171 267 5392
Fax: +44 171 267 4241
E-mail: jbf@janebalfourfilms.co.uk

J&M Entertainment Limited

Julia Palau
2 Dorset Square
London NW1 6PU
Tel: +44 171 723 6544
Fax: +44 171 724 7541
E-mail: marketing@jment.com
Website: www.jment.com

Lola Films International

Nadine Luque
19 Garrick Street
Covent Garden
London WC2E 9AX
Tel: +44 171 836 7400
Fax: +44 171 836 7778

PACT

Tommy Welensky
45 Mortimer Street
London W1N 7TD
Tel: +44 171 331 6060
Fax: +44 171 331 6700

Peakviewing TransAtlantic

Elizabeth Matthews, ceo
8 Astridge Road
Witcombe, Gloucester GL3 4SY
Tel: +44 1452 863217
Fax: +44 1452 863908
E-mail: sales@peakviewing.co.uk

Portman Entertainment

Tim Buxton
167 Wardour Street
London W1V 3TA
Tel: +44 171 468 3443
Fax: +44 171 468 3469

Renaissance Films

Stephen Evans, joint md
Angus Finney, joint md
34-35 Berwick Street
London W1V 3RF
Tel: +44 207 287 5190
Fax: +44 207 287 5191

The Sales Company

Alison Thompson, ceo
62 Shaftesbury Avenue
London W1V 7DE
Tel: +44 171 434 9061
Fax: +44 171 494 3293
E-mail: salesco@btinternet.com

Spring International UK Ltd
Massimo Graziosi, president
85 Wimpole Street
London W1M 8AJ
Tel: +44 171 935 1864
Fax: +44 171 935 1834

United Artists Films
Fiona Mitchell, senior executive vp
10 Stephen Mews
London W1P 1PP
Tel: +44 171 333 8877
Fax: +44 171 333 8878
E-mail: iilias@mgm.com

Universal Pictures International Ltd
Stewart Till, president
Graeme Mason, president, acquisitions
4th Floor, Oxford House
76 Oxford Street
London W1N 0HQ
Tel: +44 171 307 1300
Fax: +44 171 317 1301

Victor Film Company
Vic Bateman, managing director
The Floris Building
39-43 Brewer Street
London W1R 3FD
Tel: +44 171 494 4477
Fax: +44 171 494 4488
E-mail: post@victor-film-co.demon.co.uk

Vine International Pictures
Marie Vine, ceo
VIP House
Greenacres New Road Hill Downe
Orpington, Kent BR 7JA
Tel: +44 1689 854 123
Fax: +44 1689 850 990
E-mail: vine@easynet.co.uk
Website: www.vine-international.co.uk

Winchester Films
Gary Smith, ceo
Hadeel Reda, president, production & acquisitions
19 Heddon Street - Regent Street
London W1R 7LF
Tel: +44 171 434 4374
Fax: +44 171 287 4334

Australia

Beyond Films
Gary Hamilton
53-55 Brisbane Street - Surrey Hills
NSW 2010 Sydney
Tel: +612 92 81 12 66
Fax: +612 92 81 92 20
E-mail: amandah@beyond.com.au

Southern Star Film Sales
Helen Thwaites, head of film sales
Level 9, 8 West Street
NSW 2060 North Sydney
Tel: +612 92 02 85 55
Fax: +612 99 56 69 18
E-mail: hthwaite@sstar.com.au & jazzopar@sstar.com.au

USA

Alliance Atlantis Pictures International
Mark Horowitz, president
808 Wilshire Boulevard
4th Floor
Santa Monica, CA 90401
Tel: +1 310 899 8000
Fax: +1 310 899 8100

Capella
Jean-Louis Rubin, president, creative affairs
9242 Beverly Blvd.
Suite 280
CA 90210-3710 Beverly Hills
Tel: +1 310 247 4700
Fax: +1 310 247 4701

Kushner-Locke

Peter Locke/Donald Kushner, co-chairmen
11601 Wilshire Blvd., 21st Floor
Los Angeles, CA 90025
Tel: +1 310 481 2000
Fax: +1 310 481 2101
E-mail: kl@kushner-locke.com
Website: www.kushner-locke.com

Miramax International

Rick Sands, chairman, worldwide distribution
99 Hudson Street, 5th Floor
10013 New York/
7966 Beverly Boulevard
90048 Los Angeles
Tel: +1 212 941 4100
Fax: +1 212 941 3836

New Line Cinema

Ralph Borgos, vp, international distribution
& contracts
116 North Robertson Blvd.
Suite 808
CA 90048 Los Angeles
Tel: +1 310 845 5811
Fax: +1 310 854 1824

Nu Image

Avi Lerner, chairman & ceo
9145 Sunset Blvd.
CA 90069 Los Angeles
Tel: +1 310 246 0240
Fax: +1 310 246 1655
E-mail: nimage@msn.com

Overseas Filmgroup

Robert Little, co-chairman, co-ceo
8800 Sunset Boulevard
CA 90069 Los Angeles
Tel: +1 310 855 1199
Fax: +1 310 855 0719
E-mail: info@ofg.com
Website: www.ofg.com

Summit Entertainment

Patrick Wachsberger, president & ceo
1630 Stewart St, Suite 120
CA 90404 Santa Monica
Tel: +1 310 309 8400
Fax: +1 310 828 4132

4.5 Banks and financial institutions

Denmark

Unibank AJS
Lars Nolte Jakobsen
Torvegade, 2
1786 Copenhagen
Tel: +45 33 33 33 33 Ext.:3338
Fax: +45 33 33 5820

France

Banque Worms
Pierre Boisée Duplan
Le Voltaire
Place de Degres
92059 Paris la Défense-Cedex
Tel: +33 1 49 07 58 24
Fax: +33 1 49 07 53 14

Coficine
Didier Duverger
26 Rue de Montevideo
75116 Paris
Tel: +33 1 40 72 22 00
Fax: +33 1 40 72 22 01

IFCIC
Sara Goettelmann
46 Rue Victor Hugo - 75116 Paris
Tel: +33 1 53 64 55 55
Fax: +33 1 53 64 55 66

Germany

Bayerische Hypotheken-und Wechsel Bank
Arabellastrasse 12
81925 München
Tel: +49 89 92 440
Fax: +49 89 784 3188

Berliner Bank
Wolfgang Hofman
Hardenbergstrasse 32 - 10623 Berlin
Tel: +49 30 31 09 0
Fax: +49 30 31 09 2404

Hypo Bank
H. Kulmberg
Theatinerstrasse 11
80278 München
Tel: +49 89 92 44 29 60
Fax: +49 89 92 44 49 67

HypoVereinsbank
Antje Terrahe
Am Tucherpark, 16
80538 München
Tel: +49 89 378 26001
Fax: +49 89 378 25699

Investitions-Bank NRW Zentralbereich de West LB
Dr. Schumachir
Herzog, 15
40217 Düsseldorf
Tel: +49 211 826 09
Fax: +49 211 826 7691

Westdeutsche Landesbank Girozentrale
Matthias Wargers
15 Herzogstrasse
40217 Düsseldorf
Tel: +49 211 82 609
Fax: +49 211 826 62 18

Italy

Banca Nazionale del Lavoro Roma
Franza Romano
Via d Velli Scipion 267
00187 Roma
Tel: +39 06 47 021
Fax: +39 06 470 0970

Luxembourg

Banque et Caisse d'Epargne de l'Etat Luxembourg

Pierre Schmidt
Place de Metz 1
2945 Luxembourg
Tel: +352 40 15 30 20
Fax: +352 40 15 33 42

Banque Européenne European Investeringsbank

Mr Mesnar/Sabine Parisse
100 Bvr. Conrad Adenauer
2950 Luxembourg
Tel: +352 43 791
Fax: +352 43 79 31 77 04

Banque Internationale à Luxembourg

Ms. Edwige Rolin, President
Immeuble l'Indépendance
69 Route d'Esch
2953 Luxembourg
Tel: +352 45 901
Fax: +352 4590 2010

Kredietbank SA Luxembourgeoise

Jean-Paul Dekerk
43 Boulevard Royal
2955 Luxembourg
Tel: +352 461 1911
Fax: +352 47 97 73 900

Netherlands

De National Investeringsbank

Bert Habits
Cargiepleim, 4
2517 KL The Hague
Tel: +31 70 342 5449
Fax: +31 70 365 1071

Portugal

Banco de Formento Exterior

Luisa Carvalhayf/Maria Sarneiro
Rua Sao Julia 123
1100524 Lisboa
Tel: +351 1 356 1071
Fax: +351 1 321 3413

Spain

Banco Exterior de España

Mª Angeles Angulo
Goya, 14
28001 Madrid
Tel: +34 91 537 72 61
Fax: +34 91 537 74 07

The UK

Banque Internationale de Luxembourg

Ms Eddwige Rolin, Media Department
Shacklerin House, Hay's Galeria
4 Battle Bridge Lane
London SE1 2GZ
Tel: +44 171 556 3000
Fax: +44 171 556 3055

Barclays Bank Plc

G. Salmon, Media Manager
Barclays Business Centre,
Soho Square Branch
27 Soho Square
London W1A 4WA
Tel: +44 171 445 5700
Fax: +44 171 445 5864

Bank Gesellschaft

Steve Robbins, Media Director
154 Fenchurch Street
London EC3M 6JJ
Tel: +44 20 7626 2566
Fax: +44 171 572 9397/9399

Coutts & Co.
Rodney Payne, Partner Media Banking
440 Strand
London WC2R 0QS
Tel: +44 171 753 1000
Fax: +44 171 753 1069

Investec Bank
2 Gresham Street
London EC2V 7QP
Tel: +44 171 597 4000
Fax: +44 171 597 4070

Société Générale
Premila Hoon
41 Tower Hill
London EC3N 4SG
Tel: +44 171 762 4444
Fax: +44 171 676 6583

Australia

Australian Film Finance
Catriona Hughes
Level 12, 130 Elizabeth Street
NSW 2000 Sydney
Tel: +61 2 9268 2555
Fax: +61 2 9264 8581

Canada

Royal Bank of Canada
Robert D. Morrice
200 Baw Street, Royal Bank Plaza
13th Floor South Tower
M5J2J5 Toronto
Tel: +1 416 974 51 88
Fax: +1 416 955 2463

Telefilm Canada
Françoise Macerola
360 Saint Jacques Street
Suite 700
H2Y 4A9 Montreal, Quebec
Tel: +1 514 283 6363
Fax: +1 514 283 8212/2365

Japan

Long Term Credit Bank of Japan
Hirochi ("Hank") Nozaki
2-4 Otermachi 1 - chome
Chiyoda-ku
100 Tokyo
Tel: +81 35 511 5111

USA

Bank of America
Randall Friedman
2049 Century Park East
Suite 200
CA 90067 Los Angeles
Tel: +1 310 785 6077
Fax: +1 310 785 6100

Banque Paribas
Michael Mendelsohn
(Patriot Pictures – Michael Mendelsohn
for equity investment)
2029 Century Park East
Suite 3900
CA 90067 Los Angeles
Tel: +1 310 551 7300
Fax: +1 310 556 8759

Chase Securities
John Miller
1800 Century Park East
Suite 400
CA 90067 Los Angeles
Tel: +1 310 788 5600
Fax: +1 310 788 5628

City National Bank
Mary Phelm Yoel
400 North Roxbury Drive
5th Floor
CA 90210 Beverly Hills
Tel: +1 310 888 6209
Fax: +1 310 888 6238

Comerica Bank

Jeffrey Andrick
10900 Wilshire Boulevard
CA 90024 Los Angeles
Tel: +1 310 824 5700
Fax: +1 310 824 6833

Imperial Bancorp
Entertainment Industries Group

Morgan Rector
9777 Wilshire Boulevard
CA 90212 Los Angeles
Tel: +1 310 281 2400
Fax: +1 310 281 2476

JP Morgan & Co

Tracy Hampton
333 South Hope Street
35th Floor
CA 90071 Los Angeles
Tel: +1 213 437 9300
Fax: +1 213 437 9331

The Lewis Horwitz
Organisation

Lewis Horwitz, President
1840 Century Park East
10th Floor
CA 90067 Los Angeles
Tel: +1 310 275 71 71
Fax: +1 310 275 80 55

Mercantile National Bank

Melanie Krinsky
1840 Century Park East
PO Box 24830
CA 90067 Los Angeles
Tel: +1 310 282 6708
Fax: +1 310 788 0669

Newmarket Capital Group LP

William Tyrer/Chris Ball
202 North Canon Drive
CA 90210 Beverly Hills
Tel: +1 310 858 7472
Fax: +1 310 858 7473

Republic National Bank

Patrick Hines, President
445 North Bedford Drive
CA 90210-4372 Beverly Hills
Tel: +1 310 281 4281/
Irene Romero: 1 310 281 4200
Fax: +1 310 859 1628

Sumitomo Bank

Steve Mras
777 South Figueroa Street
Suite 2600
CA 90017 Los Angeles
Tel: +1 213 955 0825
Fax: +1 213 623 6832

Union Bank of California

Robert Lohmar
9401 Wilshire Boulevard
Suite 600
Beverly Hills, CA 90212
Tel: +1 310 205 3050
Fax: +1 310 273 9030

4.6 Broadcasters

Austria

ÖRF–Österreichischer Rundfunk

Gerhard Weis (Director General)
Würzburggasse 30
1136 Vienna
Tel: +43 1 87878 0
Fax: +43 1 87878 2738
E-mail: pressesprecher@orf.at
Website: www.orf.at/orf

Belgium

RTBF–Radio Télévision Belge de la Communauté Française

Christian Druytte (President)
52 Boulevard Auguste Reyers
1044 Brussels
Tel: +32 2 737 25 51
Fax: +32 2 737 44 17
E-mail: vente@rtbf.be
Webiste: www.rtbf.be

RTL–TVI–Télévision Indépendante

Paul Heyse (Managing Director)
1 Avenue Ariane
1201 Brussels
Tel: +32 2 778 68 11
Fax: +32 2 778 68 12

VRT–Flemish Radio & Television

Bert de Graeva (Director General) VRT
A Reyerslaan 52
1043 Brussels
Tel: +32 2 741 31 11
Fax: +32 2 734 93 51
E-mail: info@vrt.be
Website: www.vrt.be

Vlaamse Televisie Maatschappij

Eric Cleiys (CEO)
Medialaan 1
1800 Vilvoorde
Tel: +32 2 255 3211/3252
Fax: +32 2 252 3787/5228
E-mail: postmaster@vtm.be

Denmark

DR–Danmarks Radio TV

Christian Nissen (Director General)
TV – byen
2860 Soeborg
Tel: +45 35 20 30 40
Fax: +45 35 20 26 44
E-mail: krx@dr.dk
Website: www.dr.dk

TV 2/Danmark

Ms Christina Late (Managing Director)
Rugaardsvej 25
5100 Odense C
Tel: +45 65 91 12 44
Fax: +45 65 91 33 22
E-mail: tv2@tv2.dk
Website: www.tv2.dk

Finland

Channel 4 Finland

Mr Jorma Sairanen
(Senior VP, programming)
P.O. Box 40 - 00521 Helsinki
Tel: +358 9 45 45 1
Fax: +358 9 148 23 23

MTV Finland

Elkka Kylmala (Managing Director)
Ilmalantori 2
00240 Helsinki
Tel: +358 9 1500 1
Fax: +358 9 1500 707
Website: www.mtv3.fi

YLE-Yleisradio Oy

Arne Wessberg (Managing Director)
Radio and TV Centre
00024 Yleisradio
Tel: +358 9 14801
Fax: +358 9 1480 3391
Website: www.yle.fi

France

Arte

Jérôme Clément (Vicepresident)
2ª Rue de la Fonderie
67080 Strasbourg
Tel: +33 3 88 14 22 22
Fax: +33 3 88 14 22 00
Website: www.arte-tv.com

France 2

Marc Tessier (Managing Director)
7 esplanade Henri de France
75907 Paris Cedex 15
Tel: +33 1 56 22 42 42
Fax: +33 1 56 22 55 11
Website: www.france2.fr

France 3

Marc Tessier (Managing Director)
7 Esplanade Henri de France
75907 Paris Cedex 15
Tel: +33 1 56 22 30 30
Fax: +33 1 56 22 75 02
Website: www.france3.fr

M6 Métropole TV

Jean Drucker (Managing Director)
89 Avenue Charles de Gaulle
92575 Neuilly-sur-Seine Cedex
Tel: +33 1 41 92 66 66
Fax: +33 1 41 92 66 10
Website: www.m6.fr

TF1

Patrick Le Lay (President)
1 Quai du Point-du-Jour
92556 Boulogne Cedex
Tel: +33 1 41 41 12 34/21 23
Fax: +33 1 41 41 28 40/20 23
Website: www.tf1.fr

Canal+

Pierre Lescure (Chairman)
85-89 quai André Citroën
75711 Paris Cedex 15
Tel: +33 1 44 25 10 00
Fax: +33 1 44 25 12 34
Website: www.cplus.fr

TPS-Télévision Par Satellite

145 quai de Stalingrad
92137 Issy-les-Moulineaux Cedex
Tel: +33 1 41 33 88 00
Fax: +33 1 41 33 88 01

Germany

ARD1/German TV First Channel

Udo Reiter (Managing Director)
Arnulfstrasse 42
80335 Munich
Tel: +49 89 590 001
Fax: +49 89 5900 3249
Website: www.ard.de

NDR-Norddeutscher Rundfunk

Jobst Plog (Managing Director)
Rothenbaumchaussee 132
20149 Hamburg
Tel: +49 40 4156 0
Fax: +49 40 4156 3453

ZDF-Zweites Deutsches Fernsehen

Prof Dr Dieter Stolte (Managing Director)
Postfach 4040
55100 Mainz
Tel: +49 6131 70 2060

Fax: +49 6131 70 6822
E-mail: info@zdf.de
Website: www.zdf.de

Greece

Antenna TV SA

Minos X Kyriacou (President)
10-12 Kifissias Avenue
Maroussi
15125 Athens
Tel: +30 1 688 6100
Fax: +30 1 681 1179

ERT SA

Panayote Panayotou (President)
402 & 432 Messoghion Avenue
Agia Papaskevi
15342 Athens
Tel: +30 1 606 6000
Fax: +30 1 601 1208
E-mail: ertir@hol.gr

Mega Channel (Teletypos SA)

Elias Tsigas (Managing Director)
Messaion 117
Ambeloquepe - 11526 Athens
Tel: +30 1 690 3000
Fax: +30 1 698 3600
E-mail: webmaster@megatv.com

Iceland

Omega

Erik Eriksson (General Director)
Bolt 6 - 105 Reykjavik
Tel: +354 568 23131
Fax: +354 872 1811

RUV - Rikisutvarp Sjonvarp

Markús Öm Antonsson (Director General)
Laugavegur 176
150 Reykjavik
Tel: 1354 515 3900

Fax: +354 515 3808
Website: www.ruv.is

IBC - Icelandic Broadcasting Corporation Inc - Channel 2

Hreggvidur Jonsson (CEO)
Lynghalsi 5
PO Box 10110
130 Reykjavik
Tel: +354 515 6000
Fax: +354 515 6851

Ireland

RTE-Radio Telefis Éireann

Bob Collins (General Director)
Donnybrook
Dublin 4
Tel: +353 1 208 3111
Fax: +353 1 208 3080
Website: www.rte.ie

TnaG-Teilifis na Gaeilge

Pádhraic O Ciardha
(Editor, Development & Information)
Baile na Habhann
Co na Gaillimhe
Tel: +353 91 593636
Fax: +353 91 505021

TV 3

James Morris (Managing Director)
Westgate Business Park
Ballymount
Dublin 24
Tel: +353 1 419 3333
Fax: +353 1 419 3300
E-mail: sales@tv3.ie

Italy

Canale 5

Giorgio Gori (Managing Director)
Viale Europa 44

Cologno Monzese
20093 Milan
Tel: +39 02 25 14 1

Italia 1
Roberto Giovalli (Managing Director)
Viale Europa 44
Cologno Monzese
20093 Milan
Tel: +39 02 25 14 1
Fax: +39 02 25 14 70 63

Mediaset
Fedeli Confalonieri (President)
Viale Europa 44
Cologno Monzese
Milan 20093
Tel: +39 02 25 14 1
Fax: +39 02 25 14 70 63

Rai-Radiotelevisione Italiana
Roberto Zaccaria (Managing Director)
Viale Mazzini 14
Rome 00195
Tel: +39 06 3878
Fax: +39 06 372 5680
Website: www.rai.it

Rete 4
Vittorio Giovanelli (Managing Director)
Viale Europa 44
Cologno Monzese
Milan 20093
Tel: +39 02 25 14 1
Fax: +39 02 25 14 70 63

Rete A
Alberto Peruzzo (President)
Viale Marelli 165
Sesto S. Giovanni
Milan 20099
Tel: +39 02 24 20 21
Fax: +39 02 24 85 736

Luxembourg

CLT–UFA
Rolf Schmidt-Holtz (President)
45 Blvd Pierre Frieden
Luxembourg L-1543
Tel: +352 42 14 21sss
Fax: +352 42 142 2760
E-mail: (name)_(surname)@clt-ufa.com
Website: www.clt-ufa.com

The Netherlands

AVRO
F Maréchal (Managing Director)
PO Box 2
Hilversum 1200 JA
Tel: +31 35 671 7911
Fax: +31 35 671 7229
Website: www.omroep.nl/avro

KRO
F H Slangen (President)
PO Box 9000
1201 DH Hilversum
Tel: +31 35 671 3911
Fax: +31 35 671 3119
E-mail: kro@omroep.nl
Website: www.omroep.nl/kro

RTL 4 and RTL 5
P Porius (President)
PO Box 15000
1200 TV Hilversum
Tel: +31 35 671 8718
Fax: +31 35 623 6892
Website: www.rtl4.nl
Website: www.rtl5.nl

Veronica
Kees Gerritsen (Programming Director)
PO Box 15000
1200 TV Hilversum

Tel: +31 35 671 8718
Fax: +31 35 671 6892
Website: www.veronica.nl

Canal+ Nederland

Will Moerer (Managing Director)
Laaperculd 75
1213 VB Hilversum
Tel: +31 35 655 5808
Fax: +31 35 655 5701
E-mail: receptie@canalplus.nl
Website: www.cplus.fr

SBS 6/Net 5

PO Box 18179
1001 ZB Amsterdam
Tel: +31 20 522 5555
Fax: +31 20 522 5556
E-mail: info@sbs6.nl.nl of info@net5.nl
Website: www.sbs6.nl
Website: www.net5.nl

Norway

NRK - Norwegian Broadcasting Corporation

Aeinar Foerde (Director General)
Bjørnstjerne Bjørnsons plass 1
0340 Oslo
Tel: +47 23 04 70 00
Fax: +47 23 04 27 20
Website: www.nrk.no

TV Norge AS

Päl Traelvik (President)
Biskop Gunneruf St 6
0105 Oslo
Tel: +47 21 02 2000
Fax: +47 22 05 1000

Portugal

RTP-Radiotelevisão Portuguesa SA

Manuel Roque (Managing Director)
Avenida 5 dee Outubro, 197

Lisboa 1050
Tel: +351 1 793 1774
Fax: +351 1 793 1809/1758

SIC-Sociedade Independente de Comunicação SA

Francisco Pinto (Managing Director)
Estrada da Outurela
Carnaxinde
Tel: +351 1 279 9526
Fax: +351 21 417 3120

TVI-Televisão Independente SA, Administration

Miguel Paes do Amaral (Chief Executive)
Rua Mário Castelhano 40
Queluz de Baixo
Barcarena/Queluz 2745
Tel: +351 1 435 5181
Fax: +351 1 435 5075
Website: www.tvi.pt

Spain

Antena 3 De Televisión SA

Juan José Nieto Bueso (Managing Director)
Avenida Isla Graciosa s/n
San Sebastian de Los Reyes
28700 Madrid
Tel: +34 91 623 0875
Fax: +34 91 654 8520
E-mail: ventasa3tv@antena3tv.es
Website: www.antena3tv.es

Gestevision TeleCinco

Alejandro Echevarría (President)
Plaza Carretera de Irún
KM 11700
28049 Madrid
Tel: +34 91 396 6300
Fax: +34 91 396 6459/6135

FORTA - Federación de Organismos de Radiotelevisión Autonómicos

Goya 22, 4º
28001 Madrid

Tel: +34 91 576 1727
Fax: +34 91 576 5300

Canal+ España

Jesús de Polanco Gutiérrez
(President, Sogecable)
Gran Vía 32 3º
28013 Madrid
Tel: +34 91 396 5500
Fax: +34 91 396 5600
E-mail: cplus@cplus.es
Website: www.cplus.es

Vía Digital

Pedro Pérez Fernández de la Puente (President)
Calle Virgilio 2, Edificio 1
Ciudad de la Imagen
Ctra de Boadilla del Monte Km 2,200
28223 Pozuelo de Alarcón
Madrid
Tel: +34 91 512 9200
Fax: +34 91 512 9244

TVE-Televisión Española SA

Pio Cabanillas Alonso (Managing Director)
Prado del Rey
Pozuelo de Alarcón
28223 Madrid
Tel: +34 91 346 8000/4000/581 7000
Fax: +34 91 346 3055
E-mail: direccion.communicacion@rtve.es
Website: www.rtve.es

Sweden

SVT-Sveriges Television

Anna-Greta Leijon (Managing Director)
Oxenstiernsgatan 26-34
10510 Stockholm
Tel: +46 8 784 0000
Fax: +46 8 784 1500
E-mail: name@svt.se
Website: www.svt.se

TV4 AB

Phorbjorn Lersson (Managing Director)
Tegeluddsvägen 3
11579 Stockholm
Tel: +46 8 459 4000
Fax: +46 8 459 4444
Website: www.tv4.se

UR-Sveriges Utbildningsradio

Lars Hansson (Managing Director)
Swedish Educational Broadcasting
Tulegaten 7
Stockholm 11395
Tel: +46 8 784 4000/4141
Fax: +46 8 784 4100
Website: www.ur.se

The UK

BBC-British Broadcasting Corporation Headquarters

Christopher Bland (Chairman)
Broadcasting House
Portland Place
London W1A 1AA
Tel: +44 171 580 4468
Fax: +44 171 765 3000
Website: www.bbc.co.uk

Channel Four TV Corporation

Michael Jackson (Chief Executive)
124 Horseferry Road
London SW1P 2TX
Tel: +44 171 396 4444
Fax: +44 171 306 8347
E-mail: viewer_enqs@channel4.co.uk
Website: www.channel4.com

FilmFour Limited

Paul Webster (Chief Executive)
76-78 Charlotte Street
London W1P 1LX
Tel: +44 171 868 7700
Fax: +44 171 868 7771

Channel 5 Broadcasting

David Elstein (Managing Director)
22 Long Acre
London WC2E 9LY
Tel: +44 171 550 5555
Fax: +44 171 550 5554
Website: www.channel5.co.uk

GMTV

Charles Allen (Chairman)
London TV Centre
Upper Ground
London SE1 9TT
Tel: +44 171 827 7000
Fax: +44 171 827 7001

ITV Network Centre

Richard Eyre (Chief Executive)
200 Grays Inn Road
London WC1X 8HF
Tel: +44 171 843 8000
Fax: +44 171 843 8158

Granada Film

Pippa Cross (Head of Granada Film)
The London Television Centre
Upper Ground
South Bank
London SE1 9LT
Tel: +44 171 737 8678
Fax: +44 171 737 8682

Carlton Film

Jonathan Powell (Head of Carlton Film)
35-38 Portman Square
London W1H 0UN
Tel: +44 171 486 6688
Fax: +44 171 486 1132

BSkyB – Sky Pictures

Nadine Mellor (Commissioning Editor)
Grant Way
Isleworth
Middlesex TW7 5QD
Tel: +44 171 705 3000
Fax: +44 171 705 3030

4.7 Festivals and markets

4.7.1 Calendar of festivals and markets worldwide

January

International Film Festival of India (New Delhi)

Directorate of Film Festivals, 4th floor,
Lok Nayak Bavan, Khan Market,
New Delhi 110 001, India
Tel: +91 11 461 5953/469 4920/469
2849/461 7226
Fax: +91 11 462 3430
Festival director: Malti Sahai
Festival programmer: Shankar Mohan & S.
Santhanam
Market & Competition
Golden Peacock for Best Film by an Asian
director

Travelling – Rennes Film Festival

Université Renes 2, 6 avenue Gaston Berger,
F-35043 Rennes Cedex, France
Tel: +33-299-141143
Fax: +33-299-141145
E-mail: hussam.hindi@uhb.fr
Festival director: Hussam Hindi
Festival programmer: as above
Competition
The Jury Prize (Ffr 30 000)
Previous winner: *Junk Mail* (Pal Sletaune)

Palm Springs International Film Festival

1700 E. Tahquitz Canyon Way #3, Palm
Springs, CA 92262, USA
Tel: +1-760 322 2930
Fax: +1-760 322 4087
E-mail: jlien@psfilmfest.org
Executive director: Craig Prater

FIPA (Festival International de Programmes Audiovisuels) (Biarritz)

14 Rue Alexandre Parodi, 75010 Paris, France
Tel: +33-1-44 89 99 99
Fax: +33-1-44 89 99 60
Festival president: Marie-France Pisier
Festival programmer: Pierre-Henri Deleau
Competition
FIPA d'Or
Previous winner: *Le petit voleur* (Eric Zonca)

Solothurn Film Festival

PO Box 140, CH-4502 Solothurn, Switzerland
Tel: +41-32-625 8080
Fax: +41-32-623 6410
E-mail: filmtage@cuenet.ch
Festival director & programmer: Ivo Kummer

Tromsø The International Film Festival

PO Box 285, Tromso, N-9253 Norway
Tel: +47-77 60 51 50
Fax: +47-77 60 51 51
E-mail: filmfestival@tromsokino.no
Festival director: Hans Henrik Berg
Festival programmer: Ola Lund Renolen
Competition
Import Prize (NOK 100.000)
Previous winner: *In That Land* (Lidia Bobrova)

International Film Festival Brussels

30 Chaussée de Louvain, B-1210 Brussels, Belgium
Tel: +32-2-227 3980
Fax: +32-2-218 1860
E-mail: infoffb@netcity.be
Festival director & programmer: Christian Thomas
Competition
Crystal Star ($150,000)
Previous winner: *The Theory of Flight* (Paul Greengrass)

Sundance Film Festival (Park City)

PO Box 16450, Salt Lake City, Utah 84116, USA
Tel: +1-801-328 3456
Fax: +1-801-575 5175
Festival co-directors: Nicola Guillemet & Geoff Gilmore
Festival programmer: Geoff Gilmore
Competition
Grand Jury Prize (Drama/documentary) ($5000)
Previous winner: *Three Seasons* (Tony Bui)

Future Film Festival (Bologna)

Via Pietralata 55/a, Bologna, Italy 40123
Tel: +39 051 520 629
Fax: +39 051 523 816
E-mail: fff@clarence.com
Festival directors: Giulietta Fara, Andrea Morini, Andrea Romeo

Premiers Plans (Angers)

54 rue Beaubourg, 75003 Paris, France
Tel: 33-1-42 71 53 70
Fax: 33-1-42 71 47 55
Website: http://www.anjou.com/premiersplans/
Festival director & programmer: Claude-Eric Poiroux
Competition
Grand Prix (100.000Ff)
Previous winner: *Orphans* (Peter Mulen)

Slamdance Film Festival (Park City)

6381 Hollywood Blvd. #520, Los Angeles, CA 90028, USA
Tel: +1-213 466 1786
Fax: +1-213 466 1784
Festival director: Peter Baxter
Competition
Grand Jury Award
Previous winner: *Chi Girl* (Heidi Van Lier)

Golden Globe Awards (LA)

292 South La Cienega Blvd, Suite 316, Beverly Hills, CA 90211-3055, USA
Tel: +1-310 657 1731
Fax: +1-310 657 5576
E-mail: hfpa95@aol.com
Contact: Chantal Dennage

MIDEM (Cannes)

11 Rue du Colonel Avia, 75726, Paris, Cedex 15, France
Tel: +33-1-41 90 44 00
Fax: +33-1-41 90 44 50
Chief executive: Xavier Roy
Market

NATPE (National Association of TV Programming Executives) (New Orleans)

2425 Olympic Boulevard, Suite 550E, Santa Monica, CA 90404, US
Tel: +1-310-453 4440
Fax: +1-310-453 5258
Website: www.natpe.org
Festival director: Nick Orfanopoulos
European Offices: 454 Oakleigh Rd North, London N20 ORZ, UK
Tel: +44-81-361 3793
Fax: +44-81-368 3824
Contact: Pam Mackenzie
Market

Max Ophüls Preis Film Festival

Filmbüro, Max Ophüls Preis, Mainzer Str 8, 66111 Saarbrüken, Germany
Tel: +49-681-39452
Fax: +49-681-905 1943
E-mail: Filmhaus@aol.com
Festival director: Christel Drawer
Competition
Max Ophüls Preis
Previous winner: *Three Below Zero* (Simon Aeby)

International Film Festival Rotterdam

Karel Doormanstr. 278 B, PO Box 21696, 3001 AR Rotterdam, The Netherlands
Tel: +31-10-890 9090
Fax: +31-10-890 9091
E-mail: tiger@iffrotterdam.nl
Festival director: Simon Field
Festival programmer: Simon Field
Market and **Competition**
VPRO Tiger Award (US$10,000)
Previous winners: *Following* (Christopher Nolan), *The Iron Heel of Oligarchy* (Alexander Bashirov) and *Plus qu'hier, moins que demain* (Laurent Achard)

Internacionale Filmwochenende (Würzburg)

Gostbertsteige 2, D-97082, Würzburg, Germany
Tel: +49-931-414098/ 408561
Fax: +49-931-416279
E-mail: ifw24@aol.com
Festival director & programmer: Berthold Kremmler
Competition
Audience Award (DM 5,000)
Previous winner: *Pork Pie* (Paul Turner, UK)

Göteborg Film Festival

Box 7079, S-402 32 Göteborg, Sweden
Tel: +46-31-410 546
Fax: +46-31-410 063
E-mail: goteborg@filmfestival.org
Festival director & programmer: Gunnar Bergdahl
Competition for Scandinavian films only

Göteborgs-Posten's Nordic Film Prize (SEK 100 000)
Previous winner: *Yearning for Life* (Christen Engberg)

The International Film Festival (Belgrade)

Cika Ljubina 12, 11000 Belgrade, Yugoslavia
Tel: +381-11-625 131
Fax: +381 11 625 131
E-mail: film@scentar.co.yu
Festival director: Dinko Tucakovic
Festival programmer: Miroljub Vuckovic, Dragan Jelicic

Imagina (Monaco & Paris)

4 avenue de l'Europe, Bry-Sur-Marne, 94366, France
Tel: +33-1-4983 2693
Fax: +33-1-4983 3185
Festival coordinator: Jean-Michel Blottière
Competition
Grand Prix Imagina
Previous winner: *Bunny* (Chris Wedge)

12th Stuttgart Filmwinter

(short film, experimental film, documentary, etc)
Wand 5 e.v., Friedrichstraße 23/a, D-70174 Stuttgart, Germany
Tel: +49-711 226 9160
Fax: +49-711 226 9161
E-mail: wanda@wand 5.de
Festival director & programmer: Ulrich Wegenast and Martin Wolf
Competition
Norman Award (DM 3,000) and Teamwork Award (DM 3,000)
Previous winner: *Lenchtturm der Leidenschaft* (Nikolaus Buchholz)

Alpe Adria Cinema Film Festival (Trieste)

(Meetings with Central and Eastern European Cinema)
Via S. Rocco 1, 34143 Trieste, Italy
Tel: +39 040 311 153
Fax: +39 040 311 993

E-mail: aac@spin.it

Festival director & programmer: Annamaria Percavassi, Tiziana Finzi, Sergio Grmek Germani

Competition

Prize for the best feature film (10 mill. Itallian lira)

Previous winner: *Historia kina w Popielawach* (Jan Jakub Kolski, Poland)

The Chicago Int'l TV Competition (Chicago)

32 West Randolph Street, Suite 600, Chicago, Illinois 60601, USA

Tel: +1-312 425 9400

Fax: +1-312 425 0944

E-mail: filmfest@suba.com

Festival director: Michael Kutza

The Gold Hugo Statue

Gerardmer Fantastic Arts

36 rue Pierret, 92200 Neuilly, France

Tel: +33-1-41 34 20 00

Fax: +33-1-47 58 77 77

E-mail: publics@imaginet.fn

Festival director: Lionel Chouchan

Festival programmer: Daniel Benzakein

Competition

Grand Prix Gerardmer Fantastic Arts

Previous winner: *Cube* (Vincenzo Natali)

Kid Film Festival (Dallas)

6116 N. Central Expwy, Suite 105, Dallas 75206, Texas, USA

Tel: +1-214-821 6300

Fax: +1-214-821 6364

Website: http://www.usafilmfestival.com

Festival director: Ann Alexander

Festival programmer: Alonso Duralde

Networks in the Studio Seminar (Geneva)

Ancienne Route, 17A (European Braodcasting Union), Grand Saconnex (Geneva) Switzerland 1218

Tel: +41 22 717 2721/ 2725

Fax: +41 22 717 2749/ 10

E-mail: peters@ebu.ch

Website: www.ebu.ch

Seminar director: Jean-Jacques Peters

New York Festivals International Print & Radion Advertising Awards

780 King Street, Chappaqua, NY 10514, US

Tel: +1-914-238 4481

Fax: +1-914-238 5040

Festival director: Bilha Goldberg

Competition

Gold, Silver, Bronze World Medals and 4 Grand Awards

February

Fajr Film Festival (Tehran)

Farhang Cinema, Dr Shariati Ave, Gholhak, Tehran, 19139 Iran

Tel: +98 21 200 2088/90

Fax: +98 21 267 082/ 670 8155

Festival director: S. Daad

Festival programmer: as above

Competition

Crystal Simorgh Award (US$ 5,000)

Previous winner: *The Colour of God* (Majid Majidi, Iran)

Hungarian Film Week (Budapest)

c/o Filmunio, Varoslygeti Fasor 38, 1068 Budapest, Hungary

Tel: +36 1 351 7760

Fax: +36 1 351 6734

E-mail: filmunio@elender.hu

Festival director: Katalin Vajda

Competition for Hungarian films only

6th Annual Victoria Independent Film and Video Festival

101-610 Johnson St., Victoria, British Columbia, Canada V8W 1M4

Tel: +1-250 389 0444

Fax: +1-250 380 1547

Website: www.coastnet.com/~cinevic
Festival director: Kathy Kay

Clermont-Ferrand Short Film Festival

26, rue des Jacobins, F-63000 Clermont-Ferrand, France
Tel: +33-473 91 65 73
Fax: +33-473 92 11 93
E-mail: festival@gdebussac.fr
Festival director: Roger Gonin
Festival programmer: Roger Gonin, Christian Guinot
Competition
Grand Prix (FF20,000)
Previous winner: *Les mots magiques* (Jean-Marc Vallee, Canada)

Berlin International Film Festival

Potsdamer straße 5, D-10785 Berlin, Germany
Tel: +49-30 2592 0202
Fax: +49-30 2592 0299
E-mail: info@berlinale.de
Festival director: Moritz de Hadeln
Competition
Golden Bear
Previous winner: *The Thin Red Line* (Terence Malik)

European Film Market (Berlin)

Budapester Strasse 50, D-10787 Berlin, Germany
Tel: +49-30-25 48 92 25
Fax: +49-30-25 48 92 49
Contact: Beki Probst

International Forum of New Cinema (Berlin)

Budapester Strasse 50, D-10787 Berlin, Germany
Tel: +49-30-254 89246
Fax: +49-30-261 5025
E-mail: forum@forum-ifb.b.shuttle.de/ 10024.327@compuserve.com
Website: http://www.b.shuttle.de/forum-ifb
Festival director: Ulrich Gregor

Festival programmer: Erika & Ulrich Gregor, Klaus Dermutz, Erika Richter, Peter B. Schumann, Christoph Terhechte, Dorothee Wenner
Non-competitive, but awards are given: Wolfgang-Staudte-Preis (20.000 DM)

The Mobius Advertising Awards (Chicago)

841 North Addison Avenue, Elmhurst, 60126-1291 Illinois, USA
Tel: +1-630-834 7773
Fax: +1-630-834 5565
E-mail: filmfestivalandmobius awards@compuserve.com
The chairman: J W Anderson
Competition
The Mobius Statuette
Previous winner: *The Power of Zyrtec*

Portland International Film Festival

1219 SW Park Avenue, Portland 97205, Oregon, USA
Tel: +1-503-221 1156
Fax: +1-503-294 0874
E-mail: info@nwfilm.org
Festival director & programmer: Bill Foster
Competition
Best of Festival Award
Previous winner: *Harmonists* (Joseph Vilsmaier) & *My Name Is Joe* (Ken Loach)

Mardi Gras Film Festival (Sydney)

94 Oxford Street/PO Box 1081, Darlinghurst, NSW 2010, Australia
Tel: +61-2 9332 4938
Fax: +61-2 9331 2988
E-mail: info@queerscreen.com.au
Festival director: Tony Grierson
Competition (for Australian and New Zealand queer shorts)
My Queer Career Award (AUD 2000)
Previous winner: *Cousin* (Adam Benjamin Elliot)

MILIA (Cannes)

BP 572, 11 Rue du Colonel Pierre Avia,
75726 Paris Cedex 15, France
Tel: +33-1-41 90 44 00
Fax: +33-1-41 90 44 70
Website: http://www.reedmidem.milia.com
Programme manager: Laurine Garaude
Competition and Market
Milia d'Or
Previous winner: *Zelda Ocarina of Time*

Monte Carlo Television Festival

4Bd Jardin Exotique, Monaco MC 98000
Tel: +377-93 10 40 60
Fax: +377-93 50 70 14
Festival director: David Tomatis
Market & Competition
Golden Nymph Awards (Best TV Film,
Miniseries, News Reports, News Features)

Local Heroes

3rd Floor, 10022 103rd Street, Edmonton,
AlbertaT5J 0X2, Canada
Tel: +1-780-421 4084
Fax: +1-780-425 9099
E-mail: filmhero@nsi-canada.ca
Website: www.nsi-canada.ca
Festival director: Cheryl Ashton
Festival programmer: Anthony King
Market

Miami Film Festival

444 Brickell Ave., #229, Miami, FL 33131, US
Tel: +1-305-377 3456
Fax: +1-305-577 9768
E-mail: mff@gate.net
Festival director & programmer: Nat Chediak
Competition
Audience Award
Previous winner: *Train of Life* (Radu
Mihaileonu)

Israel Film Festival
(16th edition)

6404 Wilshire Blvd., #1240, Los Angeles, CA
90048, US
Tel: +1-323 966 4166

Fax: +1-323 658 6346
Website: www.israelfilmfestival.com
Festival director: Meir Fenigstein
Competition
Audience Award

American Film Market (AFM)

10850 Wilshire Boulevard, Los Angeles, CA
90024, USA
Tel: +1-310-446 1000
Fax: +1-310-446 1600
E-mail: afma.com
Market director: Julie Friedman
Market

Cinequest Film Festival (San Jose)

PO Box 720040, San Jose, CA 95172-0040, USA
Tel: +1-408-995 5033
Fax: +1-408-995 5713
E-mail: cineqst@wenet.net
Festival director: Halfdan Hussey
Festival programmer: Mike Rabehl
Competition
Maverick Spirit Award (US$ 500)
Previous winner: *We All Fall Down* (Davide
Ferrario)

Oporto International Film Festival– Fantasporto

Rua Da Constituição 311, P-4200 Porto,
Portugal
Tel: +351-2-507 3880
Fax: +351-2-550 8990
E-mail: fantas@caleida.pt
Festival director: Mário Dorminski
Festival programmer: Beatriz Pacheco-Pereira
Competition
Best film award
Previous winner: *Cube* (Vicenzo Natali)

Brussels Cartoon and Animated Film Festival

19 rue de la Rhétorique, 1060 Bruxelles,
Belgium
Tel: +32-2-534 4125
Fax: +32-2-534 2279

E-mail: folioscope@skynet.be

Festival director & programmer: Doris Cleven & Philippe Moins

Green Screen (London)

Festival tours 7 UK cities and foreign capitals
114 St. Martin's Lane, London WC2N 4AZ, UK
Tel: +44-171-379 7390
Fax: +44-171-379 7197
Festival director: Victoria Cliff Hodges
The Bill Travers Award (£1000)
Previous winner: *The Mahogany Trail & The Work of the Undercurrents*

Mumbai International Film Festival for Documentary, Short & Animation Films

Films Division, Ministry of Information and Broadcasting, Government of India, 24-Dr. G. Deshmuks Marg, Mumbai-400 026, India
Tel: +91-22 3864633/3873655/3861421/ 3861461
Fax: +91-22-3860308
Festival director: Mr D Gautaman
Competition and market
Various categories Golden Conch (Rs. 250,000 and Silver Conch Rs. 100,000)

Oslo Filmdager

PO Box 1584, Vika, N-0118 Oslo, Norway
Tel: +47 22 82 44 00
Fax: +47 22 82 43 68/69
Festival director: Ingeborg Moraus Hanssen

PanAfrican Film and TV Festival of Ouagadougou

Secretariat Général Permanent du Fespaco, 01BP - 2505 Ougadougou 01, Burkina Faso
Tel: +226-30 7538
Fax: +226-31 2509
Festival director: Filippe Sawadogo
Competition
Etalon de Yennega (CFA 5m)

Cine Golden Eagle Showcase (Washington DC)

1001 Connecticut Avenue NW, Suite 638, Washington, DC 20036, US

Tel: +1-202-785 1136
Fax: +1-202-785 4114
Cine Golden Eagle Award (prof.) & Cine Eagle (amateur)

Kino Festival of American Undeground Cinema (Manchester)

Kinofilm, Kino Screen, 48 Princess Street, Manchester M1 6HR, UK
Tel: +44-161 288 2494
Fax: +44-161 281 1374
E-mail: john.kino@good.co.uk
Website: www.kinofilm.org.uk
Festival director: John Wojowski
Festival co-ordinator: Abigail Christenson

Transmediale – International Media Art Festival of Berlin

Klosterstr. 68-70, Berlin, Germany, 10179
Tel: +49-30 2472 1907
Fax: +49-30 2472 1909
E-mail: info@transmediale.de
Festival director: Micky Kwella
Artistic director: Micky Kwella, Susanne Jaschko
Competition
Transmediale Award (DM 7,500)

March

Viewpoint: Documentary Now (Gent)

Sint-Annaplein 63, Gent 9000, Belgium
Tel: +32-9-225 0845
Fax: +32-9-233 7522
E-mail: studio.skoop@net7.be
Festival director: Walther Vander Cruysse
Festival programmer: Cis Bierinckx

Cartagena Film Festival

Baluarte de San Francisco, Calle San Juan de Dios, A.A. 1834, Cartagena, Colombia.
Tel: (57 5) 660 0966
Fax: (57 5) 660 0970, 660 1037
Festival director & programmer: Victor Nieto

Competition
Previous winner: *Central do Brasil* (Walter Salles)

Guadalajara Film Festival

Estudios Churubusco Azteca, Atletas 2, Edificio Luis Buñuel, Pasillo A-211, Col. Country Club, 04220 Mexico, D.F., Mexico
Tel: +525 544 6920/ 35
Fax: +525 544 6935
E-mail: muestr@latino.com
Festival director: Susana López Aranda
Festival programmer: Leonardo García Tsao

NatFilm Festival (Copenhagen)

St. Kannikestr. 6, 1169 Copenhagen K., Denmark
Tel: +45-33 12 0005
Fax: +45-33 12 7505
E-mail: info@natfilm.dk
Festival director: Peter Wolsgaard
Festival programmer: Kim Foss

Santa Barbara Film Festival

1216 State Street, Suite 710, Santa Barbara, CA 93101-2623, USA
Tel: +1-805-963 0023
Fax: +1-805-962 2524
E-mail: info@sbfilmfestival.com
Festival director: Rhea A. Lewis
Festival programmer: Renée Missel
Competition
Burning Vision Award ($US 10,000)
Previous winner: *The Power of Kangwon Province* (Hong Sang-soo)

Showest (Las Vegas)

Suite 708, 116 N Robertson Boulevard, Los Angeles, CA 90048, USA
Tel: +1-310-657 7724
Fax: +1-310-657 4758
Executive director: Herb Burton
Director: Laura Rooney
Tradeshow (convention)

The Production Show (London)

33-39 Bowling Green Lane, London, EC1R 0DA, UK
Tel: +44-171-505 8014
Fax: +44-171-505 8020
E-mail: timmac@media.emap.co.uk
Event director: Tim McPhearson

Tampere Film Festival

Box 305, 33101 Tampere, Finland
Tel: +358-3-213 0034
Fax: +358-3-223 0121
E-mail: film.festival@tt.tampere.fi
Festival co-directors: Kirsi Kinnunen, Tuula Kumpunen, Juhani Alanen
Festival programmer: Raimo Silius
Market and competition
Grand Prix FIM 25,000 and statuette "Kiss"
Previous winner: *Silk* (Mahrash Shaykh-Aleslami, Iran)

Cinema du Reel (Paris)

BPI- 19 Rue Beaubourg, 75197 Paris, Cedex 04, France
Tel: +33-1-44 78 44 21/44 78 45 16
Fax: +33-1-44 78 12 24
E-mail: cinereel@bpi.fr
Festival director & programmer: Suzette Glenadel
Competition
Prix cinema du reel (FF 50 000)
Previous winner: *Siberian Lesson* (Wojciech Sharón, Poland)

South by Southwest Film Conference and Festival

PO Box 4999, Austin, TX 78765, US
Tel: +1-512 467 7979
Fax: +1-512 451 0754
E-mail: film@sxsw.com

Fribourg Film Festival

Rue de Locarno 8, 1700 Fribourg, Switzerland
Tel: +41-26 3222 232
Fax: +41-26 3227 950
Festival director: Martial Knaebel

Festival programmer: Martial Knaebel
Competition
Grand Prix (Sfr 25,000)
Previous winner: *Life on Earth*
(Abdurahman Sissako)

Poitiers International School Film Festival

1 Place de la Cathédrale, 86000 Poitier,
France
Tel: +33-4 4941 8000
Fax: +33-5 4941 7601
E-mail: festival-poitiers@rihl.org
Website: www.rihl.org
General secretary: Franois Defaye
Programming supervisor: Bruno Nicora
Competition

San Francisco International Asian-American Film Festival

NAATA, 346 Ninth Street, 2nd Floor, San
Francisco, CA 94103 US
Tel: +1-415 863 0814
Fax: +1-415 863 7428
E-mail: festival@naatanet.org
Festival director: Brian Lau
Festival programmer: Brian Lau & Linda
Blackaby

Ann Arbor Film Festival

PO Box 8232, Ann Arbor, MI 48107, USA
Tel: +1-734-995 5356
Fax: +1-734-995 5396
E-mail: vicki@honeyman.org
Website: aafilmfest.org
Festival director: Vicki Honeyman
Festival programmer: Vicki Honeyman
Competition
Best of Festival ($2500)
Previous winner: *Shanghaied Text* (Ken
Kobland)

18th International Festival of Films on Art (Montreal)

640 Saint-Paul Street West, Suite 406,
Montréal, Québec, H3C 1L9 Canada
Tel: +1-514-874 1637

Fax: +1-514-874 9929
Festival director & programmer: René
Rozon
Competition
Grand Prix (Honorary prize)
Previous winner: *Richter, l'insoumis* (Bruno
Monsaingeon)

Action and Adventure Film Festival (Valenciennes)

6 Place Froisart, Valenciennes, France 59 300
Tel: +33-3 2725 55 40
Fax: +33-3 27 41 67 49
Festival director & programmer: Patricia
Lasou, Sylvie Lemaire, Patricia Riquet
Festival programmer: Jean-Marc Delcambre
Competition
Grand Prize (20,000 FF for the director)
Previous winner: *Elvijs and Marilyn*
(Armando Manni)

Nordic Film Festival (Rouen)

22 rue de la Champmesié, Rouen 76000, France
Tel: +33-235 98 28 46
Fax: +33-235 70 92 08
Festival director: Jean Michel Mongredien
Festival programmer: Jean Michel
Mongredien & Isabelle Dueult
Competition
Grand Jury award
Previous winner: *When the Light Comes*
(Stijn Coninx, Holland)

Cleveland International Film Festival

1621 Euclid Avenue, #428, Cleveland, Ohio
44115-2107, USA
Tel: +1-216-623 0400
Fax: +1-216-623 0103
E-mail: cfs@clevelandfilm.org
Website: www.clevefilmfest.org
Festival director & programmer: David W
Wittkowsky
Competition
Roxanne T. Mueller Award
Previous winner: *Return with Honour*
(Freida Lee Mock)

International Animation Film Festival (Stuttgart)

Int. Trick film Festival E.V., Teckstrasse 56, Stuttgart, Germany 70190
Tel: +49-711-925 460
Fax: +49-711 925 4615
E-mail: info@itfs.de
Website: www.itfs.de
Festival director: Prof. Albrecht Ade
Festival programmer: Ulrich Wegenast, Götz Gruner
Competition
State Capital Stuttgart Award/State of Baden-Württtenberg Award
Value of award: 180,000 DM (total)
Previous winner: *Un jour* (Marie Pacou)

Brussels International Festival of Fantasy Film

144 Avenue de la Reine, B-1030, Brussels, Belgium
Tel: +32-2 201 1713
Fax: +32-2 201 1469
E-mail: peymey@skypro.be
Festival director: Delmote Georges & Guy Delmote
Festival programmer: Bozzo Annie & Freddy Bozzo-Gigli
Competition
Golden Raven Award (Corbeau d'or) (US$27,000)
Previous winner: *Ring Hidio Nakata*

Bergamo Film Meeting

Via Giovanni Reich 49, Torre Boldone, Bergamo, Italy, 24020
Tel: +39-35-36 30 87
Fax: +39-35-34 12 55
E-mail: bfm@alasca.it
Festival director & programmer: Emanuela Martini & Angelo Signorelli
Competition
Rosa Camuna d'Oro
Previous winner: *La Primera noche de mi vida* (Miguel Albaladejo, Spain)

SporTel (Miami)

6040 Boulevard East, Ste. 27C, West Nerw York, NJ 07903, US
4 Boulevard de Jardin Exotique, MC-98000 Monaco, Monaco
Tel: +1-201 869 4022
Fax: +1-201 869 4335
Tel: +377-93-30 20 32
Fax: +377-93-30 20 33
Festival director: David Tomatis
Market & Competition
Golden Poldium Trophy

Diagonale–Festival of Austrian Films (Graz)

Diagonale, Obere Augerterstrasse 1, 1020 Vienna, Austria
Tel: +43-1-216 1303
Fax: +43-1-216 1303200
E-mail: wien@diagonale.at
Festival director: Christine Dollhofer & Constantin Wulff
Competition
Grosser Diagonalepreiss (210,000 ATS)
Previous winner: *Pripyat* (Nikolaus Geyrhalter)

Royal Television Society Awards (Programme Awards)

Holborn Hall, 100 Gray's Inn Road, London WC1X 1AL, UK
Tel: +44-171 430 1000
Fax: +44-171 430 0924
Contact: Nicky Harlow

African Film Festival (Milan)

Via Lazzaroni 8, 20124 Milano, Italy
Tel: +39-2 66 96 258
Fax: +39-2 6671 4338
E-mail: coe@iol.it
Festival director: tbc
Competition
Premio Agip (15,000,000 Italian Lira)
Previous winner: *La Vie sur terre* (Abderraman Sissako)

Creteil International Festival of Women's Films

Maison des Arts, Place Salvador Allende, 94000 Creteil, France
Tel: +33-1-49 80 38 98
Fax: +33-1-43 99 04 10
E-mail: filmsfemmes@wanadoo.fr
Festival director: Jackie Buet
Festival programmer: Jackie Buet, Nicole Fernandez
Competition
Grand Jury Award (FF 25,000)
Previous winner: *S dniom roddenia* (Larisa Sadilova, Russia)

East Lansing Film Festival

510 Kedzie Street, East Lansing Michigan, US 48823
Tel: +1-517 336 5802
Fax: +1-517 336 5802
E-mail: swelff@aol.com
Festival director: Susan W. Woods
Festival programmer: Jennifer L. White
Competition for the Michigan film-makers

IVCA Awards 2000 (London)

IVCA, Bolsover House, 5-6 Clipstone Street, London W1P 8LD, UK
Tel: +44-171-580 0962
Fax: +44-171 436 2606
Chief executive: Wayne Drew
Competition
Grand Prix
Previous winner: *The Nissan DQR Film*

Midwest Filmmakers Conference

Cleveland Filmmakers, 1621 Euclid Avenue, #428, Cleveland, Ohio 44115-2107, USA
Tel: +1 216 623 0400
Fax: +1 216 623 0103
Website: www. clevelandfilm.org
Festival programmer: Frank O'Grady

New Directors/New Films (New York City)

The Film Society of Lincoln Centre, 70 Lincoln Centre Plaza, New York, NY 10023, US
Tel: +1-212-875 5638
Fax: +1-212-875 5636
Website: www.filmlinc.com
Contact: Sara Bensman

Diagonale Festival of Austrian Film

Mariahilfer str. 113, A-1060 Vienna, Austria
Tel: +43-1 216 1303
Fax: +43-1 216 1303200
E-mail: wien@diagonale.at
Website: www.diagonale.at
Contact: Christine Dollhofer/Constantin Wulff

Festival du Film de Paris

7 Rue Brunel, 75017 Paris, France
Tel: +33 1 45 72 96 40
Fax: +33 1 45 72 96 41
Website: www.festival-du-film-paris.com
Festival director: Louise Maurin
Festival programmer: Olivier Pelisson
Competition
Grand Prix (FF 700 000)
Previous winner: *Karakter* (Mike Van Diem)

International Film Festival for Young People (Laon)

BP 526, 8 rue Sérurier, Laon, France Cedex 02001
Tel: +33-3-23-79 39 37
Fax: +33 3 23 793 932
E-mail: festival.cinema.laon@wanadoo.fr
Festival director & programmer: Florence Dupont
Competition
City of Laon Award (FF 30 000)
Previous winner: *Smoke Signals* (Chris Eyre)

Newport Beach International Film Festival

4400 MacArthur Blvd, #500, Newport Beach, CA 92660, USA
Tel: +1-949-851 6555
Fax: +1-949-851 6556
Website: www.nbiff.org
Festival director: Jeff Conner
Festival programmer: Michelle Parsons
Competition & Market
Grand Jury Award (US$ 8,000)
Previous winner: *Open Your Eyes* (Alejandro Amenabar)

San Diego Latino Film Festival

c/o Centro Cultural de la Raza, 2125 Park Blvd., San Diego, CA 92101, US
Tel: +1-619 230 1938
Fax: +1-619-230 1938
E-mail: latinofilm@aol.com
Festival director: Ethan van Thilo
Festival programmer: Fred Salas

Femme Totale Film Festival (Dortmund)

c/o Kulturbüro der Stadt Dortmund, Kleppingstr. 21-23, 44122 Dortmund, Germany
Tel: +49-231-50 25 162
Fax: +49-231-50 25 734
E-mail: femmetotale@compuserve.com
Festival director: Silke Johanna Räbiger

The New York Underground Film Festival

341 Lafayette St., Ste. 236, New York, NY 10012 USA
Tel: +1-212 252 3845
Fax: +1-212 925 3430
E-mail: festival@nyuff.com
Festival director: Ed Halter
Competition
Festival Choice Award (US$750)
Previous winner: *Jefftown* (Dan Kraus)

Minimalen Short Film Festival

Box 10830, Innherredsk 73, N-7002 Trondheim, Norway
Tel: +47-73 52 27 57
Fax: +47-73 53 57 40
E-mail: minimalen@mail.link.no
Festival director: Per Fikse
Festival programmer: Per Fikse
National competition
The Minimalen Festival Award (NOK 5,000)

The Kino Festival of New Irish Cinema (Manchester) & The Irish World Heritage Film Awards

48 Princess Street, Manchester M1 6HR, UK
Tel: +44-161 288 2494
Fax: +44-161 237 3423
Festival director: John S Wojowski
Competition

PILOTS (Programme for the International Launch of Television Series Workshops) (Sitges)

Diputació 279, E-08007 Barcelona, Spain
Tel: +34-93-487 3773
Fax: +34-93- 4873952
Festival director: Pera Fages

Spotlight (Ravensburg)

Location Office Bodensee-Oberschwaben, Ittenbeuren 5, 88212 Ravensburg, Germany
Tel: +49-751 24 758
Fax: +49-751 24 753
Festival director: Dr. Thomas Knubben
Festival programmer: Dr. Thomas Knubben, Peter Frey
Competition
Spotlight in Gold Award
Previous winner: *Botshaft/P & S* (Springer & Jacoby, Hamburg)

Academy Awards (Los Angeles)

Academy of Motion Picture Arts and Sciences, 8949 Wilshire Boulevard, Beverly Hills, CA 90211
Tel: +1-310-247 3000
Fax: +1-310-271-3395
Academy Awards
Prevous winner (Best Picture): *Shakespeare in Love* (John Madden)

Deutsches Kinder-Film & Fernseh-Festival (Gera)

Stiftung Goldener Spatz, Amthorstrasse 11, D-07545 Gera, Germany
Tel: +49-365-800 4874
Fax: +49-365-800 1344
E-mail: gold-spa@gera-web.de
Festival director & programmer: Margret Albers
Market & Competition
Goldener Spatz (Golden Sparrow) award
Previous winner: *A Ghost from the Grave* (Günter Meyer)

Celtic Film and Television Festival (Portree, Skye)

1 Bowmont Gardens, Glasgow, Scotland G12 9LR
Tel: +44-141 342 4947
Fax: +44-141 342 4948
E-mail: mail@celticfilm
Festival director: Mina Heulyn
Competition
Spirit of the Festival
Previous winner: *Cameleon* (Ceri Sherlock)

Festival of Yugoslav Documentary & Short Film (Belgrade)

Jugoslavia Film, Makedonska 22/VI, 11000 Beograd, Yugoslavia
Tel: +381-11 324 8554/324 8282
Fax: +381-11 324 8659
Contact: Vojislav Vucinic
Competition
Grand Prix
Previous winner: *Tamo gde smo se rastali* (Dubravko Batalica)

Bradford Film Festival

National Musuem of Photography, Film and Television, Bradford, BD1 1NQ
Tel: +44-1274- 773 399
Fax: +44-1274 770 217
Festival director: Bill Lawrence
Head of cinema: Emma Sanders
Audience award
Previous winner: *Boyfriends* (Simon Horton)

Hébraïca (Jewish Culture Events) (Montpellier)

500, Boulevard d'Antigone, Montpellier 3400, France
Tel: +33-467 15 08 76/72 32 63
Fax: +33-467 15 08 72/72 32 62
Event director: Janine Gdalia

Start the Millennium (Plymouth)

PO BOX 82, Plymouth, UK PL4 8XY
Tel: +44-1752 265 562
Fax: +44-1752 265 562
E-mail: start@sundog.zynet.co.uk
Website: http://start.at/start
Festival director: Stuart More
Festival programmer: Kayla Parker

Seoul Cable and Satellite Festival

Korea Exhibition Centre, 159 Samsung-Dong, Kangham-gu, Seoul 135-731, Korea
Tel: 822 551 1147
Fax: 822 551 1259
E-mail: chonsh@star.koex.co.kr
Festival director: Sang Hwi Chon

!Viva! Spanish Film Festival (Manchester)

70 Oxford Street, Manchester, UK MI 5NH
Tel: +44-161 228 7621
Fax: +44-161 200 1506
Festival programmer: Linda Pariser

Cairo International Film Festival for Children

17 Kasr El Nil Street, 202 Cairo, Egypt
Tel: +202 392 3562/392 3962

Fax: +202 393 8979
Festival director: Soheir Adbelkader
Competition
Golden Cairo

Cognac International Thriller Film Festival (Cognac)

36 rue Pierret, 92200 Neuilly, France
Tel: +33-1-46 40 55 00
Fax: +33-1-46 40 55 39
E-mail: publics@imaginet.fr
Festival director: Lionel Chouchan
Festival programmer: Daniel Benzakein
Competition
Grand Prix
Previous winner: *Another Day in Paradise* (Lary Clark)

International Festival of Tourist Film

ACTL, via Silvio Pellico 6, 20121 Milano, Italy
Tel: +39-02 86 46 40 80
Fax: +39-02 72 02 25 83
E-mail: info@actl.tt
Festival director: Edoardo Croci
Festival programmer: Andre Archidi
Competition
First prize
Previous winner: *373 Festino di Santa Rosalia* (Sergio Gianfalla)

Music Film Fest (Sofia)

37 Ekzarch Yossif Str., Sofia 1000, Bulgaria
Tel: +359 2 980 3911/ 880 676
Fax: +359 2 529 325
Festival director & programmer: Stefan Kitanov

Chicago Film Critics Awards

1152 North LaSalle Street, Building B, Chicago, IL 60610-2695, USA
Tel: +1-773 509 8155
Fax: +1-773 664 2925

April

Dublin Film Festival

1 Suffolk Street, Dublin, Ireland
Tel: +353-1-679 2937
Fax: +353-1-679 2939
Festival director & programmer: Maoetta Dilon

Canyonlands Film Festival (Moab)

1102 East 5th Avenue, Duragno, Co 81301, US
Tel: +1-970 382 9528
E-mail: canyonfilm@hotmail.com
Website: http://moab-utah.com/film
Festival director: Nicholas Brown
Festival programmer: Canyonlands Film Society Board of Directors
Competition
"Best of Festival" ($1,000 cash award)
Previous winner: *Bus to Queens* (Joshua Marston)

Aspen Shortfest

110 East Hallam, Suite 102, Aspen, 81611 Colorado, USA
Tel: +1-970-925 6882
Fax: +1-970-925 1967
E-mail: lthielen@aspenfilm.org
Festival director: Laura Thielen
Competition
Grand Jury Prize ($2000)

It's All True – International Documentary Film Festival (Sao Paulo/Rio De Janeiro)

Rua Simáo Alvares 784/2, Sao Paulo, Brasil 05417 020
Tel/Fax: +55-11 852 9601
E-mail: itstrue@ibm.net
Festival director: Amir Labaki
Competition
Best documentary
Previous winner: *Here We Are Waiting for You* (Marcelo Msagáo, Brazil)

Worldfest Houston

PO Box 56566, Houston, TX 77256, US
Tel: +1-713-965 9955
Fax: +1-713-965 9960
E-mail: Wolrdfest@aol.com
Website: www.worldfest.org
Festival director: J Hunter Todd
Market & Competition
Gold Remi Statuette, Gold Lone Star
Previous winner: *My American Vacation* (VV Dachin Hsu)

MIP-TV (Cannes)

Reed Midem Organisation, BP 572, 11 rue du Colonel Pierre Abia, Paris Cedex 15, 75726, France
Tel: +33-1-41 90 45 80
Fax: +33-1-41 90 45 70
Programme director: André Vaillant
International TV Market

Hong Kong International Film Festival

Level 7, Administration Building, Hong Kong Cultural Centre, 10 Salisbury Road, Tsimshatsui, Kowloon, Hong Kong
Tel: +852-2734 2903
Fax: +852-2366 5206
E-mail: hkiff@hkiff.com.hlc
Festival director: Lo Tak-Sing
Festival programmer: Li Cheuk-to, Jacob Wong

Shadow Line Film Festival (Salerno)

Via dei Principati 42, 84 100 Salerno, Italy
Tel: +39-089 275 3673
Fax: +39-089 255 1125
E-mail: pdantonio@tim.it
Festival director: Peppe D'Antonio
Competition
Shadow Line Award (5,000,000 Italian Lire)
Previous winner: *Tic Tac* (Daniel Alfredson)

National Association of Broadcasters – NAB

1771 N Street, NW, Washington, DC 20036-2891
Tel: +1-202-429 5350
Fax: +1-202 429 5406
President & CEO of NAB: Eddie Fritz

Turin Int'l Gay & Lesbian Film Fest "From Sodom to Hollywood"

Piazza San Carlo 161, Turin, Italy 10123
Tel: +39 11 534 888
Fax: +39 11 534 888
E-mail: gifilmfest@assioma.com
Festival director: Giovanni Minerba
Festival programmer: Angelo Acerbi, Luca Andreotti
Competition
Best International Feature
Previous winners: Bent (Sean Matthias)

Italian Film Festival (Glasgow/Edinburgh)

Italian Institute, 82 Nicolson Street, Edinburgh, EH8 9EW, UK
Tel: +44-131-668 2232
Fax: +44-131-668 2777
Festival director: Richard Mowe
Festival programmer: Allan Hunter

Minneapolis International Film Festival

2331 University Ave. SE, suite 130B, Minneapolis, 55414, USA
Tel: +1-612-627 4431
Fax: +1-612-627 4111
Website: www.ufilm.org
Festival director & programmer: Albert Milgrom
Competition
Best dramatic feature
Previous winner: *They Come at Night* (Lindy Laub)

International Film Festival of Uruguay (Montevideo)

Lorenzo Carnelli 1311, Montevideo 11 200, Uruguay
Tel: +598-2-408 2460/409 5795
Fax: +598-2-409 45 72
E-mail: cinemuy@chasque.apc.org
Festival director: Manuel Martínez Carril

Festival programmer: Manuel Martínez Carril & Guillermo Zapiola
Competition
Gran Premio Ciudad de Montevideo
Previous winner: *Carrier Girls* (Mike Leigh) & *Mother and Son* (Aleksander Sokurov)

Istanbul International Film Festival

Istiklal Cad: 146 Luvr Apt., 80070, Istanbul, Turkey
Tel: +90-212-293 3133 (ext. 20, 21)
Fax: +90-212 249 7771
E-mail: film@istfest-tr.org
Festival director: Hulya Ucansu
Competition
Golden Tulip Award
Previous winner: *Ayneh* (The Mirror) (Jafar Panahi, Iran)

Visions du Reel Festival International du Cinema Documentaire (Nyon)

18 rue Juste-Olivier, CP 593, CH-1260 Nyon, Switzerland,
Tel: +41-22-361 6060
Fax: +41-22-361 7071
E-mail: dosnyon@visionsdureel.ch
Festival director: Jean Perret
Competition
Grand Prix Vissions du Réel

Washington DC International Film Festival (Washington)

PO Box 21396, Washington DC 20009, US
Tel:+1-202-724 5613
Fax: +1-202-724 6578
E-mail: FilmfestDC@aol.com
Festival director & programmer: Anthony Gittens

Media Wave International Festival of Visual Arts (Győr)

Mediawave Foundation, H-9028 Győr, Soprani út 45, Hungary
Tel: +36-96-328 888
Fax: +36-96-415 285

Festival director: Hartyándi Jenö
Festival programmer: Bari Ildiko, Kadar Sandor

St Barth Film Festival (St Jean, St. Barthelemy)

410 Wst 24th Street, #16K, New York City, US 10011
Tel: +1-212 989 8004
Fax: +1-212 727 1774
E-mail: jpharris@ineractive.net
Festival directors & programmers: Ellen Lampert-Grèaux & Joshua Harrison
Focus on Caribbean films

Gen Art Film Festival (New York City)

145 W 28th Street, Suite 1101, New York, NY, USA 10001, USA
Tel: +1-212 290 0312
Fax: +1-212 290 0254
E-mail: info@genart.org
Festival director: Tobin Heminway
Festival programmer: Adam Pincus
Competition
Audience Award for Best Feature and Short
Previous winner: *Hands on a Hard Body* (Rob Bindler)

Oslo Animation Festival

PO Box 867, Sentrum, N-0104 Oslo, Norway
Tel: +47 23 119 300
Fax: +47 23 119 310
Festival director: Vibeke Christensen
Managing director: Kristine Kjølleberg
Competition
Grand Prize (£1500)
Previous winner: *Apricots* (Wotta og Uzi Geffenblad)

Philadelphia Festival of World Cinema

International House, 3701 Chestnut Street, Philadelphia, 19104 Pennsylvania, USA
Tel: +1-215-895 6593
Fax: +1-215-895 6562
E-mail: pfwc@ihphilly.org

Website: www.libertynet.org/pfwc
Festival director: Phyllis Kaufman
Festival programmer: Dave Kluft

International Documentary Film Festival Munich

Trogerstrasse 46, D-81675, Munich, Germany
Tel: +49-89-470 3237
Fax: +49-89-470 6611
Festival director & programmer: Gudrun Geyer
Competition
Der Dokumentarfilmpreis (DM 20 000)
Previous winner: *Moment of Impact* (Julia Loktev)

Ankara International Film Festival

Farabi Sokak 29/1, Çankaya, 06690 Ankara, Turkey
Tel: +90 312 468 7745/ 3892
Fax: +90 312 467 7830
Festival director: Mahmut Tali Öngören
Festival programmer: Gökhan Erkiliç
Competition
Best Long Film and Best European Documentary
Previous winner: *Sawdust Tales* (Usta beni öldürsene) Baris Pirhasan

Arizona State University Art Museum Annual Outdoor Film Festival (Tempe, Arizona)

ASU Art Museum, Tenth Street and Mill Avenue, Tempe, AZ 85287-2911
Tel: +1-602 965 2787
Fax: +1-602 965 5254
E-mail: spiak@asu.edu
Website: http://asuam.fa.asu.edu/filmfest/main-htm
Festival director: John Spiak
Festival programmer: Bob Pece
Competition
Two Juror awards and LeBlanc Audience Choice Award

Avignon/New York Film Festival

10 Montée de la Tour, 30400 Villeneuve-les-Avignon, France
Tel: +33-490 25 93 23
Fax: +33-490 25 93 24
Festival director: Jerome Henry Rudes
Tel: +1-212-343 2675/ 355 6100
Fax: +1-212-343 1849
Competition

BAFTA Film Awards

195 Picadilly, London W1V 0LN
Tel: +44-171-734 0022
Fax: +44-171-439 0473
Acting Chief executive: John Chambers
Competition
Bafta Awards
Previous winner: *Shakespeare in Love* (John Madden)

Chicago Latino Film Festival

600 South Michigan Avenue, Chicago, Illinois 60605, USA
Tel: +1-312-431 1330
Fax: +1-312-344 8030
Festival director: Pepe Vargas
Fetival programmer: Carolina Posse
Competition
Audience Award
Previous winner: *Black Tears* (Sonia Herman Doiz)

Cine Latino (Tübingen)

Osterbergstr. 9, Tübingen, Germany 72074
Tel: +49 7071 56960
Fax: +49 7071 56 96 96
E-mail: filmtage tuebingen@t-online.de
Festival director: Paolo Robert de Carvalho

European Cinema Congress (Wiesbaden)

Forum Film Mediengesellschaft m.b.H., Wiesbaden, Germany 65205
Tel: +49-611-723448
Fax: +49-611-723403

E-mail: HDFeV@aol.com.
Managing director: Wolf Verschuer

Grenzland Filmtage (Selb)

Postfach 307, D-95622 Wunsiedel, Germany
Tel:+49-923-2 4770
Fax: +49-923-2 4710
E-mail: festival@grenzland-filmtage.de
Festival director: Adele Tryr, Lena Wilfert

London Lesbian and Gay Film Festival

South Bank, Waterloo, London SE1 8XT, UK
Tel: +44-171-815 1323/815 1324
Fax: +44-171-633 0786
E-mail: jane.ivey@bfi.org.uk
Executive director: Adrian Wootton
Festival programmer: Briony Hanson

Los Angeles Independent Film Festival

5455 Wilshire Blvd., # 1500, Los Angeles, CA, 90036 USA
Tel: +1-323 937 9155
Fax: +1-323 937 7770
Festival director: Robert Faust
Festival programmer: Thomas Ethan

New England Film and Video Festival

1126 Boylston St, #201, Boston MA 02215, USA
Tel: +1-617 536 1540
Fax: +1-617 536 3576
E-mail: devon@bfvf.org
Festival director & programmer: Devon Demonte
Competition
Best of Festival (US$1,200)
Previous winner: *Floating* (William roth)

North West Film Festival Southport

33 Barrington Road, Altrincham, Cheshire WA14 1HZ, UK
Tel: I44-161-929 1423
Fax: +44-161-929 1067

Festival director: Gil Lane-Young
Festival programmer: Harry Nadler
Competition
Previous winner: *Wrestling Ernest Hemingway*

Palm Beach International Film Festival

1555 Palm Beach Lakes Blvd., 0403 West Palm Beach, Florida, 33 401, USA
Tel: +1-561 233 1044
Fax: +1-561 683 6655
Festival director: Mark Diamond

San Francisco International Film Festival

1521 Eddy Street, San Francisco, CA 94115, US
Tel: +1-415-929 5000
Fax: +1-415-921 5032
E-mail: stiff@stiff.org
Festival director: Peter Scarlett
Festival programmers: Brian Gordon, Rachel Rosen, Doug Jones,
Competition
Golden Gate Awards for documentaries, shorts, animation, experimental works and TV production

Schermi d'amore, Sentimental and Mélo Film Festival (Verona)

Comune di Verona, Corso Porta Borsari 17, 37121 Verona, Italy
Tel: +39-45 800 5348
Fax: +39-45 803 6205
E-mail: settimana.cinematografica@comune.verona.it
Festival director: Michele Placido
Festival programmer: Paolo Romano
Competition
Best Film
Previous winner: *Fire* (Depa Meta)

Silver Images Film Festival (Chicago)

Terra Nova Films, 9848 S. Winchester Ave., Chicago, IL 60643
Tel: +1-773 881 6940

Fax: +1-773 881 3368

Festival director & programmer: Martha Foster

Singapore International Film Festival

29A Keong Saik Road, Singapore, Singapore 089136

Tel: +65-738 7567

Fax: +65-738 7578

E-mail: filmfest@pacific.net.sg

Festival director: Teo Swee Leng

Festival programmer: Philip Cheah

Competition (for Asian features only)

Best Asian Feature Film

Previous winner: *Children of the Heaven* (Majid Majidi)Iran

Taos Talking Picture Festival

216M North Pueblo Road, #216, Taos, NM 87571, USA

Tel: +1-505 751 0637

Fax: +1-505 751 7385

E-mail: ttpix@taosnet.com

Website: www.taosnet.com/ttpix/

Executive director: Morten Nilssen

Festival programmer: Kelly Clement

Competition

The Taos Land Grant Award

Previous winner: *Smoke Signals* (Chris Eyre)

Trento International Festival of Mountain & Exploration Films

Via S. Croce 67, 38100 Trento, Italy

Tel: +39 0461 98 61 20

Fax: +39 0461 23 18 32

Festival director: Antanio Ciembran

Competition

Gran Premio

Udine Incontri Cinema

Via Marco Volpe 45/7 33100 Udine, Italy

Tel: +39 o432 522 717

Fax: +39 0432 601 421

E-mail: cecudine@tin.it

Festival director: Sabrina Baracetti

Festival programmers: Derek Elley,

Lorenzo Codelli

USA Film Festival (Dallas)

6116 N. Central Expwy, Suite 105, Dallas, 75206, Texas, USA

Tel: +1-214-821 6300

Fax: +1-214-821 6364

Website: http://www.usafilmfestival.com

Festival director: Ann Alexander

Festival programmer: Alonso Duralde

Competition (only for short films)

National Short Film Video Competition - Grand Prize ($1000)

Previous winner: *Lily & Jim* (Don Hertefeldt)

Vue d'Afrique (Montreal)

Les Journées du Cinema Africain et Creole, 67 rue Ste. Catherine Ouest, 5eme étage, Montreal Quebec, Canada H2X 1Z7

Tel: +1-514 284 3322

Fax: +1-514 845 0631

Festival director: Gerard Lechene

Competition

Previous winner: *Bent familia* (Nouri Bouzid)

Showlight 2001

An International Colloquium on Entertainment Lighting (every four years) 38 St Leonards Road, Eastbourne, East Sussex BN21 3UT, UK

Tel: +44-1323-642 639

Fax: +44-1323-646 905

Contact: Ruth Rossington

Cambridge Film Festival

Cambridge Arts Cinema, 8 Market Passage, Cambridge CB2 3PF, UK

Tel: +44-1223-578 944

Fax: +44-1223-578 929

E-mail: festival@cambarts.co.uk

Festival co-directors and programmers: Tony Jones & Sarley Macdonald

Cartoons on the Bay (Amalfi)

RAI Trade, Via Umberto Novaro 18, 00195 Rome, Italy

Tel: +39-06 3749 8315

Fax: +39-06 3735 3521

E-mail: cartoonsbay@raitrade.it
Website: www.raitrade.rai.it/cartoonsbay
Festival director: Alfio Basiancich
Competition
Pulcinella Awards

Festival of French Cinema

Tel Aviv Cinematheque, 2 Sprintzak Street,
Tel Aviv, Israel.
Tel: (972 3) 691 7181.
Fax: (972 3) 696 2841.

May

Int'l Television Festival "Golden Prague"

ITF "Golden Prague", Kavci Hory, 140 70,
Prague 4, Czech Republic
Tel: +420 2 6113 4028/ 4405/ 4153/ 4133
Fax: +420 2 6121 2891
E-mail: ruzena.jezkova@czech-tv.cz
Website: http://www.czech-tv.cz
Festival director: Jiri Vejvoda
Competition
Golden Prague (DM 10,000)

FIFREC (International Film and Student Directors Festival) – (Cannes)

FIFREC, BP 7144, 30913, Nimes Cedex,
France
Tel: +33-472 02 20 36
Fax: +33-472 0220 36
Festival director: Jean Sondel
Competition
Crocodil d'or

International Short Film Festival Oberhausen4–9 May 2000

Grillostrasse 34, D-46045 Oberhausen,
Germany
Tel: +49-208-825 2652
Fax: +49-208-825 5413
E-mail: info@kurzfilmtage.de
Festival director: Lars Henrik Gass
Festival programmer: selection committee

Competition & market
Grosser Preis der Stadt Oberhausen (DM 10 000)
Previous winner: *Alone. Life Wastes Andy Hardy* (Martin Arnold)

European Media Art Festival (Osnabrück)

Postfach 1861, 49008 Osnabrück, Germany
Tel: +49 541 216 58
Fax: +49 541 283 27
Festival director: Alfred Rotert

Short Film Weekend (Augsburg)

Schroeckstr. 8, Augsburg, Germany, 86152
Tel: +49-821 349 1060
Fax: +49-821 349 5218
Festival director: Erwin Schletterer
Festival programmer: as above
Competition

Toronto Jewish Film Festival

33 Prince Arthur Ave., 2nd Floor, Toronto,
Canada M5R 1B2
Tel: +1-416 324 8226
Fax: +1-416 324 8668
E-mail: tjff@interlog.com
Festival producer: Helen Zukerman
Festival programer: Shlomo Schwartzberg

Cannes Film Festival

99 Boulevard Malesherbes, 75008 Paris,
France
Tel: +33-1-45 61 66 00
Fax: +33-1-45 61 97 60
E-mail: festival@cannes.bull.net
Festival director: Pierre Viot
Festival programmer: Gilles Jacob
Market and Competition
Palme d'Or
Previous winner: *Rosetta* (Jean-Pierre Dardenne

Seattle International Film Festival

801 East Pine Street, Seattle, WA 98122, USA
Tel: +1-206-464 5830

Fax: +1-206-264 7919
E-mail: mail@seattlefilm.com
Website: www.seatllefilm.com
Festival director: Darryl Macdonald
Festival programmer: Darryl Macdonald,
Carl Spence
Competition
American Independent Award ($70 000 in
goods & services)
Previous winner: *Southie* (John Shea)

Cable & Satellite (London)
Oriel House, 26 The Quadrant, Richmond-
Upon-Thames, Surrey, TW9 1DL, UK
Tel: +44-181 910 7918
Fax: +44-181 910 7866
Contact: Sonya Gent

Int'l Festival of Animation & Computer Graphics "Anigraph" (Moscow)
3 Budaiskaya St., Moscow 129128 Russia
Tel: 7 095 187 1942/187 3498
Fax: 7 095 187 7560
Festival director: Elena Lavrenkova

Inside Out Lesbian and Gay Film & Video (Toronto)
401 Richmond St W, suite 456, Toronto,
Ontario, M5V, 3A8, Canada
Tel: +1-416 977 6847
Fax: +1-416 977 8025
Festival director: Ellen Flanders
Competition
Bulloch Award ($1500)
Previous winner: The Grace of God (Derald
L'Ecuyer)

National Educational Media Network (Oakland)
655 13th Street, Oakland, CA 94612-1222,
USA
Tel: +1-510-465 6885
Fax: +1-510-465 2835
E-mail: NEMN@AOL.COM
Festival director: Jean Paul Petraud

Festival programmer: as above
Market and competition
Gold Apple

Workshop for Young Filmmakers (Wiesbaden)
Bundesverband Jugend & Film c.v.,
Kennedyallee 105a, Frankfurt am Main,
Germany D-60596
Tel: +49 69 631 2723
Fax: +49 69 631 2922
Festival director: Berndt Güntzel-Linghet

Golden Rose of Montreux
c/o Television Suisse Romande, Quai Ernest-
Ansermet 20/CP, 234/1211 Geneva 8,
Switzerland
Tel: +41-22-708 8599
Fax: +41-22-781 5249
E-mail: gabrielle.bucher@tsr.ch
Festival director: Pierre Grandjean
Competition
Golden Rose Award
Previous winner: Yo Yo Ma Inspired by Bach:
Six Gestures (Rhombus CDN)

27th Algarve International Film Festival
Festival Internacional de Cinema do Algarve,
PO Box 8091, 1801 Lisbon.-Codex, Portugal,
Tel: +351-1 851 3615
Fax: +351-1 852 1150
E-mail: algarvefilmfest@mail.telepac.pt
Website: http://www.algarvefilmfest.com
Festival director: Carlos Manuel
Festival programmer: José Barbosa, Miguel
Valverde
Competition
The Festival Big Prize "Cidade de Portimão"
(Trophy and 500,000 Portuguese Escudos)

Children's World–International Festival of Films for Children and Teenagers (Varna)
31 Liuben Karavelov Str.,
Sofia 1000, Bulgaria
Tel: +359 2 665 564

Directory

Fax: +359 2 802 391
Festival director & programmer: Alexander Grozev
Competition
Ilko Cat Award
Previous winner: *Some Birds Can't Fly* (Petar Lalovich, Yugoslavia)

International Short Film Festival – Kraków

Ul Pychowicka 7, 30-364 Kraków, Poland
Tel: +48-12-267 2340
Fax: +48-12-267 1552
Festival director: Janusz Solarz
Festival programmer: Tadeusz Lubelsi
Market & Competition
Grand Prix - The Golden Dragon Award (12000PLN)
Previous winner: *Grieszny Czielowiek* (Yuri Shiller)

Toronto Worldwide Short Film Festival

60 Atlantic Ave, Suite 110, Toronto, Ontario, M6K 1X9, Canada
Tel: +1-416 535 8506
Fax: +1-416 535 8342
Festival director: Brenda Sherwood
Festival programmer: as above
Market & Competition
Cammy award

Int'l Film Fest Cinematograph (Innsbruck)

CineVision, c/o Cinematograph, Museumstrasse 31, Innsbruck, Austria 6020
Tel: +43-664 120 7458
Fax: +43-512-581762
E-mail: ffi.cinematograph@tirolkultur.at
Website: www.tirolkultur.at/cinema
Festival director: Helmut Groschup
Festival programmer: Helmut Groschup, Verena Teissl
Tiroler Filmpreis (5,000 Euro)
Previous winner: *Kleines Tropikana* (Daniel Diaz torres, Cuba)

Prix Jeunesse International (Munich)

c/o Bayerischer Rundfunk, D-80300 Munich, Germany
Tel: +49-89 59002058
Fax: +49-89 59003053
E-mail: prixjeunesse@papyrus.de
Contact: Ursula von Zallinger
Competition
Prix Jeunesse International

Los Angeles Asian Pacific American Film and Video Festival

Visual Communications, 263 South LA Street, Suite 307, Los Angeles, CA 90012, USA
Tel: +1-213 680 4462
Fax: +1-213-687 4848
E-mail: viscom@vc.apanet.org
Website: http://vc.apanet.org~viscom/
Festival director: Abraham Ferrer

Malaga Spanish Film Festival

Ramos Marin 2-2c, 29012 Málaga, Spain
Tel: +34 95 222 8242
Fax: +34 95 222 7760
Festival director: Salomon Castiel
Competition

June

Docfest (New York International Documentary Festival)

159 Maiden Lane, New York, NY, US 10038
Tel: +1-212 668 1100
Fax: +1-212 943 6396
E-mail: dockfest@aol.com
Website: www.docfest.org
Festival director: Gary Pollard

Emden International Film Festival

Postfach 2343, 26703 Emden, Germany
Tel: +49 4921 915 533/35
Fax: +49 4921 915 591

Festival director: Rolf Eckard, Thorsten Hecht

Festival programmer: Rolf Eckard, Thorsten Hecht

Competition for German speaking films and north-west European feature films

Emden Film Award (Dm 15,000)

Previous winner: *Left Luggage* (Jeroen Krabbe)

FICA – International Festival of Environmental Cinema and Video

Praça Cívica, n. 02, Goiânia Go Brazil 74003-010

Competition

Hudson Valley Film Festival (Poughkeepsie & Rhinebeck)

40 Garden Street, Poughkeepsie, NY, 12601, USA

Tel: +1-914 473 0318

Fax: +1-914 473 0082

E-mail: hvfo@vh.net

Festival director: Aslihan Coker

International and Open Russian Film Festivals Kinotavr (Sochi)

35 Arbat, Moscow 121835, Russia

Tel: 7 095 248 0911/248 9187

Fax: 7 095 248 0966

Festival director: Larisa Blank

Festival programmer: Michael Ufhaklv

Shots in the Dark, Mystery & Thriller Festival (Nottingham)

Broadway Media Centre, 14 Broad Street, Nottingham, England, NG1 3AL

Tel: +44-115-952 6600

Fax: +44-115-952 6622

E-mail: broadway@bwymedia.demon.co.uk

Troia International Film Festival (Setúbal)

Forum Luisa Todi, Av Luisa Todi 65, 2900 Setúbal, Portugal

Tel: +351-65-525 908

Fax: +351-65-525 681

Festival director: Mário Ventura

Festival programmer: Fernanda Silva

Competition

Golden Dolphin

Previous winner: *The Bandit* (Yavuz Turzul)

IV Festival of European Co-productions (Sofia)

Feature films only

2-A Dondukov Blvd., Sofia 1000, Bulgaria

Tel: +359 2 987 4096

Fax: +359 2 873 626

E-mail: nfc@mail.bol.bg

Festival director: Dimitar Dereliev

Festival programmer: Irina Kanousheva, Gergana Dakovska

Adriaticocinema (Bellaria, Rimini, Catolica)

Via Gambalunga 27, 47900 Rimini, Italy

Tel: +39-0541-226 27/ 26 399/ 52 038

Fax: +39-0541-24 227

Festival director: Marco Bellochio

Organising director: Gianfranco Miro Gori

International competition only for film schools

Huesca Film Festival

Avda. Parque, 1 piso, 22002 Huesca, Spain

Tel: +34-974-212582

Fax: +34-974-210065

E-mail: huescafest@fsai.es

Festival director: José María Escriche

Competition

Danzante de oro (1.000.000 pesetas)

Previous winner: *The Mirror of the Sky* (Carlos Salse)

Sydney Film Festival

PO Box 950, Glebe, NSW 2037, Sydney, Australia

Tel: +61-2-9660 3844

Fax: +61-2-9692 8793

E-mail: info@sydfilm-fest.com.au

Festival director & programmer: Gayle Lake

Competition
Dendy Awards for Australian Short Films
(A$2.500 for each award)

Annecy International Animated Film Festival

6 Avenue des Iles, b.p. 399, 74013 Annecy
Cedex, France
Tel: +33 4 50 10 09 00
Fax: +33 4 50 10 09 70
Website: www.annecy.org
Festival director: Jean-Luc Xiberraf
Festival programmer: the same
Competition
Grand Prix for best animated feature

Balticum Film and TV Festival (Gudhjem, Rønne, Svaneke)

Skippergade 8, Svaneke, DK- 3940 Denmark
Tel: +45-70 202002
Fax: +45-70202001
E-mail: balticmediacentre@bmc.dk
Website: www.bmc.dk
Festival director: Bent Nørby Bonde
Festival programmer: Karolina Lidin
Competition
Balticum Documentary Award
Previous winner: *Pavel and Layla* (Victor Kossakovsky)

The Princes' Award

The Prince's Award Foundation,
c/o European Environment Agency, Kongens
Nytorv 6, DK-1050 Copenhagen K, Denmark
Tel: +45-33 36 7100/7121
Fax: +45-33 36 7199
E-mail: princes.award@eea.dk
Website: http://www.eea.dk/events/pa97
Director of the Awards: Tage Mikkelsen
A prize for the producers of the best CD-ROM,
video and film on the environment of Europe

Filmfest Ludwigsburg/Stuttgart 1999

Filmakademie Baden-Württemberg, Mathildenstr.
20, D-1638 Ludwigsburg, Germany

Tel: +49-7141 969 361/364/360
Fax: +49-7141 969 363
E-mail: filmfest@filmakademie.de
Website: www.filmakademie.de/filmfest
Competition
Various awards for various sections

Mediterranean Film Festival (Tübingen)

Osterbergstr. 9, Tübingen, Germany 72074
Tel: +49 7071 56960
Fax: +49 7071 56 96 96
E-mail: filmtage. tuebingen@t-online.de
Festival director: Dieter Betz

Potsdam Film Fest

Dianastr. 21, 14482 Potsdam, Germany
Tel: +49 30 283 6530
Fax: +49 30 283 6533
Festival director: Heidrun Podazus
Festival programmer: festival team

Chicago Alt.film Fest

3430 N. Lake Shore Drive, suite 19N,
chicago, Il, USA 60657
Tel: +1-773 525 4559
Fax: +1-773 327 8669
E-mail: chialtfilm@aol.com
Festival director & programmer: Dennis
Neal Vaughn
Competition
Absolut Best Feature Film ($US 2000)
Previous winner: *Liar's Poker* (Jeff Santo)

U.S. International Film and Video Festival (Chicago)

841 North Addison Avenue, Elmhurst, Illinois
60126-1291
Tel: +1-630-834 7773
Fax: +1-630-834 5565
Festival director: J.W. Anderson
Competition
Gold Camera & Silver Screen Awards
Previous winner: *The Messengers of the God's Butterflies*

International Bochum Videofestival (Bochum)

Bochumer Videofestival, ASTA Kulturreferat der Ruhr-Universität, Universitätstr. 150, 44801 Bochum, Germany
Tel: +49 234 700 6712
Fax: +49 234 70 16 23
Festival director: Katarine Keller, Jessica Manscheten, Seryosha Vimmer
Competition

Montreux 1997 International Television Symposium

PO Box 1451, Rue du Théâtre 5, CH-1820 Montreux, Switzerland
Tel: +41-21 963 3220
Fax: +41-21 963 8851
E-mail: message@symposia.ch

Cologne Conference – Int'l TV & Film Festival

Im Mediapark 5b, 50670 Köln, Germany
Tel: +49-221-454 3280
Fax: +49-221-454 3289
E-mail: info@cologne-conference.de
Festival director: Lutz Hachmeister
Festival programmer: Martina Richter
Competition
Producer-Award, Casting-Award, TV-Spiel Film Award (10.000 DM each)

Fantafestival (Rome)

Viale Gioachino Rossini 9, Rome, 00198 Italy
Tel: +39-06 807 6999
Fax: +39-06 807 7199
Festival directors: Adriano Pintaldi & Alberto Ravagioli
Festival programmer: Loris Curci
Competition
Gran Premio FantaFestival
Previous winner: *Perdita Durango* (Alex de la Iglesia)

Florida Film Festival (Maitland)

Enzian Theater, 1300 S. Orlando Avenue Maitland, FL 32751, USA
Tel: +1-407 629 1088 x 222

Fax: +1-407 629 6870
E-mail: filmfest@gate.net
President: Sigrid Tiedtke
Executive director: Melanie Gasper
Festival programmer: Mathew Curtis
Competition
Grand Jury Prize
Previous winner: *The Headhunter's Sister* (Scott Saunders)

Human Rights Watch International Film Festival (New York City)

350 Fifth Avenue, 34th St., New York, NY, 10118 USA
Tel: +1-212-216 1263
Fax: +1-212-736 1300
E-mail: andersj@hrw.org
Festival director: Bruni Burres
Festival programmer: Bruni Burres, John Anderson
Competition
Nestor Almendros Award ($US 5000)
Previous winner: An *Ordinary President* (Yuri Khashchevatsky)

Banff TV Festival

1516 Railway Avenue, Canmore, Alberta, Canada, T1W 1P6
Tel: +1-403-678 9260
Fax: +1-403-678 9269
E-mail: info@banfftvfest.com
Website: www.banfftvfest.com
Festival director: Pat Ferns
Festival programmer: Jerry Ezekiel
Competition
The Banff Rockie
Previous winner: *Amongst Women* (Parallel Films for BBC Northern Ireland) (winner of 1999)

Marseille – Documentary Film Festival

3 Square Stalingrad, 13001, Marseille, France
Tel: +33-495 04 44 90
Fax: +33-495 04 44 91
Festival director: Michel Tregan

Competition
Grand Prix (FF50,000)
Previous winner: *Public Housing* (Frederic Wiseman)

National Cable TV Association 47th Annual Convention & Int'l Exposition (Chicago)

NCTA Convention/Exposition Headquarters c/o Dobson & Associates, Ltd., 1225 19th Street, NW, Suite 310, Washington, DC 20036 USA
Tel: +1-202-775 3606
Fax: +1-202 775 1028

International Hamburg Short Film Festival

Kurtzfilmagentur, D-22765 Hamburg, Germany
Tel: +49-40-398 26 122
Fax: +49-40 398 26 123
Festival director: Astrid Kühl
Competition
Hamburg Short Film Prize (5000 DM)
Previous winner: *De Zone* (Ben van Lieshout, Netherlands) (winner 1999)

Norwegian Short Film Festival (Grimstad)

Filmens Hus, Dronningens Gate 16, N-0152 Oslo, Norway
Tel: +47 22 47 46 46
Fax: +47 22 47 46 90
Website: http://www.nfi.no/krtf/welcome.html
Festival director: Torunn Nyen
Competition (Norwegian films only)
Previous winner: *Benny* (Pål Jackman)

Pesaro Film Festival

Via Villafranca 20, 00185 Rome, Italy
Tel: +39-06-445 66 43/49 11 56
Fax: +39-06-491 163
E-mail: pesarofilmfest@mclink.it
Festival director & programmer: Andrea Martini

Sunny Side of the Doc (Marseille)

3 Square Stalingrad, 13001 Marseille, France
Tel: +33-49 50 4 44 80
Fax: +33-491 84 38 34
E-mail: 100560.1511@compuserve.com
Market director: Olivier Masson
Market

Midnight Sun Film Festival (Sodankylä)

Malminkatu 36, 00100 Helsinki, Finland
Tel: +358-9-685 2242
Fax: +358-9-694 5560
Festival director: Peter von Bagh
Festival programmer: Göran Michelsson

"Message to Man" Int'l Documentary, Short & Animated Film Festival

Karavannaya 12, Saint-Petersburg, Russia 191011
Tel: +7-812 235 2660/ 230 2200
Fax: +7-812 235 2660/ 235 3995
Festival director: Mikhail Litviakov
Festival programmer: Vicotr Semeneyk
Competition
Golden Centaur Award (US$ 5000)
Previous winner: *Bread Day* (Sergei Dvordsevog)

San Francisco Lesbian and Gay Film Festival

346 Ninth Street, San Francisco, CA 94103, USA
Tel: +1-415 703 8650
Fax: +1-415 861 1404
E-mail: info@frameline.org
Festival director: Michael Lumpkin
Festival programmer: Jennifer Morris
Competition
Audience award
Previous winner: *Lilies*

Art Film Festival (Trencianske Teplice)

Konventna 8, Bratislava, Slovak Republic, 81103
Tel: (421 7) 5441 9479/81
Fax: (42 17) 5441 1679
E-mail: festival@artfilm.sk
Festival director: Peter Hledik
Festival programmer: Vladimir Stric
Market & Competition
Golden Key Award (US$ 3,000)
Previous winner: *Buttoners* (Petr Zelenka)

Bradford Animation Festival (BAF!)

National Museum of Photography, Film & TV, Pictureville, Bradford, BD1 1NQ, UK
Tel: +44-1274 725 347
Fax: +44-1274 723 155
E-mail: c.sawhney@nmsei.ac.uk or
c.fell@nmsi.ac.uk
Festival programmer: Bill Lawrence
Competition

PILOTS (Programme for the International Launch of Television Series Workshops) (Sitges)

Diputació 279, E-08007 Barcelona, Spain
Tel: +34-93-487 3773
Fax: +34-93- 4873952
Festival director: Pera Fages

Cinema Expo International (Amsterdam)

244 West 49th Street #200, New York 10019, USA
Tel: +1-212-246 6460
Fax: +1-212-265 6428
E-mail: sunshine@maestro.com
Website: www.sunshineworldwide.com
Contact person: Jun Margolis

International Advertising Film Festival (Cannes)

Woolverstone House, 61/62 Berners Street, London W1P 3AE
Tel: +44-171-636 6122
Fax: +44-171-636 6086
Website: http:/www.caneslions.com
Festival president: Roger Hatchuel
Market & Competition
Lions Award
Previous winner: *Rolo- Nestle Netherlands*

Festival of Festivals

10 Kamennoostrovsky ave, St Petersburg, 197101, Russia
Tel: +7-812-237 0304
Fax: +7-812-237 0304/ 394 5870
Festival director: Alexander Mamontov
Market & Competition
Grand-Prix
Previous winners: *Of Freaks and Men (Alexei Balabanov)*

French-American Film Workshop (New York /Avignon)

10 Montée de la Tour, 30400 Villeneuve-les-Avignon, France
Tel: +33-490 25 93 23
Fax: +33-490 25 93 24
Festival director: Jerome Henry Rudes
Tel: +1-212-343 2675/ 355 6100
Fax: +1-212-343 1849
Competition
21 Century Film-maker ($US 70,000)

Hong Kong International Film Market

38th Floor, Office Tower Convention Plaza, 1 Harbour Road, Wanchai, Hong Kong
Tel: +852 2584 4333
Fax: +852 2824 0249
E-mail: ernest.chan@tdc.org.hk
Festival director: Jenny Koo
Market

Festival of Film Schools (Munich)

Kaiser St. 39, Munich 80801, Germany
Tel: +49 89 381 9040
Fax: +49 89 381 90426
Festival director: Prof. Wolfgang Längsfeld
Competition: 6 material prizes

La Rochelle International Film Festival

16 rue Saint Sabin, 75011 Paris, France
Tel: +33-1-48 06 16 66
Fax: +33-1-48 06 15 40
E-mail: festival.de.la.rochelle@wanadoo.fr
Festival director: Jean-Loup Passek
Festival programmer: Sylvie Pras-Pruneengler
Market

Showbiz Expo West (Los Angeles)

383 Main Ave, Norwalk, CA 06851, US
Tel: +1-203 840 5945
Fax: +1-203 840 9945
E-mail: ibogardus@reedexpo.com
Festival director: Dave Bonaparte

Filmfest München

Internationale München Filmwochen GmbH,
Kaiserstraße 39, D-80801 Munich, Germany
Tel: +49-89 38 19 040
Fax: +49-89 38 19 04 26
E-mail: festivalleitung@filmfest-muenchen.de
Website: www.filmfest-muenchen.de
Festival director: Eberhard Hauff
There is no competition but special awards
are given: Top TV Award, Media Net Award

International Animation Festival (Cardiff)

18 Broadwick Street, London, UK, W1V 1FG
Tel: +44-171-494 0506
Fax: +44-171-494 0807
Festival director: Jane Williams

International Festival of Animated Film, Zagreb

Koncertna Direkcija Zagreb, Animafest,
41000 Zagreb, Kneza Mislava 18, Croatia
Tel: +385 1 461 1709
Fax: +385 1 461 1808/ 807
E-mail: kdz@zg.Tel.hr
Festival director: Margit Antauer
Artistic director: Josko Marusic

Competition
Grand Prix (18,000 Kunas)
Previous winner: *The Mermaid* (Alexandar Petrov)

European TV Sports Conference (London)

Kagan Seminars Int'l, 524 Fulham Rd,
London SW6 5NR, UK
Tel: +44-171 371 8880
Fax: +44-171 371 8715
Contact person: Alex Guthrie

Peniscola International Comedy Festival

Plaza Constitucion s/n, 12598 Pensicola,
Spain
Tel: +34-964 474 901
Fax: +34-964 481 521

Women's International Film Festival (Barcelona)

València 248 prel. 1, Barcelona, 08007 Spain
Tel: +34-93 216 0004
Fax: +34-93 215 3519
E-mail: drac.info@cambrabcn.es
Festival directors & programmers: Marya
Selva, Anna Solà

July

Age d'or Prize/Prizes for the distribution of quality films in Belgium (Cinedecouverts) (Brussels)

Royal Film Archive, Ravenstein st. 23, B-1000
Brussels, Belgium
Tel: +32-2-507 8370
Fax: +32-2-513 1272
Festival director: Gabrielle Claes
Festival programmer: as above
Competition
The Age d'or prize (500.000 BF)
Previous winner: *Xia Wu* (Jia Zhang Ke)

The Film Festival of Dhow Countries (Zanzibar)

Karume House, PO Box 3032, Zanzibar, Tanzania
Tel/Fax: +255-54 233 135
E-mail: ziff@zanzibar.org/ziff
Website: www.zanzibar.org/ziff
Festival director: Mark Leveri
Festival programmer: Yusuf Mahmoud
Managing director: Zulfikar Hirji
Competition
Golden Dhow Award (US$5000)

Karlovy Vary International Film Festival

Panska 1, 110 00 Prague 1, Czech Republic
Tel: +420-2-24 23 54 48
Fax: +420-2-24 23 3408
E-mail: iffkv@tlp.cz
Festival president: Jiri Bartoska
Festival programmer: Eva Zaoralova
Competition
Grand Prix Crystal Globe ($US 20,000)
Previous winner: *Le Coeur au poing*
(Charles Binamé)

Filmvideo 2000 – 51st International Short Film Festival (Montecatini)

Filmvideo c/o Fondazione Novaro, Corso Aurelio Saffi 9/11, 16128 Genova, Italy
Tel: +39 0242 23 704 and +39 010 553 1281
Fax: +39 010 553 1281
E-mail: novaro@tin.it
Festival director: Claudio Berieri, Ernesto G. Laura
President and organising director: Giacomo Croce
Competition & market
Golden Heron Award ($2,500)
Previous winner: *Ketchup*
(Ivan Goldschmidt, Manu Coeman, Belgium)

Mostra Internazionale del Cinema Libero/Il Cinema Ritrovato

(Festival of film restoration from the archives from all over the world)
Via Galliera 8, I-40121 Bologna, Italia
Tel: +39-051-237 088
Fax: +39-051-261 680
E-mail: cinaffcr@comune.bologna.it
Festival director: Gianluca Farinelli

International Film Festival for Children & Young People (Montevideo)

Lorenzo Carnelli 1311, 11200 Montevideo, Uruguay
Tel: +598-2 408 2460/ 409 5795
Fax: +598-2 409 4572
E-mail: cinemuy@chasque.apc.org
Festival director & programmer: Ricardo Casas
Competition
Gury Award
Previous winner: *Eno nakano bokuno mura*
(Yoichi Higashi)

Galway Film Fleadh

Cluain Mhuire, Monivea Road, Galway, Ireland
Tel: +353 91 751655
Fax: +353 91 770746
E-mail: gafleadh@iol.ie
Festival director: Fiona Kilkelly
Programme director: Pat Collins
Market & Competition
Best first feature
Previous winner: *This Is My Father* (Paul Quinn)

International Short Film Festival of Vila do Conde

Auditorio Municipal - Praga da Republica, 4480 Vila do Conde, Portugal
Tel: +351-52-641 644
Fax: +351-52-642871
Festival directors and programmers: Miguel Dias, Roi Maia, Mario Micaelo, Dario Oliveira, Nuno Rodrigues
Market and competition
Three Major awards for animation, documentary, fiction

Great Prize City of Vila do Conde (500,000 pte each)
Previous winner: *My Country* (Milos Radovic, Yugoslavia)

Outdoor Short Film Festival (Grenoble)

4 rue Hector Berlioz, Grenoble 38000, France
Tel: +33-476 544 351
Fax: +33-476 5124 43
Festival director & programmer: Michel Warren
Competition
Grand Prix (15 000 FF)
Previous winner: *A Cause d'Olivia* (Eric Assous) (winner 1999)

Alfas Del Pi (L'Alfas Del Pi)

Casa de Cultura. Cami de la Mar s/n, L'Alfas Del Pi, 03580 Spain
Tel: +34-96 588 9423
Fax: +34-96 588 9453
E-mail: jsantonja@readysoft.es
Website: www.festival-alfaz.com
Festival director: Juan Luis Iborra
Festival programmer: Javier Pascual
Competition
Faro de Plata Award (5,000,000 ptas)
Previous winner: *Rewind* (Nicolás Muõz)

Hometown Video Festival

The Alliance for Community Media, 666 11th Street, NW #806, Washington, DC 20001, USA
Tel: +1-202 393 2650
Fax: +1-202 393 2653.
Festival director: Steve Fortriede

Jerusalem Film Festival

c/o Jerusalem Cinematheque, Derech Hebron, Jerusalem 91083, Israel
Tel: +972-2-672 4131/ 671 5117
Fax: +972-2-673 3076
E-mail: festival@jer-cin.org.il and judyl@jer-cin.org.il

Festival director: Lia van Leer
Festival programmer: Lia van Leer and Avinoam Harpak
Competition
Jewish Experience Award
Previous winner: *La Vita è Bella* (Roberto Benigni)

Auckland International Film Festival

PO Box 9544, Wellington, 6001 New Zealand
Tel: +64-4-385 0162
Fax: +64-4-801 7304
E-mail: enzedff@actrix.gen.nz
Festival director: Bill Gosden
Festival programmer: Bill Gosden & Sandra Reid

5th Cairo Festival for Radio & TV Programmes

Cornish El Nile TV Building, Cairo, Egypt, 11515
Tel: +202 578 9585/574 6841
Fax: +202 773 441/ 578 2295
Festival director: Abdel Rahman-Hafez
Festival programmer: Hamdi Al Konaiesy

San Francisco Jewish Film Festival

346 Ninth St, San Francisco, CA 94103, USA
Tel: +1-415 621 0556
Fax: +1-510 548 0536
E-mail: jewishfilm@aol.com
Festival director: Janis Plotkin
Festival programmer: Janis Plotkin, Samuel Ball

28th Wellington Film Festival

PO Box 9544, Wellington 6001, New Zealand
Tel: +64-4-385 0162
Fax: +64-4-801 7304
E-mail: enzedff@actrix.gen.nz
Festival director: Bill Gosden
Festival programmer: Bill Gosden & Sandra Reid

Puchon International Fantastic Film Festival

2FI, Boksagol Cultural Center, 394-2 Sang 1-dong, Wonmi-gu, Puchon, Kyonggi-Do 420-031, Korea
Tel: +82-32 3456 313/4
Fax: +82 32 3456 315
Website: www.pifan.or.kr

Giffoni Film Festival

Piazza Umberto 1, 84095 Giffoni Valle Piana, Salerno Italy
Tel: +39-089-868 544
Fax: +39-089-866 111
E-mail: gilfonif@giffoniff.it
Festival director: Claudio Gubitosi
Festival programmer: Claudio Gubitosi
Competition
Silver Griphon Award
Previous winner: *The Mighty* (Peter Chelsom)

Moscow International Film Festival

Khokhlovski Pereulok 10/1, Moscow 109028, Russia
Tel: +7-095-917 2486/ 0944
Fax: +7-095-916 0107
Festival director: Renat Davletiarov
Festival programmer: Kiril Razlogov
Competition
Statuette of Saint George
Previous winner: *Marvin's Room* (Jerry Zaks)

Miami Gay & Lesbian Film Festival

1521 Alton Road, # 147, Miami Beach, FL 33139
Tel: +1-305 534 99 24
Fax: +1-305 535 2377
Contact: Lisa B. Palley

Stony Brook Film Festival (New York)

Staller Center for the Arts, Room 2032, Univeristy at Stony Brook, Stony Brook NY 11794-5425
Tel: +1-516 632 7235
E-mail: festival@stallercenter.com

Melbourne Intl. Film Festival

1st Floor, 207 Johnston Street, Fitzroy, Melbourne, Australia 3065
Tel: +61-3-9417 2011
Fax: +61-3-9417 3804
E-mail: miff@netspace.net.au
Festival director: Sandra Sdraulig
Festival programmer: Brett Woodward
Competition (short films only)
Grand Prix for best short film (A$5000)
Previous winner: *At Sea* (Penny Fowler-Smith)

Wine Country Film Festival

Box 303, Glen Ellen, CA 95442, US
Tel: +1-707-996 2536
Fax: +1-707-996 6964
E-mail: wcfilmfest@aol.com
Festival director: Stephen Ashton
Festival programmer: as above
Competition
Best Feature Award, Best Short Film, David Wolper Documentary Award

Fant-Asia Festival (Montreal, Toronto)

300 Léo Pariseau street, 15th floor, Montreal, Quebec H2W 2P3 Canada
Tel: +1-514 982 0020
Fax: +1-514 982 0796
E-mail: global@videotron.ca
Festival director: Pierre Corbeil
Festival programmer: Julien Fonfrede, Martin Sauvageau, Mitch Davis, André Dubois

International Film Festival (Palic)

Otvoreni Univerzitet, Trg Cara Jovana Nenada 15, 24000 Subotica, Yugoslavia
Tel: +381-24 554 726
Fax: +381-24 553 116
E-mail: opensu@fodns.openet.org
Festival director: Radoslav Zelenovic

Festival programmer: Dinko Tucakovic
Competition
Alexandar Lifka Award
Previous winner: *Full Moon* (Karen Sahnazarov)

Monitor Awards (New York)

2230 Gallows Road, Suite 310, Dunn Loring, VA 22027, USA
Tel: +1-703 319 0800
Fax: +1-703 641 8776
Contact: Jennifer Hartz

Taormina Int'l Film Festival

Palazio dei Congressi, 98039 Taormina, Italy 98039
Tel: +39 0942 21142
Fax: +39 0942 23348
Festival director: Felice Laudadio
Festival programmer: Carmelo Marabello
Competition
Cariddi d'oro & d'argento - Premio Marco Melani (75,000,000 Italian Lira in total)

Palm Springs Int'l Short Film Festival

1700 E. Tahquitz Canyon Way, # 3, Palm Springs, CA USA 92262
Tel: +1-760 322 2930
Fax: +1-760 322 4087
E-mail: jlien@psfilmfest.org
Executive director: Craig Prater
Festival programmer: Jennifer Stark
Market and competition
Best of Festival (cash awards for all categories total $10,000)
Previous winner: *The Mirror of the Sky* (Carlos Salles)

Fantasy Film Festival

(Munich-Frankfurt-Cologne-Stuttgart-Hamburg-Berlin)
Rosebud Entertainment, Herzog-Wilhelmstr. 27, 80331 Munich, Germany
Tel: +49-89-260 22838
Fax: +49-89-260 22839
E-mail: rosebud-entertainment@t.online.de

Festival directors: Rainer Stefan and Schorsch Müller
Festival programmers: as above

Dublin Lesbian and Gay Film Festival

6 Sputh William Street, Dublin 2, Ireland
Tel: +353-1- 492 0597
Fax: +353-1-670 6377
Festival director: Kevin Sexton, Yvonne O'Reilly
Festival programmer: as above

Pula Film Festival

Matka Laginje 5, Istarsko Narodno Kazaliste, Pula 52100, Croatia
Tel: +385-52 22380
Fax: +385-52 214 303
Festival director: tbc
Festival programmer: tbc
Competition
Audience Award
Previous winner: *Tri muskarca Melite Zganjer* (Snjezana Tribuson)

Festival de Films Résistances (Tarascon-sur-Ariège)

BP 23, 09400 Tarascon, France
Tel: +33-5 6105 1330
Fax: +33-5 6105 1781
Festival director & programmer: Catherine Dubuisson

Sopot Film Festival

Centar za kulturu Sopot, Kosmajski trg 7, 11450 Sopot, Yugoslavia
Tel: +381-11 825 1238/ 825 1315
Fax: +381-11 825 1315
Contact: Zivorad Milosavljevic

PIA Film Festival (Tokyo)

5-19 Sanban-cho, Chiyoda-ku, Tokyo 102-0075, Japan
Tel: +81-3-32 65 14 25
Fax:+81-3-32 65 56 59
Festival director: Keiko Araki
Festival programmer: Keiko Araki

Competition
Grand Prize (1 million Japanese yen)
Previous winner: *Sync* (Masahiro Muramatsu)

August

Yugoslav Film Festival (Herceg-Novi)

JUK Herceg-Fest, Dvorana park, Njegoseva bb, 85340 Herceg-Novi, Yugoslavia
Tel: +381-88 22 098
Fax: +381-88 22004
Festival president: Mirko Lazovic
Festival programmer: Milutin Prelevic
Competition
Grand Prix
Previous winner: *Wounds* (Srdjan Dragojevic)

Hollywood Film Festival

433 N. Camden Drive, Suite 600, Beverly Hills, CA 90210, USA
Tel: +1-310 288 1882
Fax: +1-310 475 0193
E-mail: awards@hollywoodawards.com
Festival director: Carlos de Abreu
Festival programmer: as above
Competition
Hollywood Discovery Award (US$ 20,000)

Urbanworld Film Festival (New York)

375 Greenwich St. NY, NY 10013, US
Tel: +1-212 941 3845
Fax: +1-212 941 3849
E-mail: aphill@aol.com
Festival director: Stacy Spikes
Festival programmer: tbc
Market & Competition
Best Picture

Locarno International Film Festival

Via Luini 3/A, 6601 Locarno, Switzerland
Tel: +41-91-756 2121

Fax: +41-91-756 2149
E-mail: info@pardo.ch
Festival director: Marco Müller
Festival programmer: Teresa Cavina
Market & Competition
Golden Leopard (40.000 SFR)
Previous winner: *Peau d'homme, Coeur de Bete* (*Skin of Man, Heart of Beast*) (Hélène Angel, France, winner of 99)

Hollywood Film Market

433 North Camden Drive, #600, Beverly Hills, CA 90201
Tel: +1-310 288 1882
Fax: +1-310 475 0193
E-mail: awards@hollywoodfestival.com
Website: http://www.hollywoodfestival.com
Contact: John Jacobson

International Festival "Window into Europe" (Vyborg)

Chistoprudni Blvd. 12 A, Room 601, Moscow 123242, Russia
Tel: +7095 924 8508
Fax: +7095 924 1331/ 937 7025
Festival director: Sava Koulish
Competition
Previous winner: *The Flower of Colendula* (Sergei Snjezhkin)

Motovun Int'l Film Festival

Imaginary Academy, Zagreb, Croatia, 10 000
Tel: +385 1 485 6455
Fax: +385 1 485 6459
E-mail: boris.matic@radio101.hr
Festival director: Boris Matic
Competition
Golden Tower of Motovun

Weiterstadt Open Air Filmfest

Bahnhofstrasse 70, D-64331, Weiterstadt, Germany
Tel: +49 615 012 185
Fax: +49 615 014 073
E-mail: sfk@hrzpub.tu-darmstadt.de
Website: www.home.pages.de/~sfk/weiterstadt
Festival director: Jochen Pollitt

Edinburgh International Film Festival

88 Lothian Road, Edinburgh EH3 9BZ, Scotland, UK
Tel: +44-131-228 4051
Fax: +44-131-229 5501
E-mail: info@edfilmfest.org.uk
Website: http://www.edfilmfest.org.uk
Festival director: Lizzie Francke
Festival programmer: Lizzie Francke
Market

Film Screenplay Festival (Vrnjacka Banja)

Vrnjacka 20, 36210 Vrnjacka Banja, Yugoslavia
Tel: +381-36 662 398
Fax: +381 36 662 398
Festival director: Milan Nikodijevic
Festival programmer: Milan Nikodijevic
Competition
The Best Screenplay Award
Previous winner: *Tango je tuzna misao koja se plese*

Odense International Film Festival

Vindegade 18, DK-5000 Odense C, Denmark
Tel: +45-6-613 1372
Fax: +45-6-591 4318
E-mail: filmfestival@post.odkomm.dk
Festival director: Christian Braad Thomsen
Competition
Grand Prix (DKK 25,000)
Previous winner: *The Oath* (Tiebbo Penning, Holland)

Douarnenez Film Festival

20 rue du Firt Rhu - BP 206, Douarnenes, Cedex 29172 France-Brittany
Tel: +33-2 9892 0921
Fax: +33-2 9892 2810
E-mail: fdz@wanadoo.fr
Website: kerys.com
Festival directors: Erwan Moalic & Carolin Troin
Competition only for Breton films

Espoo Ciné

PO Box 95, Espoo 02101 Finland
Tel:+358-9-466 599
Fax: +358-9-466 458
E-mail: espoocine@cultnet.fi
Festival director: Timo Kuismin

Mediterranean Film Festival (Tübingen)

Osterbergstr. 9, Tübingen, Germany 72074
Tel: +49 7071 56960
Fax: +49 7071 56 96 96
E-mail: filmtage. tuebingen@t-online.de
Festival directors and programmers: Jean-Michel Sidaine, Dieter Betz

Chichester Film Festival

Westlands, Selsey Road, Hunston, Chichester, West Sussex, PO20 6AL UK
Tel: +44-1243-784 881
Fax: +44-1243-539 853
Festival director & programmer: Roger Gibson
Competition
Audience Award for Best Preview and Best Short
Previous winner: *Lock, Stock and Two Smoking Barrels* (Guy Ritchie)

São Paulo International Short Film Festival

Rua Simao Alvares 784/2, 05417-020 São Paulo - SP Brasil
Tel/Fax: +55 11 852 9601
E-mail: spshort@ibm.net
Festival director: Zita Carvalhosa
Festival programmer: Francisco Cesar Filho

Sarajevo Film Festival

Obala Kulina Bana 10, 71000 Sarajevo, Bosnia
Tel: +387-71 665 532
Fax: +387-71 664 547
Festival director: Mirsad Purivatra
Festival programmer: Philippe Bober
Competition
Sarajevo Best Film Award
Previous winner: *Seul contre tous* (Gaspar Noé)

Norwegian International Film Festival (Haugesund)

PO Box 145, 5501 Haugesund, Norway
Tel: +47-52 73 44 30
Fax: +47-52 73 44 20
E-mail: haugfest@online.no
Festival director: Gunnar Johan Loevvik
Festival programmer: Christine Berg
Market

Montreal World Film Festival

1432 De Bleury, Montreal H3A 2JI, Canada
Tel: +1-514 848 3883
Fax: +1-514 848 3886
E-mail: ffm@interlink.net
Website: http://www.ffm-montreal org
Festival director: Serge Losique, Daniele Cauchard
Festival programmer: Serge Losique, Daniele Cauchard
Market and competition
Grand Prix of the Americas
Previous winner: *The Children of Heaven* (Majid Majidi)

Edinburgh International Television Festival

2nd floor, 24 Neal Street, London WC2H 9PS, UK
Tel: +44-171 379 4519
Fax: +44-171 836 0702
E-mail: eitf@festival.demon.co.uk
Festival director: Charlotte Ashton

International Festival of Tourist, Ecological and Sport Films – Mefest (Zlatibor)

Mefest c/o Film Danas, Bulevar Crvene Armije 38, 11 000 Beograd, Yugoslavia
Tel: +381-11 430 837/ 444 5677
Fax: as above
Festival director: Gavrilo Azinovic
Festival programmer: Dinko Tucakovic
Competition
Golden Pine
Previous winner: *A Wonderful Story Written with Water* (Gabrio Marinelli, Italy)

Love Is Folly (Varna)

31 Luben Karavelov Str., Sofia 1000, Bulgaria
Tel: +359 2 665 564
Fax: +359 2 803 791
Festival director & programmer: Alexander Grozev
Competition
Golden Aphrodita
Previous winner: *Coldblooded*

Fantoche Int'l Animation Film Festival (Baden)

Ottikerstrasse 53, 8006 Zürich, Switzerland
Tel: +41 1 361 4151
Fax: +41 1 364 0371
E-mail: fantoche@access.ch
Website: www.fantoche.ch
Contact: Otto Alder
Competition
First Prize 5000 Sfr. (Best film)
Previous winner: *Manny Happy Returns* (Majut Rimminen, UK)

Festival of Actors (Nis)

Pavla Orlovica 28 A, 18000 Nis, Yugoslavia
Tel: +381-18 47 757/ 42 849
Fax: +381-18 23 197
Festival director: Predrag Jelenkovic
Festival programmer: as above
Grand Prix for the best Actors

Gramado Film Festival – Latin and Brazilian Cinema

Rua dos Andradas 736, 3 Andar, Centro, 90 020 004 Porto Alegre Brazil
Tel: +55-51 226 3932
Fax: +55-51 226 3932
E-mail: festival@via-rs.com.br
Festival director: Esdras Rubinn
Market & Competition
Kikito
Previous winner: *For All* (Luis Carlos Laserda) & *O testamento do sinor Napomuseno* (Francisco Manso)

Hiroshima International Animation Festival

4-17 Kako-machi, Naka-ku, Hiroshima 730, Japan
Tel: +81-82-245 0245
Fax: +81-82-245 0246
E-mail: hiroanim@urban.or.jp
Website: www.city.hiroshima.jp
Festival director: Sayoko Kinoshita
Festival programmer: as above
Competition
Grand Prix (1,000,000 yen)
Previous winner: *Repete* (Michaela Pavlatova)

Brisbane International Film Festival

PO BOX 909, Brisbane 4001, Australia
Tel: +61-7 3220 0333
Fax: +61-7 220 0400

September

Festival der "Neue Heimat Film" (Freistadt, Upper Austria)

Salzgasse 25, 4240 Freistadt, Austria
Tel: +43 79 42 77722
Fax: +43 79 42 77733
Festival director: Wolfgang Steininger
Festival programmer: Wolfgang Steininger
Competition
Preis der Stadt Freistadt (30,000 ATS)

Mostra Internazionale d'arte Cinematografica (Venice)

Ca Giustinian, S Marco 1364A, I-Venice 30124, Italy
Tel: +39-041-521 8878/ 8711
Fax: +39-041-522 7639
Festival director: Alberto Barbera
Festival programmer: Silvia Menegazzi
Competition
Gold Lion Award
Previous winner: *Cosi ridevano* (Gianni Amelio)

Festival Internacional de Cinema (Figueira da Foz)

Apartado dos Correios 50407, 1709 Lisboa Codex, Portugal
Tel: +351-1-812 6231
Fax: +351-1-812 6228
Festival director: José Viera Marques
Competition
Grande premio da Figueira da Foz (a trophy)
Previous winner: *Erntezeit* (Stefan Schneider)

Deauville Festival of American Films

36 rue Pierret, Neuilly 92 200, France
Tel: +33-1-41 34 20 00
Fax: +33-1-47 58 77 77
E-mail: publics@imaginet.fr
Festival director: Lionel Chouchan, Andre Halimi
Festival programmer: Daniel Benzakin
Competition
Grand Prix "Special Deauville"
Previous winner: *Next Stop Wonderland* (Brad Anderson)

Festival of Fantastic Films (Manchester)

33 Barrington Road, Altrincham, Cheshire, WA14 1H2, UK
Tel: +44-161-929 1423
Fax: +44-161-929 1067
Festival director: Gil Lane Young
Festival programmer: Harry Nadler
Competition
Award for the best film
Previous winner: *The Long Twilight* (Atila Janish)
Best short film: *Domino* (Ori Sivan)

Latin American Film Festival (London)

79 Wardour Street, London W1V 3TH, UK
Tel: +44-171-434 3357
Fax: +44-171-287 2112
Festival director: Eva Tarr
Festival programmer: Eva Tarr

Telluride Film Festival

53 South Main Street, Suite 212, Hanover,
New Hampshire 03755, USA
Tel: +1-603-643 1255
Fax: +1-603-643 5938
E-mail: Tellufilm@aol.com
Festival director: Bill Pence, Tom Luddy

Tacoma Tortured Artists Film Festival

728A Pacific Ave., Tacoma, WA 98402, USA
Tel: +1 253 627 5932
Fax: +1 253 627 1525
E-mail: TacomaFilm@aol.com
Festival director: James Humo
Competition
The Barbie award ($1,500)

Internationales Filmfest Oldenburg

Banhof str. 15, Oldenburg 26122, Germany
Tel: +49-441 9250855
Fax: +49-441 9250856
E-mail: tnt@filmfest-oldenburg.de
Festival director: Torsten Neumann

Toronto International Film Festival

2 Carlton St, Suite 1600, Toronto, Ontario,
M5B 1J3, Canada
Tel: +1-416-967 7371
Fax: +1-416 967 9477
E-mail: tiffg@torfilm fest.ca
Website: http://www.bell.ca/toronto/filmfest
Festival director: Piers Handling
Audience Award
Air Canada Peoples Choice Award
Previous Winner: *The Hanging Garden*
(Thom Fitzgerald)

Boston Film Festival (Boston)

Box 516, Hull, MA 02045, USA
Tel: +1-781-925 1373
Fax: +1-781-925 3132
Festival director: Mark Diamond

Focus on Asia Fukuoka International Film Festival

1-8-1 Tenjin, Chuo-ku, Fukuoka 810, Japan
Tel: +81-92-733 5170
Fax: +81-92-733 5595
Festival director: Tadao Sato
Festival programmer: as above

International Broadcasting Convention, Amsterdam

Aldwych House, 81 Aldwych London, WC2B
4EL. UK
Tel: +44-171 611 7500
Fax: +44-171 611 7530
E-mail: show@ibc.org.uk
Website: www.ibc.org.uk/ibc/
Contact person: David Machon

Bogota Film Festival

Calle 26 No. 4-92, Santa Fe de Bogota,
Colombia
Tel: +57 1 282 5196, 243 1901
Fax: +57 1 342 2872
E-mail: cidc@coll.telecom.com.co.
Festival director: Henry Laguado
Competition
Gold Cycle Award
Previous winner: *La vendedora de rosas*
(Victor Gaviria)

Empire State Film Festival (Manhattan, Albany, Saratoga Springs, Syracuse, Rochester, Ithaca, Buffalo etc)

PO BOX 177, Mohawk, NY 13407, USA
Tel: +1-212-802 4679
Fax: +1-212 591 6195
E-mail: Empirefilm@aol.com
Website: www.empirefilm.com
Festival director: Michael J Zimmerman
Festival programmer: Jon Galt
Competition
Gold Torch (cash and prizes)
Previous winner: *First Daughter* (Anne
Madden)

Arsenals International Film Forum (Riga)

PO Box 626, Märstalu 14, Riga, Latvia LV 1047
Tel: +371-722 1620
Fax: +371-782 0445
E-mail: arsenals@sisenis.com.Latnet.Lv.
Festival director: Benita Sarma
Festival programmer: Ieva Pitruka, Dace Briska, Zaneta Vegnere, Vaiva Krasta

Short Cuts Cologne

c/o Kölner Filmhaus, Maybachstr. 111, 50670 Köln, Germany
Tel: +49 221 222 7100
Fax: +49 221 222 71099
Festival director: Stefan Sarasi
Competition

Breckenridge Festival of Film

P.O. Box 718, Riverwalk Center, 150 W. Adams, Breckenridge, CO 80424, US
Tel: +1-970 453 6200
Fax: +1-970 453 2692
E-mail: filmfest@brecknet.com
Festival director: Julie Bullock
Festival programmer: Terese Keil
Competition

The British Short Film Festival

BBC British Short Film Festival, BBC Centre House, Room 202, 56 Wood Lane, London W12 7SB, UK
Tel: +44-181-743 8000 ext. 62222
Fax: +44-181-740 8540
Festival director: Amanda Casson
Competition
UCI Graqnd Prize for UK and International Short (£2000)
Previous winner: *Toy Boys* (Gaby Dellal, UK)

Rio Festival (Rio De Janeiro)

Cima, Cnetro de Cultura, Informação e Meio-ambiente, Rua Fernandes Guimarães, 39, 4th floor, Botafogo, Rio de Janeiro, Brazil/ Grupo Estacão, Rua Voluntários da Pátria 97, Botafogo

Tel/Fax: +55-21 295 1060/3792/0756
Tel: +55 21 539 1505/537 9222
Fax: +55 21 539 1247
E-mail: cima@visualnet.combr
E-mail: liliamh@estacaovirtual.com
Website: http://www.estacao.com.br
Board of directors: Adriana Rattes, Iafa Britz, Ilda Santiago, Marcelo Mendes, Marcos Didonet, Nelson Krumbolz, Walkiria Barbosa

San Sebastian International Film Festival

Plaza de Oqendo s/n, 20004 San Sebastian, Spain
Tel: +34-943-48 12 12
Fax: +34-943-48 12 18
Festival director: Diego Galan
Market & Competition
Golden Shell
Previous winner: *El viento se llevó lo que* (Alejandro Agresti)

Showbiz Expo East (New York)

383 Main Ave, Norwalk, CT 06951, USA
Tel: +1-203 840 5949
Fax: +1-203 840 9949
Contact: Olivia Jonuqua

Umeå International Film Festival

PO Box 43, 90102 Umeå, Sweden
Tel: +46-90-133388
Fax: +46-90-777961
Festival director: Thom Palmen

Athens International Film Festival – Opening Nights

5 Benaki & Ag. Nektariou Str, 152-35 Vrilissia, Athens, Greece
Tel: +30-1-606 1363/606 1428
Fax: +30-1-601 4137
Festival director: Christos Mitsis
Festival programmer:
George Krassakopoulos
Audience Award (2 million Greek Drc.)
Previous winner: *La Vita è Bella* (Roberto Benigni)

Atlantic Film Festival (HaliFax)

c/o CBC 5600 Sackville St, HaliFax, Nova
Scotia B3J 3E9, Canada (PO BOX 36139)
Tel: +1-902-422 3456
Fax: +1-902-422 4006
E-mail: festival@atlanticfilm.com
Festival director: Gordon Whitteker
Festival programmer: Lia Rinaldo
Market and competition
People's Choice Award
Previous winner: *This Is My Father* (Paul
Quinn)

Helsinki Film Festival – Love and Anarchy

Mannerheimintie 22-24, Lasipalatsi, PO BOX
889, FIN 00101, Helsinki, Finland
Tel: +358-9- 684 35230
Fax: +358-9-684 35232
E-mail: lanerva@hiff.fi
Website: http://love-and-anarchy.cultnet.fi
Festival director: Pekka Lanerva

Independent Feature Film Market (New York)

104 West 29th Street, 12th Floor, New York,
NY 10001-5310, USA
Tel: +1-212-465 8200
Fax: +1-212-465 8525
E-mail: IFPNY@ifp.org
Market director: Milton Tabbot
Market
Gordon Parks Independent Film Award
($10,000, sponsored by MTV Films)

The 15th International Festival of Television Programmes for Children and Youth Prix Danube '99 (Bratislava)

Festival Secretariate, Mlynská dolina, Slovak
Television, Bratislava, Slovak Republic, 845 45
Tel: +421-7 6542 8609
Fax: +421-7 6542 8609/ 6542 5600
E-mail: prixdanube@stv.sk
Festival director: Jozef Filo
Festival programmer: Jela Kezmanová
Competition
Prix Danube award in four categories

Drama Short Film Festival (Drama)

Ag. Varvaras 9, Drama, Greece
Tel: +30-521 47575/1-330 0309
Fax: +30-521 33526/-1-330 2818
Festival director: Antonis Papandopoulos
Competition & market
Grand Prix (1,000,000 drs)
Previous winner: *My Country* (Milos
Radovic)

Cinefest The Sudbury Film Festival

Suite 218, 40 Elm Street, Sudbury, Ontario,
PC3 1S8, Canada
Tel: +1-705-688 1234
Fax: +1-705-688 1351
Executive director: Tammy Frick
Competition
Audience award/Best Canadian
Previous winners: *La Vita è Bella* (Roberto
Benigni) and *No* (Robert Lapage)

Festival Cinéma Tout Ecran

Maison des Arts du Grütli, 16 rue du Général
Dufour, Case postale 5305, CH-1211 Genève
11, Switzerland
Tel: +41 22 328 8554
Fax: +41 22 329 6802
E-mail: info@cinema-tout-ecran ch
Festival director: Leo Kaneman
Festival programmer: Stéphanie Billeter
Competition
Grand Prize (SFr10,000)
Previous winner: *No Child of Mine* (Peter
Kosminsky)

Aspen Film Fest

110 E Hallam, Suite 102, Aspen, Colorado
81611, USA
Tel: +1-970-925 6882
Fax: +1-970-925 1967
E-mail: lthielen@aspenfilm.org
Festival director: Laura Thielen

Cordoba Cartoon Forum

137 rue d'Alésia, 75014 Paris, France
Tel: +33-1 45 45 65 25

Fax: +33-1 45 45 65 35
E-mail: athol@club-internet.fr
Contact: Alexandra Tholance Conseil

Fantasy Film Festival (Lund/Malmö)

Norra Neptune Gatan 5, 21118 Malmö, Sweden
Tel: +46 40 124 666
Fax: +46 40 122 264
Festival director: Magnus Paulsson
Competition
Previous winner: *Bullet Ballet* (Chinya Tsukamoto)

Film Camera Festival Manaki Brothers (Bitola)

Vardar-Film 8 Mart 4, 91000 Skopje, Macedonia
Tel/Fax: +389-91-211 811
E-mail: ffmanaki@unec.com.mk
Festival director: Delco Mihajlov
Festival programmer: Blagoja Kunevski
Competition
Golden Camera 300
Previous winner: *Central Station* (DOP Walter Carvaillo)

Netherlands Film Festival (Utrecht)

PO Box 1581, 3500 BN Utrecht, The Netherlands
Tel: +31-30-232 2684
Fax: +31-30-213 3200
E-mail: nedfilmfest@artnet.xshall.nl
Festival director: Jacques van Heyningen
Festival programmer: Herman de Wit
Market and competition
Golden Calf ($10,000)
Previous winner: *Felice felice* (Peter Delpeut)

Bradford The Mango Film Festival (Black & Asian Film & TV)

National Museum Photography, Film & TV, Pictureville, Bradford, BD11 NQ, UK
Tel: +44-1274 203 320

Fax: +44 1274 770 217
E-mail: c.sawhney@nmsi.ac.uk or fell@nmsi.ac.uk
Festival director: Bill Lawrence
Festival programmer: Irsan Ajeeb
Market (Trade Festival of South Asian & Black Film & TV)

Festival de cinéma international Ste-Thérèse/Ste-Adèle (Ste-Thérèse et Ste-Adèle)

34 rue Blainville Ouest, Sainte-Thérèse, Québec, Canada, J7E 1W9
Tel: +1-450-434 0387
Fax: +1-450-434 7868
E-mail: festival@ odyssee.net
Festival director: André Marion
Festival programmer: Frédéric Lapierre
Competition
Best film award ($1,000)
Previous winner: *Somersault in a Coffin* (Durzis Zem, Turkey)

Festival International du Film Francophone (Namur)

175 Rue des Brasseurs, B-5000 Namur, Belgium
Tel: +32-81 24 12 36
Fax: +32-81 22 43 84
Festival director: Dany Martin
Festival programmer: Nicole Gillet
Competition
Golden Bayard for Best Film (50.000 FB)
Previous winner: *Sur terre* (Denis Villeneuve)

Films from the South (Oslo)

Fimens Hus, Dronningens Gate 16, N-0152, Oslo, Norway
Tel: +47 22 47 45 00
Fax: +47 22 47 46 90
Contact: Lasse Skagen, Susana Escobar

Holland Film Meeting (Utrecht)

PO Box 1581, 3500 BN, Utrecht, The Netherlands
Tel: +31-30-232 2684

Fax: +31-30-213 3200
Festival director: Jacques van Heijningen
Competition and Market
Golden Calf Awards

New York Film Festival

Film Society of Lincoln Center, 70 Lincoln
Center Plaza, New York, NY 10023, USA
Tel: +1-212-875 5638
Fax: +1-212-875 5610
Website: www.filmlinc.com
Festival director: Richard Peña

Vancouver International Film Festival

Suite 410, 1008 Homer St., Vancouver V6B
2X1, Canada
Tel: +1-604-685 0260
Fax: +1-604-688 8221
E-mail: viff@viff.org
Website: http://viff.org/viff/
Festival director: Alan Franey
Festival programmer: PoChu AuYeung
Audience-generated awards
Previous winner: *La Vita è Bella* (Roberto
Benigni)

Haifa International Film Festival

142, Hanassi Ave., Haifa, Israel 34633
Tel: +972 4 8353 521/522
Fax: +972 4 8384 327
E-mail: haifaff@netvision.net.il
Website: www.haifaff.co.il
Festival director & programmer: Pnina Blayer
Competition
The "Golden Anchor" award for
Mediterranean films ($US 18,000)
Previous winner: *The Powder Keg* (Goran
Paskaljevic)

Internationa Festival of New Film (Split)

PP 244, 21000 Split, Croatia
Tel/Fax: +385 21 52 59 25
E-mail: split.filmfest@st.tel.hr
Festival director: Branko Karabatic

Festival programmer: Josko Jernocic
Competition
Sculpture "The Tail"
Previous winner: *The Changing Room* (Alyson
Bell)

The Panorama of European Cinema (Athens)

Minoos 10-16, 11743 Athens, Greece
Tel: +30-1 92 96 001
Fax: +30-1 90 28 311
Director: Ninos Mikeldhs
Competition
Previous winner: *Seul contre tous* (Caspar Noe)

SporTel (Monte Carlo)

4 Boulevard de Jardin Exotique, MC-98000
Monaco, Monaco
Tel: +377-93-30 20 32
Fax: +377-93-30 20 33
E-mail: sportel@imen.com
Festival director: David Tomatis
Market & Competition
Golden Podium Award (30,000 FF) (three
categories)

Yugoslav Feature Film Festival Novi Sad Arena

Zvezda Film, Trg Slobode 2, 21000 Novi Sad
Tel: +381-21 615 759
Fax: +381-21 613 759
Festival director: Pavle Milivojev
Competition
Zlatna Arena
Previous winner: *Lajanje na zvezde* (Zdravko
Sotra)

International Computer Animation Festival (Magdeburg)

Otto-von-Guericke-Universität Magdeburg,
Institut für Simulation und Graphik,
Magdeburg, Germany
Tel: +49 391 671 8772/8342
Fax: +49 391 671 1164
Contact: Stefan Schlechtweg

FilmFest Hamburg

Friedensalee 44, D-22765 Hamburg ,
Germany
Tel: +49-40-399 19000
Fax: +49-40-399 190010
E-mail: film fest-hamburg @t-online.de
Festival director: Josef Wutz
Festival programmer: Katarin Kohlstedde

Videonale International Video and Media Festival (Bonn)

Hochstadenring 22, 53 119 Bonn, Germany
Tel/Fax: +49 228 69 28 18
Festival director: Rosanne Altstatt & Catrine
Backhaus
Competition

Rencontres d'Annecy du Cinema Italien

Bonlieu Scene Nationale, 1 rue Jean Jaures,
BP 294, Annecy 74007, France
Tel: +33-450 33 44 00
Fax: +33-450 51 82 09
Festival director: Salvador Garcia
Festival programmer: Pierre Todeschini
Competition
Grand Prix des Rencontres
Previous winner: *La stanza de lo Chirocco*
(Maurizio Schiara)

Screens on the Bay (Amalfi)

Rai Trade, Via Novaro 18, Rome 00195, Italy
Tel: +39 06 3749 8269
Fax: +39 06 370 1343
Contact: Dino Piretti
Festival du Film Britannique (Dinard)
2 Bd. Féart, 35800 Dinard, France
Tel: +33-299-88 19 04
Fax: +33-299-46 67 15
Festival director: Thierry de la Fourniere
Competition
Hitchcock award
Previous winner: *Get Real* (Simon Shore)

Alexandria International Film Festival

9 Orabi Str. 111, Cairo, Egypt
Tel: (20 2) 574 1112
Fax: (20 2) 576 8727
Competition

Cartoon Forum (each year in a different country)

Cartoon-134 bd Lambermont, 1030 Bruxelles,
Belgique
Tel: +32-2 245 1200
Fax: +32-2 245 4689
E-mail: cartoon@skynet.be
Market & Competition
Cartoon D'or (25.000 Euros)
Previous winner: *L'Enfant au Grelot* (Jacques
Remy Girerd)

Cinemayaat (Arab Film Festival) (San Francisco, Berkeley, San Jose)

2 Plaza Avenue, San Francisco, California, US
94116
Tel: +1-415 564 1100
Fax: +1-415 704 3139
E-mail: info@aff.org
Festival directors & programmers:
Tarik Elhaik & Khalil Benkirane

Int'l Festival of Film & Video for Children and Young Adults (Isfahan)

Farhang Cinema, Dr. Shariati Ave., Gholhak,
Tehran, Iran 19139
Tel: +98-21 200 2088/89/90
Fax: +98-21 267 082
Festival director: S. Daad
Festival programmer: Jamal Omid
Competition
Golden Butterfly (US$ 1,200)
Previous winner: *Benjamin Dove*
(Gisli Snaer, Iceland)

Lucas '00 – International Film Festival for Children and Young People (Frankfurt am Main)

Deutsches Filmmuseum, Schaumainkai 41, D-60596 Frankfurt am Main, Germany
Tel: +49-69-2123 3369
Fax: +49-69-2123 7881
Festival director: Prof. Walter Schobert
Festival programmer: Petra Diebold, Petra Eggensperger
Competition
Lucas Award (DM 5000)
Previous winner: *Count Me Out*
(Ari Kristinsson)

Sub Fiction – 3. Werkleitz Biennale (Werkleitz & Tornitz)

Straße des Friedens 26, 39249, Torintz, Germany
Tel: +49 39298 6750
Fax: + 49 39298 675 55
Website: www.werkleitz.de/sub-fiction
Festival director: Peter Zorn

Nextframe UFVA's Touring Festival of International Student Film & Video (Philadelphia)

09 Annenberg Hall, 13th & Diamong St., Temple University 011-00, Philadelphia PA 19122, USA
Tel: +1-215 923 3532
Fax: +1-215 204 6740
E-mail: ufva@vm.temple.edu
Festival directors and programmers: Juan Carlos Rojas and Anna Minkkinen
Competition
Several prizes

RAI Trade Screenings (Portofino)

RAI Trade, Via Umberto Novaro 18, 00195 Rome, Italy
Tel: +39-06 3749 8257
Fax: +39-06 3701 343
Website: www.raitrade.rai.it

October

Black Filmworks Festival of Film & Video (Oakland)

Black Filmmakers Hall of Fame, 405 14th Street, Suite 515, Oakland, CA, US 94612
Tel: +1-510 465 0804
Fax: +1-510 839 9858
Festival director: Dorothy Karni
Festival programmer: Felix Curtis
Market & Competition
Cash prize 2,700
Previous winner: *Morningside Prep* (Malcolm Lee)

Queerdoc – Gay and Lesbian Documenatry Festival (Sydney)

PO Box 1081 Darlinghurst, Australia, 1300
E-mail: info@queerscreen.com.au
Festival director: Tony Grierson

MIPCOM JUNIOR (Cannes)

Reed Midem Organisation, BP 572, 11 rue du Colonel Pierre Avia, Paris, France 75726
Tel: +33-1 41 90 45 80
Fax: +33-1 41 90 45 70
Programme director: André Vaillant

Film in Weimar – Festival of the Eastern European Cinema (Weimar)

Etfuster Str. 40, Jena, Germany 07745
Tel: +49 3641 45 06 30
Fax: +49 3641 61 52 34
E-mail: Klaus.Hattenbach@Jena.Thur.de
Festival director: Klaus Hattenbach
Festival programmer: Klaus Hattenbach

MIPCOM (Cannes)

BP 572, 11 rue du Colonel Pierre Avia, F-75726 Paris, France
Tel: +33-1-41 90 45 80
Fax: +33-1-41 90 45 70
Market director: André Vaillant
Market

British Film Festival (Cherbourg)

15 Passage Digard, F-50100 Cherbourg, France
Tel: +33-233 93 38 94
Fax: +33-233 01 20 78
Festival director: Catherine Tyson
Festival programmer: Yolande Forafo

Flanders International Film Festival (Gent)

1104 Kortrijksesteenweg, B-9051 Gent, Belgium
Tel: +32-9-221 8946
Fax: +32-9-221 9074
E-mail: filmfestival@infoboard.be
Website: www.rug.ac.be/filmfestival/Welcome.html
Contact: Jacques Dubrulle, Walter Provo, Peter Bouckaert, Marian Ponnet
Competition
Golden Spur Award (US$130,000)
Previous winner: *Die Sibtelbauern*

Chicago International Film Festival

32 West Randolph Street, Suite 600, Chicago, Illinois 60601, USA
Tel: +1-312 425 9400
Fax: +1-312 425 0944
E-mail: filmfest@wwa.com
Festival director: Michael J Kutza
Festival programmers: Helen Gramates, Jim Healy, Michael Kutza
Competition
The Gold Hugo Award
Previous winner: *The Hole* (Tsai Ming-Liang)

Ökomedia-International Ecology Film Festival (Freiburg)

Ökomedia Institut, Habsburger Str. 9a, 79104 Freiburg, Germany
Tel: +49 761 52024
Fax: +49 761 555 724
Festival director: Werner Kobe
Competition

Sitges International Fantasy Film Festival

Av. Josep Tarradellas 135, Esc. A 3 2, 08029 Barcelona, Spain
Tel: +34-93-419 3635
Fax: +34-93-439 7380
E-mail: cinsit@sitgestur.com
Website: www.sitges.com/cinema
Festival director: Roc Billas
Competition
Best Film Award
Previous winners: *Cube (Vicenzo Natali)*

Austin Film Festival and Heart of FilmScreenwriters

AHFF, Inc., 1600 Nueces, Austin, TX 78701
Tel: +1-512 478 4795
Fax: +1-512 478 6205
E-mail: austinfilm@aol.com
Festival directors: Barbara Morgan & Marsha Milam
Competition & market
Bronze Award ($750 for feature film)
Previous winner: *La Cucaracha* (Jack Perez)

Denver International Film Festival

1430 Larimer Square, Suite 201, Denver, CO 80202, USA
Tel: +1-303-595 3456
Fax: +1-303-595 0956
E-mail: dfs@denverfilm.org
Festival director & programmer: Ron Henderson

Mill Valley Film Festival

38 Miller Avenue, Suite 6, Mill Valley, CA 94941, USA
Tel: +1-415 383 5256
Fax: +1-415 383 8606
E-mail: info@finc.org
Festival director: Mark Fishkin
Festival programmer: Zoë Elton

Warsaw Film Festival

PO Box 816, 00-950 Warsaw 1, Poland
Tel: +48-22-853 3636
Fax: +48-22-853 1184
E-mail: festiv@wff.org.pl
Festival director: Stefan Laudyn

Leeds International Film Festival

The Town Hall, The Headrow, Leeds, LS1 3AD, UK
Tel: +44-113-247 8389
Fax: +44-113-247 8397
E-mail: filmfestival@leeds.gov.uk
Website: http://www.sensei.co.uk/films/
Festival director: Chris Fell
Festival programmer: as above

Wildscreen (Bristol)

Deanery Road, College Green, Bristol, BS1 5DB, UK
Tel: +44-117 909 6300
Fax: +44-117-909 5000
E-mail: info@wildscreen.org.uk
Website: www.wildscreen.org.uk
Festival director: Jane Krish
Competition
Golden Panda
Previous winner: *The Dragons of Galapagos* (David Parer)

International Film Festival Mannheim–Heidelberg

Collini-Center, Galerie, D-68161 Mannheim, Germany
Tel: +49-621-102943
Fax: +49-621-291564
Festival director: Dr Michael Koetz
Market & Competition
International Independent Award (DM 30,000)
Previous winner: *Max et Bobo* (Frederic Fonteyne)

New Orleans Film and Video Festival

PO Box 50819, New Orleans, 70150 LA, USA
Tel: +1-504-523 3818
Fax: +1-504-529 2430
Festival director: Carol Gniady
Festival programmer: John Despias
Competition
Lumiere Awards

Le Giornate del Cinema Muto (Sacile)

c/o Cineteca del Friuli, Via Bini Palazzo Gurizatti, I-33013 Gemona, Italy
Tel: +39-0432-980458
Fax: +39-0432-970542
E-mail: gcm@proxima.conecta.it
Website: www.cinetecadelfriuli.org/gcm/
Market director: David Robinson
Market

Raindance Film Showcase (London)

81 Berwick Street, London W1V 3PF, UK
Tel: +44-171-287 3833
Fax: +44-171-439 2243
E-mail: http://www: ftech.net/ n ind film
Festival director: Elliot Grove
Festival programmer: Suzanne Ballantyne
Market

Cork International Film Festival

Hatfield House, Tobin Street, Cork, Ireland
Tel: +353-21-271711
Fax: +353-21-275945
Festival director: Michael Hannigan
Festival programmer: as above
Competition
European Short Film (Ecu7.500)
Previous winner: *Guy's Dog* (Rory Bresnihan)

The Golden Chest International TV Festival (Plovdiv)

Bulgarian National Television, Sofia, 1504, Bulgaria
Tel: +359 2 946 1034
Fax: +359 2 946 1034
E-mail: intr@bmt.bg
Festival director: Valentin Stoyanov
Festival progammer: Veneta Gerassimova
Competition
Grand Prix 'Golden Chest"
Previous winner: *The Shooter* (Muhamed Mehmedovic, Bosnia)

PILOTS (Programme for the International Launch of Television Series Workshops) (Sitges)

Diputació 279, E-08007 Barcelona, Spain
Tel: +34-93-487 3773
Fax: +34-93- 4873952
Festival director: Pera Fages

Santa Fe de Bogota Festival

Calle 26, No 4-92, Santa Fe de Bogota, Colombia
Tel: +57 1 282 5196
Fax: +57 1 342 2872
Festival director: Henry Laguado

Dokumentart – European Film Workshop (Neubrandenburg)

Holm-Henning-Freier, Rasenstrasse 3, D-17033, Neubrandenburg, Deutschland
Tel: +49 395 566 6109
Fax: +49 395 566 6612
E-mail: latuecht@t-online.de
Festival director: Holm-Henning Freier
Competition
Latücht-Preis (7,000 DM)
Previous winner: *Castro's Tears* (Merljin Passier)

Canadian International Annual Film/Video Festival (Campbell River, British Columbia)

25 Eugenia St, Barrie, Ontario Canada, L4M 1P6
Tel/Fax: +1-705 733 8232

E-mail: ciaff@canada.com
Festival director: Ben Andrews
Festival programmer: Kevin Harrison
Competition
Best Amateur, Best Student, Best Independent

Chicago International Children's Film Festival

Facets Multimedia, 1517 W Fullerton Ave, Chicago, Illinois 60614, USA
Tel: +1-773 281 9075
Fax: +1-773 929 5437
E-mail: kidsfest@facets.org
Festival director: Rebekah Cowing
Competition
Grand Prize ($2500)
Previous winner: *The Wind in the Willows* (Terry Jones)

FCMM (Montreal International Festival of Cinema & New Media) Montreal

3536, boul. Saint-Laurent, Montréal, Queebec, Canada H2X 2V4
Tel: +1-514-847 9272
Fax: +1-514-847 0732
E-mail: montrealfest@fcmm.com
Website: www.fcmm.com
Festival director & programmer: Claude Chamberlan

IBTS – (10th Int'l Audio, Video, Broadcasting, Motion Picture and Telecommunications Show)

Via Domenichino 11, 20149, Milan, Italy
Tel: +39 02 481 5541
Fax: +39 02 498 0330
E-mail: MC 1703 @ MC Link. IT

Mostra de Valencia/ Cinema de Mediterrani

Plaza del Arzobispo 2 Bajo, 46003, Valencia, Spain
Tel: +34-96-392 1506
Fax: +34-96-391 5156
Festival director: Luís Fernández
Festival programmer: Elena Escriba
Competition

Palmera de Oro (Ptas 3 million)
Previous winner: *The 90 minutes of Mr. Baum* (Asi Dayan)

Pusan Int'l Film Festival (PIFF)

Room 208, # 1393 Woo 1 Dong, Hacuudac-Ku, Pusan, Korea
Tel: +82-51 747 3010
Fax: +82-51 747 3012
E-mail: program@piff.org
Website: www.piff.org
Festival director: Kim Dong-Ho
Festival programmer: Lee Yong Kwan, Jay Jean, Kim Ji-Seok
New Currents Award
Previous winner: *Xiao Wu* (Jiu Zhang Ke)

Yugoslav Animated Film Festival (Cacak)

Dom kulture- Foto kino-klub Cacak, 32000 Cacak, Yugoslavia
Tel: +381-32 23508
Contact: Slobodan Pajic

São Paulo International Film Festival

Al. Lorena 937 Cj.303, 01424-001 São Paolo, Brazil
Tel: +55-11-883 5137/30645819
Fax: +55-11-853 7936
E-mail: info@ mostra.org
Website: www.mostra.org.
Festival director: Leon Cakoff
Festival programmer: Leon Cakoff, Renata de Almeida
Market & Competition
Bandeira Paulista Trophy

Viennale (Vienna)

Stiftgasse 6, A-1070 Vienna, Austria
Tel: +43-1-526 5947
Fax: +43-1-523 4172
E-mail: organisation @ viennale.or.at
Festival director: Hans Hurch
Festival programmer: as above
Fipresci prize
Previous winner: *La Vie Rêvée des Anges* (Eric Zonca)

Kidscreen (Milan and Como)

Rue des Palais 112, B-1030 Brussels, Belgium
Tel: +32-2-242 5409
Fax: +32-2-242 7427
Market director: Felix van Ginderhuysen
Market

Prix Europa Berlin

SFB, Berlin 14046, Germany
Tel: +49-30-30 31 1610
Fax: +49-30-30 31 1619
Festival director: P.L. Braun
Festival programmer: Susanne Hoffmann
Competition
Prix Europa
TV programme of the year (fiction)
Previous winner: *The Polish Bride* (Karin Traïdi)

Mifed (Milan)

EA Fiera Milano, Largo Domodossoia 1, I-20145 Milano, Italy
Tel: +39-02-48 01 29 12/48 01 29 20/48 01 29 42
Fax: +39-02-49 97 70 20
E-mail: mifed @fnd.it
Director: Tullio Galleno
Market

Sport Movies & TV International Festival

FICTS - Via de Amicis 17, 20123 Milan, Italy
Tel: +39-02 8940 9076
Fax: +39-02 8375 973
E-mail: ficts@tin.it
Festival director: Prof. Franco B. Ascani
Festival programmer: Antonio Di Gregorio
Competition
Guirlande D'honneur Award (3,000,000 Italian Lira)

European Cable Communications '99 (London)

The Cable Communications Association, The Fifth Floor, Artillery House, Artillery Row, London SW1P 1RT
Tel: +44-171-222 2900
Fax: +44-171-799 1471
Contact: John Robertson

Kudzu Film Festival

P.O. Box 1461, Athens, GA 30603, USA
Tel: +1-706 227 6090
Fax: +1-706 227 6090

Sheffield International Documentary Festival

The Workstation, 15 Paternoster Row, Sheffield, S1 2BX, UK
Tel: +44-114-276 5141
Fax: +44-114-272 1849
E-mail: shefdoc@fdgroup.co.uk
Festival director: Kathy Loizou

Show East (Atlantic City)

244 West 49th Street #200, New York , NY 10019, USA
Tel: +1-212-246 6460
Fax: +1-212-265 6428
Festival director: Robert & Jimmy Sunshine

Uppsala International Short Film Festival

Box 1746, S-751 47 Uppsala, Sweden
Tel: +46-18-12 00 25
Fax: +46-18 12 13 50
E-mail: uppsala@shortfilmfestival.com
Festival director: Åsa Garnert
Festival programmer: Christopher Olofsson
Competition
Grand Prix

Lesbian and Gay Film Festival (Hamburg)

Schanzenstr. 45, 20357 Hamburg, Germany
Tel: +49 40 348 0670
Fax: +49 40 34 05 22
Festival director: Astrid Lüder, Ronald Behm
Festival programmer: Joachim Post, Sybille Bauriedl
E-mail: filmtage@hamburg.gay-web.de
Website: www.hamburg.gay-web.de/filmtage
Short film competition (only)
Ursula - Audience Award
Previous winner: *Twisted Sheets* (Chris Deacon, Canada) & *A Kiss in the Snow* (Frank Mosvold, Norway)

Yamagata International Documentary Film Festival

YIDFF, Tokyo Office, Kitagawa Bldg, 4fl, 6-42 Kagurazaka, Shinjuku-ku, Tokyo 162_0825, Japan
Tel: +81-33266-9704
Fax: +81-33266-9700
E-mail: yidff@bekkoame.ne.jp
Festival director: Yano Kazuyuki
Festival programmer: Ono Seiko, Fujioka Asako
Competition
The Grand Prize (The Robert and Frances Flaherty Prize) (¥ 3,000,000)
Previous winner: *Fragments Jerusalem* (Ron Havilio)

The Hamptons International Film Festival (East Hampton)

3 Newtown Mews, East Hampton, NY 11937, USA
Tel: +1-516-324 4600
Fax: +1-516-324 5116
Website: www.hamptonsfest.org
Festival director: Denise Kasell
Competition
Golden Starfish Award ($200,000)

Heartland Film Festivals (Indeannapolis)

613 N. East Street, Indeanapolis, IN, USA 46202
Tel: +1-317-464 9405
Fax: +1-317-635 4201
E-mail: hff@inquest.net
Festival director: Jeffrey L. Sparks
Festival programmer: Jeffrey L. Sparks
Competition
Crystal Heart Award ($100 000)

AFI Los Angeles International Film Festival

2021 N. Western Avenue, Los Angeles, CA 90027, USA
Tel: +1-323-856 7709
Fax: +1-323-462 4049
E-mail: afifest@afionline.org
Festival director: Jon Fitzgerald

Festival programmer: Nancy Collet
Grand Jury Prize/ New Directions Prize
Previous winner: *Fire Eater* (Pirjo Honksalo)
& *Free Enterprise* (Robert Meyer Burnett)

Ottawa International Student Animation Festival

2 Daly Avenue, Suite 120, Ottawa, Ontario
K1N 6E2, Canada
Tel:+1-613-232 8769
Fax: +1-613-232-6315
E-mail: crobinso@DocuWeb.ca
Festival director: Chris Robinson
Market and competition
Grand Prize
Previous winner: *Night of the Carrots* (Priit
Parn) Entry deadline for films: 1 July 1999

Virginia Film Festival (Charlottesville, Va)

Drama Department, The University of
Virginia, Culbreth Road, Charlottesville, VA
22903, USA
Tel: +1-804-982 5277
Fax: +1-804-924 1447
E-mail: rj.h2s@virginia.edu
Website: www.vafilm.com
Festival director: Richard Herskowitz

Film & Music Fest (Bielefeld)

Körnerstr. 3, 33602 Bielefeld, Germany
Tel: +49 521 677 43
Fax: +49 521 677 27
E-mail: eisenstein.filmfestival@t-online-de
Festival director: Prof. Kurt Johnen

Valladolid International Film Festival

Teatro Calderón, C/Leopoldo Cano. s/n, 4
planta, 47003, Valladolid, Spain
Tel: +34-983-305700/305777/788
Fax: +34-983-309835
E-mail: festvalladolid@seminci.com
Website: www.seminci.com
Festival director: Fernando Lara
Festival coordinator: Denise O'Keeffe
Competition

Golden Spike (Pta 3 million)
Previous winner: *My Name Is Joe* (Ken
Loach)

Cinekid (Amsterdam)

Weteringschaus 249, NL-1017 XY Amsterdam,
The Netherlands
Tel: +31-20-624 7110
Fax: +31-20-620 9965
Festival director: Sannatte Naeye
Festival programmer: Harry Peters
Competition
Cinekid Award (Dfl 5,000)
Previous winner: *On Our Own* (Lone
Scherfig, Denmark)

International Film Festival "Molodist" (Kiev)

6 Saksagansky str., Kiev, Ukraine, 252033
Tel: +380-44-227 4557/ 246 6798
Fax: +380-44-227 4557
E-mail: molodist@gu.kiev.ua
Festival director: Andrei Khalpakhtchi
Festival programmer: Alexander Shpilyuk
Competition
Scythian Deer ($10,000)
Previous winner: *Voices* (Andrei Osipov)

14the Annual Fort Lauderdale International Film Festival

1402 E. Las Olas Blvd. #007, Fort Lauderdale,
Florida 33301, USA
Tel: +1-954-760 9898
Fax: +1-954-760 9099
E-mail: Brofilm@aol.com
Website: www.ftlaudfilmfest.com
Festival director & programmer: Greg von Hausch
Competition
Best Film Award
Previous winner: *Happiness* (Tod Solontz)
and *La Vita è Bella* (Roberto Benigni)

Kinofilm (Manchester)

48 Princess St, Manchester, M1 6HR, UK
Tel: +44-161-288 2494
Fax: +44-161-237 3423
E-mail: john.kino@good.co.uk

Website: www.kinofilm.org.uk
Festival director & programmer: John Wojowski
Competition

International Leipzig Festival for Documentary and Animated Film

Box 0940, D-04009 Leipzig, Germany
Tel: +49-341-980 3921
Fax: +49-341-980 6141
Festival director: Fred Gehler
Festival programmer: Fred Gehler
Market & Competition
Golden Dove (DM 9,000)
Previous winner: *Bread Day* (Sergei Dvortsevoi, Russia)

Rencontres Internationales de cinema a Paris

Forum des Images, Porte St. Eustache, Paris, France, 75001
Tel: +33-1-44 76 62 11
Fax: +33-1-44 76 62 24
E-mail: jbledsoe@vdp.fr
Festival director: Michel Reilhac
Festival programmer: Marie-Pierre Macia
Competition
Grand Prix du Public (100,000 FF)
Previous winner: *In that Land* (Lidia Brobrowa, Russia)

International Hofer Filmtage (Hof)

Loth Str.28, D-80335 Munich, Germany
Tel: +49-89-129 7422/3079 6870
Fax: +49-89-123 6868
Festival director & programmer: Heinz Badewitz

VIPER – International Film, Video and Multimedia Festival (Lucerne)

PO Box 4929, CH-6002 Lucerne, Switzerland
Tel: +41-1-450 6262
Fax: +41-1-450 6261
E-mail: viper@dial.eunet.ch
Festival director: Conny E. Voester

Festival programmer: Conny E. Voester
Competition
Film Award, Video Award (SF5,000 each)
Previous winners: *Today* (Elja-Liisa Athila)

Geneva Film Festival "Stars of Tomorrow"

35, rue des Bains - C.P. 5615, CH-1211 Geneve 11, Switzerland
Tel: +41-22 809 9450
Fax: +41-22 809 9444/ 809 9401
President of festival: Roland Tay
Competition
European Golden Star (10 000 SFR each)
Previous winners: *Fedja Van Red*

Cinéma Meditérranéen Montpellier

78 Avenue du Pirée, , F-34000 Montpellier, France
Tel: +33-4-99 13 73 73
Fax: +33-4-99 13 73 74
E-mail: cinemed@mnet.fr
Website: www.cinemed.tm.fr
Festival director: Pierre Pitiot
Festival programmer: Pierre Pitiot
Competition
Antigone d'Or ($20,000)
Previous winner: *Express, Express* (Igor Sterk)

San Luis Obispo International Film Festival

PO Box 1449, San Luis Obispo, CA 93406, USA
Tel: +1-805-546 3456
Fax: +1-805-781 6799
E-mail: slofilmfest@slonet.org
Festival director: Mary A. Harris
Competition
George Sydney Award (US$500)
Previous winner: *Forgotten Fires* (Michael Chandler)

Saint Louis Int'l Film Festival

55 Maryland Plaza, Suite A, Saint Louis, 63108-1501 Missouri, USA
Tel: +1-314-454 0042
Fax: +1-314-454 0540

E-mail: info@sliff.org
Festival director: Delcia Corlew
Festival programmer: Audrey Hutti
Competition
The Mark Twain Banks' Audience Choice
Award (US$1000)
Previous winner: *Slam* (Marc Levin)

Festival du Cinéma International en Abitibi-Témiscamingue (Rouyn-Noranda)

215 Mercier Avenue, Rouyn-Noranda,
Québec, J9X 5W8, Canada
Tel: +1-819-762 6212
Fax: +1-819-762 6762
Festival director: Jacques Matte
Festival programmer: Jacques Matte

Tokyo International Film Festival

3F Landic Building No. 2, 1-6-5 Ginza, Chuo-
ku, Tokyo 104-0061, Japan
Tel: +81-3-3563 6305
Fax: +81-3-3563 6310
Festival director: Yasuyoshi Tokuma
Competition
Tokyo Grand Prix - Int'l Competition
Previous winner: *Open Your Eyes* (Alejandro
Amenabar)

Feminale Women's Film Festival (Cologne)

Hansaring 86, D-50670 Cologne , Germany
Tel: +49-221-130 0225
Fax: +49-221 130 0281
Contact: Katja Mildenberger
Festival programmer: Verena Mundt, Katja
Mildenberger, Carla Despineux

Framed III: Architecture on Film (London)
66 Portland Place, London W1N 4AD, UK
Tel: +44-171 307 3699
Fax: +44-171 307 3703
Festival director: Tamara Horbacka

The Golden Rhyton Nonfeature Film Fest (Plovdiv)

2-A Dondukov Blvd., Sofia 1000, Bulgaria
Tel: +359 2 987 4096/883 831
Fax: +359 2 873 626
E-mail: nfc@mail.bol.bg
Festival director: Dimitar Dereliev
Festival programmer: Karin Yanakieva
Competition
Grand Prix 'Golden Rhyton'

International Short Film Festival (Igualada)

Calle de Santa Maria 10, Bajors, 08700
Igualada, Spain
Tel/Fax: +34-93 803 4439
Festival director: Miquel Segura
Competition
Grand Award "Miquel Pique" (500,000 Ptas)

Peachtree International Film Festival (Atlanta)

Peachtree International Film Society, 2180
Pleasant Hill Rd. #A-5221, Duluth Georgia,
30096, USA
Tel: +1-770-729 8487
Fax: +1-770-263 0652
E-mail: info@peachtreefilm.org
Festival director & programmer: Michelle
Forren

San Juan Cinemafest

PO BOX , San Juan, Puerto Rico 00902-0079
Tel: +1-787-721 6125
Fax: +1-787-724 4187
Festival director: Mario Paniagua
Festival programmer: Dominique Borrell
Competition
Pitirre

Vevey International Comedy Film Festival

La Grenette CP 421, 1800 Vevey, Switzerland
Tel: +41-21-922 2027
Fax: +41-21-922 2024
Festival director: Yves Moser
Festival programmer: as above

Competition
Golden Cane (Sfr 6000)
Previous winner: *Shit* (Davide Marengo)

November

Duisburger Filmwoche (Duisburg)

Am König-Heinrich-Platz, D-47049 Duisburg, Germany
Tel: +49-203-283 4171
Fax: +49-203-283 4130
Festival director: Werner Ruzicka
Competition
German speaking documentaries only
German Film Critic Prize (DM10,000)
Previous winner: *Pelym* (Ulrich Richewsky & Andrej Klamp)

The Ohio Independent Film Festival

2258 West 10th Street, Cleveland, Ohio 44113, USA
Tel: +1-216 781 1755
E-mail: OhioIndieFilmFest@juno.com
Festival directors: Bernadette Gillota, Annetta Marion
Festival programmers: as above

Cottbus 9th Festival of Young East European Cinema

Bautzner Straße 91, D-03050 Cottbus, Germany
Tel: +49 355 431070
Fax: +49 355 4310 720
Artistic director: Roland Rust
Competition
Previous winner: *How the War Started on My Island* (Vinko Bresan)

Film Arts Festival (San Francisco)

346 Ninth St, 2nd floor, San Francisco, CA 94103, USA
Tel: +1-415-552 8760
Fax: +1-415-552 0882

E-mail: festival@filmarts.org
Festival director & programmer: Mark Taylor

News World Int'l Forum for Broadcast News (Barcelona)

39 St. James's Street, London SW1A 1JD
Tel: +44-171 491 0880
Fax: +44-171 491 0990
Managing director: Kerry Stevenson

Northampton Film Festival

351 Pleasant St. Suite 213, Northampton, MA 01060, USA
Tel: +1-413 586 3471
Fax: +1-413 584 4432
E-mail: filmfest@nohofilm.org
Festival directors & programmers: Howard Polonsky & Dee DeGeiso
Competition
Best of Fest
Previous winner: *Stuart Bliss* (Neil Grieve)

Latino Film Festival of Marin (Larkspur)

3100 Kerner Blvd., San Rafael, CA 94901, USA
Tel: +1-415 459 3530
Fax: +1-415 456 0560
E-mail: cinefest@latinofilmfestival.org
Festival director & programmer: Sylvia Perel
Competition
Numerous awards given

London Film Festival

National Film Theatre, South Bank, Waterloo, London SE1 8XT, UK
Tel: +44-171-815 1323
Fax: +44-171-633 0786
Festival director: Adrian Wootton
Festival programmer: Sandra Hebron

Cinemania French Film Festival (Montreal)

Tel: +1-514 878 2882
Fax: +1-514 878 0092

Nordic Film Days (Lübeck)

Schild Strasse 12, Germany, D-23552
Tel: +49-451 122 4109
Fax: +49-451 719 78
Festival director: Andrea Kunsemüller
Competition
NDR Promotion Prize (DM 25,000)
Previous winner: *Only Clouds Move the Stars* (Torun Lian)

4th International Short Film Festival (Rome)

Via in selci, 84/A Rome Italy 00184
Tel: +39-06 474 5585
Fax: +39-06 478 85799
E-mail: filmclub@pronet.it
Festival director: Piero Clemente
Festival programmer: Barbara Bialkowska
Competition
Grand Prix
Previous winner: *La Falaise* (Faouzi Bensaidi)

Amiens International Film Festival

MCA, Place Léon Gontier, F-80000 Amiens, France
Tel: +33-322 71 35 70
Fax: +33-322 92 53 04
E-mail: amiensfilmfestival@burotec.fr
Festival director: Jean-Pierre Garcia
Festival programmer: as above
Competition
The Golden Unicorn (50,000 FF)
Previous winners: *Bajo California, el limite del tiempo* (Carlos Bolado, Mexico)

Banff Mountain Film Festival

PO Box 1020, Stn.38, Banff, Alberta T0L 0C0, Canada
Tel: +1-403-762 6125
Fax: +1-403-762 6277
E-mail: cmc@banffcentre.ab.ca
Website: http://www.banffcentre.ab.c
Festival director & programmer: Bernadette McDonald

Market & Competition
Grand Prize (C$4,000)
Previous winner: *The Living Edens: Bhutan - The Last Shangri-La*

Children's Film Festival (Augsburg)

Schroeckstr. 6, D-86152 Augsburg, Germany
Tel: +49 821 349 1060
Fax: +49-821-349 5218
Festival director: Ellen Gratza
Festival programmers: as above

Hawaii International Film Festival (Honolulu and Neighbouring Islands)

1001 Bishop Street, Pacific Tower, Suite 745, Honolulu, Hawaii 96813, USA
Tel: +1-808-528 3456
Fax: +1-808-528 1410
Website: www.hiff.org
Festival director: Christian Gaines
Competition
First Hawaiian Bank Golden Maile
Previous winner: *Spring in My Hometown* (Kwang Mo Lee, Korea)

Ljubljana International Film Festival

Presernova 10, 1000 Ljubljana, Slovenia
Tel: +386-61-176 7150
Fax: +386-61-22 42 79
Festival director: Jelka Stergel
Kingfisher Prize
Previous winner: *La Vie Rêvée des Anges* (Eric Zonca)

Worldfest–Flagstaff Intl Film Festival

PO Box 56566, Houston, TX 77256, USA
Tel: +1-713 965 9955   .
Fax: +1-713-965 9960
E-mail: worldfest@aol.com
Website: www.worldfest.org
Festival director: J. Hunter Todd
Festival programmer: Maribel Amador

Market and competition
Golden Palm
Previous winner: *Mothertime* (Matthew Jacobs, UK)

3rd International Independent Film Festival of Ourense

1 Isabel la catòlica, Ourense, Spain, 32005
Tel: +34-988 224 127
Fax: +34-988 249 561
E-mail: turiour@fegamp.es
Festival director: Luis Rivas
Festival programmer: Jorge Maroto
Competition
Calpurnia prize (1,500,000 pesetas)
Previous winner: *Who the Hell Is Juliette?* (Carlos Marcovich)

Cinanima – International Animated Film Festival (Espinho)

Apartado 743, 4500 Espinho Codex, Portugal
Tel: +351-2-734 4611
Fax: +351-2-734 6015
Festival director: Antonio Gaio
Festival programmer: Organising Committee Cinanima
Competition
Grand Prize (Pte500)
Previous winner: *Transit* (Piet Kioon)

London Programme Market

23-24 George Street, Richmond, Surrey TW9 1HY, UK
Tel: +44-181-948 5522
Fax: +44-181-332 0495
Market director: James Laing

Rassegna Citta di Palermo/International Sport Film Festival

Via XII Gennaio 32, 90141 Palermo, Italia
Tel: +39 091 611 4968
Fax: +39 091 473 361
E-mail: sporfife@tin.it
Festival director: Vito Maggio
Competition

Paladino d'Oro (5m lir.it.)
Previous winner: *Gorodky Popular Game* (Belarus)

Festival Internazionale del cinema di Salerno

Casella Postale 137, I-84100 Salerno, Italy
Tel: +39-089-231 953
Fax: +39-089-223 632
Festival director: Ettore Capuano
Festival programmer: Mario De Cesare
Competition
Gran Trofeo Golfo di Salerno
Previous winner: *Elvijs and Marilijn* (Armando Manni)

International French Film Festival (Tübingen)

Frierichstrasse 11, D-72074 Tübingen, Germany
Tel: +49-70 71 56960
Fax: +49-70 71 59 96 96
E-mail: filmtage.tuebingen@T-online.de
Festival director: Dieter Betz, Stefanie Schneider
Festival programmer: as above
Competition
Flying Camera (DM 10,000)
Previous winner: *Petits Desordres Amoureux* (Olivier Peray)

Forum of European Cinema (Strasbourg)

10 rue Alexandre Parodi, Paris, France 75010
Tel: +33-1 44 89 99 99
Fax: +33-1 44 89 99 60
Festival president: Peter Fleischmann
Festival programmer: Pierre-Henri Deleau
Competition
Prix de l'avenir (8,000 Euros)
Previous winner: *Festen* (Thomas Vinterberg)

Brynmawr Film Festival

Blaenau Gwent Arts Development Office, Beaufort Theatre, Beaufort, Ebbw Vale, Gwent, South Wales, NP3 5QQ

Tel: +44-1495-308996
Fax: +44-1495-308996
Festival director & programmer: Geoff Cripps

Festival de Cine de Alcala de Henares

Plaza del Empecinado 1, Alcala de Henares 28801, Spain
Tel: +34-91-881 3934
Fax: +34-91-881 3906
Festival director: Pedro Medina
Competition
Primer premio nacional (800,000 pesetas)
Previous winner: *Allanamiento de Morada* (Mateo Gill)

Festival dei Popoli International Review of Social Documentary Film (Florence)

Borgo Pinti 82R, I-Firenze 50121, Italy
Tel: +39-055-244 778
Fax: +39-055-241 364
E-mail: fespopol@dada it
Festival director: Mario Simondi
Competition
Award for best Documentary Film
Previous winner: *Masud Lasghan*

Foyle Film Weekend (Derry)

2nd Floor, Northern Counties Building, 8 Custom House Street, Derry
Tel: +44-1504 267 432
Fax: +44-1504 371 738
E-mail: shaunakelpie@thenerve-centre.org.uk
Festival director: Shauna Kelpie
Festival programmer: Michael McDaid
Competition
Award: £1000

International Thessaloniki Film Festival (Thessaloniki)

Paparigopoulou 40, 11473 Athens, Greece
Tel: +30-1-645 3669
Fax: +30-1-644 8143
E-mail: info@filmfestival.gr

Website: www.filmfestival.gr
Festival director: Michel Demopoulos
Festival programmer: Michel Demopoulos
Competition
Golden Alexander (12,500,000 drs)
Previous winner: *Fishes in August* (Yoichiro Takahashi)

Stockholm International Film Festival

Po Box 3136, Stockholm, 10362 Sweden
Tel: +46-8-677 5000
Fax: +46-8-200590
E-mail: filmfestivalen@cinema.s
Website: http://www.filmfestivalen.s
Festival director: Git Scheynius
Festival programmer: Jacob Abrahamson
Competition
The Bronze Horse
Previous winner: *The Wounds* (Srdjan Dragojevic)

Encontros Internacionais de Cinema Documental (Odivelas)

Rua Angola, Olival Basto, 2675 Odivelas, Portugal
Tel: +351-1 938 8407
Fax: +351-1 938 9347
E-mail: amascultura@mail.telepc.pl
Festival director: Fernando Lopez
Competition
Grand Prix for the best documentary feature
Previous winner: *Amble Life* (Alexandar Sukurov, Russia)

The Golden Elephant, 11th International Children's Film Festival (Hyderabad)

c/o Children's Film Society, India, 24 Dr. G. Deshmukh Marg, Mumbai 400 026, India
Tel: +91-22 387 0875/6136
Fax: +91-22 380 5610
E-mail: ncyp@bom3.net.in
Chairperson: Sai Paranjpye
Festival director: S. Narayanan
Competition

The Golden Elephant for the Best Feature Film (The Golden Elephant Statue and Rs. 100,000)

Oulu International Children's Film Festival

Torikatu 8, 90100 Oulu, Finland
Tel: +358-8-881 1293
Fax: +358-8-881 1290
E-mail: raimo.kinisjarvi@oufilmcenter.inet.fi
Festival director: Pentti Kejonen
Festival programmer: Eszter Vuojala
Competition
Star Boy Award (Ecu 3000)
Previous winner: *The Glassblower's Children* (Andres Krønros)

Southern African International Film & Television Market (Cape Town)

PO Box 1176, Oakland Park, Johannesburg, 2006, South Africa
Tel: +27-11 714 3229
Fax: +27-11 714 3275
Contact: Richard Ishmail

Action and Adventure Film Festival (Antwerp)

1104 Kortrijksesteenweg, Ghent, Belgium, B-9051
Tel: +32-9-221 8946
Fax: +32-9-221 9074
E-mail: filmfestival@infoboard.be
Website: http://www.rug.ac.be/filmfestival/Welcome.html
Contact: Jacques Dubrulle, Walter Provo, Peter Bouckaert, Marian Ponnet

Birmingham International Film & TV Festival

9 Margaret Street, Birmingham B3 3SB, UK
Tel: +44-121-212 0777
Fax: +44-121-212 0666
Festival director: Sarah McKenzie
Festival programmer: Barbara Chapman
Competition for local filmmakers

Holland Animation Film Festival (Utrecht)

Hoogt 4, 3521 GW Utrecht, The Netherlands
Tel: +31-30 233 1733
Fax: +31-30 233 1079
E-mail: haff@knoware.nl
Website: www.awn.com/haff
Festival director: Gerben Schermer
Festival programmer: Metter Peters & Erik van Drunan
Competition
Previous winner: *Nestea Cool* (Dave Borthwick)

Verzaubert, Gay & Lesbian Film Festival (Munich, Cologne, Frankfurt, Stuttgart, Berlin)

Rosebud Entertainment, Herzog Wilhelm str 27, 80331 Munich, Germany
Tel: +49-89-260 22 838
Fax: +49-89-260 22 839
E-mail: rosebud-entertainment@tonline.de
Festival director: Schorsch Müller, Rainer Stefan
Festival programmer: as above

Brief Encounters (Short Film Festival) (Bristol)

PO Box 576, Bristol BS99 2BD
Tel: +44 117 922 4628
Fax: +44 117 922 2906
E-mail: brief.encounters@dial.pipex.com
Website: www.brief-encounters.org.uk
Festival manager: Louise Jannings
Competition
Audience Award
Previous winner: *Anthrakitis* (Sara Sugarman)

Cinemania (Sofia)

1 Bulgaria Square, National Palace of Culture, 1414 Sofia, Bulgaria
Tel: +359 2 54 3061/ 9166 2841
Fax: +359 2 657 053
Festival director: Christo Droumev

French Film Festival (Edinburgh/Glasgow)

French Institute, 13 Randolph Crescent, Edinburgh, UK EH3 8TX
Tel: +44-131-225 6191
Fax: +44-131-220 0648
Festival director & programmer: Richard Mowe
Hennessy Audience Award (non-monetary)
Previous winner: *Man Is a Woman* (Antoine De Caunes)

Gijon International Film Festival for Young People

Po. Begoña No 24 entlo, 33205 Gijon, Spain
Tel: +34-98-534 3739
Fax: +34-98-535 4152
E-mail: festcine@airastuz.es
Festival director: Jose Luis Cienfuegos
Festival programmer: Fran Gaio
Competition
Principado de Asturias
Previous winner: *Orphans* (Peter Mullan)

International Festival of Authorial Film (Belgrade)

Jugoslavija film, Makedonska 22/VI, 11000 Beograd, Yugoslavia
Tel: +381-11 324 8554/ 324 8282
Fax: +381-11 324 8659
Festival director: Vojislav Vucinovic
Competition
Aleksandar Petrovic Award
Previous winner: *Conte d'automne* (Eric Rohmer)

Oslo International Film Festival

Ebbellsgate 1, N-0183 Oslo - Norway
Tel: +47-22 20 07 66
Fax: +47-22 20 18 03
E-mail: filmfestival@login.eunet.no
Website: http://wit.no/filmfestival
Festival director & programmer: Tommy Lordahl

Turin International Film Festival

Via Monte di Pietá 1, Torino, Italy, 10121
Tel: +39-011-562 3309
Fax: +39-011-562 9796
E-mail: info@torinofilmfest.org
Website: www.torinofilmfest.org
Festival director: Stefano Della Casa
Festival programmer: as above
Competition
Best Film (US$ 20 000)
Previous winner: *The Fly of the Bee* (Jasmed Usmonov)

IberoAmerican Film Festival (Huelva)

Casa Colon, Plaza del Punto, 21003 Huelva, Spain
Tel: +34-959 21 0170
Fax: +34-959 210173
Festival director & programmer: Francisco López Villarejo
Competition
Colon de oro by the jury (3 mill. ptas)
Previous winner: *Traiçao* (Arthur Fontes, Claudio Torres, José Henrique Fonseca, Brasil)

Junior Dublin Film Festival

c/o Irish Film Centre, Eustache Street, Dublin 2, Ireland
Tel: +353-1 671 4095
Fax: +353 1 670 3074
Festival director & programmer: Alan Robinson

International Festival of Documentary and Short Films (Bilbao)

C/Colón de Larreategui, nº 37-4º drch, 48009 Bilbao, Spain
Tel: +34-94-424 8698/424 5507/424 7860
Fax: +34-94-424 5624
Festival director: Jaseba Inchaurraga
Festival programmer: Maria Angeles Olea
Competition
Grand Premio (Pta400,000)

Cairo International Film Festival

17th Kasr El Nil Street, Cairo, 202 Egypt
Tel: +20 2 392 3562
Fax: +20 2 393 8979
Festival director: Hasim Fahmi
Competition
Golden Pyramid
Previous winner: *The Terrorist* (India)

Festival des Trois Continents (Nantes)

19a Passage Pommeraye, BP 43302, F-44033,
Nantes Cedex 1, France
Tel: +33-240 69 74 14
Fax: +33-240 73 55 22
Festival directors: Alain Jalladeau, Philippe
Jalladeau
Festival programmers: as above
Competition (only for feature films)
Montgolfiere d'Or (FF30,000)
Previous winner: *After Life* (Kore-eda
Hirokazu) & *Xiao Wu* (Gia Zhang Ke)

International Biennale Film+Arc Graz

Hallerschloszstrasse 21, 8010 Graz, Austria
Tel: +43-316-35 6155
Fax: +43-316-356156
Festival director: Charlotte Pöchhacker
Festival programmer: as above
Competition
Grand Prix film (ATS 100,000)
Previous winners: *City of the Steppes* (Peter
Brosens, Odo Halflans)

International Documentary Film Festival Amsterdam (IDFA)

Kleine Gartmanplantsoen 10, 017 RR
Amsterdam
Tel: +31-20-627 3329
Fax: +31-20-638 5388
E-mail: idfa@xs4all.nl
Festival director: Ally Derks
Festival programmer: as above
Competition

UPRO Joris Juens Award (25.000 guilders)
Previous winner: *Photographer* (Darius
Jablonski)

Docs for Sale (Amsterdam)

Kleine Gartmanplantsoen 10, 017 RR
Amsterdam
Tel: +31-20-627 3329
Fax: +31-20-638 5388
E-mail: idfa@xs4all.nl
Market manager: Willemien Van Aalst
Market

Camerimage (Torun)

Rynek Nowomiejski 28, 87-100 Torun, Poland
Tel: +48-56-652 2179
Fax: +48-56-621 0019
Festival director: Marek Zydowicz
Festival programmer: Marek Zydowicz
Competition
The Golden Frog Award
Previous winner: *Central Station* (DOP
Walter Cavallo)

EuropaCinema (Viareggio)

Via 20 Settembre 3, 00187 Rome, Italy
Tel: +39-06 420 111 84/ 42 000 211
Fax: +39-06 4201 0599
Festival director: Monique Veaute
Competition

Taipei Golden Horse Film Festival

Floor 7, No 45, Chilin Road, Taipei, 104
Taiwan ROC
Tel: +886-2 2567 5861
Fax: +886-2 2531 8966/2521 6311
E-mail: tghffctt@ms14.hinet.net
Festival director: You-Ning Lee
Festival programmer: Johnny Yang

European Festival of Film Schools (Bologna)

Cineteca di Bologna, Via Galliera 8, Bologna,
Italy 40121
Tel: +39 051 23 70 88

Fax: +39 051 26 16 80

E-mail: cineteca@comune.bologna.it

Festival programmer: Guy Borlee

The Forum (Amsterdam)

Kleine-Gartmanplantsoen 10, 1017 RR Amsterdam, The Netherlands

Tel: +31-20-627 3329

Fax: +31-20-638 5388

E-mail: idfa@xs4all.nl

Market director: Jolanda Klarenbeek

Market

Rencontres cinématographiques (Aix-en-Provence)

Tel: +33-4 41 27 08 64

Fax: +33-4 42 38 47 83

E-mail: aixfilms@club-internet.fr

Competition for short films

International Film Festival Bratislava

Mosovskeho 16, 81103 Bratislava, Slovakia

Tel: +421-7 5441 0673

Fax: +421-7 5441 0674

Festival programmer: Peter Nagel

Competition first and second feature films

Festival of French Cinema (Acapulco)

Unifrance, 4 Villa Bosquet, 75007 Paris, France

Tel: +33-1 47 53 95 80/ 47 53 27 48

Fax: +33-1 47 05 96 55

Contact: Stephan Melchiori

Festival Primer Plano (Dijon)

4 Place Darcy BP 1002, F-21024 Dijon Cedex, France

Tel: +33-3-80 30 59 78

Fax: +33-3-80 50 18 08

Festival director: Laurence Karoibi

Competition

Previous winner: *Max et Bobo* (Frédéric Fonteyne)

PILOTS (Programme for the International Launch of Television Series Workshops) (Sitges)

Diputació 279, E-08007 Barcelona, Spain

Tel: +34-93-487 3773

Fax: +34-93- 4873952

Festival director: Pera Fages

Asian Film & video Arts Society Festival (Montreal)

300 Léo Pariseau street, 15th floor, Montreal, Quebec H2W 2P3 Canada

Tel: +1-514 982 0020

Fax: +1-514 982 0796

E-mail: cine.asie@videotrom.ca

Festival director: Anna Mijeong Lee

Festival programmer: Peter Rist, Scott Preston and the public

Golden Knight International Amateur Film and Video Festival (Valletta-Malta)

Malta Amateur Cine Circle, PO Box 450, Valetta CMR 01, Malta

Tel: +356-222345

Fax: +356-225047

Website: http://www.global.net.mt.a macc

Festival director: Alfred Stagno Navarra

Festival programmer: Vincent Lungaro Mifsud

Competition

Golden Knight Award

Women in Cinema Film Festival (Seattle)

801 East Pine St, Seattle, 98122 WA, USA

Tel: +1-206-324 9996

Fax: +1-206-324 9998

E-mail: mail@seattlefilm.com

Festival director: Darryl Macdonald

Festival programmer: Darryl Macdonald, Kathleen McInnis

Market & Competition

European Short Film Festival (London)

11 Holbein House, Holbein Place, London, SW1 W8NH, UK
Tel: +44-171 460 3901
Fax: +44-171 259 9278
E-mail: info@pearlproductions.co.uk
Website: www.pearlproductions.co.uk
Festival director: Fritz Kohle

Margaret Mead Film & Video Festival (New York)

American Museum of Natural History, 79th Street at Central Park West, New York, 10024 NY, USA
Tel: +1-212-769 5305
Fax: +1-212-769 5329
E-mail: meadfest @amnh.org
Festival director: Elaine Charnov

New York Exposition of Short Film and Video

New York Expo, 532 LaGuardia Place, Suite 330, New York, NY 10012, USA
Tel: +1-212 505 7742
Fax: +1-212 586 6391
E-mail: nyexpo@aol.com
Website: www.yrd.com/nyexpo

Northwest Film & Video Festival (Portland)

1219 SW Park Avenue, Portland, Oregon 97205, USA
Tel: +1-503-221-1156
Fax: +1-503-294 0874
E-mail: info@nwfilm.org
Festival director: Meagan Atiyeh
Competition
Best of Festival ($12, 000 in production service awards)

Tranny Fest (San Francisco)

Transgender & Transgenre Cinema
584 Castro Street, Suite 273, San Francisco, CA 94114, US
Tel/Fax: +1-415 552 4249
E-mail: trannyfest@aol. com
Festival directors: Christopher Lee & Alison Austin

Mavericks in Manchester, Festival of American Independent Film (Manchester)

70 Oxford Street, Manchester, UK MI 5NH
Tel: +44-161 228 7621
Fax: +44-161 200 1506
Festival programmer: Linda Pariser

Cinewomen (Norwich)

Cinema City, St Andrews St., Norwich, Norfolk, NR2 4AD, UK
Tel: +44-1603-622 047
Fax: +44-1603-767838

Days of Independent Film (Augsburg)

Schroeckstr. 6, 86152 Augsburg, Germany, 86152
Tel: +49-821 349 1060
Fax: +49-821-349 5218
E-mail: filmbuero@t-online.de
Festival director: Harald Munding

Cape Town International Film Festival

University of Cape Town, Private Bag, Rondebosch, Cape Town 8001, South Africa
Tel: +27-21 4238 257
Fax: +27-21 4242 355
E-mail: filmfest@hiddingh.uct.ac.za
Festival director: James A. Polley
Festival programmer: Mignon Coetzee

German Screenings

German United Distributors, Auf der Ruhr 2, Cologne 50667, Germany
Tel: +49-221 920 690
Fax: +49-221 920 6969
Market

December

International Festival of New Latin American Cinema (Havana)

Calle 23, No 1155, Vedado, Havana 10600, Cuba
Tel: +53-7-552 841/552 849

Fax: +53-7-333 078/ 334 273

Festival president: Alfredo Guevara

Festival director: Iván Giroud

Competition & Market

Coral Prizes

Previous winner: *La Vida es Silbar* (Fernando Perez, Cuba)

Cinemagic International Film Festival for Young People (Belfast)

4th Floor, 38 Dublin Road, Belfast BT2 7HN, Northern Ireland, UK

Tel: +44-1232-311 900

Fax: +44-1232-319 709

Festival director: Shauna McCarthy

Festival programmer: Frances Cassidy

Competition

Cinemagic Young Jury Award (£1,000)

Previous winner: *The Real Howard Spitz* (Vadim Jean)

European Television & Film Forum (Prague)

EIM, Kaistrasse 13, 40221 Düsseldorf, Germany

Tel: +49 211 901 0457

Fax: +49 211 901 0456

E-mail: forum@eim.org

Contact: Monique Masius

Noir In Festival (Courmayer, Italy)

Via Tirso 90, I-Rome 00198, Italy

Tel: +39-06-884 8030

Fax: + 39-06-884 0450

Festival director: Giorgio Gosetti

Festival programmer: Maria Teresa Cavina

Competition

Mystery Award

Previous winner: *Slam* (Mark Levin)

European Film Academy Awards (Berlin)

Kurfürstendamm 225, D-10719 Berlin, Germany

Tel: +49-30 887 1670

Fax: +49-30 8871 6777

Chairman of the European Film Academy: Nik Powell

Previous winner: *La vita è bella* (Roberto Begnini)

Black Night's Film Festival (Tallinn, Tarta)

Nafta Street 1, Tallinn, Estonia, 10152

Tel: +372 2 425 939

Fax: +372 6 431 351

E-mail: bnights@uninet.ee

Festival director: Endel Koplimets

Festival programmer: Tiina Lokk

Cine Asia (Hong Kong)

244 West 49th Street #200, New York 10019, USA

Tel: +1-212-246 6460

Fax: +1-212-265 6428

E-mail: sunshine@maestro.com

Festival director: Robert Suunshine

MIP-ASIA (Hong Kong)

Reed Midem Organisation, 11 rue du Colonel Pierre Avia, F-75015, Paris, France

Tel: +33-1-41 90 45 80

Fax: +33-1-41 90 45 70

Programme director: André Vaillant

Market

The First KISH International Film Festival

Kish Fress Zone Organization, Kish Street, Africa Expressway, Tehran, Iran

Tel: +98-21 879 7480

Fax: +98-21 878 3999

E-mail: kish-free0zone@kfzo.com

4.7.2 A–Z festivals and markets

Acapulco Festival of French Cinema, November

Aix-en-Province Rencontres cinématographiques, November-December

Alcala de Henares Festival de Cine, November

Alexandria Int'l Film Fest, September

Alfas Del Pi Alfas Del Pi, July

Algarve Int'l Film Fest, May

Alma Ata, Euro-Asia Film Fest, October

Amalfi Cartoons on the Bay, April

Amalfi Screens on the Bay, September-October

Amiens Int'l Film Fest, November

Amsterdam Cinema Expo, June

Amsterdam Int'l Broadcasting Convention, September

Amsterdam Cinekid, October

Amsterdam Int'l Documentary Film Fest, November-December

Amsterdam Docs for Sale November-December

Amsterdam The Forum, November-December

Angers Premiers Plans, January

Ankara, Int'l Film Fest, April-May

Ann Arbor Film Fest, March

Annecy, Int'l Animated Film Fest, June

Annecy MIFA, May

Annecy Rencontres d'Annecy du Cinema Italien, September-October

Antwerp Action & Adventure Film Fest, November

Aspen Shortfest, April

Aspen Film Fest, September

Athens Int'l Film Fest, September

Athens The Panorama of European Cinema, September-October

Athens (Georgia) Kudzu Film Fest October

Atlanta Peachtree Int'l Film Fest, October-November

Atlantic City Show East, October

Auckland, Int'l Film Fest, July

Augsburg Short Film Weekend, May

Augsburg Children's Film Fest, November

Augsburg Days of Independent Film, November

Austin South by Southwest Film Conference and Festival, March

Austin, Film Fest, October

Avignon French-American Film Workshop, June

Baden Fantoche, August-September

Banff TV Fest, June

Banff Fest of Mountain Films, November

Barcelona Women's Int'l Film Fest, June

Barcelona News World Int'l Forum for Broadcast News, November

Belfast Cinemagic Int'l Film Fest for Young People, December

Belgrade Int'l Film Fest, January-February

Belgrade Fest of Yugoslav Documenatry and Short Film, March

Belgrade Int'l Fest of Authorial Film, November

Bergamo Film Meeting, March

Berlin Int'l Film Fest, February

Berlin Int'l Forum of New Cinema, February

Berlin European Film Market, February

Berlin Video Fest, February

Berlin Prix Europa, October

Berlin European Film Academy Awards, December

Biarritz FIPA, January

Bielefeld Film & Music Fest, October

Bilbao Int'l Fest of Documentary & Short Films, November

Birmingham Int'l Film & TV Fest, November

Bitola Film Camera Fest, September

Bochum International Bochum Videofestival, June

Bogota Film Festival, September

Bologna Future Film Festival, January

Bologna Mostra Internazionale del Cinema Libero/ Il Cinema Ritrovato, July

Bologna European Festival of Film Schools, November-December

Bonn Videonale, September

Boston New England Film & Video Fest, April

Boston Film Festival, September

Bradford Film Fest, March

Bradford Animation Festival (BAF!), June

Bradford The Mango Film Fest, September-October

Bratislava Prix Danube, September

Bratislava Int'l Film Fest, November-December

Breckenridge Film Festival, September

Brisbane Int'l Film Fest, July-August

Bristol Widescreen, October

Bristol Brief Encounters Fest, November

Brussels Int'l Film Fest, January

Brussels Cartoon & Animated Film Fest, February-March

Brussels Int'l Fest of Fantasy Films, March-April

Brussels Age d'or Prize, July

Brussels Cartoon Forum, September

Brynmawr Film Fest, November

Budapest Hungarian Film Week, February

Cacak Yugoslav Animated Film Fest, October

Cairo Int'l Film Fest for Children, March

Cairo Fest for Radio & TV Programmes, July

Cairo Int'l Film Fest, November-December

Cambridge Int'l Film Fest, April

Campbell River Canadian International Annual Film/Video Festival, October

Cannes MIDEM January

Cannes MILIA, February

Cannes MIP-TV, April

Cannes Film Fest, May

Cannes FIFREC, May

Cannes Int'l Advertising Film Fest, June

Cannes MIPCOM Junior, October

Cannes MIPCOM, October

Cape Town Int'l Film Fest, November

Cape Town Southern African Int'l Film & TV Market, November

Cardiff Int'l Animation Fest, June

Cardiff Welsh Int'l Film Fest, November

Cartagena Film Fest, March

Charlotte Film & Video Fest, June

Charlottesville Virginia Film Festival, October

Cherbourg British Film Fest, October

Chicago Int'l TV Competition, January

Chicago The Mobius Advertising Awards, February

Chicago Intercom Film & Video Fest, April

Chicago Latino Film Fest, April

Chicago Silver Images Film Fest, April

Chicago Alt.film Fest, June

Chicago US Int'l Film & Video Fest, June

Chicago Alt. Film Fest, June

Chicago National Cable TV Association, June

Chicago Int'l Children's Film Fest, October

Chicago Int'l Film Fest, October

Chichester Film Fest, August-September

Clermont-Ferrand Short Film Fest, February

Cleveland Int'l Film Fest, March

Cleveland Midwest Filmmakers Conference, March

Cleveland The Ohio Independent Film Fest, November

Cognac Int'l Thriller Film Fest, March

Cologne Conference, June

Cologne Short Cuts Cologne, September

Cologne Feminale, October

Cologne (and other German cities) Verzaubert, November-December

Cologne German Screenings, November

Copenhagen NatFilm Fest, March

Copenhagen The Princes' Award, June

Cork Int'l Film Fest, October

Cottbus Film Festival, November

Creteil Int'l Fest of Women's Films, March-April

Courmayer Noir in Festival, December

Dallas Kid Film Fest, January

Dallas US Film Fest, April

Deauville Festival of American Films, September

Denver Int'l Film Fest, October

Derry Foyle Film Weekend, November

Dijon Primer Plano, November

Dinard Asociation du festival du film britannique, September-October

Dortmund Femme Totale Film Fest, March

Douarnenez Douarnenes Film Fest, August

Drama Short Film Fest, September
Dublin Film Fest, April
Dublin Lesbian & Gay Film Fest, July-August
Dublin Junior Film Fest, November-
December
Duisburg Filmwoche, November
East Hampton Hamptons Int'l Film Fest,
October
East Lansing Film Festival, March
Eastbourne Showlight, April
Edinburgh Italian Film Fest, April
Edinburgh Int'l Film Fest, August
Edinburgh Int'l TV Fest, August
Edinburgh French Film Fest, November
Edmonton Local Heroes, February
Emden International Film Festival, June
Espinho Cinanima, November
Espoo Espoo Ciné, August
Figuera da Foz Festival Internacional de
Cinema, September
Flagstaff Worldfest, November
Florence Festival dei Popoli, November
Fort Lauderdale Int'l Film Fest, October-
November
Frankfurt Lucas '00, September
Freiburg International Ecology Film
Festival, October
Freistadt Festival der "Neue Heimat Film"
September
Fribourg Film Fest, March
Fukuoka Int'l Film Fest, September
Galway Film Fleadh, July
Geneva Networks in the Studio, January
Geneva Festival Cinéma Tout Ecran,
September
Geneva Film Fest Stars of Tomorrow,
October-November
Gent Viewpoint: Documentary Now, March
Gent Flanders Int'l Film Fest, October
Gera Deutsches Kinder-film & Fernseh Fest,
March
Gerardmer Fantastic Arts, January
Giffoni Film Fest, July
Gijon Int'l Film Fest for Young People,
November
Glen Ellen Wine Country Film Fest, July-
August

Göteborg Film Fest, January-February
Gramado Film Fest - Latin & Brazilian
Cinema, August
Graz Diagonalle, March
Graz Int'l Biennale, November
Grenoble Outdoor Short Film Fest, July
Grimstadt Norwegian Short Film Fest, June
Guadalajara Film Fest, March
Györ Media Wave, April-May
Haifa Israel Film Fest, September
Halifax Atlantic Film Fest, September
Hamburg Int'l Short Film Fest, June
Hamburg FilmFest, September-October
Hamburg Lesbian and Gay Film Fest,
October
Haugesund Int'l Film Fest, August
Havana Int'l Fest of New Latin American
Cinema, December
Helsinki Film Fest - Love & Anarchy,
September
Herceg-Novi Yugoslav Film Festival,
August
Hiroshima Int'l Animation Fest, August
Hof Int'l Hofer Filmtage, October
Hollywood Film Fest, August
Hollywood Film Market, August
Hong Kong Film Fest, April
Hong Kong Int'l Film Market, June
Hong Kong Cine Asia, December
Hong Kong MIP ASIA, December
Honolulu Hawaii Int'l Film Fest, November
Houston Worldfest, April
Huelva IberoAmerican Film Fest, November
Huesca Festival de Cine, June
Hyderabad The Golden Elephant, 11th Int'l
Children's Film Fest, November
Igualada Int'l Short Film Fest, October
Indeanapolis Heartland Film Fest, October
Innsbruck Int'l Film Fest Cinematograph,
May-June
Isfahan Int'l Fest of Film & Video for
Children & Young Adults, September
Istanbul Int'l Film Fest, April-May
Jerusalem Film Fest, July
Karlovy Vary Int'l Film Fest, July
Kiev Int'l Film Fest Molodist, October
Kraków Int'l Short Film Fest, May-June

La Rochelle Int'l Film Fest, June-July

Laon Int'l Film Fest for Young People, March-April

Las Vegas Showest, March

Leeds Int'l Film Fest, October

Leipzig Int'l Fest for Documentary & Animated Film, October

Ljubljana Int'l Film Fest, November

Locarno Int'l Film Fest, August

London Green Screen, February

London Royal TV Society Awards, March

London IVCA Awards, March

London Architecture on Film, October

London The Production Show, March

London Lesbian and Gay Film Fest, April

London BAFTA Awards, April

London Cable & Satellite, May

London European TV Sports Conference, June

London Latin American Film Fest, September

London The British Short Film Fest, September

London Raindance Film Showcase, October

London Premiere Screenings, October

London European Cable Communications '99, October

London Film Fest, November

London Programme Market, November

London European Short Film Fest, November

Los Angeles Golden Globe Awards, January

Los Angeles Academy Awards Nominations, February

Los Angeles Israel Film Fest, February

Los Angeles AFM, February-March

Los Angeles Academy Awards, March

Los Angeles Independent Film Fest, April

Los Angeles Asian Pacific American Film and Video Festival, May

Los Angeles Showbiz Expo West, June

Los Angeles AFI Int'l Film Fest, October

Lübeck Nordic Film Days, November

Lucerne VIPER, October

Lund Fantasy Film Festival, September

Magdeburg International Computer Animation Festival, September

Maitland Florida Film Fest, June

Malaga Spanish Film Festival, May

Manchester Kino Festival of American Underground Cinema, February

Manchester Kino Festival of New Irish Cinema March

Manchester Viva! Spanish Film Fest, March

Manchester Festival of Fantastic Films, September

Manchester Kinofilm, October

Manchester Fest of American Independent Film, November

Mannhein Int'l Film Fest, October

Marseilles Marseilles 1999, June

Marseilles Sunny Side of the Doc, June

Melbourne Int'l Film Fest, July-August

Miami Film Fest, February

Miami Sportel, March

Miami Gay & Lesbian Film Fest, July

Milan Tourism Int'l Film Fest, March

Milan Festival Cinema Africano, March

Milan IBTS October

Milan MIFED, October

Milan Sport Movies & TV Int'l Fest, October

Milan Kidscreen, October

Mill Valley Film Festival, October

Minneapolis Int'l Film Fest, April

Moab Film and Video Festival, April

Mohawk Empire State Film Festival, September-October

Monaco Imagina, January-February

Monaco Sportel, September

Monte Carlo TV Fest, February

Monte Carlo Sportel, September

Montecatini Filmvideo 2000 -51st Int'l Short Film Fest, July

Montevideo Int'l Film Fest, April

Montevideo Int'l Film Fest for Children & Young People, July

Montpellier Cinéma Meditérráneen, October-November

Montpellier Hébraïca, March

Montreal Int'l Fest of Films on Art, March

Montreal Vues d'Afrique, April

Montreal & Toronto Fant-Asia, July-August

Montreal World Film Fest, August-September

Montreal Int'l Fest of Cinema and New Media, October

Montreal Cinemania French Film Fest, November

Montreal Asian Film & Video Arts Society Festival, November

Montreux Golden Rose, May

Montreux Int'l TV Symposium, June

Moscow 5th Int'l Festival of Animation & Computer Graphics, May

Moscow Int'l Film Fest, July

Motovun Int'l Film Fest, August

Mumbai Int'l Film Fest for Documentary, Short & Animation Films, February

Munich Int'l Documentary Film Fest, April-May

Munich Prix Jeunesse Int'l, May-June

Munich Festival of Film Schools June-July

Munich Filmfest, June-July

Munich Fantasy Filmfest, July-August

Namur Festival International du Film Francophone, September-October

Nantes Festival des Trois Continents, November

Neubrandenburg Dokumentart, October

New Delhi Int'l Film Festival of India, January

New Orleans NATPE, January

New Orleans Film & Video Fest, October

New York Festivals, January

New York Israel Film Fest, March

New York Underground Film Fest, March

New York New Directors/New Films, March-April

New York Avignon/New York Film Festival, April

New York Gen Art Film Fest, April-May

New York Docfest, June

New York Human Rights Watch Int'l Film Fest, June

New York Stony Brook Film Fest, July-August

New York Monitor Awards, July

New York Urbanworld Film Festival, August

New York Independent Feature Film Market, September

New York Film Fest, September-October

New York Showbiz Expo East, September

New York Margaret Mead Film & Video Fest, November

New York Exposition of Short Film and Video, November

Newport Beach Int'l Film Fest, March-April

Nis Actors' Fest, August

Northampton Film Fest, November

Norwich Cinewomen, November

Nottingham Shots in the Dark, Mystery & Thriller Fest, June

Novi Sad Yugoslav Feature Film Fest, September

Nyon Visions du Reel Festival Int'l du Cinema Documentaire, April

Oakland National Educational Media Network, May

Oakland Black Filmworks Festival of Film & Video, October

Oberhausen Int'l Short Film Fest, May

Odense Int'l Film Fest, August

Odivelas Encontros Internacionais de Cinema Documental, November

Oldenburg Internationale Filmfest, September

Oslo Filmdager, February

Oslo Animation Festival, April

Oslo Films from the South, September-October

Oslo Int'l Film Fest, November

Osnabrück European Media Art Festival, May

Ottawa Int'l Animation Fest, October

Ouagadougou PanAfrican Film and TV Fest, February

Oulu Int'l Children's Film Fest, November

Ourense Int'l Independent Film Fest, November

Palermo Int'l Sport Film Fest, November

Palic Int'l Film Fest, July

Palm Beach Int'l Film Fest, April

Palm Springs Int'l Film Fest, January

Palm Springs Int'l Short Film Fest, July-August

Paris Cinema du Reel, March

Paris Festival du film de Paris, March-April

Paris La Rochelle June-July

Paris Rencontres Internationales de cinema à Paris, October November

Park City Sundance Film Fest, January

Park City Slamdance Film Fest, January

Peniscola Int'l Comedy Film Festival, June

Pesaro Mostra Internazionale de nuovo cinema, June

Philadelphia Festival of World Cinema, April-May

Philadelphia UFVA's Touring Festival of Int'l Student Film & Video, September

Plovdiv The Golden Rhyton, October

Plovdiv The Golden Chest Int'l TV Fest, October

Plymouth Start the Millennium, March

Poitier Int'l School Film Fest, March

Portland Int'l Film Fest, February

Portland Northwest Film & Video Fest, November

Porto, Fantasporto, February-March

Portofino RAI Trade Screenings, September/October

Portre, Skye Celtic Film & TV Fest, March

Potsdam Film Fest Potsdam, June

Poughkeepsie Hudson Valley Film Fest, June

Prague Golden Prague, May

Prague European TV & Film Forum, December

Puchon Int'l Fantastic Film Fest, July

Pula Film Fest, July-August

Pusan Int'l Film Fest, October

Ravensburg Spotlight, March

Rennes Travelling Film Fest, January

Riga Film Forum "Arsenals", September

Rimini Adriaticocimena, June

Rio de Janeiro Rio Fest, September

Rome Fantafestival, June

Rome International Short Film Fest, November

Rotterdam Int'l Film Fest January-February

Rouen Nordic Film Fest, March

Rouyn-Noranda Festival du Cineema Int'l, October-November

Saarbrüken Max Ophüls Preis Film Fest, January

Sacile Le Giornate del Cinema Muto, October

St. Barth Film Fest, April

Saint Louis Int'l Film Fest, October-November

St Petersburg Message to Man Fest, June

St Petersburg Festival of Festivals, June

St Thérèse Festival de cinéma int'l, September-October

Salerno Shadow Line Film Fest, April

Salerno Int'l Film Fest, November

San Diego Latino Film Fest, March

San Francisco Int'l Asian-American Film Fest, March

San Francisco Int'l Film Fest, April

San Francisco Lesbian & Gay Film Festival, June

San Francisco Jewish Film Festival, July

San Francisco Cinemayaat (Arab Film Fest) September

San Francisco Film Arts Fest, November

San Francisco Tranny Fest, November

San Francisco December

San Jose Cinequest, February-March

San Juan Cinequest, October

San Luis Obispo Int'l Film Fest, October-November

San Rafael Latino Film Fest, November

San Sebastian Int'l Film Fest, September

Santa Barbara Film Fest, March

Santa Fe de Bogota Fest, October

Sao Paulo It's all True, Int'l Documentary Film Fest, April

São Paulo Int'l Short Film Fest, August

São Paulo Int'l Film Fest, October

Sarajevo Film Fest, August

Seattle Women in Cinema, November

Seattle Int'l Film Fest, May-June

Selb Internationale Grenzland Filmtage, April

Seoul Cable & Satellite Fest, March

Seoul Media & Film Expo, October

Setubal Troia Int'l Film Fest, June

Sheffield Int'l Documentary Fest, October

Singapore Int'l Film Fest, April

Sitges Int'l Fantasy Film Fest, October

Sitges Pilots Workshop for TV scriptwriters, March, June, October & November

Sochi Int'l & Open Russian Film Fests, June

Sodankylä Midnight Sun Film Fest, June

Sofia Festival of European Co-productions, June

Sofia Music Film Fest, March

Sofia Cinemania, November
Solothurn Film Fest, January
Sopot Film Fest, July
Split International Festival of New Film
September-October
Stockholm Int'l Film Fest, November
Strasbourg, Forum of European Cinema,
November
Stuttgart Filmwinter, January
Stuttgart Int'l Animation Film Fest, March
Stuttgart Filmfest Ludwigsburg June
Sudbury Cinefest, September
Svaneke-Bornholm Balticum Film & TV
Fest, June
Sydney Mardi Gras Film Fest, February
Sydney Film Fest, June
Sydney Queerdoc Fest, October
Tacoma Tortured Artists Film Fest,
September
Taipei Golden Horse Film Fest, December
Tallinn Black Night's Film Festival December
Tampere Film Fest, March
Taormina Int'l Film Fest, July
Taos Taos Talking Picture Fest, April
Tarascon-sur-Ariège Festival de films
resistances, July
Tehran Fajr Film Fest, February
Tehran Kish Int'l Film Fest, December
Tel Aviv Festival of French Cinema, April
Tellurida Film Fest, September
Tempe Arizona State Universiy Art Museum
Annual Outdoor Film Festival, April
Thessaloniki Film Fest, November
Tokyo PIA Film Fest, July
Tokyo Int'l Film Fest, October-November
Torino Film Fest, November
Tornitz Sub Fiction, September
Toronto Jewish Film Fest, May
Toronto Inside Out Lesbian & Gay Film &
Video, May
Toronto Worldwide Short Film Fest, May-
June
Toronto Int'l Film Fest, September
Torun Camerimage, November-December
Trencianske Teplice Art Film Fest, June
Trento Int'l Fest of Mountain and
Exploration Films, April

Trieste Alpe Adria Cinema Film Festival,
January
Tromso Int'l Film Fest, January
Trondheim Minimalen Short Film Fest,
March
Tübingen Cine Latino, April-May
Tübingen Mediterranean Film Fest, June
Tübingen Int'l Short Film Fest, August
Tübingen Int'l French Film Fest, November
Turin Int'l Fest of Gay & Lesbian Cinema,
April
Turin Int'l Film Fest, November
Udine Incontri Cinema, April
Umea Int'l Film Fest, September
Uppsala Int'l Short Film Fest, October
Utrecht Netherlands Film Fest, September-
October
Utrecht Holland Film Meeting, September
Utrecht Holland Animation Film Festival,
November
Valencia Mostra de Valencia/Cinema de
Mediterrani, October
Valenciennes Action and Adventure Film
Fest, March
Valladolid Int'l Film Fest, October
Valletta Golden Knight Int'l Amateur Film
and Video Fest, November
Vancouver Int'l Film Fest, September-
October
Varna Love Is Folly, August-September
Varna Int'l Fest of Films for Children and
Teenagers, May-June
Venice Mostra Internazionale d'arte
cinematografica, September
Verona Schermi d'amore, April
Vevey, Int'l Comedy Film Fest, October
Viareggio Europa Cinema, November-
December
Victoria Independent Film and Video Fest,
February
Vienna Diagonale, March-April
Vienna Viennale, October
Vila do Conde Int'l Short Film Fest, July
Vrnjacka Banja Film Screenplay Fest, August
Vyborg Int'l Fest "Window into Europe",
August
Warsaw Film Fest, October

Washington Cine Golden Eagle Showcase, February

Washington NAB, April

Washington Int'l Film Fest, April

Washington Hometown Video Fest, July

Weimar Film in Weimar Fest October

Weiterstadt Open Air Film Fest, August

Wellington Film Fest, July-August

Wiesbaden European Cinema Congress, April

Wiesbaden Workshop for Young Filmmakers, May

Würzburg Internationale Filmwochenende, January

Yamagata Int'l Documentary Film Fest, October

Zagreb Int'l Fest of Animated Film, June

Zanzibar Film Fest of Dhow Countries, July

Zlatibor Int'l Fest of Tourist, Ecological and Sport Films, August

Mike Downey

Mike Downey is the co-founder of *Moving Pictures International* and the publisher of its worldwide daily publications. Born in England of Irish parents he completed his Master's degree in Theatre Studies at L'Université de Paris-X (Nanterre) in the class of Prof. Jacqueline Jomaron, with prior stints at the Universities of Warwick, and Paris III (Sorbonne-Nouvelle). Mike spent most of the eighties as a theatre director and producer in Germany, the former Yugoslavia and the UK, where his work included productions of *Look Back in Anger*, *The Big Sleep*, *Woza Albert!*, *Decadence*, *Entertaining Mr Sloane*, *Othello*, and *In Search of Artaud*, as well as working as a correspondent, contributor and critic on such diverse titles as *Screen International* (London), *Variety* (New York), *Cinemaya* (New Delhi), *Cinema Papers* (Melbourne), *Vogue* (Madrid), *Chaplin* (Stockholm), *Stills* (London) and *Cineaste* (New York). In addition to this, Mike was also publisher of the industry trade paper, *MPTV*, and the *European Film Review* (published in association with FIPRESCI). His first book, *The Self Managing Screen*, was published by the British Film Institute. As a programmer he has created various seasons at the National Film Theatre in London as well as advising numerous festivals on programming matters. Founder of the London-based film production house Bridie Films Ltd, he was associate producer on Rajko Grlic's award winning feature film *Caruga*, co-producer of Zeljko Senecic's *Dubrovnik Twilight*, and executive producer of Indigo Filmproduktion's *Seven Days to Live*, starring Amanda Plummer. Mike has also recently completed production on the documentary feature *Brokenville – the Telling of Kosovo*, in collaboration with Heart Felt Films. He is currently a tutor on the MEGA Masters programme of the Media Business School and teaches on the Soros funded Imaginary Film Academy for filmmakers from Central Europe. In addition, Mike is a member of the board of advisors of Oklahoma University Film School and the Canada-based Silver Star Institute, as well as being president of the Council of Advisors of the Motovun International Film Festival.

Peter Dally

Peter joined Bird & Bird in 1998 as a partner in the Media and Entertainment Group having previously been a partner at Denton Hall and Marriott Harrison. Prior to qualifying in 1980 he worked for Rank Leisure, Chrysalis Records and Mainline Pictures.

His main area of practice is film and television finance production and distribution. He also handles copyright, competition issues relating to the film industry and sports broadcasting law.

He led a team of lawyers at the East/West Producers Seminars in London, Warsaw, Budapest, Prague and Bucharest between 1991 and 1995.

He is the author of "A to Z of Film Business Terminology" published in the *Media Business File* and is a contributor to *The Film Finance Handbook* published by the Media Business School.

Peter is a regular speaker and has spoken at media industry conferences in London, Vienna, Cannes and Los Angeles. He served as an expert at the Film Business School and is now in charge of Legal Affairs at the Television Business School. He has designed and taught the Common Law Module for the Master in European Audiovisual Management (MEGA) since its inception in 1997 and is a member of the course evaluation committee. Peter is also a member of the advisory board of The Script Factory.

His recent film and television credits include *Saving Grace, House!, Kurt and Courtney, A Royal Celebration, Virtual Sexuality* and *Sorted*.

Bird & Bird

International law firm Bird & Bird specialises in the media, e-commerce, communications, IT, intellectual property, pharmaceuticals and biotechnology sectors, providing a comprehensive legal service. Bird & Bird's offices in London, Brussels, Paris and Hong Kong facilitate the firm's strong transnational focus.

The Media Group works extensively with those involved in the film and television industry. Whether dealing with a first-time producer seeking sources of financing or advising on a complex tax deal, Bird & Bird is able to provide innovative solutions to complex problems.

Many of the firm's lawyers are registered or can plead in a number of jurisdictions: Australia, Belgium, France, Luxembourg, Ireland, Spain, Hong Kong, New Zealand and the United States (California, New York, Texas and Washington D.C.).

The converging synergy between the Media Group and the firm's other major practice areas gives the firm an invaluable source of industry and in-house expertise.

Clients include:

- independent film producers
- distributors
- broadcasters
- banks
- financiers
- agents.

Capabilities:

- acquisition and protection of rights
- broadcasting regulation (cable and satellite)
- clearances
- commercial advice
- contractual arrangements with talent and facilities
- co-production
- defamation
- inter-creditor agreements
- international tax and security issues
- production financing
- revolving credit facilities
- sale and leaseback arrangements
- secured lending
- tax-related financing structures.

The firm also contributes to the training of young European producers as co-sponsors of the Television Business School and MEGA (Master in European Audiovisual Management), both organised by the Media Business School.